Prentice-Hall, Inc., Englewood Cliffs, New Jersey 07632

INTERNATIONAL
MARKETING
RESEARCH

Susan P. Douglas

New York University

C. Samuel Craig

New York University

PH/ Series in Marketing

PRENTICE-HALL INTERNATIONAL SERIES IN MANAGEMENT

Library of Congress Cataloging in Publication Data

DOUGLAS, SUSAN P.
  International marketing research.

  Includes bibliographies and index.
  1. Export marketing—Research. I. Craig,
C. Samuel. II. Title.
HF1009.5.D66 1983   658.8′48   83-2991
ISBN 0-13-473132-8

Editorial / production supervision
  and interior design: Steve Young
Cover design: Wanda Lubelska
Manufacturing buyer: Ed O'Dougherty

To
Barbara and Francis Thomas
and
Charles and Catherine Craig

Printed in the United States of America

10 9 8 7 6 5 4 3 2 1

ISBN 0-13-473132-8

Prentice-Hall International, Inc., *London*
Prentice-Hall of Australia Pty. Limited, *Sydney*
Editora Prentice-Hall do Brasil, Ltda., *Rio de Janeiro*
Prentice-Hall Canada Inc., *Toronto*
Prentice-Hall of India Private Limited, *New Delhi*
Prentice-Hall of Japan, Inc., *Tokyo*
Prentice-Hall of Southeast Asia Pte. Ltd., *Singapore*
Whitehall Books Limited, *Wellington, New Zealand*

Contents

iii

3   Secondary Data Sources   56

4   Uses of Secondary Data   104

5   Issues in Primary Data Collection   131

6   Nonsurvey Data Collection Techniques   153

Appendices

306

Indices

326

Foreword

When I was asked by the authors to prepare a foreword to *International Marketing Research,* my reaction was commonplace enough—who's got the time? I'm happy to report that the manuscript was well worth the time spent on reading it. Douglas and Craig have produced a novel and useful addition to the marketing research literature.

As described in their preface, the authors are concerned with problems arising in international markets. Should corporate strategies vary by country, or can a single plan be implemented? What are the implications of competitors' actions in country A on our firm's strategy in country B? The list of such questions is almost endless, and the consequences of corporate ignorance can be fatal.

Fortunately for the reader, the authors have not taken the easy way out by writing a standard marketing research text with a thin multinational veneer. At the outset, Douglas and Craig assume some reader familiarity with marketing research. They then view their charge as showing how this basic knowledge can be modified and augmented to deal with issues that are international in scope. The authors focus on the more or less unique aspects of gathering multinational market intelligence, such as special difficulties in the collection of secondary data, respondent literacy problems, intercultural differences, and the relationship of marketing information to other functional areas, such as finance and production.

The authors take a managerial (rather than research methodologist's) slant. The result is a lively presentation that is well-laced with interesting examples of management successes and failures on the international scene. Academic jargon is kept to a minimum as Douglas and Craig carefully describe those aspects of international marketing research that differentiate it from the domestic variety. Anyone who completes this book will have a greater respect for the difficulties of implementing psychographic segmentation, brand positioning, and even market measurement studies in multinational settings.

What do the authors expect from the reader? In addition to a working familiarity with research methodology, the prospective reader should keep an open mind—many of the research practices that seem so ingrained in the United States are simply points of departure when working in international markets. However, technical requisites are kept to a minimum; this is more a book on research practice than research methodology.

I think this text will receive a lot of attention, both in the United States and abroad. It should be must reading for students in multinational business, but even the more parochial researcher will benefit from its wisdom and perspective. Douglas and Craig have demonstrated the value of product positioning right in our own backyard. Their book *is* different from the pack, and better yet, it has something useful to say. I'm glad the authors invited me to take a prepublication peek at its contents.

Paul E. Green

Preface

The internationalization of business has emerged as one of the dominant trends in the latter half of the century. For some United States and foreign-based companies, growth in foreign operations far exceeds domestic market growth. In fact, many companies derive a larger percentage of their earnings from their foreign operations. Other companies are facing intensified competition in world markets such as automobiles, steel, watches, apparel, communications, and electronics. In addition, they are increasingly being threatened in their domestic markets by the entry of foreign competition. Such trends imply an increased need for information to keep abreast of such developments, to monitor changes in world markets, and to develop more effective strategies relative to worldwide marketing activities.

Companies already involved in international markets need to collect information to assess which countries, product markets, and target segments offer the most attractive opportunities, and to determine how resources should best be allocated to exploit such potential in the light of changing market trends. In addition, research should be conducted to determine whether specific marketing tactics, such as product positioning, advertising themes, and copy execution, need to be adapted for a given country or market, or alternatively, whether standardized positionings and themes can be used, regionally or worldwide. Even companies not involved in international markets need to be aware of global market developments, since these may hold portent for domestic markets, signaling future market trends or the entry of foreign competition. All of these may necessitate reevaluation and changes in current and future marketing strategies.

The need to collect information relating to international markets, and to monitor trends in these markets, as well as to conduct research to determine which strategies are likely to be most effective in exploiting these markets is expanding rapidly. However, relatively little attention has been devoted to the problems associated with data collection in foreign markets and how these can best be resolved. The cost effectiveness and reliability of various research instruments and administration procedures in other countries, as for example, survey versus nonsurvey data collection techniques, has rarely been investigated on a systematic basis. Similarly, the need for and ways of adapting research to different sociocultural and economic environments has been little explored. The knotty issues associated with the organization of information collection in foreign markets are also seldom discussed. To the authors' knowledge, only two books concerning international marketing research have been published, and both of these are primarily concerned with the problems specific to the conduct of research in developing countries.* In addition, even the most recent texts on marketing research do not contain a section devoted to international marketing research.

The purpose of this book is to provide some direction in conducting research for international marketing decisions. International marketing research is here defined as research conducted to aid in making decisions in more than one country. These may, for example, be decisions concerning which countries or markets offer the most attractive opportunities for entry or expansion, or whether to standardize strategies across countries as opposed to adapting these to local market differences. Comparability in findings is thus required, since these decisions imply the integration or coordination of strategies across countries. Such research can be conducted sequentially, first in one or more countries, and then be extended to other countries and product markets. Alternatively, it can be conducted simultaneously in all countries being investigated.

While the main focus of the book is on research for international marketing decisions, it should be noted that many of these decisions, especially those concerned with foreign market entry, are intrafunctional in character. Thus, they have not only marketing but also financial or production aspects. Decisions to invest or establish a plant in a foreign country, for example, necessitate evaluation of foreign market risks, and the costs of producing from a foreign location. Some of the types of information required for such evaluations are covered here, but primarily insofar as these interact with marketing decisions.

The perspective adopted is that of a multinational company, that is, a company with operations in several countries, rather than that of an exporting business. Emphasis is thus placed on the collection of information to aid in de-

---

* These books are *Data Collection in Developing Countries* by D.J. Casley and D.A. Lury, published by the Oxford University Press in 1981, and *Marketing Research in the Developing Countries* by John Z. Kracmar, published by Praeger in 1971.

veloping global marketing strategy and in integrating strategies across countries and product markets. Many of the same issues, however, arise in conducting research to determine whether marketing strategies, for example, products and advertising appeals, need to be adapted for export markets.

Information requirements are also looked at primarily from the standpoint of the corporate headquarters, rather from that of a local subsidiary. In many cases, however, local management provides an important input into the global planning process. Similarly, while the perspective tends to be that of a United States company, the same principles apply to multinational companies of other national origins.

The book, thus, identifies the key issues in international marketing research. Issues relating to the design of effective international marketing research, as well as the advantages and disadvantages of the various sources of data, both secondary and primary, are examined. The various steps in primary data collection, such as establishing equivalence of data, and use of nonsurvey versus survey data collection techniques, are discussed. Instrument design, sampling, and questionnaire administration in survey research are also covered. Various problems in data analysis are discussed, as well as how the research findings and information collected can be better integrated into management decision making.

The discussion assumes familiarity with the basic principles of marketing research, as for example, nonsurvey data collection techniques, sampling, questionnaire design and administration, and data analysis. The focus is thus on issues involved in applying these principles in an international research context. For the reader who is not familiar with marketing research principles, references are made in relevant sections throughout the book to standard sources and texts.

This book is intended to have three main uses. First, specialized courses in international marketing research would find it a valuable source of material. It provides comprehensive coverage of the various issues involved in international marketing research of both a qualitative and quantitative character. Furthermore, it is applicable to problems encountered in the developing and semideveloped countries of the Far East and Africa, as well as industrialized countries such as Japan or the European nations. Second, it can be used as a supplementary text in marketing research or international marketing management courses to round out material and topics relating to international marketing research. Third, it may prove useful to practitioners of international marketing research, particularly in relation to issues of instrument design and the use of nonsurvey data collection techniques.

The book comprises a total of ten chapters. The first two are concerned with the issues arising in the conduct and design of research in the international environment. Chapter 1 focuses on the importance and need for research for international marketing decisions. It outlines the main issues in conducting such research, such as the complexity of research design, the need to establish comparability in the data, as well as organizational issues, and the economics of international marketing research. Chapter 2 outlines the stages in the design of international marketing research, including the determination of information requirements, the selection of information sources and the appropriate unit of analysis, the development of a research plan, and its administration.

The third and fourth chapters are concerned with secondary data sources. These are often more important in international marketing research due to the high costs of primary data collection. Chapter 3 identifies the various sources of international data, and outlines the main types of data available. Chapter 4 looks at the various uses of these data, as, for example, in making initial market entry decisions, or rough estimates of demand potential, or in monitoring environmental change.

Chapter 5 examines various issues in primary data collection, focusing, in particular, on the need to establish the equivalence of the constructs studied, of the measurement of these constructs, and of the samples from which data are drawn in different countries and sociocultural contexts. The emic-etic dilemma is discussed, namely, that constructs and measures adapted to specific sociocultural backgrounds are unlikely to be comparable across countries, and equally, that use of equivalent constructs or measures is unlikely to provide an optimal measuring instrument for all countries and cultures.

Chapter 6 discusses various nonsurvey data collection techniques. These include observational and quasi-observational data, protocols, projective techniques, depth interviews, and EPSYs. Use of these in the preliminary stages of research is advocated in order to identify relevant concepts to be examined in subsequent stages of research.

Chapters 7 and 8 cover instrument design, sampling, and data collection in survey research. In chapter 7, issues in instrument design, such as questionnaire formulation, instrument translation, appropriate scales, and response format, are discussed, as well as potential sources of bias arising from the respondent, or the interviewer-respondent interaction. Chapter 8 examines problems in sampling, such as identifying an efficient sampling procedure. The advantages and disadvantages of various data collection procedures such as mail, telephone, or personal interviewing in international marketing research are also discussed, in addition to field staff selection and training procedures.

Chapters 9 and 10 discuss data analysis and the development of an international information system respectively. Chapter 9 first examines issues relating to the sequencing and organization of the analysis, and the need to assess the quality and reliability of the data. Various methods of data analysis are then discussed, including both univariate and bivariate analysis as well as multivariate techniques. Chapter 10 considers how information, once collected, can be integrated into management decision making and can be updated on a regular basis. This suggests the desirability of establishing an international marketing information system. The various components of this are discussed, as well as organizational issues in data collection, processing, and maintenance, and in using the system.

We would like to thank those who, through their writing or their comments, have contributed to the development of this book. We are indebted to the many colleagues who have influenced our intellectual development and encouraged us in our professional careers. We are grateful to Professor Paul Green, University of Pennsylvania, who kindly agreed to write the foreword, despite his many other time commitments. The senior author would especially like to acknowledge her debt of gratitude to the never-failing support and inspiration provided by Professor Yoram Wind, University of Pennsylvania, Professor Harry Davis, University of Chicago, and Professor Alvin J. Silk, M.I.T. Stimulation and encouragement in the study of international marketing research has also been provided by interactions with colleagues and business professionals at the different institutions where she had been employed, and in particular, her former colleagues at C.E.S.A., Jouy-en-Josas, and the European Institute of Advanced Studies in Management, Brussels.

A special note of thanks goes to Philip Barnard of Research International, London, Dr. Gerald Albaum, University of Oregon, Dr. John U. Farley, R. C. Kopf Professor of International Marketing at Columbia University, Professor Jean-Claude Larreché, INSEAD, Fontainebleau, and Dr. Warren J. Keegan, Pace University, who reviewed the manuscript and provided many helpful and insightful comments.

We are grateful for the capable people at Prentice-Hall who assisted us through the many steps. We would like to acknowledge John Connolly, who started the project with us, and Elizabeth Classon and Steve Young, who saw it to completion.

A number of graduate students at New York University provided helpful assistance in the preparation of this book. Dave Fleischner provided invaluable help in copyediting and in verifying exhibits and references, while Carol Koch hunted down secondary data sources and other reference material. Sharon Asro, Sylvia Clark, Andrea Resnick, Stephanie Scherr, and Christine Luelys-Miksis read the manuscript in its entirety and helped us to clarify many points and perspectives.

Finally, but by no means least, we would like to acknowledge the able and cheerful support provided by the secretarial staff of the Marketing and International Business departments at New York University.

Susan P. Douglas
C. Samuel Craig

1

Marketing Research in the International Environment

Information is a key ingredient in the development of successful marketing strategies. Information has to be collected to solve specific decision problems, as for example, what advertising theme to use, whether and how to launch new products, what prices to charge, and what distribution channels to use in marketing a product. In addition, information is needed to monitor changing trends in the environment, so that strategies can be adapted accordingly. Information is also required to evaluate the effectiveness of these strategies and to assess performance.

In developing international marketing strategy, information is even more important for effective marketing decisions. All too often, decisions are made hastily, without any or with inadequate information. In the past, for example, it has not been uncommon for a company to enter a market without conducting any research, even desk research, to analyze market potential. Management takes the attitude, "It's only the cost of the shipment, and if it goes, then we can think about developing the market." In taking this attitude, they are neglecting the opportunity costs associated with entering the wrong market, or the damage done by using an ill-adapted marketing strategy initially.

Such errors can cost a company dearly. A major United States men's clothing manufacturer, for example, thought that there might be some potential for his line of ready-to-wear suits in Europe. On investigating the situation, he was advised by a leading international research consultant to conduct some desk research. He was, however, reluctant to make even a minimal outlay to study the market. Consequently, he decided to abandon the idea, and so lost the potential opportunity of expanding sales overseas.

Competition can enter the market with a better-adapted product or marketing strategy. General Mills, for example, attempted to enter the British market with its Betty Crocker cake mixes, such as those for angel's food cake, and devil's food cake. The English housewife simply could not believe that a mix would be able to produce the exotic cake pictured on the package. A competitor asked British housewives to bake their own favorite cakes, and so developed a highly successful line of the plain cakes favored by the British, such as the Victoria sandwich, the Swiss roll, the orange spongecake, and rock cakes (Ricks, Fu, and Arpan, 1974).

Alternatively, consumers can develop a negative image of a company, which can hinder their reentering the market with a better product or an improved marketing strategy. Renault, for example, entered the United States market with the Renault Dauphine—a car ill adapted to the demands of United States highway driving. The launch proved a total failure, and Renault has only just recovered to reenter the United States market with the Renault 5, "Le Car," positioned as suitable for town and suburban driving.

There are a number of reasons why companies do not collect adequate information on international markets. First is the lack of sensitivity to differences in customer tastes and preferences. Second is a limited appreciation for the very different character of the marketing environment in many foreign countries in the nature of the retail distribution network, or the availability of various communication media. Third, the lack of familiarity with alternative international and foreign data sources, and their specific advantages and disadvantages, constitutes a further problem. Fourth, reluctance to engage in the costs of conducting research in overseas markets is a major barrier. Finally, doubts about the competence and reliability of foreign research companies or of international research agencies are often a cause for hesitation.

Such attitudes are, however, largely unwarranted. While it is true that the cost of obtaining information about international markets is often greater, and the data of lower quality and reliability than comparable data in the United States market, it is, nonetheless, essential to conduct research prior to market entry. Only with the aid of such information can effective international marketing strategies be developed, and the costly errors of General Mills, Renault, the clothing manufacturer, and others, be avoided.

Collecting information about international markets is, however, by no means a simple matter. Secondary data for international markets is less readily available and less easy to obtain than that for domestic markets. Primary data collection is also more complex, since the research design has to be adapted to different cultural, linguistic, economic, and social environments. Often, exploratory research has to be conducted in order to define the problem more clearly, and to determine precisely what should be investigated, and by whom. Questionnaires have to be translated, and the research instrument adapted to the new environment. Sampling frames comparable to those available in the United States are often nonexistent.

Administration of research has to be scheduled and coordinated across national boundaries, often incurring delays, miscommunication, and other frustrations. Analysis also poses the problem of interpretation of data from a different cultural context, and hence the possibility of bias on the part of the researcher.

The following examples provide some feel for the diverse types of situations and problem areas where international marketing research can play a role. In particular, they provide an indication of the scope of problems encountered in making international marketing decisions.

Example 1: Secondary Data
to Estimate Market Potential

Mr. Bowlich, the President of National Harvester, a farming equipment manufacturer, is faced by a saturated domestic market for cornpickers. He decides he would like to investigate foreign markets, and see whether there is any potential for his product abroad, for example, in developing countries. He calls his assistant, Susan Dieserton, into his office and tells her he wants her to look into the problem, being sure to think of every possible country. He tells her to come back to him with the information in a month, and that she can only have a budget of $1,000 for out-of-pocket costs.

Susan goes back to her office wondering how she can manage to collect the information in a month, and with such a limited budget. She has never done any research on foreign markets and doesn't even know how many countries there are in the world, except a lot. Clearly, with that budget, she will have to use secondary data to provide some indication of market potential, but she doesn't know where to find any data, except she has a vague idea that the United Nations publishes some statistics on other countries.

Puzzling over the problem for a while, she decides to think of a number of factors likely to be related to demand for cornpickers, such as corn production, the number of tractors in use, the number of harvesters in use, GNP per capita, percent employment in agriculture. Tomorrow, she will go to the library to see where she can find some information about these. If she can't find them there, then she will spend her budget on going to New York, where she is sure to be able to find a library with the information, or some advice about where to go.

Example 2: Focus Groups
to Determine Product Positioning

Mr. Paul Smith, the Director of International Market Research at Kaiser Research Ltd., in London, has just come back from a meeting with one of his clients who manufactures household cleaning products, including toilet bowl cleansers, disinfectants, and general purpose household cleansing items. The client is planning to enter the European market with a disinfectant product which is positioned in the United Kingdom as a specialized toilet bowl cleanser. He wants Kaiser Research to conduct a study to determine how the product should be positioned in other European markets—as a specialized toilet bowl cleanser or as a general disinfectant. The market for household cleansing products differs significantly from one European country to another due to different attitudes toward cleanliness and the importance attached to having a spick-and-span home, as well as the availability of different products.

Mr. Smith decides that the best approach will be to conduct a series of focus group interviews, or EPSYS, in each of the European markets his client plans to enter. In these interviews he will hire local moderators and brief them to find out housewives' attitudes toward household cleaning chores, what problems and worries they have, what kind of product benefits they look for, how they feel about existing products, and in particular, about cleaning the toilet bowl. Also, he needs to know who generally buys or influences what brands of household cleaning products to buy—housewives, other family members, or cleaning help.

Mr. Smith is somewhat apprehensive about the study as he knows that the success of focus groups depends on the skill of the moderator. He has had some bad experiences in the past, particularly in the French, Spanish, and Greek markets, where there is a lack of trained moderators. He wonders whether he should get some of his own research staff, who, although not trained moderators, do speak the native language, to be present at a pilot group in each country.

Example 3: Survey Research to Determine Product Attitudes

M. Jean Lemattre, the Director of Market Research for Napoleon, a French brandy producer, has to choose a supplier to conduct a survey of consumer attitudes toward brandy, and in particular, French brandy. This information will be used by the Director of International Marketing to decide what advertising appeals should be used in marketing Napoleon brandy in various countries throughout Europe. Substantial economies can be obtained by using the same advertising campaign, but, on the other hand, if consumers have different views about brandy and perceptions of French brandy, this will result in a loss of sales.

He knows that this will require designing a base questionnaire in one language, probably English, and then translating it into different languages, pretesting it in the different countries, and deciding how to modify it and whether to add questions unique to each country. A sampling plan for each country will also have to be developed, and an appropriate sampling frame found. The best method of administering the questionnaire in each country, that is, by telephone, mail, or personal interview, will have to be decided, and also, how and where the interviews are going to be conducted, and what types of checks or controls to make. He also has to pick a supplier or suppliers, and decide how much of the job he is going to turn over to the supplier. In particular, he has to make up his mind whether the supplier should analyze the data and write up the report, or whether to do that in-house.

The two major alternatives are to turn the job over to a market research organization, such as R.I. (Research International) with offices in all the countries he is interested in, or to set up detailed specifications, and find a good local research organization in each country. The first alternative is likely to be more expensive but will require less time and effort from him.

Decision problems such as these are becoming increasingly frequent as companies throughout the world, whether of United States, European, Japanese, or Third World origin, seek to expand and to diversify, and to enter new product markets and new countries in different and unfamiliar environments. Hitachi of Japan, for example, not only manufactures transfer and container cranes, electric hoists, high speed trains, robots, compressors, and arc welders, but also video systems, TV sets, purification systems, electronic digital switching systems, main-frame computers, mini-computers, and medical equipment. Heinz now markets, not only tomato ketchup and tomato soup everywhere, but also oxtail soup in the United Kingdom, chocolate spread in the United Kingdom and Italy, canned mushrooms in the United Kingdom and Germany, and Weight Watchers throughout the world. Tatung Industries of Taiwan is currently investigating Latin American markets to determine their potential for audio equipment and videodiscs, and is seeking to expand sales of fans, refrigerators, and TV sets in Japan, and of rice cookers and fans in mainland China, and has recently acquired Racal in the United Kingdom to sell TV sets in Europe.

THE COMPLEXITY
OF INTERNATIONAL MARKETING

Marketing on an international or global scale thus poses problems that are considerably more complex than those encountered in relation to domestic markets. In the first place, it involves a diversity of modes of operation, such as licensing, joint ventures, and direct foreign investment. Secondly, it entails operation in a wide variety of different environmental contexts—in the more mature European markets, the politically unstable Latin American markets, the rapidly growing markets of the Middle and Far East, and the developing African countries. Given this complexity and diversity, research assumes a vital role in assessing the best way to enter and operate in these different countries, and how far strategy should be adapted to the different environments.

Modes of Operation
in the International Environment

Yet, while there is a need for research to determine how to enter or operate in different markets, at the same time, the degree of interest and commitment to international operations will to a large extent determine how much time and effort management is willing to spend in investigating foreign market potential, and in determining the most appropriate mode of operation. Different modes of operation imply different levels of commitment to operations overseas, both in terms of financial commitment, and also commitment of management time and effort.

In the initial stages of foreign market entry, companies typically export indirectly, filling unsolicited orders from abroad via their domestic sales organization (Bilkey, 1978). Consequently, little research is likely to be conducted in relation to international markets. More deliberate focus on foreign markets and more effective penetration of international market potential, however, requires a shift to a mode of operation providing more contact with foreign markets, and a greater degree of control over operations in markets abroad. For example, export management companies could be used, or a joint venture with a foreign partner or, wholly owned subsidiaries established to market and, or, produce the product in markets overseas. Small and medium-sized companies that want to develop export markets without making a substantial commitment of management or financial resources can employ export management companies. These not only arrange the mechanics of exporting, but also identify markets, find potential buyers, and select distributors. Ultimately, however, as these markets develop, direct contact will need to be established with a separate sales organization for international markets. This then takes over all the complex problems of research to determine which markets to enter, and with what strategy.

Licensing, while apparently a low international commitment strategy, also requires research, not only to identify the most appropriate licensee, but also, prior to the licensing decisions, to assess whether market potential will grow rapidly. In this case, alternative forms of entry such as joint venture or wholly owned subsidiaries may be preferred. Franchising, the parallel to licensing in the service industries, also requires research to find potential franchisees, and to assess how far strategies should be adapted.

Joint ventures with local companies in a foreign country also provide a means of reducing the risks associated with foreign market entry. Here, the local partner brings the expertise and familiarity with local market conditions. This reduces the need for research to determine how far products or strategies should be adapted to these conditions. If, however, a company is willing to assume all the risks associated with foreign operations, wholly owned subsidiaries may be established. In some cases, these may be independent country units, as, for example, Procter and Gamble's European operations. Research comparable to domestic marketing research is then conducted by the local subsidiary. If, however, products and strategies are to be transferred across national boundaries, some prior research is needed to assess how far standardization will result in loss of market potential.

In other cases, as for example in the automobile industry, wholly owned subsidiaries consist of a complex mass of intertwined global operations. The transmissions for the Ford Fiesta were, for example, made in Bordeaux, France; the windshields in Oklahoma; the spark plugs in the United Kingdom; and the bumperplating in Cologne. Here, research to establish the global marketing plan and to determine how far programs and strategies should be standardized or adapted to different national environments is more likely to be directed from corporate or regional headquarters, based on input from local subsidiary management.

The Diversity of the International Environment

In addition to different modes of operation, international operations are made even more complex by the diversity of environments in which such operations are conducted. Such diversity occurs particularly with regard to consumer markets, and to a lesser extent, industrial markets. An added level of complexity due to the differences in the marketing infrastructure is also encountered. For example, commercial media, banking facilities, research agencies, or postal services similar to those in the domestic market may not be available. The structure of distribution or the physical communication network may also differ. Product, pricing, advertising, and promotional regulation are specific to a given country and are important factors to be taken into consideration when developing international market entry or marketing mix strategies.

Countries and cultures also differ with regard to economic wealth and its distribution among the national population. Table 1.1 shows GNP per capita for the top ten and the bottom ten countries in the world in 1979. The range is from a low of $80 in Bhutan to $17,100 in Kuwait. Yet, such aggregate figures can be misleading when one considers that what can be purchased for the equivalent of a dollar varies from country to country, that wealth in some countries is concentrated in the hands of a few, and that in agricultural economies, many people grow their own food.

Levels of literacy vary from country to country. While levels of literacy in developed countries are typically 99 percent, it is important to remember that this is far from the case in other countries. Table 1.2 shows changes in levels of literacy from 1960 to 1976 in selected low- and middle-income countries. While it is not unexpected to discover that levels of literacy are as low as 5 percent in Upper Volta and 12 percent in Afghanistan, it is striking to note that in eight

TABLE 1.1   The top ten and bottom ten ranking countries based on per capita income

	TOP TEN			BOTTOM TEN	
	Population (millions) mid-1979	*GNP Per capita (dollars 1979)*		*Population (millions) mid-1979*	*GNP Per capita (dollars 1979)*
Kuwait	1.3	17,100	Bhutan	1.3	80
Switzerland	6.5	13,920	Bangladesh	88.9	90
Sweden	8.3	11,930	Chad	4.4	110
Denmark	5.1	11,900	Ethiopia	30.9	130
Germany, Fed. Rep.	61.2	11,730	Nepal	14.0	130
Belgium	9.8	10,920	Mali	6.8	140
Norway	4.1	10,700	Burma	32.9	160
United States	223.6	10,630	Afghanistan	15.5	170
Netherlands	14.0	10,230	Burundi	4.0	180
France	53.4	9,950	Upper Volta	5.6	180

Source: World Bank, *World Development Report.* New York: Oxford University Press, 1981.

TABLE 1.2   Levels of literacy in selected low- and middle-income countries

	ADULT LITERACY RATE (PERCENT)	
	1960	*1976*
Low-income countries		
(GNP per capita, $90–$370)		
Upper Volta	2*	5*
Niger	1	8
Mali	3*	10
Afghanistan	8	12
Middle-income countries		
(GNP per capita, $380–$4,380)		
Senegal	6*	10
Jemen Arab Republic	3*	13*
Ivory Coast	5*	20
Morocco	14	28*
Liberia	9*	30
Algeria	10*	35*
Egypt	26	44
Kenya	20*	45*
Iran	16	50

*Data for years other than indicated, but generally not more than 2 years distant.
Source: World Bank, *World Development Report.* New York: Oxford University Press, 1981.

middle-income countries, despite recent improvements and remedial programs, more than half the population was still illiterate. This seriously limits the effectiveness of written marketing communication, that is, product labeling or print advertising, and also the type of research or research tools that can be used—for example, mail or self-administered questionnaires.

Linguistic heterogeneity is yet another factor adding to the complexity of international operations. International marketers have to deal with operations spanning countries speaking a diversity of languages. For example, 159 languages are spoken by at least one million people, while twelve are spoken by more than 100 million people, and another fourteen by at least 40 million people. Some of these include Mandarin, which is spoken by 690 million people, English by 380 million, Russian by 259 million, and Spanish by 236 million (World Almanac, 1980). Furthermore, there is often a diversity of languages within a country. In many countries and cultures there are regional differences and dialects, not comprehensible in other areas. In India, where Hindi is the official language, there are thirteen major regional languages, an estimated 179 local languages, not to mention 544 dialects. Similarly, in China, Mandarin is the official language, and while six major language groups are typically identified, each of the twenty-two provinces speaks a different version, and furthermore, there are numerous local dialects. In South Africa, one of the most diverse ethnic populations in the world, there are two official languages, English and Afrikans, but these are spoken as a first language by less than 18 percent of the population. Seventy percent (that is, the black population) speak various Bantu languages, and typically nine major ethnic groups are identified. Another 10 percent are coloreds of mixed racial origin, speaking a smattering of different languages, while 3 percent are Asian, speaking predominantly Indian languages.

Similarly, though most evidence is anecdotal, the diversity of observed behavior in different countries suggests that cultural values and dispositions vary from country to country (Hall, 1976). Hall (1959) has, for example, pointed out marked differences in the way people communicate in different countries and cultures. Thus, for example, while in Western society a smile is a sign of happiness and approval, in Oriental culture it is used to cover embarrassment. Similarly, socially acceptable distances for interpersonal conversation differ. In Anglo-Saxon cultures, four distances are commonly used in social relations: six to eighteen inches for intimate relationships, one and a half to two feet for one-to-one conversations, four to seven feet for business or formal occasions, and more than seven feet for public addresses and communications. Touching is reserved for intimate relationships or moments of intimacy in personal relationships. In Latin or Southern European cultures, on the other hand, the dimensions of personal and social space are considerably closer, and demonstrative behavior habitual.

Availability of different communications media also varies from one country to another. Table 1.3 shows, for example, variation in selected media

TABLE 1.3 Communications media in 14 countries

	POPULATION (Millions) mid-1979[a]	DAILY NEWSPAPERS (Copies per 1,000) 1978[b]	RADIOS (% households) 1978[b]	TV SETS (% households) 1980[c]	DOMESTIC MAIL (Per capita) 1977[b]	TELEPHONES (% households) 1980[c]
N. America						
U.S.	223.6	287	100	99	397.8	97
Canada	23.7	221	100		237.8	na
W. Europe						
W. Germany	61.2	423	100	97	202.1	70
U.K.	55.9	409	99	97	158.1	69
Italy	56.8	97	96	87	53.5	50
Spain	37.0	123	97	97	96.7	40
Greece	9.3	107	56	95	30.7	60
Asia						
Japan	115.8	546	98		105.2	na
India	650.9	16	14	50*	11.4	13*
Thailand	45.5	na	71	67*	4.1	18*
Indonesia	142.9	na	20	35	1.3	7
Africa						
Nigeria	82.6	9	59	8*	11.6	
South Africa	28.5	66	70	white 81 nw 2	48.5	white 78 nw 1
Ghana	11.3	42	41	na	5.1	na

*% Urban households

[a] World Bank, *World Development Report.* New York: Oxford University Press, 1981.
[b] Euromonitor staff, *International Marketing Data and Statistics.* London: Euromonitor Publications, 1981. Euromonitor staff, *European Marketing Data and Statistics.* London: Euromonitor Publications, 1981.
[c] Philip Barnard, "The World of Research," *Marketing Research Society Newsletter,* June 1980 (London: Marketing Research Society).

for different countries in four major continents. Here, it is striking to note not only the differences that exist between the highly developed nations of North America and Western Europe, and the developing nations in Asia and Africa, but also the differences within these regions.

Advertising regulations also vary from country to country. While in the United States, comparative advertising is encouraged, in France and Germany it is banned. In Italy direct comparisons are banned, though indirect comparisons can be made if they are substantiated. The extent and the way in which advertising to children is regulated also varies. In Austria direct appeals are forbidden, while in Italy, children cannot be shown eating, and in France prebroadcast screening of commercials is required. Similarly, limitations on advertising of different types of products differ. While in the United States, tobacco advertising is restricted to print media, in Italy and Switzerland it is banned in all media. In addition, Switzerland also bans advertising of drugs and medicine (Dunn and Barban, 1978).

Such differences in economic wealth and levels of literacy, coupled with the linguistic heterogeneity and cultural diversity in marketing environments throughout the world, imply that management should not assume that a strategy that works in the home market will be equally effective abroad. In addition, certain barriers—such as the absence of certain communications media, or advertising or product regulation—may impede the use of domestic marketing tactics in markets overseas.

THE IMPORTANCE OF RESEARCH
FOR INTERNATIONAL MARKETING DECISIONS

The diversity and complexity of the international environment, coupled with the frequent lack of familiarity with a foreign country, underscores the importance of undertaking research prior to making decisions. This is true whether with regard to initial market entry decisions, product positioning, or marketing mix decisions. Research is necessary to avoid the costly mistakes of inappropriate strategy and the possibility of lost opportunities, and to determine how far international operations can be coordinated across countries to take advantage of the potential synergies arising from marketing in a global environment. Some illustrations of the mistakes that can be made if research is not undertaken are next discussed. Then, the ways and types of information that can aid in developing international marketing strategy are examined.

Research as a Basis for Marketing Strategy

First of all, research can aid in preventing inappropriate market entry strategies. It can help to avoid mistakes such as those made by General Mills in entering the United Kingdom market (Ricks, Fu, and Arpan, 1974). Their breakfast cereal package showed a freckled, red-haired crew-cut kid saying,

"Gee kids, it's great." General Mills failed to recognize that the British family is not as child oriented and permissive as the American family, and that parent-children relationships tend to be more authoritarian. Consequently, the package repelled the housewife and wound up untouched on grocery shelves.

The possibility of lost opportunity can also be lessened by research. In the early 1960s, a United States cereal manufacturer looked at the French market for breakfast food and observed that the French did not eat cereal for breakfast, but typically ate bread and croissants. They decided there was no market for their products. A competitor examined the market and, observing an increasing number of working wives, pressures on time available for food preparation, and at the same time an increasing concern for nutrition, decided there was an opportunity for a correctly positioned product. The product line was launched using a quick and easy-to-prepare appeal, as well as emphasizing it as nutritious and "starting the day off right." He encountered a captive market and effectively shut his competitor out of the market.

Research can also be used to determine appropriate product formulation for each country. Nestlé, for example, produces one blend of coffee for the British, who take coffee heavily diluted with milk; one for the French, who commonly drink it black and like chicory; and one for the Brazilians, who like an even stronger blend.

Product positioning decisions can also be guided by research. An English chocolate manufacturer, for example, was thinking of entering the French market with his line of chocolate after-dinner mints. Research revealed that the French regarded the combination of mint with chocolate as quite unthinkable. The mints were thus positioned as a sophisticated English after-dinner candy, and no mention was made of the mint flavor. The advertising campaign showed the mints being served in an aristocratic setting, after dinner in an English castle. The launching was a huge success and the mints have now captured a sizable share of the confectionery market.

Prior investigation of the market also aided Renault in correctly positioning the Renault 5 in Europe. The car was initially launched in France using a humorous appeal, with an animated cartoon showing a little super car bouncing along the road with eyes drawn in the headlights and a smile on the bumper. A more serious appeal had to be adopted in other countries. In Italy, in view of competition from Fiat and the Italians' concern with road handling and performance, the car was positioned as "the citizen of the world"—a comfortable car with good road-handling abilities. In Germany, with competition from Volkswagen and the Germans' preoccupation with good performance, the advertising campaign focused on the car's technical features, showing its solid body work, its engine power and speed capacity on highways, its braking power and tire durability, as well as its gasoline mileage and oil consumption. In Sweden, due to competition from Volvo and Swedish concern with safety, greater emphasis was placed on the safety features, such as the locking mechanism on the wheel, the strength of the windshield glass, the front and rear braking system, and the body seatbelts.

The appropriateness of advertising appeals also needs to be assessed through research. Some prior research would, for example, have aided in avoiding the error made by Binoca in launching its talcum powder in India (Ricks, Fu, and Arpan, 1974). Its advertising, placed in leading local newspapers, showed an attractive, though apparently nude, woman dousing herself with talcum powder. The caption covering strategic portions of her body read: "Don't go wild—just enough is all you need of Binoca talc." The Indian public, traditionally conservative, found the ad indecent and highly distasteful, and developed strong negative associations with the brand name.

A similar though less damaging mistake was made by a United States manufacturer of dishwashers in Switzerland. No research was undertaken to test the effectiveness of a convenience appeal to market dishwashers. The Swiss housewife, highly involved in her domestic role, rejected the appeal. She interpreted this as implying that she was being replaced by a machine. Consequently sales did not take off as expected. Some in-depth research revealed the source of the problem and led to the identification of a hygiene appeal—centering on the concept that dishwashers killed germs and bacteria. This was highly effective with the Swiss housewife, who attaches considerable importance to cleanliness.

Packaging decisions can also be aided by research. An international manufacturer of water recreation products encountered a somewhat mysterious problem in Malaysia. Although initial orders appeared promising, distributors failed to place repeat orders and were left with large stocks on their hands (Ricks, Fu, and Arpan, 1974). Investigation of the problem revealed that the main cause was the packaging. In Malaysia, green symbolizes the jungle with all its dangers and diseases. Unfortunately for the manufacturer, green was a predominant color in its packaging, particularly in its logo stamped on the outside of the package. Consequently the Malays shied away from a package with such a fearful omen.

International marketing thus entails operations in a diverse and complex environment and requires extensive research in order to gain familiarity with this environment. Research provides information about this environment and generates increased understanding and ability to cope effectively with these complexities. It prevents management from making mistakes, either by missing potential opportunities or from failing to adapt strategy and tactics to this very different environment. Marketing in an international environment is thus substantially different and more complex than domestic marketing management.

Role of Research
in International Marketing Strategy

In addition to aiding in making appropriate marketing mix decisions, as, for example, product positioning, product formulation, advertising appeals, and packaging decisions, research can also aid in developing *global* marketing strategy. Operation in a multicountry situation implies that in addition to the basic marketing decisions—such as product positioning and the elements of the marketing mix—a number of decisions relating to the multicountry aspect of multinational operations have to be made. These concern the extent to which marketing mix strategies are standardized or coordinated across country units and also decisions relating to the choice of foreign markets.

The marketing mix decisions about product positioning, price, distribution, advertising, and personal selling are made in the context of an unfamiliar environment, especially the economic, social, and cultural aspects. There may be differences in the availability or effectiveness of the marketing infrastructure, as for example, transportation facilities, the distribution network, or different communications media. This implies that more extensive research will need to be conducted than might be the case in domestic markets, in order to avoid the mistakes of the companies cited earlier.

In particular, research is required *prior* to developing or implementing strategy, in order to avoid the mistakes of the cereal manufacturer and of the manufacturers of appliances and talcum powder. Often relatively low-cost research can be undertaken. For example, some desk research involving only a few phone calls may rapidly indicate whether similar distribution channel strategies are likely to be feasible. A case in point is Japan, where the length and complexity of distribution channels, as well as their domination by key trading companies, typically rule out use of direct distribution channels.

Decisions about *which* countries to enter, in what order, what modes of entry or operation to use in these countries, which products or product lines to transfer across national boundaries, how to schedule market entry, and whether to pursue similar target segments in each country have to be made also. These are decisions that should be made relative to a number of countries simultaneously, rather than on a country-by-country basis. Otherwise profit will be maximized by local national profit centers, but not necessarily at a global level.

These decisions thus concern the integration of country-level operations on a global basis. They are *inter*country as opposed to *intra*country decisions, and hence comprise a level of decision making that does not occur in domestic marketing management. Such decisions are unique to international marketing management, and therefore require the collection of specific types of information.

In particular, two types of information will be required. First, information relating to the business and market environment is necessary in order to assess the risks and returns likely to be associated with operating in different foreign markets. These might include, for example, information relating to the *political* risks and returns, such as the likelihood of expropriation or subsidies to foreign companies; or to *financial* risks and returns, such as the rates of inflation or of currency exchange fluctuations; or to potential *economic* risks and returns, such as the likelihood of economic growth or depression. Information enabling assessment of the *favorability* of the investment and market climate, such as demographic characteristics, sociocultural and life style patterns, market size and growth rate, competing and substitute products, and the degree and nature of competition in that market is a crucial component of such decisions. Information enabling evaluation of the costs of operating in a given market will also be required, as, for example, information about wage and labor costs, management training and skills, and electricity and energy costs.

Secondly, in markets where the company is already operating, information relating to measures of performance, at different levels of the organization ranging from the corporate level down to the product line or brand, will be required. These might include measures such as ROI, market share, sales growth, and net profit, and, depending on the nature of the market, might be broken down by region or target market segment, where relevant panel data are available.

International marketing decisions will, therefore, require the collection of information or research under conditions different from those required for domestic marketing decisions. In the first place, greater attention to the collection of information about the business environment—that is, political, financial, and legal factors; economic and technological trends; as well as unique social and cultural patterns—in other countries will be needed. Secondly, research will be conducted in a variety of unfamiliar and different environments and contexts, thus posing a number of unique, conceptual, methodological, and organizational issues.

In sum, it is important to undertake international marketing research because the environment of international marketing operations is highly complex and diverse, and because there are a multiplicity of different ways in which firms can operate in this environment. The various pitfalls that firms can encounter illustrate that operation in this environment is rarely simple. Rather, it poses innumerable challenges in developing successful marketing strategies. Yet, if the task facing the international manager is a complex and challenging one, that facing the international researcher is no less so. In particular, it poses a number of conceptual and operational issues that do not arise, or at least not in the same magnitude, in domestic marketing research. These are next highlighted.

ISSUES IN INTERNATIONAL MARKETING RESEARCH

A number of conceptual, methodological, and organizational issues hamper the collection of data and the conduct of research for international marketing decisions. These stem essentially from the diversity of international operations, and the synergies arising from coordination of these operations, and also from their conduct in complex and highly diverse environments. Principal among these are

1. the complexity of research design, due to operation in a multicountry, multicultural, and multilinguistic environment,
2. the lack of secondary data available for many countries and product markets,
3. the high costs of collecting primary data, particularly in developing countries,
4. the problems associated with coordinating research and data collection in different countries,
5. the difficulties of establishing the comparability and equivalence of data and research conducted in different contexts,
6. the intrafunctional character of many international marketing decisions,
7. the economics of many international investment and marketing decisions.

Complexity of Research Design

In the first place, designing research for international marketing decisions is considerably more complex than where a single country is concerned. The conduct of research in different countries implies much greater attention to defining the relevant unit and level of analysis, that is, countries versus segments versus regions will be needed. In addition, problem definition and assessment of whether this is similar in structure and relevant parameters—as, for example, whether the same products should be studied—will be required.

While countries are convenient units of analysis due to the existence of political and organizational boundaries, and also because much secondary data are available by country, these may not be the most appropriate units from a marketing standpoint. Management might prefer to target teenagers throughout the world; hence the relevant unit of analysis is a "culti-unit," that is, a subgroup or segment with similar needs, interests, and response patterns throughout the world (see Naroll, 1971).

Similarly, the relevant respondent may differ from country to country. While in the United States, children may play an important role in decisions with regard to the purchase of chocolate or cereals, in other countries that are less child oriented and more authoritarian in child-rearing practices, the housewife may be the relevant decision maker. Furthermore, while women in the United States have an important role in insurance and automobile purchase decisions, in other countries, characterized by more male-dominant philosophies as, for example, the Middle Eastern countries, they may have little or no influence at all.

Analysis can become yet more complex where attention is focused on examination of similar subgroups and entities across countries. This requires implicit or explicit identification of the comparability of the groups in each country, followed by comparison across countries. Both aspects suggest the need for a multistage approach to research design and analysis, and also the importance of establishing the equivalence and comparability of the units examined in the different countries.

Lack of Secondary Data

A second issue concerns the lack of secondary data with regard to many countries and product markets. Researchers accustomed to the plethora of data available in domestic markets are likely to be confounded by the absence in many developing countries of data on variables such as income or product sales, which are the basic tools of the domestic researcher's trade.

Furthermore, even where such data are available, their accuracy and reliability are often open to some question. Population censuses may, for example, be collected based on estimates made by village elders or local priests. Similarly, national income statistics or retail sales turnover may be compiled from tax returns, where much income or sales are undeclared. Such problems imply that frequently it is necessary to work with data that are of poorer quality than those which are available for domestic marketing research.

This suggests that, in many cases, international marketing decisions may have to be made on the basis of more limited and less reliable data than are available in relation to domestic marketing decisions. Similarly, greater attention may need to be paid to the use of qualitative research, in order to define the problem to be examined—as, for example, the relevant product class, or factors that influence consumer purchase decisions for a specific product within a class, such as soft drinks in the class of cold beverages. These may differ substantially in a foreign market.

Costs of Collecting Primary Data

Such difficulties are compounded by the costs of primary data collection in foreign markets. This is particularly likely to be the case in developing countries, where there is no marketing research infrastructure or experience in conducting research in such countries. Frequently, this entails substantial investment costs to develop basic information relating, for example, to sampling frames, or, alternatively, to train qualified interviewers.

This implies that greater reliance may need to be placed on secondary data, despite their somewhat doubtful reliability. Also, greater reliance may need to be placed on data extrapolation techniques. In other words, data collected in one country may be used as a basis for collecting data, determining strategy, or developing sales forecasts in another country. For example, hypotheses might be generated about the ability to predict sales of TV sets with three-dimensional screens in a foreign country, based on the observed relationship between income and purchase of color TV sets or other innovative products.

Coordination of Research
and Data Collection Across Countries

The conduct of research in the international environment not only adds considerably to the complexity of research design and data collection, but also gives rise to a number of issues pertaining to the organization and administration of research in different countries.

Concern with the coordination, design, and execution of research across different countries implies that agreement has to be reached with regard to research objectives in every country in which research is to be conducted. The design of the research instrument and data collection procedures have also to be harmonized. This can add considerably to research costs, due to the need for a coordinating agency, and may also result in considerable time delays.

The way in which coordination is organized, and the type of coordination problems likely to be encountered, are often closely related to the organizational structure of the company. If international marketing operations are under the control of an international division at corporate headquarters, research may be directed from this location, and internal coordination problems will be minimal. If, on the other hand, the company is organized by product divisions, then research is likely to be conducted by product line in each country and coordinated across countries by the product division staff at corporate headquarters. Thus, there may be a lack of coordination and a danger of duplication of research by different product divisions within a country. If, however, the company has a geographic organizational structure, then research is likely to be decentralized and conducted by local operating units. This may then be coordinated by committees at the intercountry level.

Such factors suggest the need for skill in the organization of research design—balancing the need for knowledge of, and familiarity with, the local market environment, with knowledge of the specific product or service, and the type of information required to develop effective marketing programs for the product. This can in some cases be achieved by the use of a matrix-type structure, in which dual responsibility for an area and a product division are combined. Such structures are, however, often somewhat unwieldy and highly complex.

Difficulty of Establishing Comparability
and Equivalence

Considerable difficulties are likely to be encountered in establishing equivalence and comparability of research in different countries, both with regard to secondary and primary data and with methods of data collection. An example relating to secondary data is the case of motor vehicle registration. In some countries, for example, the United States, a company car is often provided to salespersons and hence may be counted as a commercial vehicle. It may, however, also be used extensively for personal transport.

Similarly, many of the concepts, measurement instruments, and procedures for primary data collection have been developed and tested in the United States. Their relevance and applicability in other countries, is, however, far from clear. Explicit administrative and analytic procedures for modifying concepts and measures developed in one country, and testing their relevance in another, should thus be incorporated into the research design. In addition, such procedures should enable the identification of concepts and measures unique to a specific country or culture (Wind and Douglas, 1982).

Establishment of the comparability of data administration procedures poses further difficulties (Webster, 1966). In one country a certain method of data collection—for example, mail questionnaires—may be known to have a given level of reliability. In another country, personal interviews rather than mail questionnaires may have an equivalent level of reliability. Levels of reliability associated with comparable research techniques thus differ and suggest the desirability of using techniques with equivalent levels of reliability rather than techniques that are strictly comparable.

Intrafunctional Character
of International Marketing Decisions

The intrafunctional character of many international decisions, as, for example, which countries to enter, or what methods of operations to use in these countries, also suggests the need for intrafunctional research. In selecting countries, for example, an important issue may well be not only the development or market growth in that country, but also the possible sources of supply that it offers. This suggests that market research should be coordinated with research in purchasing and identifying and evaluating alternative suppliers or sources of supply. Similarly, decisions about the mode of operation also entail decisions about the degree of equity exposure and the location of foreign production. Consequently, analysis of political risk, foreign exchange rates, and financial markets; and investigation of the production and shipment costs associated with alternative logistical strategies will be required. Similarly, pricing decisions need take into consideration currency fluctuations, foreign exchange risk, and market factors.

This poses a number of conceptual and operational problems in defining the units to be examined. The production department might, for example, want to examine markets at the divisional level, such as the toiletries division versus writing implements, while the marketing department might want to examine them at the product business level, such as shampoos versus fragrances.

Similarly, the accounting department or the finance department might want to focus on measures of profitability, such as cash flow or ROI, while the marketing department is more concerned with market share.

Yet, while such difficulties may be encountered, an intrafunctional orientation implies that research will have stronger conceptual and methodological foundations. Greater precision is introduced in the conceptual and operational definition of the variables and constructs to be studied, and these are more closely linked and integrated with the specific decisions to be made.

In addition, such research will lead to improved coordination of strategic decisions made by different departments and also of information collection relative to international markets. Duplication of research effort in international markets can be avoided, and economies of scale in research costs can be achieved, by organizing and conducting research at the corporate or divisional level.

Economics of International Investment and Marketing Decisions

A final factor to be considered is the economics of international investment and marketing decisions. For such decisions, the time horizon required is typically considerably greater than that required in relation to comparable domestic decisions. This is in part due to the much more rapid rates of growth and change in many overseas markets, as for example, the Far Eastern or Latin American markets. In addition, it is important to take a longer-term view of market potential, and to consider entry at an early stage of market development, to avoid allowing the market to be captured by competitors. The fight for market share on a global level in many industries—such as automobiles, electronics, or color TV sets, implies the importance of monitoring trends in national markets worldwide. The impact of different environmental scenarios, in relation to, for example, inflation or oil prices, on these markets needs also to be assessed.

Such considerations imply that the payoff period for evaluating the costs associated with the conduct of international marketing research will need to be considerably longer than that in relation to comparable domestic research. While in the domestic market, a payoff period of one year might be appropriate for research conducted to aid in developing the marketing plan, in international markets, a period of five years might be more appropriate.

Similarly, the lack of familiarity with foreign environments, and with operations within these environments, implies that much research, especially in the initial entry stages, should be viewed as an investment rather than a current expense. It aids in the avoidance of costly entry mistakes, and enables the development of more effective long-run international market expansion strategies.

SCOPE OF THE BOOK

While the basic principles of marketing research are the same whether research is conducted in an international or a domestic context, the international marketing researcher is likely to encounter greater difficulties than his or her domestic research counterpart. These difficulties stem from operating across national boundaries and in a diverse range of sociocultural environments. Examples of issues that may arise include how to obtain response from illiterate or semiliterate populations, how to develop a sampling frame in the absence of reliable census data or sampling lists, or simply how to find or train competent interviewers. Frequently, creativity and resourcefulness are required in coping with unexpected problems. In addition, an ability to manage and to deal with and organize researchers of different cultural backgrounds and value systems is essential to successful international marketing research.

The main focus of this book is on identifying and highlighting the problems unique to international marketing research. Approaches that help to avoid these are discussed, as well as procedures to minimize their impact. Certain aspects of international marketing research are no different from domestic research—for example, report writing—and are thus not discussed here. Similarly techniques for data analysis are not covered in detail, though their application in the context of international marketing research is illustrated.

In the following nine chapters, the various stages typically involved in the conduct of international marketing research are examined. Chapter 2 looks at the issues associated with the design of international marketing research, focusing in particular on those related to the organization of international marketing research, the choice of supplier, the determination of information requirements, the selection of information sources and the appropriate unit of analysis, and the development of a research plan and its administration.

Chapters 3 and 4 are concerned with secondary data sources. These are often more important in international marketing research, due to the high costs of primary data collection. Chapter 3 identifies the various sources of international data, and outlines the main types of data available. Chapter 4 looks at the uses of these data, as, for example, in making initial market entry decisions or rough estimates of demand potential, or in monitoring environmental change.

Chapter 5 examines various issues in primary data collection, focusing in particular on the need to establish the equivalence of the constructs studied, of the measurement of these constructs, and of the samples from which data are drawn in different countries and sociocultural contexts. The emic-etic dilemma is discussed, namely, that constructs and measures adapted to specific sociocultural backgrounds are unlikely to be comparable across countries, and equally, that use of identical constructs or measures is unlikely to provide an optimal measuring instrument for all countries and cultures.

Chapter 6 discusses various nonsurvey data collection techniques. These include observational and quasi-observational data, protocols, projective techniques, depth interviews, and EPSYs. Use of these in the preliminary stages of research is advocated in order to identify relevant concepts to be examined in subsequent stages of research.

Chapters 7 and 8 cover instrument design, sampling, and data collection in survey research. In Chapter 7, issues in instrument design, such as questionnaire formulation, instrument translation, appropriate scales, and response format, are discussed, as well as potential sources of bias arising from the respondent, or the interviewer-respondent interaction. Chapter 8 examines problems in sampling, such as identifying an efficient sampling procedure. The advantages and disadvantages of various data collection procedures, such as mail, telephone, or personal interviewing, in international marketing research are also discussed.

Chapter 9 deals with the analysis of international marketing data. Issues relating to the sequencing and organization of the analysis, and the need to assess the quality and reliability of the data, are examined. Various methods of data analysis are then discussed, including univariate and bivariate analysis, followed by a discussion of multivariate techniques ranging from regression techniques to factor analysis, scaling, and mapping. Use of each of these techniques is illustrated by examples from the literature.

Chapter 10 examines the steps involved in the development of an international information system. This covers how information is collected, and updated on a regular basis. The various components of the system are discussed, as well as how data relating to these might be collected and fed into the system. Issues relating to the processing and maintenance of the system are also examined. In addition, the question of integration of information into decision making is considered.

REFERENCES

BILKEY, WARREN J., "An Attempted Integration of the Literature of the Export Behavior of Firms," *Journal of International Business Studies* 9 (Spring/Summer 1978), 33–46.

DUNN, S. WATSON and ARNOLD M. BARBAN, *Advertising,* 4th ed. Hindsdale, IL: The Dryden Press, 1978.

EUROMONITOR PUBLICATIONS LTD., *International Marketing Data and Statistics.* London: Euromonitor Publications, 1981.

HALL, EDWARD T., *The Silent Language.* Garden City, NY: Doubleday and Co., 1959.

HALL, EDWARD T., *Beyond Culture.* Garden City, NY: Anchor/Doubleday, 1976.

NAROLL, RAOUL, "Some Thoughts on Comparative Method in Cultural Anthropology" in Hubert M. Blalock, Jr. and Ann B. Blalock, *Methodology in Social Research.* New York: McGraw-Hill, 1971.

RICKS, DAVID A., Y.C. FU, and S. ARPAN, *International Business Blunders.* Columbus, OH: Grid, 1974.

WEBSTER, LUCY, "Comparability in Multi-Country Surveys," *Journal of Advertising Research,* 6 (December 1966), 14–18.

WIND, YORAM and SUSAN P. DOUGLAS, "Comparative Consumer Research: the Next Frontier," *Management Decision,* 20 (September 1982), 24–35.

World Almanac, New York: Newspaper Enterprise Association, Inc., 1980.

WORLD BANK, *World Development Report.* New York: Oxford University Press, 1981.

Designing International Marketing Research

In terms of a formal definition, international marketing research is research conducted to aid in making decisions in more than one country. As in domestic marketing research, management decisions provide the basis for the determination of information needs and for the development of the research design. In the international environment, however, not only are the decisions facing management more complex, but the actual task of conducting research is also more difficult. International business decisions tend to be hierarchical in nature, pertaining to different areas, regions, countries, and groupings within countries. Also, as pointed out in Chapter 1, these decisions tend to be multifaceted in character. Such factors add to the complexity of information requirements and to the organization of appropriate data collection and analysis procedures. Frequently, this will require a multistage approach, with a preliminary phase to determine what information is available and how it can best be collected, before field research is conducted. In addition, the integration of research into the planning process, and more particularly, into management decision making, poses a number of difficulties.

A unique feature of international marketing research is that many relevant decisions, whether made at regional or corporate headquarters, concern operations spanning several countries rather than a single country and, consequently, require information relating to a number of different countries and environmental contexts. This, in turn, entails the coordination of research across each of these country units and gives rise to a number of design and organizational issues. Since decisions such as selection of target markets, segmentation strategy, or standardizing marketing mix tactics cover several countries, it is important that the information on which such decisions are based be comparable and consistent from one country to another. Furthermore, decisions have to be made about where research is designed, how and where it is implemented, and by whom. Here, three major alternatives may be identified: 1) the design organization and control of research are centralized at corporate headquarters; 2) research design and implementation are delegated to an international research organization; 3) details of design and implementation are organized by local country subsidiaries or sales offices. In all cases considerable coordination of research activities will be required.

Such considerations imply that research design and organization depend not only on management information requirements, but also on the organization and planning of field operations and, in particular, on the degree of centralization in planning and decision making. In organizations characterized by centralized planning and decision making, research design and administration may frequently be centralized. If, on the other hand, considerable autonomy is given to local subsidiaries or operating units, then details of research design may be developed locally, as well as control of the implementation of research. This may also depend on the type of decision. While research for strategic decisions is likely to be centralized, research for tactical decisions is more likely to be organized locally. However, even in this case corporate headquarters may exercise some control to ensure a degree of comparability across different operations.

In addition, whether research is conducted in-house or purchased outside needs to be considered. It is generally unlikely that corporate headquarters will have adequate research staff to conduct more than secondary data analysis for strategic decisions or set the specifications for research design. Similarly, relatively few local subsidiaries or operating units have their own field organization or staff specialized in all aspects of research design. Consequently, in many cases research services, whether for design or implementation of international research, will be purchased outside. Here four major alternatives may be identified: 1) large multinational research companies, who will design, coordinate, and implement international research; 2) loosely linked research chains, where an office in one country will commission studies from sister organizations in other countries; 3) national research suppliers commissioned directly by corporate or regional headquarters, local subsidiaries, or a coordinating research agency; and 4) traveling research executives who will organize local studies in each country (Barnard, 1982).

The conduct of international marketing research thus involves a number of interrelated stages, each of which has to be carefully planned, coordinated, and integrated into the management decision process. The remainder of this chapter is devoted to examining the issues involved in each of these stages in the design and implementation of an international marketing research plan. The various stages outlined here are then covered in more detail in subsequent chapters.

THE INTERNATIONAL MARKETING
RESEARCH PROCESS

The first step in the international marketing research process frequently incorporates a preliminary phase of assessing information needs and availability. Rarely is one likely to be in a position to design a detailed research plan at the outset of the project. Rather, some exploratory investigation will need to be conducted to pinpoint more precisely the relevant dimensions of the decision problem and to relate it to information needs. In addition, some preliminary research will be needed to provide input into elements such as instrument design, the sampling plan, or data collection procedures, as well as how the research process is best organized.

In many cases, this preliminary phase will involve some desk research based on secondary data. In selecting which markets to enter, investigation of trends in different countries—as for example, growth in GNP—political or financial stability may help to narrow the choice, and to select those to be investigated in more depth. Qualitative research, personal or depth interviews, focus groups, or observational research may also be conducted to determine relevant questions to be examined in subsequent phases of research. In deciding whether or not to market and, if so, how to market in a given country or set of countries, qualitative research can provide some initial indication as to likely responses, as well as attributes used in evaluating products, and different scenarios in which products might be used. In addition, qualitative research may be useful in determining the relevant competitive product set or in defining the target market, and hence in providing guidelines for the sampling plan. It should, however, be noted that the time and effort devoted to such exploratory research will depend on the research budget, as well as experience conducting research in a given country environment.

Organizational and administrative issues may also be examined in the preliminary phase of research. These might include, for example, investigation of the availability and quality of research services in the various countries where research is to be conducted, as well as the costs of these services. In some cases, for example, particularly in developing countries in the Far East and Africa, qualified field staff and interviewers trained in conducting qualitative research may not be available. Consequently, local staff may have to be recruited and trained, or, alternatively, trained researchers from other countries utilized. Initial estimates of the cost of alternative procedures may also be obtained, to determine which is likely to prove the most cost efficient and to draw up the budget for the research.

Once the preliminary phase of the research has been completed, the next step is the design of the international marketing research plan. This in turn may involve a number of stages, and is frequently considerably more complex than domestic marketing research. (This process is outlined in Figure 2.1.)

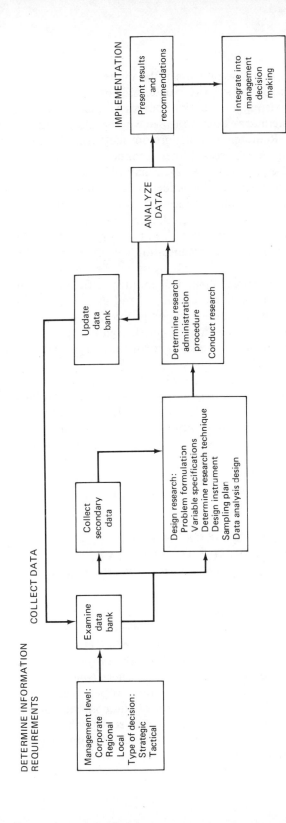

FIGURE 2-1 The international market research process

First, the nature of the decision to be made has to be specified, and a problem statement formulated so as to determine management information requirements. Next, existing information sources available to management or in the information system are examined to see whether they meet any or some of these requirements. Requirements that are not met from these sources have to be obtained from outside sources. Either secondary data sources may be consulted, or, alternatively, primary research may be conducted.

Where primary research is conducted, an important consideration is whether this is purchased from outside sources—for example, a research consultant or organization—or, alternatively, designed or executed in-house. In general, this is likely to depend on the size of the organization and its research staff, as well as the degree of the organization's involvement and experience in international operations.

The design of the research plan will entail specification of the data to be collected, as well as the research techniques and instruments to be used, the sampling plan, and research administration procedures and analyses to be conducted. This plan has then to be implemented. Again, this may either be done in-house, where a company possesses its own field organization, or, alternatively, purchased from outside sources.

The final step is the analysis of the information collected and its presentation to management. The findings have to be examined, some conclusions drawn, and recommendations made with regard to alternative courses of action. A key problem in this context is their presentation to management so as to maximize the likelihood of acceptance and use in the decision process. Procedures to incorporate findings into the information system need also be established to ensure that the findings are assimilated and become part of the stock of accumulated knowledge and experience in international markets.

DETERMINING INFORMATION REQUIREMENTS: THE LEVEL OF ANALYSIS AND TYPE OF DECISION

In determining information requirements, a primary consideration is the specific level and type of decision for which the research is being conducted. As in domestic research, information may be required in relation to decisions made at different levels in the organization, from the *corporate* level, relating to strategic issues, down to local operating units where concerns tend to be more tactical. Such decisions vary in focus and scope, from corporate decisions—determining the long-run direction of the company and implicit corporate objectives, spanning a diversity of different product lines—to operational decisions such as modification of advertising copy or packaging for a specific brand in a given country.

Where responsibility for different decisions is located in the organization, and hence specific problems investigated, will depend to a large extent on a company's organizational structure. In companies that have a highly diversified range of products and are organized by product division or strategic business unit, new product research and development may be conducted within the product division or strategic business unit at corporate headquarters. In companies that are decentralized or organized by geographic units, such research may be conducted at regional headquarters or linked to local operating units.

In general, however, irrespective of the level and location where research is conducted, two major types of decisions can be identified—strategic decisions and tactical decisions. These differ significantly in their information requirements, or rather in the types of data most commonly used to aid in such decision making. Strategic decision making in international markets is likely to rely heavily on secondary data sources, in addition to management experience accumulated through operating in different countries and marketing environments. In some cases, however, primary data collection may be required. Tactical decisions, on the other hand, are likely to require primary data collection and research tailored to the specific decision to be made.

Information for Strategic Decisions

Global strategic decisions are made primarily at the corporate level. These concern decisions with regard to market expansion and development strategies—that is, whether and which new countries or product markets should be entered—and what modes of entry—that is, exporting, licensing, joint venture—should be used in entering these countries and product markets. In addition, decisions have to be made with regard to market segmentation strategies, that is, whether markets are segmented on a country-by-country or on a transnational basis, and what positioning strategies should be used relative to each target segment.

Such decisions thus imply determining the overall allocation of company resources across countries, product markets, and target segments. As such, they go beyond the marketing function, encompassing other functional areas such as financial and production management; and entail decisions relating to capital budgeting, accounting procedures, or production scheduling. Different modes of entry, for example, imply different levels of financial and resource commitment.

For instance, licensing typically entails a minimal financial commitment and risk in international markets, but also more limited returns. Exporting does not require the establishment of a production facility, although in some cases a sales organization may be set up. Direct investment, on the other hand, implies greater commitment of financial resources but a higher return. Thus, the risks associated with operating in a particular country or product market may be mitigated by the specific mode of entry or operation.

In addition, given limited resources, decisions to enter different countries or product markets are highly interrelated, since decisions to develop new products, to expand existing product lines, or to extend them to other countries and product markets involve commitment of resources to specific countries or product markets. The potential for economies of scale associated with multiple product operations in a given country, or in multiple countries, suggests the need for an integrated perspective in making such decisions, coordinating international operations across product lines and divisions and across geographic or regional areas. Evaluation of entry into new countries or product markets or target segments should thus be made relative to expansion and development (or divestment) of existing operations in other countries and product markets.

Adoption of an integrated approach in making such decisions implies that information will be required at different levels corresponding to different entities in relation to which decisions have to be made, that is, regions, countries, product markets, and target segments. These will vary, depending on the organizational structure of the company by, for example, product division, geographical area, or strategic business unit. Furthermore, information will be required relating not only to marketing factors such as sales volume or product ownership, but also to financial variables such as rates of inflation and foreign exchange risk, to legal factors such as product or advertising regulation, and to political factors such as expropriations.

Some illustrations of the type of information likely to be required at each of these levels is summarized in Table 2.1. It should, however, be noted that these examples are illustrative only. The specific information to be collected by management will need to be determined in each case, depending on management and corporate objectives, company resources, and the relevant product market and target segment.

At the country level, two major dimensions need to be taken into consideration in making resource allocation decisions. These relate to the *risks* and the *opportunities* associated with operating in different countries. Surrogate indicators of these can be developed. As indicated in Table 2.1, risks might be assessed based on factors such as the number of expropriations, rates of inflation, and foreign exchange risk; and opportunities based on indicators such as GNP per capita, growth of GNP, and population size and density.

As noted previously, different modes of operation and marketing strategies entail different costs. The costs associated with these can be estimated based on factors such as costs of electricity, energy, water, and labor; retail margins; media costs; and transportation rates. At the product market level, information relating to current and projected performance levels—as, for example, ROI or market share—is likely to be required. This information will, however, only be available in relation to product markets in which the firm is currently operating. In product markets where the firm is not currently in-

TABLE 2.1   Sample indicators for assessing risks and opportunities

	Type of indicators	Sample indicators
Country entry decisions	Political risk	Number of expropriations, expert ratings of stability
Risks	Financial risk	Rate of inflation, foreign exchange risk, restrictions on capital flow
	Legal risk	Import-export restrictions, restrictions on ownership
Opportunities	Macromarket potential	GNP per capita, growth of GNP, ratio of investment to GNP, population size, density, urbanization, educational level
Modes of entry decisions	Production and marketing costs	Electricity, energy costs, labor skills and costs, management training, capital and technology availability and costs, rates of interest
Product market decisions	Product market size	Sales volume of product, ownership of product, sales of complementary and substitute products, number, and size of competing firms

Source: Adapted from Susan P. Douglas and C. Samuel Craig, "Information for International Marketing Decisions" in Ingo Walter (ed.), *Handbook of International Business*. New York: John Wiley, 1982.

volved, surrogate indicators can be developed—as, for example, sales volume of products, product ownership, sales of complementary products, and number of competing firms.

Once this information has been collected, it can then be integrated into a computerized international data bank and updated on a regular basis. This will considerably facilitate integration of information into the management decision process. Some problems are likely to be encountered in developing such an information bank, due to lack of comparability in data collected in different countries and different environmental contexts. Such issues need to be resolved, and procedures need to be developed for rapid access to and retrieval of data in a form suitable to the relevant management decision. These issues are discussed further in Chapter 10.

Information for Tactical Decisions

The second type of information required in making international marketing decisions aids in determining the specific tactics to be used in different countries and product markets. These are closely linked to market segmentation and positioning decisions. It is, for example, necessary to determine, given a specific positioning strategy, what advertising copy to use, how far a standardized theme can be used, or what adjustments to a standard prototype campaign will be required. Examples of the types of decisions and related research are shown in Table 2.2.

Decisions with regard to new product development will, for example, require product benefit and attribute research, concept testing, and, often, test marketing in all the countries in which it is planned to market the product. Questions may arise as to whether products should be adapted to meet differing environmental and market conditions, such as competing products and differing customer tastes, needs, and interests in other countries. Similarly, new products may be developed in response to these conditions, or new outlets for existing products may be found in new target markets or countries investigated.

The effectiveness of using the same advertising theme or similar sales promotion tools in different countries or cultures may also be tested to determine whether these should be applied, or whether specific appeals and promotional tools geared to the particular market environment will be required. Research may also be desirable to assess whether price elasticities are similar in different countries, and hence, whether similar pricing strategies can be used. The idiosyncratic characteristics of the media and distribution infrastructure in each country are likely to dictate appropriate policies in making media and distribution decisions, and hence, research will focus on identifying such characteristics.

The type of information required in relation to these decisions is essentially the same as that required in comparable domestic marketing research and often entails similar research procedures. Greater use may, however, be made of qualitative research techniques, especially in the initial stages of market entry, due to lack of familiarity with the environment. Furthermore, the research

TABLE 2.2 Tactical international marketing decisions requiring international marketing research

Marketing mix decision	Type of research
Product policy decision	Focus groups and qualitative research to generate ideas for new products
	Survey research to evaluate new product ideas
	Concept testing, test marketing
	Product benefit and attitude research
	Product formulation and feature testing
Pricing decisions	Price sensitivity studies
Distribution decisions	Survey of shopping patterns and behavior
	Consumer attitudes to different store types
	Survey of distributor attitudes and policies
Advertising decisions	Advertising pretesting
	Advertising posttesting, recall scores
	Surveys of media habits
Sales promotion decisions	Surveys of response to alternative types of promotion
Sales force decisions	Tests of alternative sales presentations

process tends to be more complex since it is conducted in a variety of different cultural and environmental contexts, and there is a need for comparability across these different units.

UNIT OF ANALYSIS

Once information requirements have been determined, the next step is to determine the appropriate unit of analysis, that is, region, country, subgroup or segment within country, industry, and so on. Data may be collected relative to one or more of these, depending on the specific research problem, the type of information required, and the size of the research budget. The advantages and limitations of each of these units of analysis are next considered in more detail.

Region or Country Grouping

The first unit in relation to which analysis may be conducted is that of the geographic region or groups of countries. Secondary data are sometimes available for such units, as, for example, for the European Economic Community, or the LAFTA (Latin America Free Trade Association) group. In general, however, such data are more likely to be broken down by country.

In primary data collection, the rationale for using the region or country grouping as the unit of analysis is that, in some cases, patterns of behavior within these areas tend to be similar. Hence, it may be appropriate to design marketing strategies for specific geographic regions such as Europe or Central America. In the automobile industry, for example, regional groupings of countries often define the relevant target market, due to the existence of economies of scale and the need for the integration of small markets. The same also applies to the pharmaceutical industry. Use of regions as units of analysis is, however, not appropriate if there is substantial heterogeneity of behavior within the region.

Country

The unit of analysis most commonly used in international marketing research is the country. As in the case of the region or country grouping, much secondary data are collected at the country level, for example, GNP, population, steel or energy consumption, price trends, and private consumption expenditures. Many market reports and industry studies are also conducted relative to a given country. Furthermore, in primary data collection, research organizations and networks are often organized by country.

The main advantage of using the country as the unit of analysis is thus that many data are already collected and available on this basis. The country is also frequently an important unit in the organization of international operations. Companies frequently establish national sales or marketing organizations or subsidiaries with responsibility for specific national markets.

If, however, the country is used as the unit of analysis, this implies that data are aggregated across regions or subgroups within countries, and it may in many cases give an illusion of homogeneity, masking the existence of wide diversity between regions within many countries. In Europe, for example, the wealthiest of the 119 regions of the Common Market, Hamburg, had an income in 1970, seven times as great as that of the poorest region, the Irish West Country (Morello, 1977). Substantial differences in economic conditions and life style may also be observed between Northern and Southern Italy. Similarly, data relating to aggregate values or living patterns, as, for example, the Yankelovich Monitor data (de Vulpian, 1974) or the *Reader's Digest* European survey may hide significant differences with regard to values or living standards among different sectors of the population.

In general, therefore, it is important to realize that, while the country has traditionally been used as the relevant unit of analysis in international marketing research, it is not necessarily the most appropriate. Countries are often highly heterogeneous with regard to a variety of factors such as language diversity, socioeconomic and technological development, social cohesion and wealth, and other factors affecting behavior patterns. Consequently, it is often desirable to pay attention to subgroupings within countries, such as cities, regions, or communities; or cultural subgroups, such as teenagers or blue-collar workers, when determining the appropriate unit(s) of analysis.

Subgroups Within Countries

In some cases subgroups or entities within countries provide an appropriate unit of analysis in international marketing research. These can be geographic units—as, for example, regions within countries, cities, or communities—or, alternatively, organizational, cultural, and social subgroups such as specific industries, firms of a given size, teenagers, working women, or businessmen.

Use of such groupings as relevant units of analysis is to a large extent based on the assumption that since these groups and organizations face similar problems and decision situations from country to country, they may be expected to have similar behavior and response patterns (Douglas, 1976). In some cases these may be closer to those of a comparable segment in another country than to other groups within the same country (Thorelli, Becker, and Engledow, 1975). Consequently, marketing strategies may be most effectively designed relative to such segments considered transnationally or on a global basis.

The primary disadvantage of such segments as units of analysis is the limited availability of secondary data relating to such units. Primary data collection costs may also tend to be high due to the difficulty of identifying such segments. Furthermore, it is not always clear to what extent such groupings provide clear-cut and unambiguous units for the purposes of analysis. Industries may be concentrated in specific regions. Particularly in the case of sociocultural subgroupings, boundaries of different subgroups may be overlapping. Catholic French Canadian teenagers, are, for example, members of the Catholic subculture as also the French Canadian subculture. Consequently, which affiliation will affect behavior in specific roles is an important consideration.

The complex and hierarchical character of many international marketing decisions, as well as the interrelationship between information requirements and organizational structure, implies that frequently the research design will require the use of a multiple-tier structure incorporating units at different levels. Thus, for example, while regional groupings of countries might provide the focal unit of analysis, data collection might be organized by countries within those regions, and from specific cities within those countries.

Thus, in marked contrast to domestic marketing research, which typically entails use of a single level or unit of analysis, selection of appropriate units of analysis in international marketing research is likely to follow a highly complex multistage structure. This structure in essence provides the framework for the research design and the organization of the research plan and, more specifically, for the determination of the sampling frame and subsequent data analysis (Chapters 8 and 9).

SELECTING INFORMATION SOURCES

The next stage in the research process is to investigate alternative data sources for the required information. Here, as in domestic research, two major types of data may be identified—secondary versus primary data. They can be obtained from sources that are external, that is, outside the company, or internal, that is, intracompany sources. Each has a number of advantages and limitations. These relate primarily to their cost relative to their availability, reliability, and applicability to the problem at hand. Each of these factors is next discussed in relation to the different types of data.

Secondary Versus Primary Data

Secondary data often play an important role in international marketing research, particularly in the initial phases of research. Various types of secondary data are available, ranging from government, economic, and social statistics, to reports published by trade associations, industry reports, and other commercial publications. The specific sources of such information are discussed in Chapter 3 and hence are not listed in detail here.

The primary advantage of such data is their low cost and ready availability. For example, government and United Nations statistics are to be found in most libraries. Access to world data banks, such as Business International, can be obtained by paying a small subscription fee and, in addition, analyses tailored to specific company problems may be obtained. Similarly, trade publications are generally available at only moderate cost. Such data are also particularly useful in providing initial indications concerning aggregate economic, social, and political markets. They thus help in pinpointing geographic areas and decision problems that need to be investigated more closely, and provide an indication as to what further information is required. This may lead to the collection of additional secondary data, or, alternatively, primary data.

The main disadvantage of such data is that they are typically collected on a regional or country basis, and hence may not be comparable. This is the case even for data such as population and GNP. These data are also frequently somewhat out of date. This is often critical given the rapid pace of change in many international markets. Furthermore, they are primarily macroindicators, relating to factors such as income, population, and economic and social trends, rather than specific market data required for marketing decisions. Similarly, industry reports and trade publications tend to be concerned predominantly with industry trends and growth. These are, therefore, only of limited relevance for specific problems faced by individual companies in the light of their own corporate objectives and position relative to such trends.

Where secondary data do not provide adequate information input for management decision making, primary data collection will be required. Collection of such data does, however, tend to entail high costs relative to its perceived value, that is, the extent to which it leads to improved management decision making. This stems in part from the difficulties encountered in international marketing research, and the lack of experience in conducting such research in many countries, which may result in data that are less reliable and accurate than those obtained in comparable domestic research.

Collection of primary data is nonetheless important for many strategic marketing decisions, for example, market segmentation. It is essential in relation to many tactical marketing decisions such as testing new products or new concepts or advertising copy, or in evaluating price sensitivity. In conducting such research, different types of data collection techniques may be used, ranging from qualitative data collection techniques such as focus groups, observation, and in-depth interviews, which require small sample sizes, to survey data collection techniques, which entail large sample sizes.

Qualitative data collection techniques are useful in the initial phases of research, since they enable identification of constructs, product class definitions, or relevant attitudes and behavior to be examined in subsequent phases of research. In international marketing research such techniques are particularly advantageous insofar as the researcher is often unfamiliar with the market environment and needs information about such parameters. Furthermore, they avoid the imposition of a cultural bias, since no prespecified conceptual model is imposed a priori by the researcher. On the other hand, the burden of interpretation is placed on the researcher to determine which concepts, attitudes, or behavior are considered relevant. Consequently, it is important to incorporate explicit procedures in the research design, to eliminate or reduce any potential sources of cultural bias.

In subsequent phases of research, and particularly where more precise estimation is required, survey research is likely to be desirable. Such data collection techniques are widely used in international marketing research and have the advantage that data can be collected and processed from large samples.

Use of the survey in international marketing research is, however, fraught with a number of difficulties, stemming largely from operation in a range of diverse sociocultural and linguistic environments. Such factors imply that considerable care needs to be exercised in instrument design to avoid errors of interpretation on the part of respondents, particularly among those of low socioeconomic status or those with low levels of literacy. Similarly, sampling and survey administration procedures need to be designed to avoid bias arising from nonresponse or respondent-interviewer interaction.

A number of pitfalls thus lie in the path of international marketing research and are especially pronounced in the case of primary data collection. These are examined in Chapters 5, 6, 7, and 8 along with appropriate procedures to avoid or mitigate their impact on the validity and reliability of the data obtained.

External Versus Internal Data

Another important distinction in the type of data used in international marketing research is that between external data, that is, collected outside the firm, and internal data, that is, drawn from within company data sources. Secondary data can be both external or internal, while primary data are generally external, though in some cases may be collected within the organization.

External data provide information primarily with regard to environmental trends, demand patterns, competition, and the distributor network. In particular, this can be useful in providing insights about current economic, social, and political developments, and their impact on general business and industry conditions. External data can also provide insights concerning competitive factors, such as market share, characteristics of leading competitive products and services, and the strategies and policies of leading competitors. Data concerning the number of current and potential customers, customer characteristics, where customers live, what motivates and interests them, where and how frequently they purchase, how much they purchase and how they purchase, that is, by cash or credit, are also typically obtained from external data sources.

Internal secondary data are likely to come predominantly from the firm's accounting records, particularly relating to sales and cost data. These data are primarily useful insofar as they provide information about profitability and growth trends for specific products, product lines, geographic regions, channels of distribution, and the effectiveness of different marketing tools such as advertising, merchandising, sales promotions, personal selling, and price cuts. But a number of problems in the use of such data in international marketing research result from different national accounting systems and procedures, and different fiscal and taxation systems. Consequently, extensive reworking of existing information may be required in order to produce information comparable from one country to another as well as adapted to management needs.

Internal resources may also be utilized to collect primary data. This is likely to be particularly appropriate in industrial markets where sales representatives often provide a valuable source of information with regard to potential customers and the needs and interests of existing customers. Surveys of salespersons' opinions may be taken in order to provide input for new product development decisions, product modification decisions, and changes in promotional or delivery policies. Use of such procedures helps to reduce costs associated with surveys of clients and potential customers. Various caveats need, however, be issued, especially in the use of sales representatives' opinions, since bias might be a factor if information supplied will influence establishment of sales quotas.

Headquarters may also survey the opinions and attitudes of management in local subsidiaries, sales, or marketing organizations, toward current trends and developments in local national markets. These might, for example, focus on changes in customer needs and interests, receptivity to new products, response to changes in marketing strategy and tactics, as well as likely reactions and retaliatory strategies by competitors and distributors. Such inputs are often crucial to effective international marketing planning.

RESEARCH PLAN

Once secondary data sources have been investigated, the next step is to draw up a plan for primary data collection. Essentially the same steps as those involved in designing domestic marketing research will need to be followed. It should, however, be remembered that the plan will frequently be more complex than in domestic research, entailing a number of successive stages and, often, the integration of secondary data with collection of primary data.

First, the specific variables or factors to be examined, and also categorization of these variables, have to be specified. Then, relevant relationships between these variables are hypothesized. Appropriate research techniques have to be determined—for example, whether qualitative research should be conducted to examine the hypothesized relationships. Research instruments suitable for use in all the countries covered must be developed, sampling procedures determined, and appropriate administration procedures selected. Once the data have been collected, they have then to be analyzed and presented in a form that can be clearly understood by management.

The major differences between international and domestic marketing research stem from operation in a multicountry, and therefore multicultural and multilinguistic, environment. This gives rise to a number of issues relating to the comparability of data collected in such diverse research environments, and also the extent to which similar research instruments and procedures are equally adapted or suitable and, hence, will yield comparable results in each environment. This implies that phases such as problem formulation, and specification of relevant data and of instrument design, assume paramount importance and pose a number of somewhat different issues from those encountered in domestic marketing research.

Problem Formulation, Variable Specification, and Categorization

Problems may not always be couched in the same terms in different countries or cultural contexts. This may reflect differences in socioeconomic conditions, levels of economic development, cultural factors, or competitive market structure. Differences in levels of economic development may, for example, imply that the relevant set of competing products and services, or the relevant product attributes, differ. In Asian countries, for example, cars remain luxury items, and hence small compacts may be competing with scooters or mopeds. Similarly, products such as washing machines may be competing with low-cost laundry services or in-home help.

Even more complex differences may arise in the case of attitudinal data where differences in sociocultural variables and life style factors may imply existence of different attitudinal constructs that underlie preferences for different products or desired product benefits. Customers in different countries vary with regard to the significance and prestige value attached to brand names such as Lincoln Continental, Dior, or Cardin, and to the possession of different items such as cars, clothing, or household appliances. Similarly, the importance attached to saving time, or to product reliability, varies, and this influences customer interest in products such as "instant breakfast" or Minute Rice, or their concern with product quality and engineering.

All of these factors imply that, in specifying the scope and specific content of the research design, careful attention needs to be given to the equivalence of consumption and purchase behavior and relevant factors influencing them. These issues are addressed in Chapter 5.

Choice of Research Techniques

Selection of appropriate research techniques also poses a number of issues with regard to their comparability and cost effectiveness in different countries and cultural contexts, and in the relation of research techniques to specific research problems. Essentially, this involves a decision as to whether to conduct a survey; make use of experimental techniques; collect data by observation or other qualitative procedures, for example, focus group or projective techniques; or use some combination of these.

Survey research is the procedure most commonly used in multicountry research. The effectiveness of this method varies considerably from country to country, since it essentially assumes the existence of a population with a certain minimal level of education, able to comprehend and respond to oral or written questions; and the availability of sampling lists or profile data from which to draw samples. These conditions are not always met, particularly in developing countries. Consequently, considerable ingenuity may be required in devising research instruments and procedures to overcome potential communication and comprehension problems.

Experimental techniques are, at least in theory, potentially applicable to all cultural and socioeconomic backgrounds. In practice, however, it is often difficult to design an experiment that is comparable or equivalent in all respects in every country or sociocultural context. Experiments, particularly field experiments, typically incorporate certain elements of the specific sociocultural context in which they are conducted. This is particularly the case when experimental techniques are applied to marketing problems, such as in market tests. Here, it is, for example, likely that differences in the structure of distribution or in the competitive structure will make such tests not strictly comparable.

Observational and projective techniques avoid some of the problems associated with survey techniques since they do not impose any prestructured frame of reference on respondents. This may reflect the specific cultural referents of the researcher and hence be a potential source of bias. On the other hand, the lack of structure implies that the onus of interpretation of the data and their meaning lies on the researcher, and hence may be subject to criticisms of cultural bias at the analysis stage. Various types of nonsurvey research techniques are covered in Chapter 6.

Instrument Design

Differences in sociocultural factors in different countries also require that extreme care be taken in instrument design. In particular, it is necessary to ensure that potential problems of miscommunication between respondents and researcher are eliminated. In essence, the prime issue is to ensure translation of the research instrument into concepts and terms that have equivalent meaning and relevance in all contexts and cultures studied.

Where research occurs in settings that involve different linguistic backgrounds, translation of the research instrument and response format to ensure equivalence across these different contexts is necessary. Frequently, this gives rise to considerable difficulties in obtaining equivalence, due to the language or culture-bound nature of many terms and concepts. Use of nonverbal, as opposed to verbal, stimuli or response measures can aid in facilitating comprehension, but does not totally eliminate miscommunication problems, since nonverbal stimuli will also require translation to ensure stimuli of equivalent meaning in each cultural context.

Different types of cultural bias in the research interaction, such as yea-saying, nay-saying, social acquiescence, or cultural stereotyping, need as far as possible to be minimized, or at least carefully assessed. This should be taken into consideration, not only in the design of the research instrument—for example, the questionnaire in a survey or an experiment—but also of the response format, since different types of formats tend to be more or less prone to different types of response bias. These issues are discussed in Chapter 7.

Sampling and Survey Administration Techniques

Yet another consideration in international marketing research is that of sampling and survey administration procedures. Here, important issues include the difficulties of obtaining sampling lists in many countries, achieving comparability in sample composition and representativity, as well as differences in the feasibility and cost effectiveness of using different data collection procedures.

Given the absence of population lists, and other lists commonly used as sampling frames, difficulties may be encountered in applying random sampling techniques. Consequently, use of nonrandom procedures may be desirable and more cost efficient. Sampling procedures, such as random walk, cluster, or area sampling, may also vary in reliability and accuracy from one country to another, and hence, a mix of these may be needed to obtain roughly comparable samples.

Similarly, data collection techniques such as mail or telephone surveys and personal interviewing vary in relative cost, feasibility, and coverage of the population. In international research, low levels of literacy may preclude the use of mail surveys, and low levels of telephone ownership, telephone surveys. Consequently, greater reliance may be placed on personal interviewing. However, this requires the availability of trained interviewers conversant with the relevant language. These issues are discussed in Chapter 8.

Data Analysis

Data analysis also poses certain unique problems in international research. While the specific analytic techniques applied depend on the problem format and the nature of the data collected, procedures to test for and minimize sources of cultural bias need to be incorporated in the research design.

Normalization or standardization of data, to adjust for the impact of cultural referent points and response biases, is typically desirable. This is particularly necessary in the case of attitudinal and opinion variables where tendencies for specific response set biases may be prevalent. The multitier character of international marketing research also suggests the desirability of following a sequential procedure in analyzing multicountry data. Data are thus examined first for each country or other relevant unit independently, and cultural biases are identified. Issues of equivalence and comparability are examined, and then data are compared or analyzed across different countries. In this context, it should be noted that existing statistical procedures are not well suited to the multilevel hierarchical character of much international marketing research, and frequently hybrid or analytic solutions are required. These issues are discussed in Chapter 9.

ISSUES IN ADMINISTERING INTERNATIONAL MARKETING RESEARCH

Once the research plan has been established, there are still a number of organizational and administrative issues that need to be resolved in order to implement the plan. While such details tend to be procedural, they are nonetheless important for successful international marketing research and plan implementation. Three major issues in this regard are the degree of centralization in coordinating the overall research effort, the extent to which research services are obtained outside the firm, and the cost of conducting research. Each of these is further discussed in the next section.

The Degree of Centralization in Research

The appropriate degree of centralization depends to a large extent on the organizational structure of the company, the nature of the decision, and the level and location in the organization where the decision is made. In international operations, companies vary considerably in structure and, in particular, with regard to the degree of centralization. In a highly centralized organization, plans are established at corporate headquarters, and local subsidiaries or operating units implement these plans with only minor modifications to local market conditions. In a highly decentralized organization, operations are organized on a country-by-country basis. Local operating units develop their own marketing plans and adapt tactics to local market conditions. Central headquarters thus exercises little control over local operations other than in financial terms. Between these two extremes are a number of alternatives, such as providing mechanisms like regional committees to coordinate and integrate operations across geographic areas.

In essence, three major approaches to organizing international marketing research may be identified: 1) centralized, 2) coordinated, and 3) decentralized (Ewen, 1981). These are outlined in Figure 2.2. Centralized research, directed and controlled at corporate headquarters, may be the most appropriate where the purpose of the research is to provide input into corporate policy and strategic decision making. There is, however, a danger of misinterpreting local nuances and downplaying environmental factors. In coordinated research, an outside research agency is used to design and coordinate research conducted in different countries. Management in local subsidiary operations is thus likely to review the research plan and to monitor its implementation. In the case of

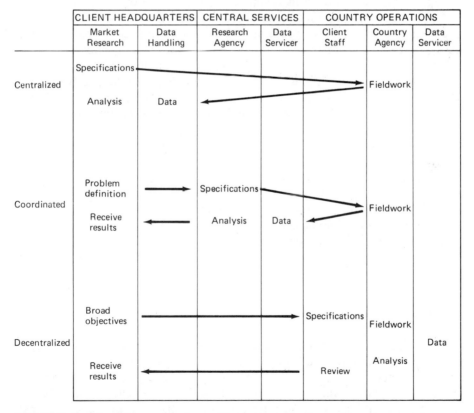

FIGURE 2-2 Alternative modes of organizing and coordinating multicountry research

Source: Adapted from John W. Ewen, "Industrial Research in International Markets," American Marketing Association/Market Research Society Conference, New York, October 20, 1981.

decentralized research, responsibility for the establishment of research specifications and organization is delegated to local country management, once broad guidelines have been established by corporate headquarters. This may, however, result in the collection of data that are not comparable across countries as well as substantial emphasis on local country-specific issues.

Centralized Organization

Where a centralized mode of organization is adopted, the research unit at corporate headquarters establishes the specifications for the research that is to be conducted in each country. The research may use secondary data where, for example, country screening studies are concerned, or it may entail primary data collection. In either case the details of the research design and data analysis are specified at corporate headquarters. Secondary data or fieldwork may be purchased from an outside organization, that is, a local research agency or organization, but data analysis is conducted at headquarters.

This approach provides maximum control and also ensures comparability in data across countries. In addition, it may help to hold down costs. Often, however, the international research staff at corporate headquarters will not be sufficiently large or have the technical expertise to handle large-scale and complex projects. Consequently, it is better suited for simple studies, such as initial market entry or country-screening studies, or in situations involving confidential data, where it may be desirable to limit the number of external participants involved.

On the other hand, there is the danger of ethnocentric cultural bias. Central headquarters will prefer a uniform research design with minimal adaptation to differences in local conditions, since this facilitates control of research and is consistent with a strategic, as opposed to a tactical, orientation (Adler, 1975). Problems of communication and coordination can, however, arise when research findings are implemented by local operating units, since they did not participate in the research process. They may complain of a lack of attention to specific local factors and environmental conditions and hence of inappropriate or unimplementable corporate policy.

Coordinated Organization

In the case of coordinated organization, corporate headquarters will participate in the definition of the research to be conducted, but an external research agency or organization will spell out the details of the research design, take charge of the administration and coordination of the fieldwork in different countries and data analysis. They then report results to corporate or regional headquarters. This may result in some of the same problems of communication and coordination between corporate headquarters and local operating units if responsibility for research design and field operations is delegated to an external agency. This can, to some extent, be alleviated by requesting management or research staff in local operating units to examine the research design and data collection plan. They may then indicate their opinion, based on their experience with previous research and knowledge of local market conditions, concerning the suitability and likely cost efficiency of the proposed plan. They may also control the fieldwork, data collection, and analysis.

This may ease local country management objections to plans based on such research. On the other hand, it may also result in some problems with regard to lack of comparability in the data, if modifications are made locally in research design or data collection procedures.

Decentralized Organization

The third major alternative is decentralization. Here, corporate headquarters establishes research objectives in broad terms, and leaves the detailed specifications of the research design and management of the research process to local country operating units. Local management is thus responsible for data collection and analysis and, once this is concluded, presents a report on relevant findings to corporate headquarters. This approach is likely to be most appropriate where research is intended as an input to tactical, as opposed to strategic, decisions.

The primary advantage of this type of approach is that it provides optimal adaptation to differences in local market conditions and in research capabilities and services in different countries. It is thus also likely to be appropriate where qualitative research is to be conducted. Here, there will often be a need for the adaptation of research to the local environment. Consequently, allowance for local input and modifications is highly desirable.

On the other hand, problems with regard to comparability in research design or data collection procedures may arise. In addition, an inclination to adopt a country-specific perspective and to focus on aspects specific to a given national environment may occur. This can to some extent be alleviated by establishing international or regional coordinating committees and meetings (Adler, 1975). Such procedures can, however, add to administrative costs, as well as prolonging the research process. Scheduling of fieldwork and of reports also need to be coordinated, to ensure comparability in the timing of the research. Sometimes, this can give rise to difficulties, due to operation across geographic distances and international boundaries. Delays can, for example, occur in mailing or receipt of data and reports. Standardized procedures for coding and categorization of data, as well as for data analysis and report preparation, may also to be desirable in order to ensure comparability (Franzen and Light, 1976). Development of standardized procedures is in fact often critical to ensure effective communication and coordination of local research.

This is especially the case where research is undertaken by researchers of different cultural backgrounds, and hence, research traditions, especially if these are far apart.

Such problems can become particularly acute when conducting research in developing countries. This suggests that in such cases a centralized or coordinated approach may be preferable. This is particularly desirable if highly sophisticated quantitative data collection procedures are to be utilized. Questionnaires can thus be centrally developed and administered by local branch units. This may also involve decentralized pretesting with the preliminary results being telexed to a central location for coordination and modification.

Ideally, the organization of international research should strike a delicate balance between centralization and direction of research from the central administrative unit, or corporate headquarters, and decentralization or local autonomy in research design and implementation. The former may result in lack of attention to specific local idiosyncracies and problems of implementation. The latter is likely to lead to research and data that are not comparable across countries. In either case, however, mechanisms to ensure effective communication and control between local operating units and central administrative units are essential.

In-House Versus Outside Research Services

A second issue concerns the use of in-house research capabilities versus the purchase of outside research services. As noted previously, it is unlikely that many companies will have the in-house expertise to design and implement all the types of research required in all international markets. This is particularly the case where primary data collection is involved. The need for familiarity with the local research environment and for multiple linguistic competence is typically critical for effective field research. Consequently, unless a study entails predominantly desk research, purchase of outside services is likely to be required.

The ten largest research organizations are shown in Table 2.3. The four largest organizations essentially offer specialized services. Nielsen, for example, provides retail store audit data predominantly. Its drug index and bimonthly food index are available in all the 22 countries in which it has operations. Test-marketing services are available in all but two countries, and controlled store tests and product pick-up service in all but five. SAMI offers as its main service, a warehouse withdrawal monitoring service, but it operates in only the United States and Canada.

Some organizations specialize in particular product markets. IMS International, the second largest research organization in volume of sales, is the dominant researcher in the pharmaceutical area and conducts audits of pharmaceutical products and panels of physicians worldwide. Other organizations,

TABLE 2.3   Top ten market research companies worldwide, 1980

	Research revenues	Countries with office	International head office
	($m)		
1. A. C. Nielsen	363	22	U.S.A.
2. IMS International	102	57	U.K. (U.S.A. parentage)
3. SAMI	63	2	U.S.A.
4. Arbitron	55	1	U.S.A.
5. Research International	51	29	U.K.
6. Infratest	49	6	Germany
7. AGB	46	9	U.K.
8. GfK	40	8	Germany
9. Burke Marketing Services	33	7	U.S.A.
10. Market Facts	26	2	U.S.A.

Source: Philip Barnard, "Conducting and Co-ordinating Multicountry Quantitative Studies Across Europe," *Journal of the Market Research Society,* 24 (1982), 46–64.

such as Market Behavior, headquartered in the United Kingdom, specialize in qualitative market research, including discussion groups and projective techniques.

The full-service organizations offer a range of services including consumer, industrial, agricultural and feasibility studies as well as a variety of data collection and processing services. The largest international research supplier is Research International, headquartered in the United Kingdom. With two exceptions, R.I.'s local offices have at least 10 permanent staff members. All offices have their own staff of interviewers. Omnibus surveys are conducted in 14 countries, which are typically the smaller markets, and the offices run consumer panels for product tests and surveys in 13 countries. Other major services include fixed location test centers and minitest markets. Other organizations, such as INRA or Gallup International, also supply international research services. These are, however, essentially research chains in which each national office operates independently but has an arrangement for cooperation on field work if a client of a specific national office wishes to conduct a multicountry study.

Much research tends to be ad hoc,—that is, product development and testing, and attitude and image studies—and hence focuses primarily on tactical decisions and qualitative studies. The profile of the "typical" research market in Table 2.4 indicates the types of research most commonly conducted. In the more industrialized countries, however, a higher proportion of the research budget is spent on continuous, that is, audit or monitoring, research, than is indicated in Table 2.4.

Understanding of the market, the primary purposes of ad hoc research, has already been gained, and, hence, the main focus is on monitoring performance. There is, however, variation from country to country in the type of

TABLE 2.4a   Profile of "typical" research market (by value)

	%
Continuous research	35
Ad hoc research	
Habit/attitude/image studies	15
Product development and testing (quantitative)	15
Qualitative	10
Industrial/agricultural/pharmaceutical/other nonconsumer	10
Others	5
Media research	5
Omnibuses	5

b. European marketing research market structure (by value)

	Ad hoc	Continuous
		%
Austria	62	38
Belgium	52	48
Denmark	75	25
Finland	60	40
France	69	31
Germany (F.D.R.)	65	35
Greece	75	25
Ireland	67	33
Italy	50	50
Netherlands	65	35
Norway	55	45
Portugal	59	41
Spain	47	53
Sweden	48	52
Switzerland	59	41
U.K.	65	35

Source: Philip Barnard, "Market Research in the World Economy," *Market Research Society Newsletter,* 150 (September 1978), 9–14.

research conducted. In Australia, Malaysia, Denmark, and Finland, for example, substantial use is made of omnibuses. These are surveys conducted by research agencies and sold to a number of clients. In some cases the clients will add their own questions. Also, the type of research conducted changes over time. In India, for example, there is less product testing than previously, as understanding of consumer tastes has grown, and greater emphasis is placed on market monitoring.

Choice of organizations or type of service depends to a large extent on the type of research required, and, in particular, the degree of methodological sophistication required. In the case of exploratory marketing research, use of traveling research executives and qualitative research may be appropriate. If more extensive ad hoc market surveys are required, use of one of the large international full-service research organizations with offices and experience in the countries to be investigated may be desirable. Similarly, if highly specialized research is required, such as in pharmaceuticals, use of organizations specialized in the product market is likely to be preferable.

Other considerations include the size and resources of the supplier, adequate facilities for qualitative research, software for data analysis, access to corporate facilities, and the range of services offered. Technical capability and experience with more sophisticated research techniques such as conjoint analysis, multidimensional scaling, simulation, or preference modeling may also be important. Experience in international marketing research and in the countries to be investigated is frequently the critical determinant.

In purchasing outside services, another issue is whether to purchase all services from the same supplier, or whether to "patch together" services from different suppliers. Use of a single supplier helps in building a working relationship and minimizes the administrative effort required, but can, on the other hand, lead to a monopoly situation. However, only a limited number of companies provide a complete range of services and are likely to cover all countries desired. Alternatively, services can be purchased from multiple suppliers, that is, medium-sized and small ad hoc agencies. However, this may entail greater costs, inconvenience, and difficulties for management, particularly in research organization and administration. Use of different suppliers for different projects and types of research—that is, qualitative versus survey research—may, therefore, be desirable.

The Cost of International Marketing Research

The cost of conducting research in international markets is often higher than for a comparable study in the domestic market. This stems in part from differences in the degree of development of the marketing research infrastructure, and the availability, efficiency, and experience of marketing research organizations. Costs may also be higher, depending on the nature and quality of the data collected, and the difficulties associated with the data-collection process.

These costs, which may be high relative to expected market size, may constitute a psychological barrier in undertaking international marketing research, especially for small and medium-sized companies with little experience in overseas markets. As a result, research is often conducted after the fact, when some blunder has been made, rather than prior to making a strategic or tactical decision. Furthermore, the bulk of the research is concentrated in the major industrial nations where expected market size is sufficiently large to justify the ex-

TABLE 2.5 Marketing research expenditures worldwide, 1980

Area	Expenditure in dollars (000,000)
North America	$ 1,350
Europe	1,000
Asia/Oceania	270
Central and South America	70
Africa	40
Middle East	20
Total	$ 2,750

Source: Philip Barnard, "Conducting and Co-ordinating Multi-Country Quantitative Studies Across Europe," *Journal of the Market Research Society,* 24 (1982), 46–64.

penditure. As Table 2.5 indicates, of the nearly $3 billion spent on commissioned marketing research in 1980, more than 85 percent was conducted in North America or Western Europe.

It also implies that few companies other than the major multinationals, who in fact account for the majority of marketing research expenditure, will conduct research prior to market entry or making a decision to prevent what may become costly errors.

Little research is, for example, conducted in certain parts of the world, notably Central and South America, Africa, and the Middle East. However, these are markets with which management is less likely to have experience, and hence may be more prone to make mistakes. Also, in these areas the marketing research infrastructure is not likely to be as well developed, and hence, conducting marketing research will be more difficult.

Comparisons of levels of expenditure are, however, somewhat misleading, since the costs of conducting research in various parts of the world vary. These costs do not always parallel wage and salary levels in each country, but also depend on the efficiency and experience of marketing research organizations. Trained psychologists may, for example, be used in qualitative research, and charge higher rates than a marketing researcher. Similarly, funded social costs may add considerably to field interviewing expenses. For example, in France an additional 50 percent must be added to the basic interviewer fee for funded social costs. In the United Kingdom there are no such costs unless the interviewer earns more than $200 per month, in which case it is 9 percent (Barnard, 1982). In Europe, research costs are substantially lower in the United Kingdom than in other countries, as indicated in Table 2.6.

Strict cost comparisons between the European cost levels and the United States are also difficult, as the nature of the research supply industry differs (Barnard, 1982). In the United States, research design and analysis are more

TABLE 2.6   Cost of research in Europe relative to U.K.

	AGENCY A	AGENCY B	AGENCY A	
	Fieldwork out of pocket expenses	*Field/punching*	*Executive cost rates*	*Consumer packaged good product and ad tests*
	1980	*1978/79*	*1980*	*1975–1978*
U.K.	1.0	1.0	1.0	1.0
Belgium	1.7	2.1	2.4	1.7
Denmark	2.6	1.9	1.2	2.5
France	2.2	2.1	2.4	3.2
Germany	2.4	2.4	1.4	3.1
Italy	2.0	1.8	1.3	2.2
Netherlands	1.7	2.1	2.3	2.3
Sweden	3.4	3.0	1.5	3.3
Spain	1.6	2.0	1.1	—

Source: Adapted from Eileen Cole, "Where Are We Starting From: Where Are We Going" XXXIII ESOMAR Congress, Monte Carlo (September 14–18, 1980).

likely to be handled by the client, with executive cost being covered in the gross margin rather than covered separately. United States suppliers are more likely to subcontract fieldwork while European firms are more likely to have their own. Finally, while mall intercept and telephone interviews are used extensively in the United States, personal interviewing at home is still the most common form of data collection in Europe (Barnard, 1982).

These cost variations imply that the same study executed in different countries may vary in expense. This must be incorporated into the overall planning of a multicountry research project. The research budget must be based on the actual costs likely to be encountered in all countries, not just in those of the home country.

Furthermore, if research organizations have the capacity to conduct research in several countries, it may be desirable to select a country where executive costs are lower or research organizations more cost effective, and to use these as the preferred location from which to conduct international marketing research. This should not, however, be done at the expense of quality research, based on the lowest bid. Careful examination of the relation between costs and delivered product, quality controls, and so on should, therefore, be made before a supplier is selected.

While the absolute level of marketing research costs vary by country, the cost relative to the level of sales in each country may vary even more dramatically. Many marketing costs are essentially variable and will be proportional to the level of business activity in a particular country. However, given that sample size requirements do not vary directly with the size of the universe being sampled, smaller countries may account for disproportionately high marketing research costs. Table 2.7 presents hypothetical data on a multinational corpora-

TABLE 2.7   Hypothetical sales/research cost relationship for a multinational company

Operations	Sales volume (000)	Cost of research survey	Percent of sales
Domestic			
U.S.	$600,000	$50,000	.0083
International			
Country A	60,000	50,000	.083
Country B	50,000	50,000	.100
Country C	40,000	50,000	.125
Country D	30,000	50,000	.167
Country E	20,000	50,000	.250
40 Remaining Countries	200,000	2,000,000	1.000
Total International	400,000	2,500,000	.625
Total Sales	1,000,000		

tion with $1 billion annual sales.[1] The research costs shown are for cross-sectional surveys in each of forty-six countries in which the company does business. For simplicity, all costs are assumed to be the same; however, as already indicated, these costs would also differ. The cost of the surveys as a percent of sales varies considerably; so much so in fact that in some countries the level of sales would not justify the survey cost, and executive judgment or secondary data would have to be relied upon.

In situations where it is difficult to justify a customized survey, omnibuses provide a convenient means of reducing costs for small and fragmented markets. A number of research organizations conduct omnibus surveys at regular intervals; in some cases they relate to specialized product markets or segments such as baby products. Companies can buy the results of these surveys and in some cases may negotiate specific additional questions to be included in the survey. Costs are lower since the cost of collecting data relating to demographic or socioeconomic data or product purchase data is spread across a number of companies.

The frequency with which omnibuses are conducted depends on the nature and degree of development of the product market (Webb, 1982). In Britain or Germany, for example, an omnibus might be conducted fortnightly, whereas in Italy or Austria, it might be conducted monthly, and in Indonesia or Malaysia, quarterly. In addition, omnibuses are not very appropriate for sensitive topics, such as political reactions or response to advertising. They are, however, very useful for investigations of more enduring attitudes, such as company image or major consumer durable ownership.

International research budgets also need to take into account problems

---

[1] This example was suggested by Edwin Sonnecken, Chairman, Marketing Science Institute.

caused by delays in delivery of research, and by transportation and communication delays in international markets. Problems may occur with regard to the shipment of data, getting test products through customs, unreliability of carriers and mail services, and so on. Field services may not meet target dates, thus causing scheduling problems. Delays may creep in, as key personnel or executives on visits to foreign countries may succumb to local diseases such as malaria. Consequently, some margin needs to be allowed for such factors.

Fluctuating foreign exchange rates and differing rates of inflation are also crucial factors to be considered, since these can have a dramatic impact on international research costs. This is particularly the case when research is being conducted in countries that are politically and economically unstable, as, for example, many of the South American countries. Yet, even in a country such as France, these factors can give rise to problems, as the impact of the 1981 election on exchange rates demonstrates. This issue becomes particularly important when the research project is a major one involving a number of countries, and is spread out over one or two years. Cost escalation clauses may have to be built into contracts to account for these types of contingencies.

SUMMARY

As with domestic marketing research, the decisions facing management provide the basis for determining information requirements and, hence, for the conduct of international marketing research. Yet, while the management decision problems provide direction for marketing research, the complexity of the international environment, and in particular its linguistic and sociocultural diversity, give rise to a number of conceptual, methodological, and organizational problems in the conduct of that research. The first stage in the process is frequently an assessment of information needs and availability. Second, the level at which various decisions are made in the organization,—that is, corporate, strategic business unit, or product—and the type of decisions have to be determined. Decisions can either be strategic or tactical in nature. Strategic decisions are based primarily on secondary data. This can eventually lead to the establishment of an information bank that will need to be continually updated. Tactical decisions, on the other hand, are more likely to require the collection of primary data. Management can thus use either primary or secondary data, which may come from sources internal to the firm or from external sources.

A key consideration in the overall design of international marketing research is the unit of analysis. The units sampled can be regions, country groupings, countries, or subunits within countries. The selection of the unit(s) of analysis provides the framework for establishing the actual research plan. The first step in this plan involves problem formulation, variable specification, and categorization. Next, the appropriate research technique has to be selected.

Here, nonsurvey techniques are often helpful in the initial phases of research, and may provide guidelines for survey research in the latter stages of the research process. If a survey is to be conducted, then the instrument must be designed and adapted to each country or cultural context in which it is administered. The next step is to develop appropriate sampling techniques and survey administration procedures, that is, personal interview, telephone interview, or mail. Finally, the data must be analyzed to provide some insight into the questions initially posed by management.

Related to design issues in international research are issues concerned with how the research is administered. Here, the major trade-offs center around whether the research effort is highly centralized or decentralized. Also, the firm must decide whether it has the in-house capability to conduct and coordinate all phases of the research or whether outside suppliers are to be used. Frequently, some balance between centralization and decentralization should be struck, as well as between in-house control and purchase of outside services. Another important consideration is the cost of conducting international marketing research. This may vary considerably from country to country.

REFERENCES

ADLER, LEE, "Managing Marketing Research in the Diversified Multinational Corporation" in Edward M. Mazze (ed.), *Marketing in Turbulent Times and Marketing: The Challenges and Opportunities, Combined Proceedings*. Chicago: American Marketing Association, 1975, pp. 305–8.

BARNARD, PHILIP, "The Role and Implementation of International Marketing Research," *International Marketing Research ESOMAR Seminar*. Brussels: ESOMAR, 1976, pp. 49–65.

——, "Market Research in the World Economy," *Market Research Society Newsletter,* 150 (September 1978), 9–14.

——, "The World of Research," *Market Research Society Newsletter, 171,* (June 1980).

——, "Conducting and Co-ordinating Multicountry Quantitative Studies Across Europe," *Journal of Market Research Society,* 24 (1982), 46–64.

BERENT, PAUL-HOWARD, "International Research is Different," in Edward M. Mazze (ed.), *Marketing in Turbulent Times and Marketing: The Challenges and the Opportunities, Combined Proceedings*. Chicago: American Marketing Association, 1975, pp. 293–97.

COLE, EILEEN, "Where Are We Starting From: Where Are We Going," *Taking Stock: What Have We Learned and Where Are We Going,* XXXIII ESOMAR Congress, Monte Carlo, September, 1980.

DOUGLAS, SUSAN P., "Cross-National Comparisons and Consumer Stereotypes: A Case Study of Working and Non-Working Wives in the U.S. and France," *Journal of Consumer Research,* 3 (June 1976), 12–20.

―――― and C. SAMUEL CRAIG, "Information for International Marketing Decisions," in Ingo Walter (ed.), *Handbook of International Business*. New York: John Wiley, 1982.

EWEN, JOHN W., "Industrial Research in International Markets," American Marketing Association/Market Research Society Conference, New York, October 20, 1981.

FRANZEN, M.P. and LARRY LIGHT, "Standardize Process Not Programs," *International Marketing Research Seminar*. Brussels: ESOMAR, 1976, pp. 49–65.

MORELLO, GABRIELE, "Understanding the European Market," paper presented at the 60th AMA Conference on the New Role of the Marketing Professional, May 1977, Cleveland, OH.

READER'S DIGEST STAFF, "A Survey of Europe Today," London: Reader's Digest Association, 1970.

THORELLI, HANS, HELMUT BECKER, and JACK ENGLEDOW, *The Information Seekers: An International Study of Consumer Information and Advertising Image*. Cambridge, MA: Ballinger Publishing Co., 1975.

DE VULPIAN, ALAIN, "Les Courants Socio-culturels en France," *Les Styles de Vie,* in *Journées de l'IREP,* (May 1974), pp. 27–28.

WEBB, NORMAN, "International Omnibuses," *Market Research Society Newsletter,* 192 (March 1982), 24.

Secondary Data Sources

Secondary data are a key source of information for conducting international marketing research. This is in part due to their ready availability, the high cost of collecting primary data versus the relatively low cost of secondary data, and the usefulness of secondary data in assessing whether specific problems need to be investigated, and if so, how. Further, secondary data sources are particularly valuable in assessing opportunities in countries with which management has little familiarity, and in product markets at an early stage of market development, as for example, the developing countries.

Secondary data sources provide an easy means of rapidly gaining some initial awareness of the market environment in a foreign country, and of the problems that are likely to be encountered there. They are available either in libraries or, at low cost, from the organization or institution that publishes them. They can be quickly consulted in order to pinpoint areas of concern, and provide an overview of the context in which the company's products and services are to be marketed.

The high costs and difficulties of collecting primary data in foreign countries make secondary data especially valuable. This is particularly the case in relation to countries where market potential is small and, hence, does not warrant an elaborate full-scale study. It is also the case in countries where there are no organizations experienced in conducting research and, hence, there is the lack of a market research infrastructure and a research tradition.

Secondary data are also useful insofar as it may be desirable to adopt a two-step approach in international marketing research. Secondary data are used initially to identify areas of potential concern that merit in-depth investigation based on primary research. For example, secondary data might be used to identify which of the 150 or so countries in the world appear likely to offer the most attractive prospects or potential and should therefore be examined in-depth.

Secondary data are also relatively inexpensive to collect. Where a good business library is available, it merely requires the time of a research assistant to consult relevant sources and to amass the desired information. In many respects, the key problem here is the plethora of data available and the need for selectivity in identifying appropriate sources.

The objective of this chapter is to provide some indication of the types of secondary data that are available and their specific advantages and limitations. The focus here is on *external,* that is, publicly available, secondary data sources. *Internal* sources, that is, company-specific data, which are also important, are discussed in Chapter 10. Some illustrative examples of the major external sources are provided, focusing in particular on sources that provide data for all or most countries in the world. Chapter 4 then discusses how these data may be used. An extensive list of sources of information and assistance can be found in *Sources of Aid and Information for United States Exporters* (Washington Researchers, 1979). In addition, Appendix I contains a listing of selected secondary data sources and their addresses.

INFORMATION SOURCES

A wide variety of secondary data sources is available. These range from sources that provide general economic, social, and demographic data for almost all countries in the world, such as Business International or the World Bank, to sources that focus on specific industries worldwide, such as the *Global Market Surveys* of the U.S. Department of Commerce, or the *Worldcasts* service of *Predicasts*. This distinction between general and industry sources is somewhat arbitrary, as the general sources also provide some industry data and often the industry-specific sources provide some general indicators. Nonetheless, the specific focus and intent, in terms of relevance to specific industries, does vary. Sources also vary considerably in their accuracy and in the frequency with which they are updated.

The information sources that may be useful in comparing prospects in different countries, and in making decisions relating to market entry and expansion strategies, are first discussed. Both general economic data sources and also industry-specific data sources are covered. Primary emphasis is placed on sources that provide worldwide coverage and are widely available. Other sources providing regional or national coverage are, however, available. These often provide more detailed or in-depth information, and thus are also highly valuable, especially in making initial country entry and investment decisions. Next, the different types of information that may be required in deciding which countries to enter and what modes of operation to use within specific countries are examined. These include not only marketing data, but also data relating to political, financial, and legal factors; the development of the distributive and communication networks; service organizations; and physical, human, and capital resources. Some sources of such data are also indicated, though this is far from a comprehensive listing.

Economic Data

A host of sources of macroeconomic data are to be found, ranging widely in the number of countries or regions covered. Many of these are based on or derived from United Nations and World Bank data. Those covered here are merely intended to illustrate the type of data sources that are available, rather than to provide exhaustive coverage.

United Nations

The United Nations *Statistical and Demographic Yearbooks* and the UNESCO *Statistical Yearbooks* and data, are the official sources of many demographic and social statistics. These statistics are extremely detailed and cover an extensive number of countries. There is typically a world volume, and several regional volumes that provide more detailed information. The focus is predominantly on economic and demographic data, such as income; population; birth, death, and marriage rates; literacy; educational levels; unemployment; wages; consumer prices; and production of primary commodities and manufactured goods. The United Nations *Statistical Yearbook,* for example, contains data on 215 factors. The topics covered are listed in Table 3.1.

These data are carefully compiled and collected and are probably the most reliable of their type. The degree of detail is illustrated by the page from the *Statistical Yearbook* shown in Table 3.2. Their major limitation is that their focus is not always the most relevant for marketing decisions. Emphasis is placed on analysis of past trends rather than on future trends.

World Bank

The World Bank also publishes a number of statistics for 124 countries throughout the world (World Bank, 1981). These include basic indicators such as population, GNP per capita, inflation, literacy, and food production; as well as statistics relating to the economy, that is, growth of production by sector,

TABLE 3.1 Topics covered in the U.N. statistical yearbook

Population	Education
Manpower	Science and technology
Agriculture	Culture
Forestry	Internal trade
Fishing	External trade
Industrial production	Transport
Mining and quarrying	Communications
Manufacturing	Consumption
Conservation	Balance of payments
Energy	Wages and price
Development assistance	National accounts
Health	Finance
Housing	Public finance

growth of consumption, trade movements, and capital movements; and various demographic and social statistics. These are listed in Table 3.3.

Data are organized by country. Five country groups are identified. These include thirty-six low-income countries with per capita income of $370 or less in 1979, sixty middle-income countries with a per capita income of $380 to $4,380, eighteen industrialized countries with a per capita income of more than $4,210, four capital surplus oil-exporting countries, and six centrally planned economies. Countries with populations of less than one million are not reported. (See Table 3.4 for representative data.)

The main advantage of these data is that they are highly comprehensive and cover almost all countries. They are carefully compiled, in many cases using United Nations or UNESCO data, and are highly reliable. On the other hand, they suffer from the same limitations as the United Nations data—namely, that the latest figures, published in 1981, were for 1979; and the primary focus is on the analysis of past trends rather than on future developments.

In addition, the World Bank also publishes highly comprehensive country reports, covering both macroeconomic and industry-specific trends. These are published in two series, initially as working documents and then as *Country Economic Reports*. The primary concern of these reports is, however, which industries or sectors can and should provide the basis for economic growth, rather than the competitive structure of the market environment.

Business International

Of the macroeconomic country data sources, those collected by Business International tend to be the most frequently updated. As indicated in Table 3.5, they comprise a number of variables covering key indicators of economic struc-

TABLE 3.2 Sample data from the *United Nations Statistical Year Book*

18. *Population by sex, rate of population increase, surface area and density for each country or area of the world: latest census, and mid-year estimates for 1970 and 1977. [Unless otherwise specified, population figures are present-in-surface area estimates for the present territory; surface area estimates include inland waters.]*

Continent and country or area	POPULATION							Surface area (km²) 1977	Density 1977
	Latest census (in units)				Mid-year estimates (in thousands)		Annual rate of increase 1970–77 (%)		
	Date	Both sexes	Male	Female	1970	1977			
Africa									
Algeria	4-IV-66	11 821 679	5 817 145	6 004 534	14 330	17 910	3.2	2 381 741	8
Angola	15-XII-70	*5 646 466	*2 943 974	*2 702 192	...	...	...	1 246 700	...
Benin	25-V—	2 106 000	1 020 558	1 061 953	2 718	3 286	2.7	112 622	29
Botswana	30-IX-61	608 656	...	...	579	710	3.0	600 372	1
British Indian Ocean Territory	31-VIII-71	...	...	...	[x]2	[x]2	...	78	26
Burundi	1970-71	3 350 000	...	...	3 544	[x]3 900	...	27 834	142
Cape Verde	15-XII-70	272 071	131 211	140 860	[x]268	[x]300	*1.9*	4 033	76
Central African Empire	...	...	...	...	...	...	...	622 984	...
Chad	XII-63—VIII-64	3 254 000	...	...	*3 640*	*4 213*	*2.1*	1 284 000	3
Comoros	VII-IX-66	243 948	119 909	124 039	[x]270	*370	*4.6*	2 171	170
Congo	7-11-74	*1 300 120	*641 059	*659 061	[x]1 191	*1 440	*2.8*	342 000	4
Djibouti	1960—61	81 200	...	...	[x]95	[x]111	*2.2*	22 000	5
Egypt	22-23-XI-76	*36 656 180	*18 698 904	*17 957 276	33 329	38 741	*2.2*	1 001 449	39
Equatorial Guinea	31-XII-60	245 989	132 293	113 696	[x]285	[x]322	*1.8*	28 051	11

Italics indicate estimates of questionable reliability.

*Provisional.

[x]United Nations estimate.

Source: *United Nations Statistical Yearbook*, 1980.

TABLE 3.3.   World Bank statistics

1. Basic Indicators
     Population
     Area
     GNP per capita
     Rate of inflation
     Adult literacy
     Life expectancy
     Food production per capita (1969–71 = 100)
2. Growth and structure of production; growth of consumption and investment in GDP; and agriculture, industry, manufacturing, and services sectors
3. Structure of demand (GDP by public consumption, private consumption, gross domestic investment and saving, exports of goods and nonfactor services resource balance)
4. Industrialization (value added by food and agriculture, textiles and clothing, machinery and transport equipment, chemicals, other manufacturing)
5. Commercial energy—annual growth rate, production, and consumption per capita
6. Growth, structure, and destination of merchandise trade
7. Trade in manufactured goods
8. Balance of payments and debt service ratios, flow of external capital, public debt, and reserves, development assistance
9. Population growth, past and projected; demographic and fertility-related indicators; labor force; urbanization
10. Health indicators, and life expectancy
11. Education and income distribution
12. Defense and social expenditure

ture, historical population and labor force statistics, wages and prices, foreign trade, and production and consumption data. Though in some cases data are not available for all countries, 131 countries in the world are covered. For example, national income and GDP data are available for some small developing countries. The Business International printout summary contains a selected number of these variables, and changes for the previous five and ten years, as indicated in Table 3.6.

There are two files, an historical file containing data beginning in 1960, up to the latest available year; and a forecast file for thirty-five key countries. The latter is in two parts. The first is a brief summary of key factors affecting the economy, such as the political situation, upcoming elections, and the labor situation. The second is a forecast in current and constant terms for the current and forthcoming year of key variables, such as GDP, private consumption expenditure, government consumption, and the Consumer Price Index.

Forecasts are updated quarterly for seven countries, the United States, the United Kingdom, Japan, France, Brazil, Germany, and Italy; semiannually for another sixteen countries including Canada, Mexico, Spain, Sweden, and Switzerland; and annually for the remaining thirteen countries.

The primary advantage of this data bank is that it is computerized and is regularly updated. The annual subscription fee provides access to the data base.

TABLE 3.4 Sample data showing the basic indicators in the *World Development Report*, 1981

| | Population (millions) Mid-1979 | Area (thousands of square kilometers) | GNP PER CAPITA | | Average annual rate of inflation (percent) | | Adult literacy rate (percent) 1976 | Life expectancy at birth (years) 1979 | Average index of food production per capita (1969-71 = 100) 1977-79 |
			Dollars 1979	Average annual growth (percent) 1960-79	1960-70	1970-79			
Low-income countries	2,260.2	33,778	230	1.6	3.0	10.8	51	57	105
China and India	1,623.7	12,885	230	..	..	..	54	59	108
Other low-income	636.5	20,893	240	1.8	3.0	10.9	43	50	97
1 Kampuchea, Dem.	..	181	..	..	3.8	..	..	..	..
2 Lao PDR	3.3	237	..	..	..	..	..	42	87
3 Bhutan	1.3	47	80	−0.1	..	..	..	44	100
4 Bangladesh	88.9	144	90	−0.1	3.7	15.8	26	49	92
5 Chad	4.4	1,284	110	−1.4	4.6	7.9	15	41	91
6 Ethiopia	30.9	1,222	130	1.3	2.1	4.3	15	40	84
7 Nepal	14.0	141	130	0.2	7.7	8.7	19	44	88
8 Somalia	3.8	638	..	−0.5	4.5	11.3	60	44	85
9 Mali	6.8	1,240	140	1.1	5.0	9.7	10	43	88
10 Burma	32.9	677	160	1.1	2.7	12.1	67	54	97
11 Afghanistan	15.5	648	170	0.5	11.9	4.4	12	41	94
12 Viet Nam	52.9	330	..	..	..	..	87	63	106
13 Burundi	4.0	28	180	2.1	2.8	11.2	25	42	105
14 Upper Volta	5.6	274	180	0.3	1.3	9.8	..	43	93
15 India	659.2	3,288	190	1.4	7.1	7.8	36	52	99
16 Malawi	5.8	118	200	2.9	2.4	9.1	25	47	100

17 Rwanda	4.9	26	200	1.5	13.1	14.6	..	47	107
18 Sri Lanka	14.5	66	230	2.2	1.8	12.3	85	66	124
19 Benin	3.4	113	250	0.6	1.9	9.2	..	47	97
20 Mozambique	10.2	783	250	0.1	2.8	11.0	..	47	75
21 Sierra Leone	3.4	72	250	0.4	2.9	11.3	..	47	87
22 China	964.5	9,597	260	..	..	..	66	64	114
23 Haiti	4.9	28	260	0.3	4.1	10.9	..	53	90
24 Pakistan	79.7	804	260	2.9	3.3	13.9	24	52	101
25 Tanzania	18.0	945	260	2.3	1.8	13.0	66	52	94
26 Zaire	27.5	2,345	260	0.7	29.9	31.4	15	47	90
27 Niger	5.2	1,267	270	-1.3	2.1	10.8	8	43	89
28 Guinea	5.3	246	280	0.3	1.5	4.4	20	44	86
29 Central African Rep.	2.0	623	290	0.7	4.1	9.1	..	44	102
30 Madagascar	8.5	587	290	-0.4	3.2	10.1	50	47	94
31 Uganda	12.8	236	290	-0.2	3.0	28.3	..	54	90
32 Mauritania	1.6	1,031	320	1.9	1.6	10.1	17	43	75
33 Lesotho	1.3	30	340	6.0	2.5	11.6	52	51	100
34 Togo	2.4	57	350	3.6	1.1	10.3	18	47	81
35 Indonesia	142.9	1,919	370	4.1	..	20.1	62	53	103
36 Sudan	17.9	2,506	370	0.6	3.7	6.8	20	47	105
Middle-income countries	985.0	38,705	1,420	3.8	3.0	13.3	72	61	107
Oil exporters	324.8	13,781	1,120	3.1	3.0	14.0	64	57	97
Oil importers	660.2	24,924	1,550	4.1	3.0	12.2	76	63	113
37 Kenya	15.3	583	380	2.7	1.5	11.1	45	55	92
38 Ghana	11.3	239	400	-0.8	7.6	22.4	..	49	82
39 Yemen Arab Rep.	5.7	195	420	10.9	..	17.8	13	42	95
40 Senegal	5.5	197	430	-0.2	1.7	7.6	10	43	88
41 Angola	6.9	1,247	440	-2.1	3.3	21.6	..	42	85
42 Zimbabwe	7.1	391	470	0.8	1.3	8.4	..	55	100

Source: World Bank, *World Development Report*. New York: Oxford University Press, 1981.

TABLE 3.5 Business International data

Key economic indicators	Wages and prices
Demographic data	Average hourly wages in manufacturing
National income	Wholesale price index
Gross domestic product	Consumer price index
Private consumption expenditure	Commercial bank prime rate
Fixed capital formation	
Exports of goods and services	Foreign trade
Imports	Trade balance
Industrial production	Total exports (FOB, CIF)
Exchange	Exports to U.S., EEC, Japan
	Imports from U.S., EEC, Japan
GDP by activity	
Agriculture	Selected production and consumption data
Construction	Passenger cars in use
Manufacturing	Trucks and buses in use
	Telephones in use
Population and labor force statistics	Steel consumption
Total population	Cement production
% urban	Energy use
% 16–64	Electricity production
Total employed	Consumption of newsprint
% labor force in manufacturing	Residential construction

In addition, special analyses of these data can be made using in-house or standardized programs, or alternatively, the data can be merged with company data. Analyses tailored to specific company situations or to specific countries can thus be made, and the data can be related to internal company sales and performance data. The cost varies with the computer time required and the complexity of the analysis.

The primary limitation of these data is that they only cover a relatively limited range of variables, focusing in particular on economic and macroeconomic trade data. They thus provide an indication of the general investment climate, but the link to the specific product market or target segment has to be established. A country such as Brazil might appear to offer attractive investment opportunities. Yet, the potential for a product such as video games may be limited. Similarly, while Argentina may not on the surface appear attractive, the upper social strata of high-income consumers may provide a small, highly lucrative target segment for luxury products such as automobiles, wristwatches, and highly priced cosmetics and fragrances. Again, Japan may appear an attractive market for video games, VCRs, or computers and related peripheral equipment; yet severe local competition suggests that considerable difficulty may be encountered in attempting to exploit this market.

Euromonitor

A substantially broader range of indicators is to be found in the Euromonitor publications headquartered in London. Two volumes are published, one on the European markets, the other on all other countries in the world. The types of statistics available in the international volume are shown in Table 3.7. The information and data available for the European markets is considerably more detailed, though the principal categories are the same. A sample page is shown in Table 3.8. In some cases, the statistics are taken from official sources—such as the United Nations *Statistical Yearbook,* the United Nations *Yearbook of International Trade Statistics,* The Foreign Affairs Office, the National Statistical Offices, and the United Nations *Monthly Bulletin of Statistics*—or from trade association sources; and in some cases, the estimates are compiled by Euromonitor.

The primary advantage of these data is the wealth of information contained and the breadth of coverage. On the other hand, they are only updated as revised statistics become available. Furthermore, they are not computerized and, hence, are not in a form convenient for analysis. Reliability varies, depending on the specific data source. Also, data are frequently missing, especially for developing countries.

Worldcasts

The *Worldcasts* division of *Predicasts* also publishes annually information on general economic variables such as population, gross domestic product, industrial and agricultural consumption and production, public utilities, and passenger cars or commercial vehicles in use. These are published for the world, and for regions such as North America, Latin America, and the European Economic Community (E.E.C.), as well as for individual countries within these regions. A summary page from *Worldcasts* is shown in Table 3.9. In addition to data for the current year, historical data for preceding base years (three-year averages starting with 1963–65) and projections for the subsequent year, as well as for 1985, 1990, and 1995, are provided, along with the expected growth rate from the current year to 1990.

The primary advantage of these data is that they provide both historical and future projections, which can be seen at a glance. Furthermore, these are summarized across countries by region, so that comparisons can be made of the outlook for a country, or countries, relative to the region, both in terms of past performance and future prospects; and in the immediate short run and also in the more distant future. On the other hand, these are forecasts based on information collected from a variety of sources, and hence, their accuracy will depend on the extent to which the underlying assumptions made by different forecasters about future trends prove correct, and the extent to which unex-

TABLE 3.6. Sample data from *The BI World Economic Indicators*

193 Australia

Key economic indicators:	Values (US \$ billions)				% Change p.a. (local currency)			
	1977	1978	1979	1980E	Previous 10 years	Previous 5 years	Previous year	Latest year
National income	85.29	95.61	105.26	120.42	14.53	13.29	12.18	1980
Gross domestic product	92.28	103.33	113.00	129.59	14.16	13.19	12.54	1980
GDP—1975 prices	85.99	86.82	90.24	92.21	3.47	2.82	2.17	1980
Private consumption—1975 prices	50.14	51.84	53.34	54.56	3.72	3.18	2.29	1980
Fixed capital formation—1975 prices	18.80	18.70	19.22	19.06	1.05	0.50	-0.86	1980
Exports of goods and services	14.59	15.96	18.32	24.42	16.31	16.62	30.71	1980
Imports of goods and services	14.74	16.56	19.26	22.93	15.51	14.97	16.74	1980
Industrial production (1975 = 100)	104.0	105.0	112.0	115.0	2.38	2.83	2.68	1980
Exchange rate to US\$ (average)	0.9017	0.8737	0.8950	0.8776				

GDP by activity (current prices):	Percentage distribution				% Change p.a. (local currency)			
	1960	1970	1978	1979	Previous 10 years	Previous 5 years	Previous year	Latest year
Agriculture	---	7.07	4.36	---	8.09	5.18	-2.53	1978
Construction	---	7.39	7.03	---	13.53	15.30	6.14	1978
Manufacturing	---	22.99	18.40	---	11.24	13.16	8.57	1978

Population and labor force statistics:				Annual percentage increase			
	1970	1975	1980E	Previous 10 years	Previous 5 years	Previous year	Latest year
Total population (000)	12552.0	13627.0	14487.0	1.44	1.23	1.14	1980
% Urban	84.8	86.0	87.2	1.73	1.51	1.52	1980
% 16–64 yrs	62.8	64.0	65.8	1.92	1.79	1.79	1980
Total employed (000)	5306.0	5841.3	6236.9	1.63	1.32	-2.67	1980
% of labor force empl. in mfg.	28.7	23.4	---	---	-2.58	-6.00	1978

	Current values				Annual percentage increase			
	1976	1977	1978	1979E	Previous 10 years	Previous 5 years	Previous year	Latest year
Wages and prices:								
Ave. hourly wages in mfg (lc)	3.01	3.35	3.58	3.84	---	12.54	7.24	1979
Ave. hourly wages in mfg (US$)	3.68	3.71	4.10	4.29	---	6.96	4.68	1979
Wholesale price index (1975 = 100)	111.4	122.7	132.7	152.4	9.68	11.89	14.85	1979
Consumer price index (1975 = 100)	113.5	127.5	137.6	150.1	9.77	11.55	9.08	1979
Commercial bank prime rate	11.5	11.5	11.5	11.0				
Foreign trade, millions of US$:								
Trade balance	766	-163	-1152	436				
Total exports (fob)	13155	13352	14416	18667	16.03	11.11	29.49	1979
Total imports (cif)	12389	13515	15568	18231	14.92	8.02	17.11	1979
Exports to the US	1220	1235	1629	2220	14.36	16.47	36.28	1979
Exports to the EEC	2112	2006	2084	2584	9.87	8.49	23.99	1979
Exports to Japan	4465	4428	4362	5197	17.18	10.25	19.14	1979
Imports from the US	2296	2538	3030	3774	14.09	10.23	24.55	1979
Imports from the EEC	2786	3085	3539	4196	11.59	6.18	18.56	1979
Imports from Japan	2345	2383	2717	2580	17.75	4.61	-5.04	1979
Misc. production and consumption data:								
Passenger cars in use (000)	5284	5604	5642	---	5.06	4.54	0.68	1978
Trucks and buses in use (000)	1290	1282	1388	---	4.18	5.18	8.27	1978
Telephones (000)	5501	5835	6266	---	6.33	6.11	7.39	1978
Steel consumption (000 m. tons)	4720	5131	---	---	-0.27	-3.76	8.71	1977
Cement production (000 m. tons)	5004	5040	5016	5112	2.13	-1.13	1.91	1979
Energy use (million mt coal equiv.)	91	93	94	---	4.51	3.90	0.85	1978
Electricity production (million kwh)	76598	82524	88524	93696	6.74	6.08	5.84	1979

Source: *BI World Economic Indicators.* New York: Business International, 1980.

TABLE 3.7 Euromonitor international marketing data

Population

Total population
Area, population distribution and density
Population growth and forecasts

Vital statistics
Household population
Demographic breakdowns by age and sex

Employment

Labor force by age
Unemployment
Average working week
Industrial disputes

Accidents at work
Female working population
Economically active population
Employment by activity

Production

Land use and irrigation
Indices of agricultural and food production
Livestock
Meat production
Animal and fishery products
Fruit and vegetables
Cereals
Forestry products
Other crops
Manufactured foods

Beverages and tobacco
Natural resources
Refined metals
Building materials
Energy resources and production
Electrical energy
Chemical products
Clothing and textiles
Automotives
Consumer durables

Trade

Balance of trade
Direction of trade (imports and exports)

Trade by basic commodity groups
Imports of selected manufactured goods

Economy

Economic indicators
Gross national product
Productivity
State budget

Gross domestic product origin & distribution
Money reserves & supply
Exchange rates

Standard of living

Comparative wages and earnings
Consumer prices
Comparative costs
Radios and TVs in use

Car ownership
Ownership levels for consumer durables
Household expenditures
Retail trade

Consumption

Industrial products
Energy
Agricultural requisites
Food

Beverages
Tobacco
Sales of durables

TABLE 3.7   Euromonitor international marketing data (*cont.*)

Housing, health, education

Dwelling stock	Primary education
Size of dwellings	Secondary education
Facilities in dwellings	Higher education
Hospital establishment	Expenditure on education
Health personnel	Illiteracy level

Communications

Cultural indicators	Transport statistics
Libraries, museums, books, newspapers	Roads, railways, air traffic, shipping
Communication services	Tourist statistics
Telephones, telegrams, mail	

Source: *European Marketing Data and Statistics*. London: Euromonitor Publications Ltd., 1982.

TABLE 3.8   Comparative costs of selected consumer goods 1980

U.S. dollars	22-inch color television	Refrigerator	Gas cooker	Vacuum cleaner	Men's lounge suit	Ladies' summer dress	Men's shoes (1 pair)	Ladies' shoes (1 pair)	Men's haircut	Ladies' hair-do
Austria	1,088	229	442	177	181	98	76	54	13	20
Belgium	1,079	476	460	209	349	79	82	79	11	13
Denmark	998	233	333	133	274	50	54	47	12	10
Eire	1,015	332	541	176	190	66	71	66	42	8
Finland	701	336	431	210	299	52	117	65	13	13
France	928	487	354	188	332	111	93	89	13	22
Germany, W. (F.D.R.)	766	434	357	128	255	89	69	55	5	10
Greece	1,461	623	441[1]	251	172	82	54	49	6	12
Italy	1,075	349	349	202	269	107	107	86	12	21
Netherlands	1,031	328	406	156	278	100	61	49	8	13
Norway	1,139	462	520[1]	218	275	97	75	68	11	34
Portugal	283[2]	518	324	160	127	113	52	42	2	4
Spain	1,009	347	215	126	221	88	44	50	5	8
Sweden	796	480	572	212	274	126	86	80	14	29
Switzerland	1,022	312	312	284	239	68	68	62	17	23
United Kingdom	775	382	644	187	167	95	76	48	6	13

Notes: [1]Electric [2]Black and White

Source: *European Marketing Data And Statistics,* London: Euromonitor Publications Ltd., 1982.

TABLE 3.9 Sample data from *Worldcasts*

WORLD—PRODUCT—CASTS
SUMMARY—ECONOMIC OUTLOOK

per capita GDP
(1975 $) continued

| COUNTRY | BASE YEARS | | | | | 1978 AND PROJECTIONS | | | | | | ANNUAL GROWTH |
	1963/65	1966/68	1969/71	1972/74	1975/77	1978	1979	1980	1985	1990	1995	1990/99
East Europe	1931	2217	2462	2753	3014	3186	3194	3236	3710	4300	4905	2.7%
Albania	358	407	468	519	570	651	693	733	902	1059	1253	3.9%
Bulgaria	1353	1616	1796	2003	2262	2378	2435	2452	3072	3481	4297	3.3%
Czechoslovakia	2765	3039	3278	3557	3798	3980	3977	4026	4492	5067	5919	2.2%
East Germany	2664	2932	3203	3534	3968	4245	4349	4426	5174	6006	6896	3.0%
Hungary	1767	1960	2078	2253	2384	2499	2523	2577	2831	3348	3812	2.6%
Poland	1578	1785	1932	2306	2586	2689	2671	2555	3013	3482	4027	2.4%
Romania	1302	1584	1736	2049	2375	2570	2662	2758	3532	4525	5640	4.9%
U.S.S.R.	2048	2372	2655	2951	3212	3390	3378	3430	3878	4450	4987	2.5%
Yugoslavia	960	1057	1226	1404	1595	1780	1889	1982	2468	3119	3857	4.7%
Africa–Mideast	442	492	568	664	742	780	787	800	943	1108	1281	3.2%
Egypt	273	293	305	325	360	398	408	433	505	607	738	3.7%
Nigeria	247	255	389	497	537	549	558	571	672	834	967	3.7%
South Africa	1126	1217	1329	1394	1439	1399	1414	1431	1592	1750	1908	2.0%
Iran	694	869	1127	1499	1666	1625	1259	1007	1215	1506	1815	1.6%
Israel	2099	2278	2875	3403	3491	3545	3648	3718	4341	5118	5960	3.1%
Saudi Arabia	2111	2905	3365	5047	5953	6661	7164	7653	9388	11217	12889	4.2%
Turkey	580	654	725	809	936	972	954	997	1109	1297	1484	2.8%
Other Africa—Mid East	346	371	403	438	497	540	575	599	708	814	937	3.2%

Source: *Worldcasts*. Cleveland, OH: Predicasts, Inc., 1982.

pected events affecting the world economic outlook, such as the situation in Iran or the Falkland crisis, occur.

There are numerous sources of general economic and business environment data available. Those cited here are not intended to be exhaustive, but rather to provide a flavor for the range and content of easily accessible data. These can provide the starting point for the investigation of international markets, and particularly for the evaluation of different country markets.

Industry Data

The preceding data sources, with the exception of Euromonitor, relate to the general business environment. They therefore do not provide much indication as to market potential for specific industries. Where attention is focused on specific industries, as is generally the case, further data on these specific industries, and the linking of the economic and environmental data to specific industries, will be required. A number of sources of industry-specific data may be identified; these include government sources such as the U.S. Department of Commerce, and private companies such as Predicasts.

The United Nations Yearbooks

The United Nations *Yearbook of Industrial Statistics* contains such valuable information for certain industries as follows:

extractive industries
   mining and quarrying
   coal
   crude production
   ferrous and nonferrous production
   nonmetallic minerals and fertilizers
manufacturing industries
   food, beverages
   textiles, wearing apparel, and leather products
   wood and wood products
   paper and paper products
   chemicals and chemical products
   petrochemicals
   other nonmetallic industries
   iron and steel
   nonferrous metal products
   fabricated metal products
   transportation
   miscellaneous manufactured articles
electricity and gas
   electricity
   manufactured gas

The data are predominantly production data and cover only certain developed countries.

Information about the number of establishments, persons employed, supplements to wages and salaries, number of operators, wages and salaries of operators, hours or days worked by operators, quantity of electricity consumed, gross output, cost of goods and industrial services consumed, cost of materials and supplies consumed, cost of fuels and electricity consumption, value added, gross fixed capital formation, total value of stocks, value of materials stocks, fuel supply, value of stocks of work in progress, and value of stocks of finished goods is also to be found for thirty-six three-digit ISIC industries, for all member nations. (See Table 3.10.)

The U.S. Department of Commerce

A valuable source of industry data is the U.S. Department of Commerce. The department publishes global market surveys—in-depth reports covering twenty to thirty of the best foreign markets for individual United States industries, such as graphics, industrial equipment, medical equipment, metalworking and finishing equipment, building products and construction equipment, and food processing and packaging. These reports cover the current-year United States industrial outlook, including export and import data for each given industry, and then provide country-by-country reports for the fifteen to twenty-five countries identified as the most promising for the industry. This covers potential customers and competing United States and third-country suppliers. Key data for the major product categories in the industry are provided, as well as a list of products considered to provide the best sales potential for the country.

The primary advantage of these reports is that they provide an easily accessible and predigested survey of world markets for the company interested in investigating international market potential. The exporting company can select which of the countries it wishes to investigate in greater depth, based on the match with the type of products in which the company has a competitive advantage, and on the level of competition in the country. The primary limitation of these data is that they are only available for a limited number of industries, identified by the Department of Commerce as prime prospects for the development of export potential. These include, for example, electrical energy systems, medical equipment, computers and peripheral equipment, production equipment, and test equipment and materials for the electrical industries. These are all industries in which the United States is known to have a technological advantage.

The U.S. Department of Commerce also publishes *Overseas Business Reports* for almost every country throughout the world. These provide a highly comprehensive survey of each country, including the outlook for foreign trade

TABLE 3.10 Sample data from the *U.N. Yearbook of Industrial Statistics*

AUSTRALIA

ISIC	Industry	1. NUMBER OF ESTABLISHMENTS a/b/ (NUMBER)			c/		2. AVERAGE NUMBER OF PERSONS ENGAGED a/b/d/ (THOUSANDS)			c/	c/	ISIC
		1975	1976	1977	1978	1979	1975	1976	1977	1978	1979	
210	Coal mining	132	131	129	129	134	25	26	27	27	28	210
220	Petroleum and gas	212	193	188	166	178	36	34	34	31	31	220
230	Metal ore mining											230
290	Other mining	966	951	964	1057	1056	9	9	8	9	9	290
2	Mining, quarrying	1310	1275	1281	1352	1368	70	69	69	67	68	2
311/2	Food products	2973	3002	2892	2902	2891	166	166	167	167	163	311/2
313	Beverages	507	524	483	449	428	25	24	23	23	22	313
314	Tobacco	9	9	7	7	7	6	6	5	5	5	314
321	Textiles	1027	1025	990	948	915	59	60	55	53	51	321
3211	Spinning, weaving etc. ...	306	302	293	267	262	29	30	26	24	24	3211
322	Wearing apparel	1960	1874	1748	1609	1526	60	59	55	53	53	322
323	Leather and products	251	252	229	225	214	6	6	5	5	5	323
324	Footwear	221	217	193	213	209	11	11	9	13	13	324
331	Wood products	2713	2785	2699	2526	2539	52	52	52	49	48	331
332	Furniture, fixtures	1182	1255	1257	1225	1278	26	26	26	26	26	332
341	Paper and products.......	306	300	288	280	267	30	27	28	27	26	341
3411	Pulp, paper etc.	20	18	18	16	16	11	10	11	10	9	3411
342	Printing, publishing......	2294	2350	2315	2293	2345	73	71	70	70	72	342

Note. For certain differences in classification, see country note.
a/ Twelve months ending 30 June of the year indicated.
b/ Manufacturing: excluding single-establishment enterprises with fewer than 4 employees.
c/ Data are compiled by a revised industry classification.
d/ Mining and electricity and gas: at 30 June of the year indicated.

Source: *1980 Yearbook of Industrial Statistics*. New York: United Nations, 1980.

and the best industry prospects. The major sectors of the economy are briefly described, as well as channels of distribution and sales practices. The climate for foreign investment is discussed, along with trade policy and regulation, taxation, and foreign exchange regulation.

The Economist

The Economist Intelligence Unit in London also publishes a variety of reports that can be useful in evaluating international marketing opportunities. In the first place, they publish annually the *E.I.U. World Outlook,* providing forecasts of industry trends in the economies of more than 160 countries. Two are concerned with trends in commodities: one covering industrial raw materials, and the other, food, foodstuffs, and beverages.

Marketing in Europe, a quarterly, also publishes surveys of specific country product markets in Europe. These are divided into three groups: 1) food, drink, and tobacco; 2) clothing, furniture, and leisure goods; and 3) chemist goods, household goods, and domestic appliances. In February, 1982, for example, studies were published on furniture and furnishing in Belgium, France, and the Netherlands; carpets in Belgium; skiwear in Germany; and car hire in Italy.

A number of special reports are also published, covering different country prospects, industries, and aspects of international marketing. These include, for example, a survey of prospects in Australia, the *New Industrialized Countries and their Impact on World Manufacturing, Chips in the 1980s, Applications of Micro-electronics,* the *United States Passenger Car Market,* the *World Textile Industry in the 1980s,* the *Economic and Social Impact of Tourism on Developing Countries,* and the *Growing Role of Export Processing Zones.* These tend to be detailed and systematic reports, based on both qualitative and quantitative data. They are, however, not synchronized either by country or by industry, and although they are in some respects comparable with one another, they rarely provide global coverage, or identical coverage.

In addition, the Economist Intelligence Unit has an international economic appraisal service, which provides a continuously updated collection of important macroeconomic statistics, covering eighty countries. Reviews covering 160 countries are published quarterly, providing a business-oriented analysis of the latest economic trends.

Worldcasts

The *Worldcasts* division of *Predicasts* also publishes detailed statistics, including both historical data and projections for various product markets. These are organized both geographically and by product. The World *Regional* casts are organized by four major regions: the Common Market countries; other

European countries, including Eastern Europe; Canada, Central America, and South America; and Africa, Asia, and Oceania. Regional summaries are available, as well as country-by-country summaries (Table 3.11). The World *Product* casts are organized by product, which are broken down into three major categories: agriculture, mining, forestry, textiles, wood, and paper; chemicals, polymers, petroleum, oil and rubber, drugs, leather, stone clay, and glass; and primary metals, machinery, electrical machinery, instruments, and transportation equipment. These are presented by region, and major country with region, and include historic data as well as one-, six-, ten-, and fifteen-year projections of key production, consumption, and trade data.

The primary advantages of these data are the level of detail and the projections that are provided. Their main focus is, however, on commodity and industrial product market data, such as chemicals, metals, instruments, and transportation equipment, rather than on consumer markets.

Background Data

Numerous other sources specific to individual countries or product markets are also to be found. Country handbooks, reports, or economic surveys provide much valuable information with regard to the business environment in a given country. These may be published by government or other official bodies within a country, in which case they may not be strictly comparable from country to country. Alternatively, they may be published by private international or multinational organizations.

The U.S. Department of Commerce, for example, publishes an *International Marketing Handbook* in two volumes, providing profiles of 138 countries, as well as special information about doing business with Eastern Bloc countries and in the Near East and North Africa. The profiles are compiled from their *Overseas Business Reports* and contain information about

> Foreign Trade Outlook
> Industry Trends
> Trade Regulations
> Trade Customs
> Distribution and Sales Channels
> Transportation and Utilities
> Advertising and Marketing Research
> Credit
> Investment
> Taxation
> Guidance for Business Travelers Abroad
> Sources of Economic and Commercial Information
> Market Profile

TABLE 3.11 Sample data from *Worldcasts*

Venezuela

SIC NO	Product A	Event	Product B	Years B	Years S	Years L	Quantities B	Quantities S	Quantities L	Unit of measure	Source Journal	Source Date	Source Page	Annual growth
	Intnl financial transactions (Cont)													
	E57 14 00 Balance on current account			79	80	81	-.3	2.7	2.5	bil US$	ChemBLEcon	12/23/80	8	-7.4%
	E57 14 00 Balance on current account	(planned)		79	80	81	-.3	3.	4.7	bil US$	Fin Times	5/14/81	20	56.7%
	E57 14 00 Balance on current account			80	—	85	3215.	—	2590.	mil US$	Venez UID	no/3/80	5	-4.2%
	Agriculture, Forestry, Fishing (010)													
	0101 Agriculture													
	01010 007 Agricultural programs	expend by	national government	811	to	851	—	4.3	—	bil US$	OBR 81-06	4/ /81	5	—%
	01010 007 Agricultural programs	expend by	national government	—	811	—	—	6249. ±	—	mil bolivar	BOLSA	11/ /80	267	—%
	0102 Crop farms													
	Grains													
	01100 005 Grains	production		79s	80s	81s	1.5	1.4	1.9	mil m tons	USDA WAS	12/ /80	41	35.7%
	01100 005 Grains	net imports		79s	80s	81s	1.9	2.	1.8	mil m tons	USDA WAS	12/ /80	41	-10.0%
	01100 005 Grains	consumption		79s	80s	81s	3.4	3.4	3.7	mil m tons	USDA WAS	12/ /80	41	8.8%
	01100 008 Grains ex rice	production		79s	80s	81s	1189.	940.	1599.	000 m tons	FAC Grains	12/16/80	2	70.1%
	01100 105 Feed grains	production		79s	80s	81s	1188.	939.	1598.	000 m tons	FAC Grains	1/28/81	120	70.2%
	01100 105 Feed grains	production		79s	80s	81s	1.2	.9	1.6	mil m tons	USDA WAS	12/ /80	42	77.8%
	01100 105 Feed grains	net imports		79s	80s	81s	1.1	1.2	.9	mil m tons	USDA WAS	12/ /80	42	-25.0%
	01100 105 Feed grains	imports		80s	81s	82s	1072.	1230.	1150.	000 m tons	FAC Grains	8/14/81	15	3.6%
	01100 105 Feed grains	consumption		79s	80s	81s	2252.	2148.	2468.	000 m tons	FAC Grains	1/28/81	120	14.9%
	01100 105 Feed grains	consumption		79s	80s	81s	2.3	2.1	2.5	mil m tons	USDA WAS	12/ /80	42	19.0%
	01100 105 Feed grains	used for	feed	79s	80s	81s	1019.	1196.	1103.	000 m tons	FAC Grains	1/28/81	120	-7.8%

Source: *Worldcasts*. Cleveland, OH: Predicasts, Inc., 1982.

Foreign Trade
Foreign Investment
Finance
Economy
Basic Economic Facilities
Natural Resources
Population

The Council for Mutual Economic Assistance, for example, publishes a statistical yearbook for member countries, Bulgaria, Hungary, East Germany (G.D.R.), Cuba, Mongolia, Poland, Romania, U.S.S.R., and Czechoslovakia. This provides data similar to that provided by the United Nations in the following areas:

Area and Population
Major Economic Indicators
Industry
Capital Investment
Agriculture and Forestry
Transport and Communication
Internal Trade
Foreign Trade
Labor and Wages
Education, Culture, and Art
Public and Social Services

Governments or other public bodies frequently publish national yearbooks, or statistical data books. The Australian Bureau of Statistics, for example, publishes the *Australia Yearbook.* The Council for Economic Planning in the Republic of China publishes the *Taiwan Statistical Data Book.* Policies vary, however, as to whether these are published in a language other than that of the country. The Central Bureau of Statistics of Norway, for example, publishes its official statistics in Norwegian and English, while the Swiss Federal Office of Statistics publishes its statistical yearbook in French and German.

Various private sources also publish regional and country handbooks. The *World of Information,* for example, publishes an *Africa Guide,* a *Middle East Review,* a *Latin America and Caribbean Review,* and the *Asia and Pacific Review.* Each volume includes topics such as business and economic prospects in the continent; relations with other trading blocs, such as the Soviet Union, the European Economic Community, and the United States; availability of natural resources; and major growth markets. This is followed by more detailed profiles for each country. These cover trends in economic and social development, major industrial developments, the political situation, the government's foreign policy, and some summary market facts.

Business International also publishes regional and country reports that contain information relating to the political and economic outlook; the operating climate; labor laws; the tax bill; financing operations; technology; marketing factors such as distribution, regional markets, sales force, advertising and promotion, price controls, and tariffs and import barriers; and barriers and aids to exporting and importing to particular countries, such as access to credit, export credit, insurance, import duty relief, and free zones. Surveys of "Asia in the 80's," and "Trading in Latin America" were, for example, published in 1981. In 1980, surveys of Puerto Rico, Egypt, and Kenya were published.

The American University also publishes area handbooks for most countries in the world, which contain background information related to the physical environment and population; living conditions, such as income, consumption patterns, living costs, housing, sanitation and pollution control, and health and medical services; political dynamics and values; and the character and structure of the economy relating, for example, to agriculture, industry, and foreign economic relations. These vary considerably in their recentness, as they are only revised every eight or ten years. The handbook for Thailand was, for example, revised in 1981, and that for Jordan in 1980; but that for India dates back to 1975.

Price Waterhouse publishes information guides on many countries, covering foreign investment opportunities—that is, basic resources, major industries, and growth areas—and more detailed information about exchange controls and restrictions, and accounting procedures. Dun and Bradstreet also publishes an *Exporter's Encyclopedia,* which provides information about market basics, trade regulations related to exporting and importing, product and packaging regulation, and transportation in countries throughout the world. The main focus is on information relevant to potential exporters to the country.

Trade associations, banks, trade journals, and other periodicals such as *Business Week, Business International, The New York Times, Advertising Age,* or the *Economist* often publish special world, regional, or country reports, which constitute valuable sources of information in assessing foreign market or industry potential. These sources are too numerous to be covered exhaustively here. The appropriate source will depend to a large extent on specific research objectives as well as on availability and accessibility of different data sources.

Data Accuracy and Equivalence

Both economic and industry data vary considerably in their accuracy and equivalence. This is particularly marked in the case of macroeconomic data and in relation to developing countries, where data are less readily available. It may also be a hidden danger, though less apparent, in relation to industry data.

First, different sources often report different values for a given statistic such as GNP per capita, number of TV sets in use, vehicle registration, or number of retail institutions. Clearly this casts some doubt on the accuracy of the data. Certain discrepancies can sometimes be observed in macroeconomic data such as GNP, GDP, or number of telephones in use. This may result from differences in the way the unit is defined; for example, GDP may include income of nationals in foreign countries in some cases and not in others. Similarly, the frequency with which estimates are updated—for example, whether estimates are made to update population data, or income is adjusted for inflation—may vary. In general, it is desirable to understand how a specific statistic is defined in each information source so that differences can be reconciled. Then the statistic best suited for the specific problem can be selected.

Accuracy of data also varies from one country to another. Data from the United States and the highly industrialized nations are likely to have a higher level of accuracy than that from developing countries. This is largely due to the mechanisms for collecting data. In the United States and other industrialized nations, relatively reliable and sophisticated procedures for collecting population or industry census, national accounting, or other macrodata are utilized. In developing countries, where a substantial proportion of the population is illiterate, however, such data may be based on estimates, or rudimentary procedures incorporating a high component of measurement error. In China, for example, personal interviews are conducted with the head of the household. If it appears that the head of the household has not understood, the interviewer "guesses" the number in the household.

Similarly, business statistics and income data are affected by the taxation structure and the level of tax evasion. In EEC countries, production statistics are often inaccurate, because taxes are collected based on domestic sales figures. Thus, companies may underestimate production statistics in order to reduce their tax burden. Similarly in France, taxes are declared and paid in the subsequent fiscal year. The amount to be paid is frequently "negotiated" with the local tax inspector, and tax evasion is a national hobby. Consequently, income statistics frequently underestimate actual income, especially among self-employed persons.

Comparability of data varies from country to country. Population censuses may not only be inaccurate, but also vary in the frequency and year in which they are collected. While in the United States a population census is conducted every ten years, in Bolivia there was a twenty-five-year gap between the 1950 and the 1976 censuses, and it was estimated that during that period the population doubled. In Ethiopia and Chad, no census has ever been conducted, and the first census in Saudi Arabia was conducted in 1974. Similarly, in the People's Republic of China, there was a twenty-nine-year gap between the 1953 and the 1982 censuses. These are, however, considered inaccurate, since in rural areas of China, ancestor worship is so strong that names are kept on registers even after they die.

Consequently, population figures are not for the same year in each country, or where updated—as for example, by Business International or the World Bank—they are based on estimates of population growth. Similar difficulties arise in relation to income or consumption statistics, where reporting systems, particularly in the developing countries, are not as efficient or up to date as in the United States and other industrialized countries. The rapid rates of population growth and rise in living standards in Far Eastern and other developing countries make such problems particularly acute.

Measurement units are not necessarily equivalent from country to country. In the case of income, for example, all salaried workers in France and Belgium are paid for a "thirteenth month" as an automatic bonus. This is reported as part of annual income, producing a measurement construct different from that in other countries. Similarly, German expenditure for recreation and entertainment includes the purchase of television sets, while in the United States this is included as furniture, furnishing, and household equipment.

The definition of "urban" used to establish the proportion of the urban population in the United Nations *Demographic Yearbook* varies substantially from country to country, depending largely on the population density. In Japan, for example, urban population is defined as a *shi* (city) with 50,000 inhabitants or more, or *shis* (population usually 30,000 inhabitants) with urban facilities. In India it includes all places with 5,000 inhabitants or more. In Nigeria, it includes the forty largest towns; and in Kenya and Zaire, agglomerations with at least 2,000 inhabitants. Similarly, in France and West Germany, it includes communities with 2,000 or more inhabitants, while in Norway and Sweden it goes down to localities or built-up areas with as few as 200 inhabitants.

Interpretation of apparently equivalent measures also poses a number of problems. Comparisons of GNP per capita may, for example, be misleading. Differences in personal taxation structures; in the provision of socialized services such as medicine or education, or of retirement pensions or family allowances; or in the existence of private pension plans or health schemes may occur. In addition, the extent to which people grow their own food, what they require to achieve an equivalent standard of living, or differences in relative prices may imply that purchasing power is not necessarily equivalent. In Sweden, for example, high rates of personal taxation, coupled with socialized services, imply a lower standard of living than their high per capita income would suggest. Procedures to adjust national income statistics for purchasing power equivalents have been developed for sixteen countries. These are shown in Table 3.12. This tends to result in significant adjustments of apparent relative wealth, especially for developing economies. Often subsistence requirements in terms of clothing are low and the provision of much food and services does not enter into the monetary economy.

TABLE 3.12 Population and per capita gross domestic product in national currencies, in U.S. dollars at official exchange rates, and in international dollars, 1970 and 1973

Country	Currency unit	Population (thousands) (1)	PER CAPITA GDP						Exchange rate—deviation index (7) = (5) ÷ (3) (7)
			In national currency (2)	In U.S. dollars converted at official exchange rates		In international dollars			
				U.S. dollars (3)	U.S. = 100 (4)	International dollars (5)	U.S. = 100 (6)		
			1973						
Kenya	shilling	12,480	1,291	184	2.97	379	6.12		2.06
India	rupee	577,000	1,000	129	2.08	394	6.37		3.06
Philippines	peso	40,120	1,751	259	4.18	755	12.2		2.91
Korea, Republic of	won	34,070	145,750	366	5.91	904	14.6		2.47
Colombia	peso	22,500	10,487	440	7.11	1,106	17.9		2.51
Malaysia	M. dollar	11,310	1,546	633	10.2	1,180	19.1		1.86
Iran	rial	31,410	62,776	914	14.8	1,809	29.2		1.98
Hungary	forint	10,430	39,799	1,619	26.2	2,793	45.1		1.72
Italy	lira	54,910	1,471,828	2,525	40.8	2,913	47.0		1.15
Japan	yen	109,100	1,017,451	3,738	60.4	3,962	64.0		1.06
United Kingdom	pound	56,020	1,279	3,136	50.6	3,750	60.6		1.20
Netherlands	guilder	13,440	12,305	4,402	71.1	4,234	68.4		0.96
Belgium	B. franc	9,740	179,984	4,618	74.6	4,663	75.3		1.01
France	franc	52,130	21,275	4,777	77.2	4,709	76.1		0.99
Germany, F.D.R.	DM	61,980	14,791	5,535	89.4	4,791	77.4		0.87
United States	dollar	210,410	6,192	6,192	100.0	6,192	100.0		1.00

Column 1 contains mid-year population estimates: Kenya, Hungary, Italy, Malaysia, the Netherlands, and the Philippines.

Source: Irving B. Kravis, Alan Heston, and Robert Summers, *International Comparisons of Real Product and Purchasing Power*. Published for the World Bank by The Johns Hopkins University Press, Baltimore and London, 1978.

Thus, while there is an extensive number of secondary data sources available, these vary considerably in the data covered, as also in their accuracy and recency. In general, there is a trade-off between these two. The United Nations and World Bank statistics, while highly reliable, are not as recent as those provided by commercial services. Similarly, sources vary in the extent to which they focus on analysis of historical trends, or alternatively, on the forecasting of future trends. Management has to select the most appropriate sources based on its specific objectives and concerns, suitability of sources for the industry or product, and the particular decision concerned.

INFORMATION REQUIREMENTS

In making decisions about the appropriate mode of operation in a given country and the specific marketing strategy to employ, more specific sources of information will be required in addition to the general sources discussed earlier. This includes information not only directly related to marketing decisions, but also to other aspects of the firm's operations, such as financial production or legal questions.

More specifically, four major types of information requirements can be identified. These are

1. political, financial, and legal data, which provide indicators of the risks associated with operation in an overseas market;
2. data relating to the infrastructure, which are needed to estimate probable costs associated with alternative modes of operation;
3. marketing data, which can be used to assess market potential and the costs associated with different marketing strategies;
4. product-specific data, which are required to develop initial evaluations of current market potential and profitability.

Each of these is further discussed in the next section.

Political, Financial, and Legal Data

In the first place, management is likely to be concerned with examining the risks associated with operating in a specific national or country environment. This requires the collection of political, financial, and legal data to assess the different types of risks involved in marketing in various countries. These can have a significant impact on both the short- and long-run profitability of operations in a foreign environment.

Political Data

Collection of information relating to political factors such as the number of expropriations, hostility to foreign investment, or internal political stability and insurrection is necessary to assess the likelihood of expropriation, confiscation of assets, insurrection, or the imposition of restrictions on foreign corporations by host governments. The uprising in Iran in 1978, resulting in overexposure of United States companies estimated at more than $1 billion, provides ample evidence of this.

The importance of assessing this risk does, however, vary with the company and industry and with the mode of entry envisaged. The extractive industries, such as oil refining or mining, are particularly susceptible to expropriation as they do not entail any sophisticated management or marketing technology and they have large capital assets in plant and equipment (Bradley, 1977). Similarly, the banking, insurance, utility, and transportation industries are prime candidates for confiscation, since they form an integral part of the economic infrastructure and are key to economic growth. Large multinational concerns such as I.B.M. also need to pay attention to political risk due to the feelings of nationalism and hostility they tend to arouse.

A variety of approaches can be used to assess political risk. Expropriations, for example, can be assessed on the basis of historical data, that is, the number of expropriations that have taken place in a particular country (Bradley, 1977). It should, however, be noted that such indicators are not always the most accurate, due to changes in government. Consequently, use of a more comprehensive approach, combining both qualitative and quantitative methods of assessing political risk may be desirable. Qualitative approaches typically use expert opinion, either based on impressions or assessed more systematically through the use of Delphi techniques. This entails successive rounds or iterations of discussion, with feedback on the results of each round, until finally consensus is reached. Quantitative methods use a number of indicators to assess political risk (Rummell and Heenan, 1978). One of the more comprehensive approaches advocates the use of four major dimensions. These are 1) domestic stability, measured by indicators such as riots, purges, and assassination; 2) foreign conflict, measured by variables such as diplomatic expulsions or military violence; 3) the political climate, measured by the size of the country's communist party and the number of socialist seats in the legislature; and 4) the economic climate, measured by gross national product, inflation, external debt levels, and so on.

Some companies undertake their own evaluation of political risk. American Can, for example, has a computer program PRISM, which reduces 200 variables collected from various data sources, to an index of economic desirability and one of risk payback, or of economic and political stability. The attractiveness of a country can thus be weighed against its economic and political stability. United Technologies Corporation uses data from question-naires filled out by overseas managers to identify countries such as Zaire and Indonesia, where conditions are not attractive today but may be candidates for increased future involvement (Thomas, 1980).

Borg Warner integrates country risk assessment into strategic planning. Company executives are interviewed and provide ratings for thirty-seven coun-tries, based on political stability, economic conditions, the labor situation, government controls, and external considerations (Business International, 1981). Each country is then ranked according to its investment attractiveness. Foreign strategic business units (SBU) are then identified, and their status plotted in a matrix. One of the dimensions of the matrix is the investment at-tractiveness of the country (as derived from the survey); and the other, the business strength of the SBU, that is, ability to compete in its market. Strategy is thus guided by position in this matrix, and specific products that are not do-ing well even though they are in an attractive country are identified. For an in-depth examination of the different methodologies, see Kobrin (1981).

If management does not wish to use in-house staff for the evaluation of risk, syndicated services for evaluating risk can be used. These include, for ex-ample, the Business Environment Risk Index and the Political Risk Index of BERI Ltd., the Business International Risk and the World Political Risk ser-vices. The Business Environment Risk Index rates the business environment of a country. Countries are ranked, by a panel of 105 experts around the world, on a scale of 1 to 100, based on the evaluation of fifteen economic, political, and social factors in foreign countries (Hanes, 1981). The Political Risk Index also uses a panel of experts, but they have in this case a political science, rather than business, orientation. Countries are ranked on a scale of 0 to 100, based on various symptoms of internal and external causes of political risk—under pres-ent conditions, in five years time, and in ten years time.

The World Political Risk Forecast of Frost and Sullivan offers a similar service. Business International also has a service rating fifty-seven major coun-tries on a scale of 0 to 100, based on risk and opportunity (Business Interna-tional, 1981). The ratings are based on three subindexes. The first comprises ten political, legal, and social variables; the second, ten economic criteria relating to the size and development of a market; and the third covers monetary and financial aspects.

Financial and Foreign Exchange Data

Examination of financial and foreign exchange risk factors, such as the rate of inflation, currency depreciation, restrictions on capital flows, and repatriation of earnings, is important insofar as these have a critical impact on overall levels of profitability and expected ROI. Such factors are thus a major consideration in making international investment and resource allocation deci-sions.

Assessment of foreign exchange risk is particularly critical where foreign based production is concerned and goods or services will move across national boundaries. A manufacturer of color TV sets, planning the acquisition of a company in the United Kingdom to supply European markets, will, for example, need to make a careful evaluation of the anticipated movement of the pound relative to other European currencies. Similarly, the movement of inflation and interest rates may be an important factor for companies with high credit exposure, as for example, consumer credit card companies or retailers.

Data on many of the relevant variables are to be found in International Financial Statistics, if a company wishes to make its own evaluation of financial risk. With the advent of floating exchange rates and rising oil prices, this has, however, become increasingly complex. Consequently, a number of commercial services for predicting different types of financial risks have been established. These include services for predicting foreign exchange rates in the long run, such as those provided by the major international banks, such as Chemical Bank, Citibank, and Chase Manhattan; or specialized econometric forecasters, such as Chase Econometrics, Data Resources, Inc., or the Wharton Econometric Forecasting Associates. A number of smaller organizations specialized in assessing foreign exchange rates have also developed; these include Predex, Mureenbeld, Conti Currency, and the European-American Bank. The accuracy and reliability of these services have been extensively investigated, and show variation, depending on the currency and time horizon (Levich, 1980). Summary indicators are also provided, such as the rating of over 100 countries' credit worthiness by international bankers, published in the Institutional Investor every six months.

Legal and Regulatory Data

Information on legal and regulatory factors, such as import-export restrictions on various forms of ownership, modes of operation, tariff barriers, taxation, and product regulation and legislation, must also be collected. These are often a major impediment to market entry and limit the modes of operation that can be used. They also affect the extent to which modifications in products or in marketing strategies will be required.

A company considering entry into Mexico, India, or Sri Lanka can, for example, only do so via a joint venture, although in India, some exceptions may be made in the high-export-oriented industries. Other countries prohibit foreign investment in certain industries. In Italy, for example, foreign investment is not permissible in the cigarette, cigar, and match industries, which are run by government monopolies. Similarly, in many European nations the airlines, railroads, telephone and telegraph, and electricity services are public monopolies. In Morocco, joint ventures are required in certain industries such as leasing, wine distribution, banking, insurance, and tobacco.

Some countries have indirect controls on entry by foreign companies. In

Japan, for example, an extensive system of import licensing exists. Companies have to obtain approval from the relevant regulatory body for their products and also for their proposed distributors (Jetro, 1979). In electrical appliances, for example, authorization in the form of the T-mark has to be obtained from JAS, the trade regulatory body, and often significant delays may be encountered in industries such as those relating to color TV sets or electronics. Stiff sanitation and packaging requirements are also imposed, and food and pharmaceutical packaging must indicate ingredients in Japanese.

Information about such factors must generally be analyzed on a country-by-country basis for a specific product category, and is to be found in sources such as the *Price Waterhouse Information Guides,* or Dun and Bradstreet's *Exporter's Encyclopedia* or Business International's *Investment, Licensing and Trading Conditions Abroad* series. The types of information contained in these guides are shown in Table 3.13.

TABLE 3.13   Foreign regulatory information

THE PRICE WATERHOUSE INFORMATION GUIDES

Foreign investment opportunities
   Basic resources
   Major industries
   Growth areas
Exchange controls and restrictions on foreign investment
   Repatriation of capital
   Restrictions on foreign investment
   Regulation of business, price controls, monopolies, acquisitions
Investment incentives
   Banking and local finance
   Import restrictions
   Forms of business enterprise
   Labor relations and social security
Accounting
   Audit requests
   Accounting principles
   Corporate taxation
   Individual taxation

DUN AND BRADSTREET 1979 EXPORTER'S ENCYCLOPEDIA

Foreign commerce, language, weights, and measures
Exchange and import regulation
Price controls
Distributor agreements
Commercial practices law
Marking and labeling

Infrastructure Data

The second type of data on which information is required relates to the existence of integrative networks such as the physical transportation structure; the retail distribution network; and the availability and cost of certain basic resources such as electricity, work skills, management, and financial resources. These affect, and to a large extent determine, the costs of exploiting market potential, and also the feasibility of utilizing specific types of marketing programs and strategies.

Integrative Networks

Three types of integrative networks can be identified: *distributive* networks, which affect physical distribution and channel decisions; *communication* networks, which affect advertising and communication decisions; and *service organizations* such as market researching agencies or banks, which determine the extent to which a company can buy outside services such as marketing research or media planning as opposed to developing its own capabilities in-house.

Distributive Networks. Information will be required in relation to both the physical distribution network and the nature of the channels of distribution. The physical distribution network is an important consideration insofar as if this is poor, it could add significantly to distribution costs; also delays might be incurred, which implies that capital would be tied up in inventory. With rising rates of inflation, this clearly poses an increasing problem. The character of the retail and wholesale network is also an important consideration, particularly in terms of the availability of mass-merchandising outlets such as supermarkets or department stores. Absence of these may, for example, severely limit ability to adopt a "pull" strategy, as is commonly used in industrialized countries for many consumer packaged goods.

The development of the physical distribution network is particularly critical in countries with a difficult terrain, or where a significant proportion of the market is in rural areas, as is the case in many developing countries. Some countries with a rugged topography, such as Switzerland, have a well-developed transportation infrastructure, and hence distribution does not pose a major problem. In other countries, however, such as Peru, this is not the case. Consequently, this can add significantly to distribution costs. This might, for example, be an important issue for a company marketing bulky products, such as tires; or products that require refrigeration, such as milk and whey-based products. Similar considerations apply in the case of countries such as Thailand or many African countries where much of the population lives in remote hinterlands or in jungle areas that are not easily accessible. The nature of the physical distribution network can be gauged with the aid of transportation statistics, such as kilometers of railroads, roads relative to the physical size of the country, ton kilometer of freight per kilometer of road and railroad, or the number of commercial and consumer vehicles per capita. These can be found in many international information sources, such as Euromonitor's *European and International Marketing Data,* or world almanacs. More detailed statistics can be found in country almanacs and handbooks.

Examination of the distribution network is also an important consideration insofar as this may affect ability to use mass-merchandising techniques. In many of the developing Asian and African nations, for example, the majority of retailers are small, self-operated family businesses that are open from 8 A.M. until late at night, in a space little larger than a front room. A cigarette manufacturer might thus be limited in its ability to use mass-merchandising techniques, and might have to resort to strategies such as selling cigarettes in singles through kiosks and newspaper stands, rather than in packs or cartons with heavy advertising. Similarly, in order to ensure·that their products are widely available and reach the consumer in good condition, a processor and distributor of perishable products might have to provide on a leasing basis to small retailers, small refrigerated units to stock fresh products.

Information relating to the availability of different channels of distribution is somewhat difficult to obtain on a global basis. Some data sources, such as Euromonitor, provide information on the number of wholesalers and retailers in a country. Euromonitor's *European Marketing Data* also provides information about the number of supermarkets, department stores, and voluntary chain groups, and their relative importance in food distribution. Information about the number of supermarkets or self-service outlets can also be obtained for some countries from international trade association sources, such as the International Association of Department Stores, or the International Supermarket Association. In general, however, these provide coverage predominantly with regard to the major industrialized nations, and are less accurate for the developing nations where such networks are changing rapidly.

More detailed information is contained in country-specific sources such as National Censuses of Distribution, or in publications of regional or national trade associations such as the European Federation of the Footwear Industry. Such sources do not, however, provide an indication of the more subtle aspects of channel control. In Germany, for example, wholesalers are often in a dominant position, and hence, direct distribution strategies cannot be used without a payoff to wholesalers.

Communication Networks.   Two types of communication networks need be considered, since they affect the feasibility and costs of using alternative communication and promotional strategies. The first are the mass media such as TV, radio, magazines, and newspapers. These affect the feasibility of using "different" strategies, and also the extent to which different appeals can be targeted to specific market segments. The second is the network of intrapersonal communications such as the telephone and postal systems. This affects the costs and efficiency of different promotional strategies, such as the use of salespersons, and also of alternative modes of organization or of conducting operations within a country.

Mass Media.   In the case of the mass media, information is needed about factors such as the availability of such media for commercial purposes, and about the reach and audience characteristics of each medium, media costs, and regulation of the content of advertising in different media. In some countries, advertising is not permitted in certain media. In Sweden, Norway, Denmark, Belgium, and Israel, for example, advertising is not permitted on TV. In the United Kingdom, there are three TV networks—one, a government-sponsored network, the BBC, with two channels on which no commercial advertising is permitted; and two commercial networks on which advertising is permitted.

Similarly, in Belgium, Denmark, Sweden, and Switzerland, no advertising is permitted on radio. This may be an important condition to consider in market entry decisions since it severely limits the feasibility of adopting the heavy advertising push strategies used by many packaged goods companies in the United States, such as detergent manufacturers or consumer packaged goods manufacturers.

The reach and audience characteristics of different media may also vary considerably from one country to another. In the developing countries, high levels of illiteracy, and low levels of TV ownership imply that both print media and TV will only reach a relatively limited upscale target segment. In countries such as Nigeria, Morocco, and Algeria, which have illiteracy levels of more than 63 percent, print media can, by definition, only reach a limited segment of the population. Similarly, levels of TV ownership below four per thousand, in 1980, in countries such as Ghana, India, and Kenya imply very limited TV audiences (Starch INRA Hooper, 1981). In some developing countries, however, the level of TV ownership is surprisingly high. In 1979, Saudi Arabia had 125 sets per thousand population; and in 1980, South Korea, 157, and Taiwan, 225.

Even in the developed countries, there are substantial differences in reach and audience characteristics from one country to another. In the United States, print media tend to be highly segmented, and there are, for example, few national newspapers. In other countries such as Germany, France, or the United Kingdom, there are national newspapers such as the *Bild Zeitung, France Soir,* the *Daily Mirror,* and the *News of the World,* which have a relatively broad-based circulation. Similarly, although cinema advertising is a good way to reach young adults throughout Europe, attendance varies substantially. In Italy, the average number of cinema admissions per person in 1978 was 9.4, one of the highest in Europe; but in the United Kingdom, it was only 2.3, and in the Netherlands, 2.2, suggesting substantial differences in exposure (UNESCO, 1981).

General information about aspects such as the number of TV sets or radio ownership is contained in most information sources cited previously. The Euromonitor's *European and International Marketing Data* also contains more detailed statistics concerning circulation for national and regional newspapers. Circulation figures are also published periodically by *Advertising World*. This information is particularly comprehensive for the major European countries. More detailed information about costs of different media, audience characteristics, time and space availability, and regulation will require consultation of more specific sources such as the *World Radio and TV Handbook* or the *Media Guide International for Business and Professional Publications and Newspapers,* or trade publications such as the International Advertising Association's survey of promotional regulation, *Advertising Age, Advertising World,* or specific country sources.

Some indication of how the availability and suitability of media affect expenditures is provided in Table 3.14. Print allocations range from a low of 25 percent in Brazil to a high of 65 percent in Germany. The percent allocated to television is highest in Greece (51 percent) and lowest in France (9 percent). These differences have implications for the development of marketing and advertising strategy, as well as for the types of research that are conducted.

Intrapersonal Media.   The second type of communication network on which information is required concerns intrapersonal communication. This includes factors such as the development of the telephone system, and the calling, waiting, or answering services available; the linkage with international net-

TABLE 3.14   Profiles of advertising expenditure, 1980; percent allocation to various media

| | COUNTRIES | | | | | | | |
Media	Norway	France	Germany (F.D.R.)	U.S.A.	U.K.	Japan	Brazil	Greece
Cinema	1	1	1	—	1	—	1	—
Radio	*	7	3	7	2	5	13	6
TV	*	9	10	21	25	35	32	51
Print	62	40	65	38	58	37	25	42
All others (Outdoor, direct, etc.)	37	43	21	34	14	23	29	1

*data not available

Source: *World Advertising Expenditures.* Mamaroneck: Starch, INRA Hooper, 1981.

works; and the efficiency of the postal system, the speed of delivery, and the cost and availability of different postal services. These have an important impact both on the costs of doing business in a country, the speed with which communication can be maintained between operations in different parts of the country, and also the extent to which manpower resources such as sales representatives' time can be efficiently managed.

In many developing countries, for example, telephone systems are not well developed, and linkages are often poor. In Indonesia and Thailand, for example, there were seven phones per thousand persons and two phones per thousand persons respectively, thus, considerably limiting this as a means of communication. This also implies that control of operations would have to be carried on predominantly by personal visits, or alternatively, by mail. Even in countries such as Spain and Italy, in 1979, the number of phones per thousand persons was only 280 and 301, respectively, of which 49 percent and 36 percent, respectively, were business phones (A.T. & T., 1979). Again although the networks and linkages are fairly well-developed, few countries have the range of telephone answering services that are available throughout the United States. This implies that the ability of salespersons to improve their productivity and efficiency by using answering, recording, or remote control answering services may be restricted.

Similarly, the development of the postal system varies considerably. In Thailand, for example, the average number of units of internal mail was only four per capita in 1977, and even in Greece in 1977, it had only reached a level of 30, compared with 202 in Germany for the same period. Yet, even where the postal system is well-developed, its efficiency may vary considerably. In countries such as Brazil, it has been estimated that approximately 30 percent of the mail is never delivered, and consequently, businesses in urban areas make extensive use of messenger services. Even where the postal system is relatively widespread, there are few countries that offer services such as the express delivery available from the U.S. Postal Service, or commercial mail metering.

General information about factors such as the number of telephones in use is available in most standard information sources. Euromonitor also contains information about domestic and foreign mail flow, number of telegrams sent, use of telegraph, and so on. More detailed information about costs and further breakdowns of statistics will, however, require consultation of more specific trade or country sources, such as the International Telephone and Trade Association, or the A.T. & T. "The World's Telephones," or local consulates.

Service Organizations. The third type of integrative networks about which information will be required are the marketing support or service organizations, such as banks, financial or credit institutions, advertising agencies, and marketing research organizations. It is important to obtain information concerning the availability of such services, since otherwise the company itself will have to undertake the organization of such services, which may add considerably to costs, as well as pose a number of implementation problems. If, for example, no advertising agencies are available, a company will have to organize its own advertising campaign and media buying. Similarly, if there are no official marketing research organizations, means of obtaining the desired information will have to be devised. A company interested in investigating market potential, for example, for rice cookers in China, would need to train its own interviewers and use, perhaps, university students or foreign interviewers skilled in the relevant language or dialect.

Information about the availability of banking and other financial or credit services can be obtained from international sources and associations such as the *Investor's Chronicle's World Banking Survey,* which provides information about the major banks in seventy-one countries. Alternatively, more detailed information about the existence of branches in different countries and about the services provided can be obtained from the major international banks such as Barclays, the Midland Bank, Citibank, Bank of America, Caisse National de Credit Agricole, and Deutschebank. More detailed information about availability of different services can be obtained from specific country sources or consulates.

Similarly, in the case of advertising associations, information about advertising agencies in different countries can be obtained from the International Advertising Association. The major international advertising agencies, such as McCann-Erickson, J. Walter Thompson, S.S.C. & B., Young & Rubicam, Ogilvy & Mather, and Ted Bates, can provide listings of offices in different countries. More detailed information about specific local agencies and services provided can be obtained from regional or country-specific sources.

Similar sources can be used to obtain information about the availability of marketing research organizations. Although there is no international marketing research association, the New York chapter of the American Marketing Association has published a listing of research organizations in foreign countries. (See Appendix III.) These are, however, in some instances, branches of American marketing research organizations. The Market Research Society of the United Kingdom and the British Overseas Trade Board publishes an extensive international directory of marketing research companies in fifty-nine countries throughout the world, including the principal marketing research and marketing associations. More detailed information can be obtained from national marketing research organizations such as the Market Research Society of Australia, the Danish Market Research Society, or the South African Market Research Association. (See Appendix II for a more complete listing of associations.) Furthermore, the major international research agencies, such as Nielsen, IMS, R.I., and Burke, can provide listings of offices in other countries, and of services and coverage of other countries.

Resource Requirements

The second type of infrastructure data consists of data that are needed to assess the costs of operating in a specific country environment. This is primarily of concern when management is considering the establishment of a production facility in a country, but may also be of some importance if a sales or marketing organization is to be established within a foreign market. The factors that will be important are, for example, energy costs, wage rates, availability of labor skills, and capital resources and technology.

Three major types of resources can be identified:

Physical Resources.   Where the establishment of a physical plant is being considered, examination of the availability and costs of physical resources such as electricity, oil, coal, or water is particularly important. It is, for example, of critical importance in many heavy industries, such as steel or construction. Such factors are also important if a sales or marketing organization is to be established in the country, but are less crucial in this context.

General information indicating the availability of such resources, as for example, energy consumption and production and their costs, is available in the general sources cited earlier, such as the United Nations *Yearbook of Industrial Statistics.* Specific regional or site availability will, however, need to be investigated in more detail, based on country-specific sources, since frequently there are significant regional variations in availability and cost.

Human Resources.   Investigation of the availability and costs of different types of labor and management skills is also an important consideration. For companies considering foreign-based production, wage rates and the availability of certain technological skills are frequently important factors. Low wage rates in Asian countries such as Taiwan and South Korea, have, for example, been an important factor in inducing the movement of the textile and electronics industries to these locations. Availability of technological skills is also an important consideration for companies that require engineering skills, such as those in the construction industry, since otherwise expatriate engineers have to be employed, thus adding substantially to production costs. Availability of trained management and sales personnel may also be an important consideration, even in industries such as fast foods, because otherwise, management or sales training programs have to be developed for franchisees, in order to ensure uniform service and quality, thus adding substantially to costs.

Information about the availability of labor and of wage rates in different industries can be found in the general sources cited earlier, and notably in the United Nations *Yearbook of Industrial Statistics.* Information relating to management and specific skills is somewhat more complex, and may require the use of surrogate indicators, such as the number of management training programs and the number of graduates from such programs.

Capital Resources.   Availability of capital and financial resources may in some cases be an important consideration. This is more likely to be important where a local production facility is to be considered. Factors to be examined include the availability of local capital; the cost and normal terms of borrowing, as for example, interest rates, government credit aids, and tax incentives to new businesses; and the country's rating as a borrower by United States, European, or other sources. In addition, opportunities for reinvestment of earnings may be an important consideration, especially where there are restrictions on the repatriation of earnings. In countries such as Ireland, for example, the government grants substantial tax reliefs in order to encourage foreign investment and the development of employment opportunities by foreign companies. In countries such as India and Taiwan, repatriation of capital or earnings is restricted, and consequently convertible currencies are only available on the black market at a slightly discounted rate.

Information with regard to such factors is to be found in general sources such as *International Financial Statistics* country guides, or relevant business publications. These sources will, however, only provide a general indication, since there is likely to be considerable variation in the extent to which such resources are readily available or can be negotiated, and also variation in relevant rates and terms from one industry or one company to another.

Marketing Data

Furthermore, information is needed concerning key characteristics of the marketing environment in a country, such as its demographic, economic, geographic, technological, and sociocultural characteristics. While some of these are to be found in the general sources discussed earlier, more specific and detailed information is often required to make a better assessment of market potential and likely market development. In essence, these characteristics can be viewed as surrogate indicators of market size and rates of growth. Some illustrations of the types of indicators that might be used are provided in the next section. It should, however, be emphasized that these are only examples, and that management will need to select the specific indicators relevant to the company's international corporate objectives, and to the specific industry or product market concerned.

Demographic Characteristics

Information about demographic characteristics provides an important indication of potential market size. The estimated population of one billion in the People's Republic of China is, for example, an important element encouraging interest in entry into this market. Conversely, small countries such as Iceland, Qatar, or the Bahamas are rarely of interest to international marketers due to their small population size (less than 200,000). The types of general demographic variables that are often examined, in addition to population size, include rate of population growth, degree of urbanization, age structure, and composition.

The importance of such factors varies from product to product. For some products, such as baby foods, geriatric products, or records, demographic characteristics may be key indicators of market potential. In selling diapers, for example, the number of married women of childbearing age, rates of fertility, and the degree of urbanization may be critical factors delineating market size.

Data on certain demographic factors, notably population size and growth, are included in most of the international data sources cited earlier. More detailed statistics and breakdowns can be obtained from the United Nations Population Center and relevant publications such as their *Demographic Yearbook,* the *Statistical Yearbook,* and UNESCO sources. As noted previously, the data contained in commercial data sources are typically based on these sources, with some updating of estimates.

Economic Characteristics

Information about economic characteristics is important in evaluating the affluence of a market. While population delineates market size, large countries that are poor, such as China or India, may not provide very attractive markets. This is especially the case for items such as cosmetics, perfume, designer clothing, or videocassettes. The possible existence of small, affluent segments within such countries implies that information is required not only about aggregate economic data such as GDP, GNP, and rates of growth, but also about income distribution within a country.

A marketer of an expensive women's face cream or of designer jeans might be more concerned with identifying the existence of a small upscale target segment within a country than with average per capita income. For example, this marketer might identify an important target segment in Brazil or Mexico, although average per capita income is less than $3,500.

Information about aggregate economic characteristics such as GDP or GNP is typically contained in most general information sources such as those cited previously. More detailed breakdowns are to be found in sources such as the United Nations, the World Bank, or UNESCO. In some cases, such as income distribution, these are not available for all countries, particularly the poorer developing countries.

Geographic Characteristics

The geographic characteristics of a country play an important role in influencing ability and ease of exploiting marketing opportunities. A country's physical size and the nature of its terrain will in particular affect physical distribution costs and ease of communication with potential target markets. For some products, such as snowmobiles, fur coats, sunglasses, or electric fans, geographic or climatic factors are important indicators of market potential.

In sparsely populated countries such as Zaire, Nigeria, or Australia, considerable difficulty may be encountered in reaching the rural population in outlying areas. In African countries, reaching such populations may require a complex system of distribution, combining railroad with riverboat, train, or cart. In Australia or other developed countries, this population may best be reached, as in the United States, by mail catalog. Similarly, in several Latin-American countries such as Peru, the Andean mountains constitute an important barrier separating markets.

Information about some of these characteristics is contained in the general information sources cited earlier. More detailed information can typically be found in geographic atlases. World almanacs, tourist guidebooks, and country guides also provide a useful source of information.

Technological Characteristics

Technological characteristics, such as the level of technological skills or education, affect the costs of alternative modes of operation and entry into a country, and in some cases can also provide indicators of market potential. The availability of managerial and technological skills may influence whether direct investment, as opposed to exporting, is considered, since the cost of expatriate management tends to be higher than the cost of local personnel. Levels of education, or management skills, may provide important indicators of potential for products such as electronic games, books, sales management training modules, and personal computers.

A company interested in marketing sales management training programs that make use of much audio-visual equipment might be concerned with examining a number of these factors. First, the number of companies with substantial sales forces would need to be determined; then, factors such as the number and size of computers, the size of undergraduate business programs, the extent of management education, and sales of film projectors might also be investigated.

General information about the level of technological development can be found in the macro information sources cited earlier, as for example, those on energy and steel consumption, or agricultural production as a percentage of GNP. Indications of the level of consumption technology can be evaluated from the levels of household appliance ownership, the number of libraries and museums, consumption of newsprint, or expenditure on higher education. This information is contained in the United Nations handbooks and in UNESCO sources, or in summary form in sources such as Euromonitor's *European Marketing Data* and *International Marketing Data*.

Sociocultural Characteristics

Sociocultural characteristics such as cultural values, life style patterns, linguistic fragmentation, and cultural or ethnic homogeneity are often important factors influencing market response. This is particularly the case for products that tend to be culturally embedded, such as food products, drinks, and certain personal clothing items.

A marketer of instant breakfast drink might, for example, be concerned with obtaining data on eating and drinking habits at breakfast, the types of beverages typically consumed at other times, the consumption of milk products or of fruit drinks, and the level of food processing and consumer receptivity to such processed products. Cultural factors can also affect the cost of marketing in a country, especially where multiple languages require the development of multilingual packages, or separate communication appeals. Information about specific aspects such as linguistic fragmentation and the number of ethnic or subcultural groups can be obtained from United Nations demographic and statistical handbooks, and from UNESCO sources. Similarly, information concerning magazine circulation and the number of museums and libraries can be found in Euromonitor. Considerably more difficulty is likely to be encountered in obtaining hard data and quantified measures of sociocultural values and life styles, especially in developing countries. Even where available, knowing how to interpret them poses some problems, since sociocultural patterns are subject to change, and their relevance depends on the strategy adopted by the international marketer.

Detailed studies of cultural values and life style patterns have been conducted in relation to a number of countries, typically the more industrialized countries (Plummer, 1977; Segnit and Broadbent, 1973; McCann-Erickson, 1978). Leo Burnett has, for example, conducted life style studies in Canada, the United Kingdom, Germany, Spain, Italy, France, Denmark, South Africa, Australia, Mexico, Japan, and Brazil. Similarly, McCann-Erickson has conducted a survey of the youth market in the major West European countries, Japan, Canada, and Australia.

These provide some general indications of current trends in life style or cultural values, and can be helpful in diagnosing the way in which these may affect demand for certain products, for example, fast foods, and market response patterns, for example, advertising themes. In general, however, the link with each specific product market needs to be explicitly evaluated (Douglas and Macquin, 1977).

Product Market Data

In addition, wherever feasible, data relating to the specific product markets should be collected. The type of data required varies, depending on the type of product, that is, industrial versus consumer product, its stage in the product life cycle, and so on. In the case of industrial products, consumption and production data are required and, where possible, market share data as well as information relating to the growth of end user industries. For consumer products, product usage data or product market data, and information relating to complementary or substitute products and the competitive market structure are desirable. The ease of obtaining such data is likely to vary substantially, depending on the specific product, its recency and rate of growth, and the country.

Industrial Products

For industrial products, many of the sources cited previously provide consumption and production data as well as market surveys. The United Nations *Handbook of Industrial Statistics,* for example, provides extensive coverage of industries in different nations. The U.S. Department of Commerce *Global Market Surveys* furnishes in-depth surveys of key markets for selected products.

Predicasts, on the other hand, provides highly detailed production and consumption data and forecasts for fifty industries in fifty countries. They also have a service, PROMT, that provides monthly abstracts of articles published on twenty-eight industry sectors throughout the world. Another service, *Predibriefs,* is a monthly industry news report containing statistical summaries and discussion of trends in a given industry for selected products.

Information with regard to end user industries may also be found in such sources, though this varies depending on the specific industry. Alternatively, trade sources and trade publications may provide useful information, though typically these are likely to provide information for specific countries or regions, rather than providing worldwide surveys. Information on market share, product replacement and usage, and competitive activity may be considerably more difficult to obtain. The U.S. Department of Commerce reports provide this information, but only for selected industries. In other cases, trade publications may be the best sources for obtaining information about competitive market conditions and structure, though these may tend to be somewhat patchy. In some cases, government, industry, or trade sources in a given country may provide such information. In Japan, the Yano Economic Research Institute has published detailed information on market share for twelve major industrial and consumer industries.

Consumer Products

Somewhat greater difficulty is likely to be encountered in obtaining product market data for consumer markets. This is particularly likely to be the case in developing countries, and also in relation to emerging markets or markets where the structure of the market is changing rapidly, such as home entertainment, toys, or beverages. In cases where a product is already marketed in other countries, information relating to current product usage or consumption patterns is useful in attempting to assess current levels of market saturation and future development potential. It provides some indication of the level of market development for the product line or product class, as well as the extent to which effort will need to be devoted to developing primary demand as opposed to a more selective positioning.

Product Usage Data.   In the case of durable products, data relating to levels of product ownership is often desirable, for example, ownership of TV sets, washing machines, and other durables. A manufacturer of microwave ovens might, for example, be interested in current levels of microwave oven ownership. Information on the recency of purchase—that is, the average age of the item—and on the existence of a second-hand market—for example, in automobiles or mopeds—might also be valuable. Furthermore, to the extent that purchase of durables tends to follow a sequence—that is, oven, refrigerator, washing machine, dishwasher, microwave oven, and so on—information pertaining to not only the specific durable, but also to related durables, may be useful. Information about ownership of different consumer durables can be obtained from some of the general information sources cited earlier. The Euromonitor sources, for example, provide much useful data about ownership of standard consumer durables. Surveys such as those conducted by the Economist Intelligence Unit provide a more accurate and up-to-date source of information. For nondurables, data relating to current sales trends, repeat purchase rates, and usage patterns are likely to be more relevant. Marketers of consumer packaged goods, or basic staples such as coffee or soups, are more likely to be concerned with trends in per capita consumption, repeat patterns, and other usage conditions for these products in different countries.

In the case of soups, for example, a manufacturer might be interested not only in per capita consumption, but also in differences in consumption and usage of different product variants, that is, canned versus dehydrated soups. Some of this information, especially that related to usage, is to be found in product market surveys or in trade publications. In general, however, these tend to cover only a specific country or region rather than being global in character.

Nielsen data are available for many nations. More specifically, their drug index and bimonthly food index are available in twenty-two countries. Coverage with regard to other industries tends, however, to vary. IMS provides coverage on pharmaceutical, health, and personal care industries for thirty-one countries. In addition, national and regional store audits and panels can be very useful. Infratest has, for example, extensive panel and audit services in many European countries. Some research organizations such as Research International also develop their own panels. Research International runs product usage panels in thirty countries where such information would not otherwise be available.

Usage of Related Complementary or Substitute Products.   Information relating to usage of substitute, complementary, or related products may also be valuable. An important concern is the nature of the product market and how to define relevant product market boundaries. A product such as bleach might, for example, be positioned as a household cleanser, or alternatively, as part of the detergent market. This raises a number of questions about how different products and product variants are perceived, and various issues with regard to the equivalence and comparability of product markets in different countries. These are discussed in further detail in Chapter 5.

Information about the dimensions of the product market is especially useful in contexts where the product is new and different and where there are no well-established markets for the product, or alternatively, where there are important interrelated production or marketing costs. A tire manufacturer might be concerned with sales of trucks and passenger cars, as well as average truck and passenger car mileage.

Equally, a manufacturer of jellied cranberry sauce might want to look not only at turkey consumption and sales data, but also at other sweet or tart meat accompaniments such as mint jelly, crab apple jelly, chutenies or other relishes, as well as at gelatin-based desserts or molds in which cranberry sauce might be used.

Competition.   Examination of competition is also an important consideration insofar as it affects ease of market entry, the need to emphasize promotional or distribution strategy, and the potential profitability from entering different product markets. The domination of a market by a few large companies may, for example, suggest difficulties in market entry and obtaining distribution. A more fragmented structure may pose fewer problems. In examining competition, a number of factors might be considered. These range from the number and size of competitors, to their sales volume, rates of growth, or relative market share; to the identity of these competitors—that is, multinational versus local competitors, and their relative resources.

The specific factors will depend to a large extent on the particular industry. In the computer or detergent industries, for example, the key factor may be the presence of a major multinational competitor with extensive financial and other resources, such as I.B.M., or Procter & Gamble. Local competitors are, however, not to be ignored, as they may have less administrative overhead, lower operating costs, and greater competitive flexibility. In each case, however, the feasibility of obtaining such data is likely to vary significantly with the specific product. Difficulties are likely to be encountered, particularly in obtaining worldwide marketing information. Nielsen and other audit data are available for a number of countries. In addition, national and international trade sources may be helpful, but in general, information may be patchy.

SUMMARY

There is a wide variety of secondary data sources available for conducting international marketing research. In essence, the problem is not one of the scarcity of data, but rather one of the plethora of information available. Hence, it becomes important to be selective in picking information sources that provide up-to-date and accurate data relevant to the specific product or service and the decision problem concerned.

Secondary data provide an excellent starting point for many international marketing research projects. They are readily available and relatively inexpensive, and can be quickly consulted. They are particularly useful in pinpointing specific problems and key areas that need to be investigated in further depth, and should provide the major focus in subsequent research.

Secondary data also provide information relating to a wide variety of different aspects of international operations. They cover, for example, economic data relating to the general business environment in a country. They include specific industry data with a worldwide coverage. In addition, other sources contain data relevant to specific marketing strategy decisions, such as information about demographic, economic, geographic, technological, and sociocultural characteristics. Also, they provide information about political, financial, foreign exchange, legal, and regulatory data; data relating to the availability and character of distributive and communication networks and service organizations; and data about other physical, human, and capital resources, which are needed in making market entry and investment decisions.

The specific sources that are selected, and the degree of detail in which information is collected, will, however, depend on specific corporate objectives and resources. In particular, the degree of commitment to international market expansion and involvement is an important consideration, as is the size of the company and its experience in international and other country markets. The relevant management decision problem will also dictate to a large extent the time and resources allocated to secondary data collection. The uses of secondary data are discussed in a subsequent chapter.

REFERENCES

Area Handbook Series. Washington, DC: Foreign Area Studies of the American University.

A.T.&T. STAFF, "The World's Telephones." Bedminster, NJ: A.T.&T. Long Lines, 1979.

BRADLEY, DAVID G., "Managing Against Expropriation," *Harvard Business Review,* 55 (July–August 1977), 75–83.

BUSINESS INTERNATIONAL, *Worldwide Economic Indicators.* New York: Business International, 1981.

——, *Managing and Evaluating Country Risk.* New York: Business International, 1981.

——, *Country and Regional Reports.* New York: Business International.

——, *Investment, Licensing and Trading Conditions Abroad.* New York: Business International.

COUNCIL FOR MUTUAL ECONOMIC ASSISTANCE, *Statistical Yearbook of Member States.* London: IPC Industrial Press, Inc.

DOUGLAS, SUSAN P. and ANNE MACQUIN, "L'Utilisation du Style de Vie dans le Media Planning." Paris: Jours de France, 1977.

DUN and BRADSTREET, *Exporters Encyclopedia.* New York: Dun and Bradstreet, Annual edition.

ECONOMIST INTELLIGENCE UNIT, *Marketing in Europe* (Monthly). London: The Economist Intelligence Unit.

——, *Quarterly Economic Reviews.* London: The Economist Intelligence Unit.

EUROMONITOR PUBLICATIONS LTD., *European Marketing Data and Statistics,* 17th ed. London: Euromonitor Publications, 1981.

——, *International Marketing Data and Statistics,* 6th ed., London: Euromonitor Publications, Ltd., 1981.

HANES, F.T., "Construction and Forecast Techniques for a Measure of a Country's Willingness and Capacity to Permit Repatriation of Funds," Long Beach, CA: B.E.R.I. Ltd., 1981.

The Institutional Investor Country Credit (March and September issues).

INTERNATIONAL ADVERTISING ASSOCIATION, *Premiums, Gifts and Competitions: An International Survey.* New York: International Advertising Association, 1978.

International Directory of Marketing Research Houses and Services, Green Book, 20th ed. Pat Ryan (Ed.) New York: American Marketing Association, 1982.

International Financial Statistics (Monthly). Washington: International Monetary Fund.

The International Research Directory of Market Research Organizations, 6th ed. London: The Market Research Society, British Overseas Trade Board, 1982.

JETRO, *Sales Promotion in the Japanese Market.* Tokyo: Jetro, 1979.

KOBRIN, STEPHEN J., "Political Assessment by International Firms: 'Models or Methodologies,' " *Journal of Policy Modeling,* 3 (1981), 251–70.

KRAVIS, IRVING B., ALAN HESTON, and ROBERT SUMMERS, *International Comparisons of Real Product and Purchasing Power,* United Nations International Comparison Project: Phase II. Baltimore and London: The Johns Hopkins University Press, 1978.

LEVICH, RICHARD M., "Analyzing the Accuracy of Foreign Exchange Advisory Services Theory and Evidence," in Richard M. Levich and Clas G. Wihlborg, *Exchange Risk and Exposure.* pp. 99–128. Lexington, MA: D. C. Heath & Co., 1980.

MCCANN-ERICKSON, *Youth in Europe.* London: McCann-Erickson, 1978.

Media Guide International. New York: Directories International. (Annual editions.)

PLUMMER, JOSEPH, "Consumer Focus in Cross-National Research," *Journal of Advertising,* 6 (Spring 1977), 5–15.

Predicasts. Cleveland, OH: Predicasts.

PRICE WATERHOUSE INFORMATION GUIDES, *Doing Business in . . . , Value Added Tax, Foreign Exchange Information.* New York: Price Waterhouse.

RUMMEL, R. and DAVID HEENAN, "How Multinationals Analyze Political Risk," *Harvard Business Review,* 56 (January–February 1978), 67–76.

SEGNIT, SUSANNA and SIMON BROADBENT, "Lifestyle Research," *European Research,* 1, (January 1973), 6–19; 1, (March 1973).

STARCH INRA HOOPER, *World Advertising Expenditures.* Mamaroneck: Starch INRA Hooper, 1981.

THOMAS, PHILIP S., "Environmental Scanning—The State of the Art," *Long Range Planning,* 13 (February 1980), 27–28.

UNESCO Statistical Yearbook. (Annual edition.) Paris: UNESCO.

UNITED NATIONS, *The Demographic Yearbook.* New York: United Nations. (Annual edition.)

——, *The Statistical Yearbook.* New York: United Nations. (Annual edition.)

——, *Yearbook of International Trade Statistics.* New York: United Nations. (Annual edition.)

——, *Yearbook of Industrial Statistics,* vol. 1, *General Industrial Statistics;* vol. II, *Commercial Production Data.* New York: United Nations. (Annual editions.)

——, *Yearbook of Labor Statistics.* New York: United Nations. (Annual edition.)

U.S. DEPARTMENT OF COMMERCE, *Global Market Surveys.* Washington, DC: U.S. Department of Commerce.

——, *International Marketing Handbook,* vol. I, II. Washington, DC: Department of Commerce, 1981.

——, *Overseas Business Reports.* Washington, DC: U.S. Department of Commerce.

WASHINGTON RESEARCHERS, *Sources of Aid and Information for U.S. Exporters.* Donna M. Jablonski, ed., Washington, DC: Washington Researchers, 1979.

World Almanac. New York: Newspaper Enterprise Association. (Annual edition.)

WORLD BANK, *World Tables,* 2nd ed. Baltimore and London: Johns Hopkins University Press, 1980.

——, *World Development Report.* New York: Oxford University Press, 1981.

Worldcasts. Cleveland, OH: Predicasts.

World of Information, Regional Guides. Saffron Walden: World of Information.

World Radio and T.V. Handbook. London and New York: Billboard Publications. (Annual edition.)

4

Uses of Secondary Data

The wide variety of secondary data available for use in the preliminary stages of international marketing research was discussed in Chapter 3. These are particularly useful in evaluating country or market environments, whether in making initial market entry decisions or in attempting to assess future trends and developments. They thus form an integral part of the international marketing research process. More specifically, three major uses of secondary data may be identified: 1) in selecting countries or markets that merit in-depth investigation, 2) in making an initial estimate of demand potential in a given country or set of countries, and 3) in monitoring environmental change.

In the first case, secondary data can be used to screen, on a systematic basis, market potential, the risks, and the likely costs of operating in different countries throughout the world. Those that appear to offer the most promising potential and are prime candidates for in-depth investigation can be identified. Secondly, once these have been singled out, secondary data can be used to develop more precise and quantified estimates of demand and market size. Finally, secondary data can be useful in assessing changes in economic and environmental conditions throughout the world. It can, thus, facilitate detection of countries that should provide the prime focus for market expansion and growth, and those where operations should be curtailed.

MARKET ENTRY

For companies entering international markets for the first time, a dual decision has to be made concerning the appropriate combination of countries and modes of entry to be used. This requires the collection of information to assess the investment climate and market potential in all countries to be considered, as well as the risks and costs associated with operation in these different environments.

A major problem in the initial stages of international market entry is the bewildering array of countries and markets that could be entered. Since it is clearly prohibitive to examine all possible countries and markets, an initial screening procedure to determine which countries to investigate in-depth is required. Secondary data can provide the basis for this evaluation, either being used in standard or generalized classification schemata or indicators, or in customized models geared to specific company objectives and industries.

Generalized Procedures

Two types of generalized (that is, noncompany- and nonindustry-specific) procedures can be identified. The first is based on the development of classification schemata to group countries with similar business environments, and the second uses secondary data to develop composite indices of market potential in different countries throughout the world.

Classification Schemata of Countries

Macroindicators have been used in a number of studies to classify countries according to their business environments, and hence, investment potential. The classic study of this type was that conducted by the Marketing Science Institute (Liander and others, 1967). In addition to a regional-typological approach, two approaches were adopted. One was based on two dimensions—a country's degree of demographic and economic mobility, and its domestic stability and cohesion. Position on the economic demographic dimension was measured by twenty-one variables relating to development and industrialization, marketing orientation, communications, transportation, organization of population, and education and health. The second dimension, internal stability and cohesion, was measured by three indicators—deaths from group violence, cultural homogeneity and fragmentation, and duration of national identity. In the second approach, countries were first classified into Berry's five levels of technological development: most highly developed, developed, semideveloped, underdeveloped, very underdeveloped. Similarity among countries within each level was then examined, based on twelve environmental and societal characteristics such as population growth, urban population, and religious and racial homogeneity.

Litvak and Banking (1968) have proposed that investment climates be evaluated in terms of seven major categories of variables, including political stability, cultural homogeneity, geocultural distance, market opportunity, and economic development. Sheth and Lutz (1973) have developed an operational means of applying this framework, using fifty-nine readily available environmental indicators, to classify investment climates into the three categories of hot, warm, and cold.

Another schema is that developed by Sethi (1971), which uses twenty-nine variables relating to political and socioeconomic factors, trade, transportation, communications, biological, and personal consumption data, to classify ninety-one countries. In a later study, (Sethi and Curry, 1973) more sociocultural variables were added, resulting in the classification of ninety-three countries on fifty-six variables. A more recent study (Johansson and Moinpour, 1977) classifies countries within the Pacific Rim and Atlantic Ocean region, based on twenty-nine economic, social, and political variables.

Similarly, Doyle and Gigendil (1976) used twenty-six indicators drawn from the United Nations *Statistical and Demographic Yearbook,* the UNESCO *Yearbook,* and Business International data to identify countries with similar characteristics and, hence, hypothesized to have equivalent market potential. The matching of countries based on their profiles was then investigated as a basis for grouping countries for market entry or strategy development.

Piper (1971), in an early investigation of factors used by United States firms to evaluate investment opportunities, also found similar types of information were used in investment studies. These are shown in Table 4.1. In addition to the macroeconomic indicators, and as might be anticipated in an investment study, a number of financial variables were also included.

The major limitation of such classification schemata is, however, that they are based solely on macroeconomic, social, and political indicators. Consequently, they assume that the same indicators are equally relevant for all product markets and companies. While this may be true for some indicators such as GNP or population size, it is not true for others. Political factors are, for example, likely to be more important where a substantial equity involvement is being considered or for companies in strategic industries, such as the extraction industries, or high-technology industries, such as telecommunications, than for companies primarily concerned with exporting. Furthermore, such schemata do not contain any information concerning specific industries. These schemata are nonetheless likely to provide an important input in assessing market potential in a given country.

TABLE 4.1   Decision variables identified in 16 investment studies

Financial considerations

1. Capital acquisition plan
2. Length of payback period
3. Projected cash inflows (years one, two, and so forth)
4. Projected cash outflows (years one, two, and so forth)
5. Return on investment
6. Monetary-exchange considerations

Technical and engineering feasibility considerations

7. Raw-materials availability (construction/support/supplies)
8. Raw-materials availability (products)
9. Geography/climate
10. Site locations and access
11. Availability of local labor
12. Availability of local management
13. Economic infrastructure (roads, water, electricity, and so forth)
14. Facilities planning (preliminary or detailed)

Marketing considerations

15. Market size
16. Market potential
17. Distribution costs
18. Competition

19. Time necessary to establish distribution/sales channels
20. Promotion costs
21. Social/cultural factors affecting products

Economic and legal considerations

22. Legal systems
23. Host-government attitudes toward foreign investment
24. Host attitude toward this particular investment
25. Restrictions on ownership
26. Tax laws
27. Import/export restrictions
28. Capital-flow restrictions
29. Land-title acquisitions
30. Inflation

Political and social considerations

31. Internal political stability
32. Relations with neighboring countries
33. Political/social traditions
34. Communist influence
35. Religious racial/language homogeneity
36. Labor organizations and attitudes
37. Skill/technical level of the labor force
38. Socioeconomic infrastructure to support American families

Source: James R. Piper, "How U.S. Firms Evaluate Foreign Investment Opportunities," *M.S.U. Business Topics* (Summer 1971), pp. 11–20.

Multiple-Factor Indexes

Multiple-factor indexes are also published by various commercial services. Business International, for example, each year publishes information based on three indexes: 1) market growth, 2) market intensity, and 3) market size, for countries in Western and Eastern Europe, the Middle East, Latin America, Asia, Africa, and Australia. A summary of these regional analyses for the twenty-two largest markets in the world is shown in Figure 4.1. The specific variables included in each of these indexes vary somewhat from region to region, reflecting different market characteristics. The market growth index

7

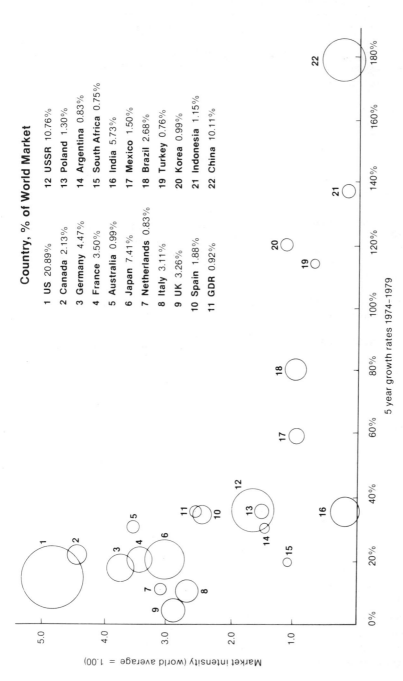

FIGURE 4.1 1979 B.I. market indexes: size, growth and intensity of 22 largest markets

Note: The center of each circle shows the intensity of the market (when measured against the vertical axis) and its cumulative growth over the 1974–79 period (when measured against the horizontal axis). The size of the circles indicates the relative size of the market in terms of its percentage of the global market. The graph identifies only those countries whose share of the world market was 0.75% or more in 1979.

Source: Reprinted from the January 8, 1982 issue of *Business International* (BI), page 16, with the permission of the publisher, Business International Corporation (New York).

is based on the average of a number of indicators of percent growth over the past five years. In Europe, these are population, steel consumption, cement production, electricity production, passenger cars in use, GDP, national income, private consumption, expenditures, and telephones and TV sets in use. In Latin America, the last five are omitted, and energy consumption and trucks and buses in use, added. The average growth in this region over the past five years was 42 percent, with Paraguay as the leader at 82 percent, followed by Brazil at 75 percent.

Market intensity is an index that measures the "richness" of a market, or the degree of concentrated purchasing power. The region is taken as the base, and a score for each country is calculated based on certain indicators. In Europe these are the same indicators as for market growth, with double weighting of private consumption expenditure and ownership of passenger cars. In Latin America, per capita energy and steel consumption, and telephones and TV sets in use are used in addition to private consumption expenditure, ownership of passenger cars, and the proportion of the urban population that receives double weighting. A score is calculated for each country in a region and expressed relative to the regional norm of 1.00. For example, in Latin America, in 1978, the Antilles had the highest intensity, with a score of 4.14; followed by Puerto Rico with 2.79. Honduras and Bolivia were the lowest, with scores of .26 and .29 respectively.

The market size index measures the relative size of each national market as a percent of the region. In Latin America, this ranking is based on population; urban population (double-weighted); private consumption expenditure; energy and steel consumption; cement production; and telephones, cars, and TV sets in use. Scores are calculated for each country in the region and expressed as a percent of the regional total. For example, in 1978, Brazil accounted for 33.7 percent of market potential in Latin America, followed by Mexico with 20.4 percent.

The principal limitation of these indexes is that they focus on macrocountry indicators. These are used as surrogate indicators or proxy variables for evaluating the general business climate. As such, they are useful as a first step in identifying countries that are likely to be attractive candidates for initial entry or expansion of international operations. Individual companies will, however, need more detailed analyses, tailored to corporate objectives and the specific product markets in which they are involved. Consequently, their use is somewhat limited, particularly for companies that wish to make a serious commitment to international operations.

Customized Models

An alternative approach is to develop customized models using secondary data geared to specific company objectives and industry characteristics. The variables to be used to screen countries are thus selected on the basis of management objectives with regard to international marketing operations, and are adapted to the particular industry and product lines concerned. Some companies may, for example, attach greater importance to political risk than other factors, while other companies may be more concerned with the rates of inflation or future market growth. Similarly, the kinds of criteria that may be relevant for one industry may not be the same for other industries. Companies marketing minicomputers might, for example, be concerned with the number of banking and financial institutions and retail businesses. Agricultural equipment manufacturers, on the other hand, would be more concerned with agricultural production and the percentage of the population employed in agriculture.

A selection of such indicators can be used to make a subjective evaluation of countries and areas that appear to offer the best prospects for market entry. Alternatively, more systematic procedures, combining selection of these variables with a screening or scanning routine to evaluate countries on the basis of relevant variables, can be developed.

One such model integrating management judgment has been developed (Douglas, Lemaire, and Wind, 1972). This uses management judgment to select relevant variables and to weight them according to their perceived importance. A rank order of countries is then obtained, indicating priority for further investigation. A modified version of the conceptual framework underlying this procedure, integrating international information needs, is outlined in Figure 4.2. This procedure involves three stages. First, criteria for examining countries are identified. Next, criteria for evaluating countries and the weights to be assigned to them under different modes of operation or entry are determined. Finally, countries are evaluated based on these criteria, utilizing information relating to the general business and investment climate and, where available, to the specific product market. A sensitivity analysis is then conducted to assess the robustness of the classifications.

Step 1: Preliminary Screening Criteria

The first step is to establish the preliminary screening requirements. These consist of GO/NO-GO criteria applied by management to establish the feasible list of countries for the evaluation process. This assumes that countries may be excluded from further consideration on the basis of certain attributes.

Two types of attributes may be relevant:

1. *prohibitions* or restrictions on the sale of specific products or services by foreign companies, such as firearms or narcotics; or restrictions by home governments on marketing to certain countries, as for example, to the U.S.S.R.; and
2. *a priori rules of thumb* established by management for eliminating countries. The latter may reflect ideological or political influences. For example, a United States company might eliminate South Africa, or a company selling pork products might

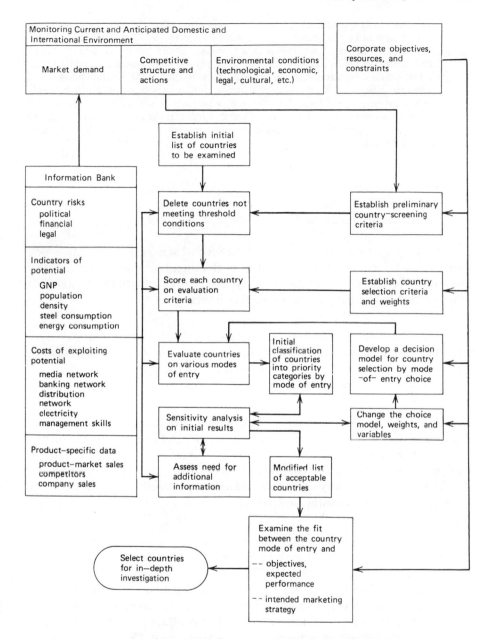

FIGURE 4.2 A conceptual framework for country/mode-of-entry selection

Source: Adapted from Susan P. Douglas, Patrick LeMaire, and Yoram Wind, "Selection of Global Target Markets: A Decision-Theoretic Approach," *Proceedings of the XXIII Esomar Congress*. Cannes, France: European Society for Opinion and Market Research, 1972.

eliminate Moslem countries. These rules might also reflect the need for a minimum level of demand or minimum market size. For example, a manufacturer of fur coats might eliminate countries with a tropical climate; or a cigarette manufacturer, countries below a certain level of GNP per capita or below a certain population size. The specific criteria will depend on the nature of the product market and corporate objectives. Companies marketing similar products will not necessarily use similar sets of criteria. For example, interest and willingness to trade with Communist countries or to assume risk may vary with the individual company. In any given situation, therefore, the onus is on management to identify the set of relevant criteria.

Step 2: Selecting Variables and Determining Weights for Evaluating Countries

Identifying Relevant Variables.   The second step is to determine which country characteristics are to be used in evaluating marketing opportunities, and how these should be weighted. Four types of variables need to be taken into consideration in evaluating international markets:

1. The *risks* associated with operating in a given national or product market.
2. The market *potential,* and growth of the country and the specific product market.
3. The *costs* of operating in that environment.
4. The strength of potential *competition.*

This would include variables that indicate market potential, political, financial, and legal risks, or relating to integrative networks and resource requirements, or other characteristics that might be used in evaluating international marketing opportunities. In each specific case, however, the specific variables to be included need to be carefully selected by mangement, based on the nature of the product market and corporate objectives.

Establishing the Relative Importance of Each Variable.   Once the relevant variables to be included have been selected, the weight to be assigned to each of these has to be determined. These are likely to vary from company to company. For example, one company may be willing to accept a higher degree of political risk and less economic stability than another company. Similarly, a company emphasizing a mass media approach may attach importance to a well-developed communication structure, or the existence of TV advertising. This implies that the weights should be provided by the judgments of relevant decision makers within the firm. Such judges should be selected on the basis of their involvement and importance in decisions to enter international markets.

Various data collection and analytical procedures may be utilized to generate these weights. If, for example, decisions to enter an overseas market are typically made on the basis of group judgments, a Delphi technique may be appropriate. Weights initially attributed by individual judges are modified by group discussions. If, on the other hand, a hierarchical decision-making procedure is used, independent judgments may be collected from all relevant decision makers, and weighted according to their relative importance in the decision-making process.

Such judgments may be collected using different scaling techniques, ranging from a simple rank order to the more rigorous interval scales. For example, each decision maker might be presented with a set of variables. He or she then assigns a value of 0 to the variable rated lowest, and 100 to that rated most important. Values ranging from 0 to 100 are then assigned to the remaining variables corresponding to their relative importance. Aggregating across decision makers, an interval scale for the weights is obtained. More complex procedures such as conjoint or trade-off analysis may also be developed.

Country selection decisions are also affected by, and interact with, the mode of entry or operation decision. The size of tariff barriers is, for example, critical when exporting, and may encourage local production. Similarly, factors such as the level of local technological, mechanical, or managerial skills are substantially more important if local production, as opposed to licensing or exporting, is envisaged.

The variables included in the evaluation procedure and the importance attached to them, therefore, need to be adjusted according to the mode of entry. Judges or decision makers can be asked to select and weight variables under different modes of operation and entry as, for example, exporting, licensing, contract manufacturing, joint venture, or local production. Where significantly different variables or weights are assigned for different modes of entry, these can then be incorporated into the evaluation model.

Step 3: Country Evaluation

Countries can then be evaluated based on these variables and rank ordered according to their score. If more than one set of weights is used, evaluations can be made sequentially, based on the different sets. The highest ranking obtained for the country on any one of these sets is then retained as its score. The rank orderings of countries and the implied financial investment is then reviewed, and the initial list of countries for in-depth evaluation selected.

Next, the robustness of this procedure and overall congruence with initial management objectives is examined. A sensitivity analysis is conducted to evaluate the explicit and implicit decision rules used by management, and their implications. At the same time, the need for more accurate information about countries where minor changes—either in the value of variables or their weights—would affect acceptance or rejection, may be assessed. This sensitivity analysis thus consists of two subphases: analysis of the weights used for each mode of entry or operation; and analysis of the effect of variation in the value of a variable, for the country rating. In both cases, simulation procedures are used to assess the impact of alternative weights and values for variables, on country scores. Particular attention is focused on cases that would shift the country dramatically from a high priority to a medium or low priority.

The possibility of collecting additional information or redefining information needs can also be considered. This may entail either collecting more accurate or detailed information with regard to a particular variable for a given country or set of countries, or reassessing a particular variable and the way in which it is defined or measured. A reevaluation of countries is thus conducted, leading to the development of a modified list of acceptable countries.

Finally, the congruence of the procedure with initial management objectives is assessed. The rank ordering of countries for in-depth investigation is then examined. Each country ranking implies a specific mode of entry or operation, for example, exporting to Venezuela or local production in the Philippines. The compatibility of this country/mode-of-entry alternative with initial management expansion and financial objectives can be assessed. If the country rankings do not appear to be consistent with these objectives, reassessment of the procedure is required. More explicit incorporation of financial or other investment criteria may, for example, be desirable.

Other procedures can be developed for evaluating target countries based on secondary data. These vary in the degree of complexity and sophistication, depending on company size and resources available for international market evaluation. Simple country rating schemata may, for example, be used, or more intricate models developed incorporating political and financial risk analysis (Stobaugh, 1969). In either case, however, careful selection of country indicators relevant to the specific company or product market, and availability of appropriate information sources is crucial to effective country market assessment.

DEMAND ESTIMATION

Once the appropriate countries and markets to be investigated in-depth have been determined, the next step is to make an explicit evaluation of demand in that country or market. This is important when considering initial market entry, due to the high costs and uncertainty associated with entering new markets. Here, management will need both to make an initial estimate of demand potential, and also to project future market trends.

Where the industry or product market is already well developed, and historical sales data are available, procedures similar to those used in the domestic market can be followed. For example, time-series, trend or double exponential smoothing analyses can be conducted. Since their applications are identical to those in the domestic market situation, these are not discussed here.

If, however, management is considering entry into new markets, or is in the initial stages of market development, other procedures will be required. Often, many of these markets, particularly in developing countries, are small and fragmented, and little secondary data are available (Moyer, 1968). Their small size, as well as the difficulty and high costs of undertaking research under such conditions, suggests that techniques commonly used in domestic markets, such as surveys of buying intentions or market tests, are likely to be prohibitively expensive. In some cases, they may in fact be infeasible. Consequently, the use of low-cost rudimentary procedures will be required.

Data extrapolation techniques offer considerable potential in this regard, since they make use of experience and data collected in one or more countries to develop estimates or forecasts of potential in other countries. Such extrapolations may be made using either time-series or cross-sectional data.

It is, however, important to note that use of extrapolation techniques requires a number of assumptions concerning the relevance of data collected in one country, to another country. It requires, first, that countries be equivalent units or comparable in certain relevant respects. Thus, for example, extrapolation between countries that have similar market structures or demand characteristics is likely to be the most successful. Second, it assumes that the measurement units are comparable or equivalent in all countries. Thus, for example, if monetary units are used, their currency equivalents have to be established. Third, it assumes that the relationship between demand determinants and sales is the same in all countries—that is, if GNP is related to cement consumption in one country, it will be related to cement consumption in another country. Finally, it requires that product classes are comparable and equivalent in all countries. For example, comparability of different shampoo variants or detergents in all countries has to be established. Furthermore, if projections over time are to be made, the rate of change in all markets should be approximately equivalent.

Lead-Lag Analysis

The first and most simplistic method of data extrapolation is lead-lag analysis. This is based on the use of time-series data from one country to project sales in other countries. It assumes that the determinants of demand in the two countries are identical, and the only factor that separates them is time. Thus, for example, sales trends in France can be predicted on the basis of sales trends in the United States, with a lag of x years. Figures 4.3a and 4.3b show this for TV sets in the United States, the United Kingdom, and Germany. This method is, however, generally not widely used, due to the difficulty of identifying the relevant time lag. Furthermore, the accuracy of the estimate is open to some question. It is likely to be most effective in the case of innovations that have the same penetration or diffusion rate in different countries. For a more complex application of lead-lag analysis, see Lindberg (1982).

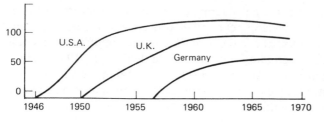

FIGURE 4.3a
Percentage of households
owning television sets

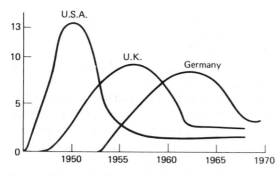

FIGURE 4.3b
Yearly percentage increase
in household ownership of
television sets

Source: Warren J. Keegan, *Multinational Marketing Management,* 2nd ed., © 1980, p. 219.
Reprinted by permission of Prentice-Hall, Inc., Englewood Cliffs, NJ.

Surrogate Indicators

A second procedure is the use of surrogate indicators. This is similar to the use
of general macroindicators, but develops these relative to a specific industry or
product market. Data on these indicators can then be collected from surveys or
other secondary data sources. Two types of indicators may be used, market
potential indexes for countries where survey data are available, and
macrosurveys where greater reliance has to be placed on visual indicators or
observational methods.

Market Potential Indexes

Indexes composed of a number of surrogate indicators hypothesized to be
related to market potential for a product or industry can be developed. Dickens-
sheets (1963) has, for example, developed a market potential index for
refrigerators with larger storage capacity, consisting of eleven indicators, including food shopping habits, number of supermarkets and self-service food
stores, auto ownership, consumption of frozen foods, per capita private con-

sumption expenditure, employment of women, availability of domestic help, availability of consumer credit, cost of electricity for residential use, dwelling construction and size of new dwellings, and refrigerator saturation in high-income families.

If either the rank order of importance of these variables or specific weights are developed, such indexes can be used to rank countries in terms of their relative attractiveness. Alternatively, they can be estimated for regions within a country, and used to evaluate the sales potential of different regions within a country. Erickson (1963), for example, constructed an index for Brazil to rank submarkets within the country. This index was based on population, domestic income, and retail store sales, in each state as a percent of the national total. This provided a measure of relative sales potential in each Brazilian state. Such indicators are, however, somewhat unwieldy. In addition, it is not always clear to what extent similar indicators may be relevant from one country to another.

A more general approach has been developed by Samli (1977) to approximate market potential in East Europe as a percent of United States market potential. The approach adjusts market size to reflect the quality of the market. Market quality is expressed in terms of eight general indicators that capture aspects of the degree of economic development (per capita income, manufacturing employment, steel consumption, kilowatt hours produced) and quality of life (motor vehicle registration, and telephones, radios, and TV sets in use). The approach has not been validated, but it does suggest how secondary data might be used to obtain a rough estimate of market potential.

The Macrosurvey

An analogous procedure based on observational rather than survey data is the macrosurvey. This is particularly effective in developing countries, where there is low market potential, predominantly in scattered rural areas (Carr, 1978). A scale has first to be developed consisting of several indicators, composed of items or objects that can be observed. The presence of each of these is hypothesized to correspond to a given level of market potential. An example of such a scale developed to assess the potential for United States products in rural Thailand is shown in Table 4.2. Here, presence of a market square is considered to indicate a potential market for piece-good cloth and light agricultural implements, while existence of a fiber mill, a Buddhist temple, an elementary school, and some shops, suggests markets for mopeds, hardware, school supplies, and simple motorized agricultural equipment.

In general, such scales are likely to be cumulative in nature, that is, the presence of an item higher in the scale is invariably associated with the presence of items lower in the scale. An example of a scale for which this has been explicitly tested using Guttman scaling techniques is shown in Table 4.3. Thus, if

TABLE 4.2 Differentiation scale of rural Thailand and associated markets

Step number	Item content	Estimated population	Markets
1	Market square	1,000 to 3,000	Piece-good cloth and light agricultural implements (e.g., shovels).
2	Fair ground; agricultural support shops (e.g., hand forges, wheel wrights); food shops.	3,000 to 8,000	Manufactured clothes (e.g., work clothes, sandals); canned/dried foods (e.g., evaporated milk, dried shrimp and squid); radios, bicycles, and mopeds.
3	Raimie *fiber* mill and pond, Buddhist temple, elementary school; urban support shops (e.g., auto repair shop).	5,000 to 10,000	Service for mopeds; hardware (e.g., hammers, saws, roofing material); school supplies; 1-man motorized agricultural equipment (e.g., front end tiller).
4	Government administration building; ambulatory health care, secondary school, police services.	7,000 to 10,000	Window/door screen material, glass; social dresses; primitive plumbing equipment (e.g., lavatories, shower heads, etc. with support piping).
5	Raimie *sack* mill and water reservoir; high school and/or technical college; sewer and water purification systems.	22,000 to 30,000	Light industrial machinery (welding, pipe threading equipment); air conditioning; cement; construction services; office supplies and equipment.

Source: Richard P. Carr, Jr., "Identifying Trade Areas for Consumer Goods in Foreign Markets," *Journal of Marketing* 42 (October 1978), 76–80.

a church exists, there are likely to be one or more organizations in the village, more than one street, some government officials, and an autonomous locality group. The relation of each level to sales potential has again to be established. For example, the presence of a church in a village might be worth a sales call, but the community might need to have several phones before it was considered worthwhile to establish a distribution facility.

Data have then to be collected on the presence or absence of these various items. This may be accomplished by aerial photography, or in some cases, the equivalent of the Yellow Pages can be useful. The most comprehensive approach would include a community visit in order to complete and update the index.

Barometric Analysis

A third technique, which relies on the use of cross-sectional data, is analogous to the use of barometric procedures in domestic sales forecasting. This assumes that if there is a direct relationship between consumption of a product, service, or

TABLE 4.3 Guttman scale of differentiation for 24 Mexican villages

Step number	Item content	Proportion discriminated
1	Named and autonomous locality group.	1.00
2	One or more governmentally designated officials; more than one street.	.92
3	One or more organizations in village.	.88
4	A church.	.84
5	A school building; a government organization; Mass said in the village more than annually.	.80
6	A functional school.	.76
7	Has access to a railroad or informant voluntarily includes railroad in list of village needs.	.63
8	Access to electric power; informant estimates that a majority have electricity; six or more streets.	.46
9	Railroad station; four or more bus or train trips daily.	.41
10	School has four or more grades.	.37
11	Village has a public square; village market patronized by people in other villages.	.29
12	Doctor; priest resides in village; ten or more streets; school has six or more grades; six or more stores; two or more television sets in village; public monument.	.20
13	Has one or more telephones.	.16
14	Forty percent or more have radios; settlement area one square mile or more.	.12
15	Secondary school; 20 or more stores.	.08
	(Coefficient of scalability is .92)[a]	

[a]The coefficient of scalability is a measure which "varies from 0 to 1, and should be above .6 if the scale is truly unidimensional and cumulative."

Source: Richard P. Carr, Jr., "Identifying Trade Areas for Consumer Goods in Foreign Markets," *Journal of Marketing* 42 (October 1978), 76–80.

commodity and an indicator in one country, the same relationship will hold in other countries. This relation can be assumed to hold either at the aggregate level—that is, for the entire market—or alternatively, for specific segments within the market.

Aggregate Barometers

In a number of markets, and particularly in industrial markets, where the factors underlying demand are likely to be similar, barometric procedures can be used to extrapolate the relationship between an aggregate indicator and consumption or sales in certain countries to other countries. Particularly in relation to basic commodities such as paper, glass, or cement, there is often a relation between consumption and GNP. Figure 4.4 shows this relationship for glass consumption and GNP in various countries.

Alternative models can be applied to these data, including linear regres-

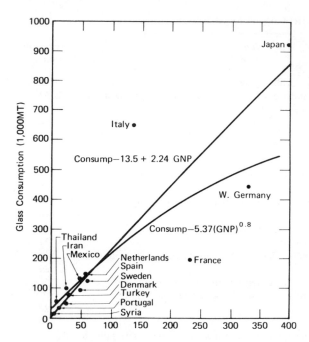

FIGURE 4.4 Glass consumption and GNP

Source: J. Cowen, et al., *International Expansion of PPG Float Glass Technology* (unpublished working paper, 1979).

sion, logarithmic, exponential, or more complex models, to develop relevant model parameters as in Table 4.4. These can then be used to predict sales based on the level of GNP in other countries. This procedure is typically most effective in less industrialized markets where levels of GNP are below 100 billion dollars.

Segment Extrapolation

Another version of the barometric procedure is segment extrapolation. The barometric procedure assumes that certain gross indicators are related to aggregate market potential. In some cases, there may be different market segments, where different factors underlie demand. Alternatively, different market segments may have different levels or rates of market penetration.

In the first case, different indicators will have to be developed for each market segment. In the case of diesel engines for small boats, for example, there may be two potential markets, that of pleasure boats, and that of fishing boats. In the first case, the relevant indicators might include, for example, per capita disposable income, while in the second case, the length of the coastline, or

TABLE 4.4 Regression models for predicting glass consumption based on GNP

Country	Glass consumption (metric tons)	GNP ($ Billion)
Syria	15	3
Portugal	36	13
Thailand	46	11
Turkey	50	23
Denmark	74	26
Iran	95	28
Sweden	99	48
Mexico	128	50
Netherlands	138	58
Spain	132	59
France	197	230
West Germany	454	330
Italy	686	135
Japan	1,230	393

Model I $C = A + B(GNP) = 13.5 + 2.24GNP$ $R^2 = .71$
Model II $C = A(GNP)^B = 5.37(GNP)^{.8}$ $R^2 = .88$

Source: J. Cowen, et al., *International Expansion of PPG Float Glass Technology* (unpublished working paper, 1979).

estimates of fish haul, would be more appropriate. Similarly, in the case of hotels, there may be two potential market segments, one of tourist and one of business travel. The first may be estimated on the basis of the number of tourists traveling to different countries, and the second on the basis of growth in GNP.

In the second case, where different market segments have different rates of consumption or market penetration, extrapolation by segment, rather than for the total market, is desirable. This is particularly likely to be appropriate in relation to upscale luxury goods such as premium wine or wristwatches. If, for example, market penetration of expensive wristwatches is related to income, the number of units sold to different income groups can be identified in one country, for example, the United States. The number of household units in each of these income groups is then identified in the second country, and multiplied by the relevant group penetration rate to obtain potential market size by subgroup. This procedure is shown in Table 4.5.

Similarly, in relation to industrial markets, different user industries can be identified, and rates of penetration in each of these industries determined for one country. The number of companies in each of these industries in another country can then be assessed, and multiplied by the relevant penetration rate in order to determine potential market size. In the case of minicomputers, for example, the key user industries might be financial institutions or commercial data processing and marketing research companies.

TABLE 4.5 Predicting sales of wristwatches

| | COUNTRY 1 | COUNTRY 2 | | |
| | | | | |
Household income	Number sold annually	Number household units (thousands)	=	Potential sales volume (units)
$35,000 and over	0.51	240	=	122
$30,000–34,999	0.47	300	=	141
$25,000–29,999	0.39	310	=	121
$20,000–24,999	0.38	600	=	228
$15,000–19,999	0.35	580	=	203
$10,000–14,999	0.21	610	=	128
$ 5,000– 9,999	0.20	1920	=	384
$ Under 4,999	0.19	2040	=	388
				1715

Source: Susan P. Douglas and C. Samuel Craig, "Information for International Marketing Decisions," in I. Walter and T. Murray, eds., *Handbook of International Business*. Copyright © 1982 by John Wiley & Sons, Inc. Reprinted by permission of John Wiley & Sons, Inc.

This technique can be further refined by breaking down companies within each of these industries by size, sales volume, or other factors indicative of sales potential. Penetration rates in each of these within-industry segments are estimated in the base country. The number of companies in each of these segments in the second country is determined, and multiplied by the relevant segment penetration rates. Thus, for example, in estimating market potential for microwave ovens in the industrial sector, three major groups of potential users might be identified—hotels, fast food chains, and restaurant chains. For hotels, the number of units likely to be purchased might vary with the number of rooms. Sales potential is thus estimated by size class in the base country. The number of hotels in each size class in the second country is then evaluated from tourist board data or tourist guides. This is multiplied by the relevant size class sales potential figure to obtain market potential estimates. This is shown in Table 4.6. Similarly, in the case of fast food chains, if the number of units purchased varies with sales volume, penetration rates by size groups can be estimated in the base country. Again, these rates can be multiplied by the number of chains in each size group in the second country to obtain market potential estimates.

Econometric Forecasting Models

More complex forecasting models can also be developed using econometric procedures. These typically require both cross-sectional data on factors underlying sales for a given product market for a number of countries, and time-series data for these factors. The first step is to identify the key factors

TABLE 4.6 Estimating market potential of microwave ovens by user segment (market segment—hotels)

Number of rooms	Number of units purchased	×	Hotels	Potential market
50–100	5		200	1000
30–49	2		100	200
<30	0		50	0
				1200

Source: Susan P. Douglas and C. Samuel Craig, "Information for International Marketing Decisions," in I. Walter and T. Murray, eds., *Handbook of International Business.* Copyright © 1982 by John Wiley & Sons, Inc. Reprinted by permission of John Wiley & Sons, Inc.

related to sales of the product. These might include, for example, factors such as population, income, literacy, or proportion of the agricultural population. Armstrong (1970), in developing a model to predict sales of still cameras, identified eleven variables that explained variation in sales. These were

Beckerman's standard of living index
price of camera goods
buying units index (households per adult)
temperature
rainfall
proportion of children in population
growth in per capita income per year
total population
literacy rate
proportion of population age 15–64
proportion of nonagricultural employment

Data on these were then collected for thirty countries for the period 1960–1965. A regression model was applied to the data for nineteen of these countries to obtain estimates of model parameters. A multiplicative or "log-log" model was used to minimize percentage error, and give "unit-free" results. This provided an excellent fit to the data and the resulting R^2's were over .99. The predictive validity of the model was tested by applying the model to the remaining eleven countries, and comparing the results with actual trade estimates. The average deviation was in the range of 31 percent. A backcasting procedure, using the model to predict sales for a prior period (1953–55), was applied. This led to a reduction in mean absolute percentage error from 30 percent to 23 percent compared with backcasts based on trade data only. This suggested that the model provided a reasonable fit with the data.

Such models do, however, require the availability of historical sales data for a number of countries, and assume that similar factors underlie sales in all of these countries. They also assume that extrapolation of these data will enable prediction of future sales. This is likely to be the case only in relation to products that are in a mature or stable phase of the product life cycle. It also requires that there is no change in the relationship between underlying factors and sales. Econometric procedures are thus only valid to the extent that no new events occur that change existing relationships. The failure of many general econometric models to develop accurate predictions over the past decade has, for example, been largely due to the explosion of oil prices and inflation, and the growing interdependence of the world economy.

Trends, and hence underlying relationships between sales and indicators, often change very rapidly in international markets. Consequently, such econometric procedures are likely to be often subject to substantial error. Furthermore, the models are complex to develop, and frequent updating of relevant model parameters is required.

MONITORING ENVIRONMENTAL CHANGE

A third use of secondary data is in monitoring environmental change. Here, it can be argued that all companies, whether or not they are currently involved in international operations, should monitor the international environment and consider the implications, as well as potential sources of foreign competition for domestic operations. Otherwise, the fate of the United States automobile, electronics, and textile industry may befall them.

Companies *not* currently engaged in international operations should monitor developments in international markets, since these may provide better growth opportunities than domestic markets. In cases where rates of growth in domestic markets are slackening, international markets may offer improved horizons for expansion and exploitation of existing product lines and for the firm's research and development, and marketing technology. Even where such opportunities do not exist, awareness of trends in other markets is essential, since these may hold portent for domestic markets, signaling, for example, future market trends, entry of foreign competition, and other changes that might require a reexamination of the current marketing strategies of the firm.

Companies *already* involved in international operations need to evaluate systematically the degree of their involvement in different countries and product markets. This requires examining how the market environment is evolving in each country, as well as monitoring competitive developments in each of these markets. Profitability and long-run market growth may be improved either by developing new products or by changing strategies in existing markets, or alternatively, by shifting effort from one country or product market to another.

Monitoring the international environment is particularly crucial insofar as that environment is highly dynamic. Events such as the Solidarity strikes and suppression in Poland, the invasion of Afghanistan, or the conflict over the Falkland Islands can have a dramatic effect on international operations, and on the nature and relative attractiveness of opportunities in different countries.

Various environmental factors affect international operations. These range from coups, such as those experienced in Iran, or expropriations, which are becoming increasingly frequent in the Middle East, to more gradual changes such as the increase in the standard of living in African or Asian countries, giving rise to new markets for consumer goods. This implies that there is a variety of different aspects of the international environment that require monitoring. These are discussed in more detail in the next section.

Indicators for Monitoring Environmental Change

Monitoring environmental change requires surveillance of a number of key indicators. These should be carefully selected and tailored to the specific product or range of products with which management is concerned. Two types of indicators are required. The first monitors the general health and growth of a country, and its economy and society; the second, that of a specific industry or product market. Again, information with regard to these indicators can be obtained from the sources cited in Chapter 3.

The first type of indicator might include factors such as the growth of GNP, population growth, percentage of GDP in agriculture, level of steel or cement consumption, imports of gasoline, and employment in service industries. In this context, it is helpful to include indicators that relate not only to general economic and business trends and market growth, but in addition, financial data, such as the rate of inflation or balance-of-payment figures, and foreign exchange rates, which provide indicators of the financial health of the economy. These are likely to be particularly critical where a company is involved in exporting or in sourcing across international boundaries.

The second type of indicator might include data relating to product sales in units and in dollar volume, market share data, prices of leading competitors, number and growth of user industries, and so on. If such data are not available or the product market is not well developed, surrogate indicators of potential demand may be developed, such as those discussed earlier. In the case of personal computers, level of education or number of students in higher education might be used. In each case, however, the particular indicators to be included should be tailored to the specific objectives and strategy of the company and the nature of the product market. Companies reluctant to assume financial risk might, for example, place greater emphasis on financial indicators and rates of inflation.

Approaches for Monitoring
Environmental Change

A variety of different procedures can be used to analyze the impact of environmental factors on world trends or individual countries, and on product markets, as well as the implications for market growth and appropriate marketing strategies. These range from relatively simple trend projections or tracking studies and the use of leading indicators, to the more complex scenario evaluation studies.

Trend Analysis
and Tracking Procedures

In the case of trend analysis or tracking procedures, the indicators that are selected as relevant for the specific product market or corporate objectives are monitored in each country or group of countries. For example, in the minicomputer market, the growth of the service industry, or of banks and other financial institutions, might be monitored, as well as other industries that appear to offer potential. Furthermore, these might be monitored not only in European markets, where there is clearly substantial market potential, but also in markets such as the Far East, where latent potential may be emerging.

In addition to assessing purely economic factors, there are more general environmental conditions with which a computer manufacturer might be concerned. For example, I.B.M. monitors trends in consumerism, privacy, and data security in each country, along with international political and economic relationships. C.P.C. International scans political, social, and economic trends regionally, such as the trend toward European integration, as well as legal developments, consumer behavior trends, labor organization, and changes in market structure within countries (Thomas, 1980).

Where quantitative indicators can be identified, various statistical procedures may be used to assess trends, such as analysis of life cycle trend curves, moving averages, linear or logarithmic extrapolation, power series expansion, and double exponential smoothing. The appropriate technique will depend to a large extent on the nature of the data available, and in particular, the number of years for which it is available. Those unique to international marketing, such as data extrapolation techniques, have already been discussed in relation to demand estimation, and hence, do not merit further discussion here. Use of such an approach, however, implies that past trends provide an indication of future developments.

This type of analysis is particularly useful insofar as it provides insights into future growth and investment prospects. It can, for example, suggest which markets or countries are likely to become rapidly saturated, and hence may be candidates for future divestment. In addition, those countries that should be watched as future potential markets may be identified. Monitoring of the growth and risks in the Middle East and Far East markets may, for example, be advisable for products such as office equipment or construction materials.

Scenario Analysis

A somewhat more complex procedure is that of scenario analysis. Here, different world or country environmental scenarios are developed. These might, for example, include assumptions about rates of growth or inflation in different countries, trends in oil prices, and anticipated political unrest. The impact of alternative scenarios on the product market or business is then evaluated either in terms of world market share, or of profitability in individual countries. The implications for international and national strategic plans are then assessed.

This approach has been adopted by a number of multinational companies such as Shell and General Electric (G.E.). It combines the use of secondary data with management experience and, in some cases, expert opinion. The way in which scenario analysis is applied by Shell and by G. E. is next discussed to illustrate how secondary data can be used in conjunction with management or expert judgment in strategic planning.

Shell's Approach. Shell adopts a three-level approach to scenario planning. The first level looks at long-term world scenarios, with a timespan of up to twenty years. These focus predominantly on economic factors. Where possible, these are quantified, for example, in terms of GNP and oil prices. More recently, an analysis of social trends has been included. The second tier of global scenarios examines developments insignificant in a ten- to fifteen-year timeframe, but important for near-term planning. These focus on business cycles, and give less attention to changes in social climate. The third tier is comprised of local scenarios developed by individual business sectors and operating companies. These are more detailed local country scenarios and include variables specific to local operating units, but of less importance at the global unit level. Currency fluctuation is, for example, vital to a national unit such as Shell United Kingdom, but of less consequence to a multinational corporation as large as Shell.

Scenarios are developed in contrasting pairs, rather than around a central scenario. This is said to encourage a tendency by management to gravitate to the middle when considering the impact of these scenarios. The two long-term world scenarios currently being used are "the World of Internal Contradictions," which represents the higher limit of economic growth, and "Restructured Growth," which denotes the lower limit. For example, the World of Internal Contradictions assumes continued aversion to risk taking and an associated slump in economic growth worldwide. This suggests an average annual rate of growth of 2.5 percent in Europe and the United States, and about 4 percent in Japan.

Local subsidiaries are urged to use these scenarios in developing their strategies and planning projects for local markets. The use of two dramatic opposites is intended to make managers question their assumptions and hence be prepared for all eventualities, or at least to adapt to rapidly changing circumstances. The global scenarios are, however, too general for specific uses such as predicting the expansion of service station networks. Here, the development of local scenarios, and in some cases of specific scenarios relevant to individual projects, is encouraged.

General Electric's Approach.   G.E. uses a similar approach but focuses on variants of a central scenario, rather than the twin-scenario approach used by Shell. First, the major elements of alternative world scenarios are identified. These might, for example, include the rate of economic growth, energy prices, levels of inflation, or trends in trade restrictions. The most likely or central scenarios are then developed, using expert opinion or other judgmental procedures. These might, for example, hypothesize generally stable rates of growth, a gradual rise in energy prices, rates of inflation around 12 percent, and more restrictive trade practices. Variants on these are then developed, as for example, rampant inflation, rapid rises in oil prices, and inflation at moderate levels. The likelihood of each of these scenarios occurring can then be assessed based on expert opinion or using Delphi techniques.

The next step of the G.E. approach is to identify the major external forces affecting each product business studied. These can, for example, include rates of economic growth, demographic growth, life style, energy costs, and inflation. The impact of these on the market for each product business, such as air conditioners, refrigerators, and so on, is then assessed. A matrix is constructed, indicating whether the factor is estimated to have a positive, negative, or negligible effect.

The final step is to evaluate by country the impact of alternative world scenarios on each product business. Thus, for example, assuming the central scenario or each of the variants, an evaluation is made as to whether the projected marketing strategy and underlying assumptions for the product-country business appear to be sound. Based on this analysis, and the estimated likelihood of the different scenarios, some conclusions can be reached as to whether planned marketing strategies appear basically sound, should be questioned, or seem inappropriate.

SUMMARY

In brief, secondary data can be highly useful in international marketing research. Such uses are more extensive than in domestic marketing research, due to the high costs of primary data collection relative to potential market size.

In this chapter, three major uses of secondary data have been identified: determining which countries to enter, developing estimates of demand in these countries, and monitoring environmental change.

In evaluating which countries to enter, two major approaches have been applied. The first is based on clustering or rating countries based on environmental criteria. The second uses a customized approach geared to the specific product market or company. While the clustering or rating scheme may provide an initial approximation, adoption of a customized approach is likely to prove more relevant to specific management and corporate objectives.

Similarly, four main categories of demand estimation techniques can be identified: lead-lag analysis, use of surrogate indicators, barometric analysis, and econometric forecasting models. Lead-lag analysis and econometric forecasting models both assume that data can be extrapolated over time, and hence, that there are no major underlying changes in the factors influencing sales trends. To the extent that this is rarely the case in international markets, use of surrogate indicators or barometric procedures may be more desirable. The former are most useful in markets where little data are available, market potential is limited, and relatively crude estimates will suffice. The latter provide more precise estimates at either the aggregate market level or for specific market segments. The technique that is most appropriate, will, however, depend on the availability of data and the nature of the product market.

Finally, secondary data can be used to monitor environmental change. Here, change may be monitored both at the world or country environmental level, and also at the industry or product market level. Again, different monitoring techniques can be used, ranging from tracking to more complex scenario evaluation.

Thus, secondary data perform an important function in international marketing research. This is particularly significant in the initial evaluation of marketing opportunities and in pinpointing key areas for in-depth examination. Yet, it also provides a useful ongoing contribution in forecasting and updating the emergence of new opportunities and in signaling needs for adaptation of marketing strategy and tactics.

REFERENCES

ARMSTRONG, J. SCOTT,   "An Application of Econometric Models to International Marketing," *Journal of Marketing Research, 7* (1970), 190–198.

BUSINESS INTERNATIONAL,   *B.I. Data.* New York: Business International, 1982.

CARR, RICHARD P.,   "Identifying Trade Areas for Consumer Goods in Foreign Markets," *Journal of Marketing, 42* (1978), 76–80.

COWEN, J., R. R. GALAN, F. GALLIONE, B. GARDNER, C. SULLIVAN and J. C. TSHISHIMBI, *International Expansion of PPG Float Glass Technology* (unpublished working paper, 1979).

DICKENSHEETS, R. J., "Basic and Economical Approaches to International Marketing Research," *Proceedings American Marketing Association* (1963), Chicago: American Marketing Association, pp. 359–377.

DOUGLAS, SUSAN P., PATRICK LEMAIRE, and YORAM WIND, "Selection of Global Target Markets: A Decision-Theoretic Approach," *Proceedings of the XXII ESOMAR Congress,* Cannes, France, (September 1972), pp. 237–51.

——— and C. SAMUEL CRAIG, "Information for International Marketing Decisions," in I. Walter and T. Murray, eds., *Handbook of International Business.* New York: John Wiley, 1982.

DOYLE, PETER and ZEKI GIDENGIL, "A Strategic Approach to International Market Selection," *Proceedings, European Academy for Advanced Research in Marketing,* Copenhagen, Denmark, 1976.

ERICKSON, LEO G., "Analyzing Brazilian Consumer Markets," *Business Topics,* 11, (Summer 1963), 7–26.

JOHANSSON, J. K. and REZA MOINPOUR, "Objective and Perceived Similarity of Pacific Rim Countries," *Columbia Journal of World Business* (Winter 1977), pp. 65–76.

KEEGAN, WARREN J., *Multinational Marketing Management,* 2nd ed. Englewood Cliffs, NJ: Prentice-Hall, Inc., 1980.

LIANDER, BERTIL, ed., *Comparative Analysis for International Marketing,* Marketing Science Institute. Boston: Allyn & Bacon, 1967.

LINDBERG, BERTIL C., "International Comparison of Growth in Demand for a New Durable Consumer Product," *Journal of Marketing Research,* 19 (August, 1982), 364–71.

LITVAK, ISAIAH A. and PETER M. BANTING, "A Conceptual Framework for International Business Arrangement," in Robert L. King, ed., *Marketing and the New Science of Planning,* pp. 460–67. Chicago: American Marketing Association, 1968.

MOYER, REED, "International Market Analysis," *Journal of Marketing Research,* 5, (November 1968), 353–60.

PIPER, JAMES A., "How U.S. Firms Evaluate Foreign Investment Opportunities," *M.S.U. Business Topics* (Summer 1971), pp. 11–20.

SAMLI, COSKUN A., "An Approach for Estimating Market Potential in East Europe," *Journal of International Business Studies* (Fall-Winter 1977), 49–53.

SETHI, S. PRAKASH, "Comparative Cluster Analysis for World Markets," *Journal of Marketing Research,* 8 (1971), 348–354.

——— and DAVID CURRY, "Variable and Object Clustering of Cross-Cultural Data: Some Implications for Comparative Research and Policy Formulation," in S. Prakash Sethi and Jagdish N. Sheth, *Multinational Business Operations,* pp. 31–61. Pacific Palisades, CA: Goodyear Publishing Company, 1973.

SHETH, JAGDISH and RICHARD LUTZ, "A Multivariate Model of Multinational Business Expansion" in S. Prakash Sethi and Jagdish N. Sheth, *Multinational Business Operations,* pp. 96–103. Pacific Palisades, CA: Goodyear Publishing Company, 1973.

STOBAUGH, ROBERT, "How to Analyze Foreign Investment Climates," *Harvard Business Review* (September-October 1969), pp. 100–108.

THOMAS, PHILIP S., "Environmental Scanning—The State of the Art," *Long Range Planning,* 13 (February 1980), 27–28.

5

Issues in Primary Data Collection

Once secondary data sources have been examined, the next step is collection of primary data, tailored to meet the specific information requirements of international management decisions. Here, a key concern is to establish the comparability between data collected in different cultural contexts. Comparability in this sense is defined as data that have, as far as possible, the same meaning or interpretation, and the same level of accuracy, precision of measurement, or reliability in all countries and cultures. This is important insofar as international marketing decisions are concerned with the development of strategic and tactical decisions relative to several countries, as opposed to a single national market. Consequently, the question arises as to whether similar strategies and tactics can be used in different countries.

Standardization of tactical decisions across countries offers a number of advantages to the extent that it enables realization of potential synergies arising from operation in a multicountry context. Good ideas, whether for new products, advertising appeals, promotions, or distribution strategies, can be exploited on a wider geographic scale. Cost savings are achieved in, for example, expenditure on product research and development, or the development of advertising copy. Furthermore, consistency of product, service, or company image across countries or regions, and in some cases worldwide, has certain advantages. This is becoming increasingly so as there is growing communication and travel across national boundaries. Furthermore, coordination and control of activities in different countries is facilitated.

Comparability of data is important irrespective of whether research is conducted in a single country or a multicountry context. Where research is only conducted in a single country, it is important to bear in mind that research relating to a similar problem may subsequently be conducted in another country. For example, a product developed in relation to one national market might be test marketed in a single foreign market. Yet, if it is successfully introduced in that market, management might wish to test market it in other countries. Consequently, it is important that research designs are developed in such a way that findings from different test markets can be compared.

Comparability in research design and data is even more crucial where simultaneous multicountry research is conducted. Multicountry research may be conducted when decisions are being made as to which country or market to enter, and whether and how far to integrate strategies across different countries and product markets, as, for example, whether to adopt a standardized advertising strategy. Here, comparability in content and quality is necessary in order to ensure that findings reflect similarities and differences between countries, rather than the spurious effect of sociocultural differences in response to a research instrument, administration procedures, or lack of adaptation of the research design and plan to a specific sociocultural environment.

The need for comparability gives rise to a number of important methodological issues in the design of primary data collection. These stem in large measure from the conduct of research in different sociocultural environments. In particular, their diversity in language and in levels of literacy can give rise to difficulties of communication between researcher and respondent, or between researchers from different cultural backgrounds.

In the first place, this diversity implies that different behavioral and attitudinal phenomena may occur or be relevant to a specific problem. Consequently, the issue of whether similar research designs can be used or are relevant in different environments arises. In the social sciences, this is known as the emic-etic dilemma (Pike, 1966). In the second place, given the pragmatic needs of the marketing researcher to establish, or at least estimate, the limits of comparability or equivalence in these data, a number of different types of equivalence have to be considered. These include the functional, conceptual, and category equivalence of constructs, the linguistic and metric equivalence of the measurement instruments, and the equivalence and independence of samples. Finally, the establishment of control procedures to reduce cultural bias in data interpretation is needed to limit nonequivalence arising in the administration and interpretation of the research instrument. Each of these issues is next discussed in more detail.

THE EMIC VERSUS THE ETIC DILEMMA

The issue of comparability has traditionally haunted cross-national research in the social sciences. To the extent that each country has certain idiosyncratic features, and is characterized by a unique pattern of sociocultural behavior patterns and values, attitudinal and behavioral phenomena may be expressed in unique ways. Consequently, relevant constructs will be unique to a given country. Furthermore, measures of those specific to a particular country will be required. This does, however, also imply that these may not be comparable. On the other hand, insofar as there is commonality between countries, comparable constructs and concepts can be identified. Equivalent and standardized measures of these can thus be developed, though these may entail some loss of precision and accuracy in any given culture and country (Elder, 1976; Przeworski and Teune, 1966–67). Alternatively, even though common constructs are identified, idiosyncratic or country-specific measures may be required.

Given this dilemma, two alternative approaches or schools of thought—the "emic" and the "etic"—have typically dominated research in the social sciences (Pike, 1966). The "emic" school holds that attitudinal and behavioral phenomena are unique to a culture, and best understood in their own terms. Consequently, emphasis is placed on studying the particularities of each country, identifying and understanding its unique facets. Following this point of view, widely held by many anthropologists, will require measures specifically adapted to each cultural context. This, to a large extent, implies making inferences about cross national differences and similarities in qualitative or judgmental terms, since each measure is "culture-specific." The "etic" school, on the other hand, is primarily concerned with identifying and assessing universal attitudinal and behavioral concepts and developing pancultural or "culture-free" measures (Elder, 1976). The use of such measures facilitates comparison but can give rise to a number of methodological problems. In particular, it can lead to the adoption of a "pseudo-etic" approach, in which constructs and measures developed in one country are applied without, or with minimal adaptation to, other countries (Triandis, 1972).

Following a recent review of the issues involved in cross-cultural research, these two approaches can be characterized in terms of their implications for 1) the perspective taken by the researcher, 2) the number of countries or cultures studied, 3) the structure or constructs guiding research, and 4) the criteria against which to examine and understand behavior in each country or culture. These characteristics are summarized in Table 5.1.

These two approaches or schools of thought represent, in essence, two polar extremes on the continuum of cross-national research methodology, the one emphasizing cultural uniqueness, the other pan-culturalism in behavioral

TABLE 5.1 Characteristics of emic versus etic approaches

	APPROACH	
Characteristic	*Emic*	*Etic*
Perspective taken by researcher	Studies behavior from within the system	Studies behavior from a position outside the system
Number of cultures studied	Examines only one culture	Examines many cultures, comparing them
Structure guiding research	Structure discovered by the analyst	Structure created by the analyst
Criteria used to compare behavior in the culture(s)	Criteria are relative to internal characteristics	Criteria are considered absolute or universal

Source: John W. Berry, "Introduction to Methodology," in Harry C. Triandis and John W. Berry, eds., *Handbook of Cross-Cultural Psychology,* vol. 2, *Methodology.* (Boston, MA: Allyn and Bacon Inc., 1980) p. 11.

patterns and the underlying processes. The international marketer is primarily interested in identifying similarities, since these offer the most attractive opportunities for the transfer of products and services and for the integration of strategies across national markets. Consequently, adoption of an orientation reflecting an "etic" philosophy is likely to be preferable in international marketing research. Thus, the prime emphasis is on identifying and developing constructs and measures that are as comparable as possible across countries and cultures.

Different procedures may, however, be used to establish this comparability. In some cases, clearly identified unidimensional concepts and measures of those concepts, validated in at least one national context, are available, as for example, personality trait measures, or ecology and community attitude scales. These can be translated and administered in another country, and "decentered," that is, adapted to that specific cultural context. If, on the other hand, concepts are not clearly defined and identified in different countries, an alternative approach is to identify relevant concepts and measures in each country. Analytic techniques such as factor analysis are then applied to examine interrelationships and identify similar dimensions or factors in each country.

If the first type of approach is adopted, there is a danger of introducing a "pseudo-etic" bias (Triandis, 1972) or, in other words, using an "emic" construct or measure and assuming that this will work as an etic approach. It is, thus, important to allow for "decentering," that is, eliminating any cultural bias arising from development in the country of origin, and adaptation to the specific national or cultural context of interest. The construct validity of a standardized measure in another culture has thus to be established and, where modified, its equivalence examined.

Construct validity is essentially concerned with the extent to which an operationalization measures the concept that it purports to measure (Zaltman,

Pinson, and Angelmar, 1973). While it is recognized that other kinds of concept validity, such as face or predictive validity, may also be of concern, the issues that arise are the same as in domestic marketing research, and hence are not discussed further here. An in-depth treatment is to be found in Zaltman, Pinson, and Angelmar (1973).

Validity of standardized measures, and equivalence of modified measures can be examined, either by comparing patterns of internal variance across countries (that is, internal validity), or, alternatively, by examining the correlation of a measure with another measure of the same or associated constructs (that is, external validity). Various different procedures may be used to examine similarity in the patterns of internal variance and homogeneity of measures, ranging from split-half test-retest reliability tests to factor analysis. These are further discussed in Chapter 9. Personality tests, such as the California Psychological Inventory, the Eysenck Personality Questionnaire, Gordon's Survey of Interpersonal Values, and the S-F test of authoritarianism have, for example, been tested in this way (Eysenck and others, 1977; Kikuchi and Gordon, 1966; Irvine, 1969; Levin and Karni, 1970). Criterion or external validity tests, based on correlation of measures with other measures of the same or associated constructs, can also be conducted. The California Psychological Inventory, Kohn's Authoritarian scale, the California F Scale, and the C scale of conservatism have all been investigated using such procedures (Bennett, 1977; Gough, 1964; Kohn, 1974; Kagitcibasi, 1970; Lapslye and Enright, 1979).

Yet, while such approaches enable the development of cross-national measures that have equivalent construct validity, the extent to which measures are truly "decentered," and hence have content validity, remains open to some question (Triandis, 1972). This becomes particularly apparent when this approach is adopted in studies where some national or cultural specificity is likely to exist. Little allowance is made for explicit identification of culture-specific constructs that might be more relevant to the problem studied. This is likely to be particularly crucial where an important concern is making generalizations about cross-national similarities and differences (Roberts, 1970).

The second approach, commonly used in the exploratory stages of cross-national or cultural research, is more appropriate where relevant constructs are ill defined and need to be determined. Several of the classic comparative sociological and political studies applied this approach. Cattell (1949), for example, factor-analyzed seventy-two variables derived from secondary sources, and identified twelve main factors of national syntality, including thoughtful industriousness versus emotionality, and fastidiousness versus forcefulness. He held these to be the key dimensions on which Western societies could be meaningfully compared. Osgood and others (1976), in their development of the semantic differential, have used a similar type of approach to identify three elements: evaluation, potency, and activity. These they postulate to underlie semantic space in any language, and hence provide the basis for developing cross-culturally equivalent semantic differential scales.

A number of recent studies of consumer attitudes and life styles have followed along the same line (Anderson and Engledow, 1977; Douglas, 1976; Douglas and Urban, 1977; Urban, 1976, 1977). Attitudinal or life style items are developed and administered to national samples, and then factor-analyzed to identify key factors.

While this approach is useful in generating hypotheses about appropriate concepts to examine, it suffers from the lack of any theoretical foundations to validate or guide interpretation of the concepts identified. These will depend on the battery of items examined, and its balance; that is, the number of items introduced relating to each concept (Berrien, 1968; Douglas and LeMaire, 1974). Extensive retesting and replication on similar and other samples, the reemergence of the same constructs within batteries of differing item composition, and evidence of systematic relationship to other relevant constructs in each given national or cultural context is required before these are established as appropriate concepts for cross-national analysis (Bruno and Pessemier, 1972; Pessemier and Bruno, 1971; Villani and Lehmann, 1975; Wells, 1975).

The specific advantages offered by each approach suggest the desirability of developing procedures that allow examination of both the reliability of existing available constructs and measures of them, as well as the identification of "emic" or culture-specific constructs and measures (Wind and Douglas, 1982). Experience gained in identifying relevant constructs, and appropriate measures of them in specific national contexts, can thus be utilized in developing measures more specifically adapted to other national contexts.

An orientation in cross-national research that includes both emic and etic elements should be adopted. Wherever available, country-specific concepts and measures of them are identified; these are compared and, where similar, combined. Concepts that are unique to a single country are tested in other countries, and may in some cases be modified. Wherever possible, pan-cultural concepts that do not have any specific cultural bias are identified. Allowance should, however, be made for the existence of certain concepts that are idiosyncratic to an individual country or group of countries. Similarly, as far as possible, pan-cultural measures of concepts are identified, though in some cases, modification to a specific research context may be required.

In the latter case (that is, pan-cultural measures), equivalence of cross-national measurement requires consideration not only of the stimuli presented to respondents in different countries, but also of procedures for scoring or coding response to such stimuli. Where a pan-cultural construct has been identified, a phenomenally identical stimulus may be used, and in some cases, phenomenally identical modes of quantifying may be used in each society. However, use of phenomenally identical measures does not necessarily result in conceptual equivalence. For example, scoring on attitudinal variables, such as role norms or intelligence tests, may need to be adapted, or culturally ipsatized, to provide equivalent measures across cultures (Straus, 1969).

Similarly, constructs that are conceptually equivalent but not operationally defined in the same way in different countries may be identified, as for example, innovativeness. In some cases, similar measurement procedures, such as six-point Likert rating scales, may be used, and in others, culture-specific measurement procedures may be preferable.

Comparability or equivalence has thus to be established in relation to a number of different aspects of the data collection procedure, including the concepts examined, the measures of these that are applied, and the specific sample in relation to which concepts are studied. Each of these different types of cquivalence is next studied in more detail.

ESTABLISHING DATA EQUIVALENCE

The importance of generating data that are comparable from one country to another suggests that the equivalence of various aspects of the data collection process needs to be examined. First, whether the constructs being studied are equivalent has to be established. Secondly, the equivalence of the measures of the concepts being studied has to be assessed. Finally, the equivalence of the sample studied in each country or culture has to be taken into consideration.

Construct Equivalence

Examination of construct equivalence entails three distinct aspects. First, the researcher must assess whether a given concept or behavior serves the same function from country to country; that is, its *functional* equivalence. Secondly, the researcher must determine whether the same concepts or behavior occur in different countries, and whether the way in which they are expressed is similar; that is, their *conceptual* equivalence. Finally, the reseacher must examine whether the same classification scheme of objects can be used across countries, or, in other words, the degree of *category* equivalence.

Functional Equivalence

In examining equivalence, a first issue to consider is that the concepts, objects, or behaviors studied may not necessarily be *functionally* equivalent, that is, have the same role or function in all countries studied (Berry, 1969). For example, while in the United States, bicycles are predominantly used for recreation, in the Netherlands and in various developing countries, they provide a basic mode of transportation. This implies that the relevant competing product set must be defined differently. In the United States it will include other recreational products, while in the Netherlands it will include alternative modes of transportation.

Apparently similar activities may also have different functions. In some countries, such as the United States, for example, adult education courses may be regarded primarily as a leisure activity designed to provide broader cultural awareness. In other countries—for example, Japan—adult education is geared primarily to improving work performance. Similarly, while for many United States families, grocery shopping is a chore and a work activity to be accomplished as efficiently and conveniently as possible, in other countries it plays an important social function. Interaction with local shopkeepers and vendors or with other neighbors and acquaintances in stores or in the marketplace is an integral part of day-to-day living.

Objects may also have different functions or significance in different countries or cultures. While in the United States, possession of a car is no longer a status symbol (although in certain circles, makes such as Mercedes or Rolls Royce may carry prestige), in other less-developed countries, ownership or nonownership of a car is still an important denoter of status. Similarly, in Mexico, ownership of a refrigerator is a symbol of status and, hence, it is frequently placed in the living room. In African nations, ownership of small household appliances, symbols of the white man's power, may play the same role, even though the owner's home has no electricity and, hence, he cannot make use of them.

Conceptual Equivalence

While functional equivalence is concerned with the role of objects and behavior in society from a macrocultural level, conceptual equivalence is concerned with the interpretation that individuals place on objects, stimuli, or behavior, and whether these exist or are expressed in similar ways in different countries and cultures. The focus is thus on individual variation in attitudes and behavior, rather than on identifying societal and cultural norms. It is in this context that some scholars (notably in cross-cultural psychology) have expressed doubt as to whether truly pan-cultural measures can be developed. While the basic cognitive and behavioral processes are the same, the way in which they are expressed is conditioned by their context, which by definition varies from country to country (Frijda and Jahoda, 1966).

Personality traits such as aggressiveness, authoritarianism, or affiliation needs may not be relevant in all countries and cultures, or may be expressed in different types of behavior, hence requiring different measures. Some attitudes or behavior might be unique to a specific country. The concept of "philotimo," or behaving in the way members of one's ingroup expect, for example, is said to be unique to the Greek culture (Triandis and Vassilou, 1972). This includes meeting obligations and sacrificing self to help ingroup members, which include family, friends, and guests.

Even where the same concept or construct is identified, it may be expressed by different types of behavior in different cultural settings. Innovativeness, for example, may be a relevant concept in both the United States and France. In the United States, this is reflected not only in the purchase and trial of new products, but also in conversations and providing information to friends and neighbors about new products and brands. In France, however, to be innovative is not socially valued, and consequently, those who purchase new products will rarely discuss these products with others (Green and Langeard, 1975).

Similarly, in many Western societies, social interaction and sociability is frequently reflected in having dinner with friends, going to parties, bars, and so on. In other cultural contexts, such as developing countries, dining with friends may not be a common practice, as meals are taken almost exclusively with family, and similarly, parties may not be given. Social interaction may take other forms such as participation in communal dancing or other festivities.

Rites such as betrothal or death rituals may also vary from one country or culture to another. In the United Kingdom an engagement is a formal commitment to be married, while in Italy and Spain it merely implies having a boyfriend. Similarly, while high school proms are an important social function in the United States, their counterpart may not exist in other countries and cultures, where education may take different forms and end at different stages.

Category Equivalence

Yet, a third type of construct equivalence relates to the category in which objects or other stimuli are placed. Relevant product class definitions may, for example, differ from one country to another. In the soft drink and alcoholic beverage market, for example, forms of soft drinks such as carbonated sodas, fruit juices, and powdered and liquid concentrates vary significantly from one culture to another, and hence, how these are defined and delineated differs. In Mediterranean cultures, for example, beer is considered to be a soft drink (Berent, 1975). Similarly, in the dessert market, items that are included will vary substantially, ranging from apple pie, jellies, and ice cream, to baklava, rice pudding, and zabaglione. In some societies, cakes or cookies are included as desserts, while in China, sweet items do not form part of the meal. This implies that what is included in the relevant competing product set will vary. Careful attention to such factors is thus an important consideration when developing product-related measures. In addition, the characteristics or attributes perceived by consumers as relevant in evaluating a product class may differ from one country to another. In France, for example, the hot-cold continuum is a key attribute in characterizing consumers' perceptions of fragrance. In the United States and the United Kingdom, however, this is not an attribute that is perceived as relevant by consumers.

Differences in background or sociodemographic classes have also to be considered. In the case of marital status, for example, in various African countries it is not uncommon for a male to have several wives, and in some cases, women may have several husbands. Occupational categories also do not always have strict equivalence in all countries. The counterpart of the United States lawyer, the English barrister, or the Japanese subway packer may, for example, be difficult to find. Occupations may also differ in status from one country or society to another. Being a priest, religious minister, or teacher is, for example, often more prestigious in less-developed than in the more-literate industrialized nations. Similarly, the social prestige attached to government administrative positions or to being a lawyer varies from society to society.

Measure Equivalence

Once construct equivalence has been examined, the next step is to consider measure equivalence. Construct and measure equivalence are highly inter-related insofar as the measure is an operational definition of the construct. It is, nonetheless, useful to separate the concept or item to be measured from the actual measurement procedure. Here, equivalence with regard to three aspects has to be considered: 1) the calibration system used in measurement, 2) the translation of the research instrument, and 3) the metric or scale equivalence of the instrument.

Calibration Equivalence

First, in developing a research instrument, equivalence has to be established with regard to the calibration system used in measurement. This includes not only equivalence with regard to monetary units and measures of weight, distance, and volume, but also other perceptual cues, such as color, shape, or form, which are used to interpret visual stimuli.

The need to establish equivalence with regard to monetary and physical measurement units is clearly apparent. Standard procedures or tables for conversion are readily available. Comparability with regard to measurement standards and procedures needs also to be considered, as these may vary from one context to another. Similarly, comparability with regard to standards such as product grading, or product quality and safety regulations, should also be investigated, since these are not uniform from one country to another.

More subtle differences in instrument calibration, which are particularly relevant in the case of nonverbal instruments, relate to perceptual cues such as color, form, or shape. Studies in cognitive and cross-cultural psychology suggest that a substantial degree of commonality exists with regard to the manifestations of these in different countries and cultures (Deregowski, 1980; Pick, 1980). However, ability to differentiate and to develop gradations in these schemata appears to differ.

Studies of color in different cultures have shown the existence of an identical color spectrum throughout cultures (Berlin and Kay, 1969), but the ability of cultures to differentiate between different points on the color spectrum varies. Berlin and Kay claim that there are never more than eleven basic color classes, but that there may be less. Western subjects, for example, typically have more color classes than African subjects, and some primitive people have only a two-term color language (Heider, 1971, 1972; Heider and Olivier, 1972). The Bantu of South Africa, for example, do not distinguish between blue and green. Consequently, they do not discriminate between objects or symbols of these colors.

Interpretation of the meaning attached to these may also vary from one culture or cultural context to another. White, for example, is a color of mourning in Japan; while in Chinese culture, red is a symbol of happiness and plays a focal role in weddings—from invitations being printed in red and monetary gifts given in red envelopes, to the red dresses worn by the bride. Green, in Malaysia, symbolizes the jungle, and hence has connotations of danger (Ricks, Fu, and Arpan, 1974). Awareness of such nuances is thus an important consideration in instrument design and development, especially in relation to visual stimuli.

Translation Equivalence

A second aspect of measure equivalence concerns translation of the instrument so that it is understood by respondents in different countries, and has equivalent meaning in each research context. The need for translation of questionnaires and other verbal stimuli where research is conducted in countries with different languages is readily apparent. The need to translate nonverbal stimuli to ensure that they evoke the desired image and to avoid problems of miscommunication is less widely recognized.

Translation equivalence is a central issue in the establishment of construct validity, since this is the stage in the research design at which the construct is defined in operational terms. The translation procedure thus frequently helps to pinpoint problems with regard to whether a concept can be measured by using the same or similar questions in each cultural context, and whether a question has the same meaning in different research contexts. If different questions are used, then issues arise with regard to the minimal level of equivalence necessary for two questions to be considered the same, and what criteria for equivalence can be established.

Translation of nonverbal stimuli requires attention to how perceptual cues are interpreted in each research context. Misunderstanding may arise because the respondent is not familiar with a product or other stimulus, for example, with an electrical appliance, or with the way in which it is depicted. Alternatively, respondents may misinterpret stimuli because the associations evoked by the stimuli differ from one country or culture to another.

Translation of verbal and nonverbal stimuli thus plays a key role in the establishment of equivalence. Often it provides a focal point both for uncovering and for making pragmatic decisions as to how to resolve equivalence issues. These issues are covered in greater detail in Chapter 7.

Metric Equivalence

A final concern is metric equivalence. This is the scoring or scalar equivalence of the measure used. Two aspects have to be considered in determining metric equivalence: the first concerns the specific scale or scoring procedure used to establish the measure; the second, the equivalence of response to a given measure in different countries. The greater the emphasis placed on quantitative measurement and data interpretation, the more important the establishment of metric equivalence becomes. It is thus an integral part of decisions relating to data analysis, especially where attitudinal scaling or multivariate procedures are entailed.

Metric equivalence in scale and scoring procedures is of particular relevance insofar as different scales or scoring procedures may be most effective in different countries and cultures. This depends essentially on familiarity with different scales and scaling procedures. While in the United States, use of a five- or seven-point scale is common, in other countries twenty-point or ten-point scales may more commonly be used (Douglas and LeMaire, 1974). Similarly, use of nonverbal response procedures requires consideration of the comparability of these across countries and cultures.

A second aspect of metric equivalence concerns the response to a score obtained on a measure. Here the question arises as to whether a score obtained in one research context has the same meaning and interpretation in another context. For example, on an intentions-to-purchase scale, do the top two boxes, commonly used to predict the proportion of likely buyers, indicate a similar likelihood of purchase from one country to another, or does a position on a Likert scale have the same meaning in all cultures.

Metric equivalence can be examined by using multiple measurement methods. Thus, different measures that have different potential biases may be applied, and the results compared to establish equivalence. This is, however, relatively time-consuming and expensive. An alternative procedure is to apply statistical techniques; for example, normalizing, standardizing, or ipsatizing the data to achieve some degree of equivalence.

In contrast to other types of equivalence, metric equivalence can only be examined once the data have been collected. Prior experience or examination of similar types of measures in the relevant country or culture may provide some guidelines as to appropriate scales and typical response patterns. This may also suggest the types of data analysis and statistical procedures that will be required to test for metric equivalence, and are appropriate in view of typical response patterns.

Sampling Equivalence

The third and final form of equivalence concerns the comparability of samples drawn from different countries. Here, two issues need to be examined. The first concerns the relevant respondent, that is, individual(s) within the household, or in the organization, to be sampled. The second concerns the extent to which the samples can be considered to be independent and representative of the country.

Individual Versus Group

In sampling, an important issue to consider is whether a single respondent or multiple respondents within the household or organization should be used. In addition, it is necessary to assess whether these respondents should be the same in all countries. In the purchase of many major household durables, such as automobiles and household appliances, several family members may be involved. Consequently, it may be desirable to obtain data from multiple household members rather than from a single individual. While more time-consuming and adding to research costs and complexity, obtaining data from several respondents in the household provides a more complete and accurate conceptual basis for data collection and analysis. All relevant participants in the decision-making process are included, and hence, a biased perspective that might be obtained from use of a single respondent is avoided.

In addition, it is necessary to assess whether or not the respondents should be the same in all countries. In the United States it is not uncommon for children to exercise substantial influence in the purchases of cereal, toys, desserts, and other items. In other countries, where families are less child oriented, children have much less influence. Similarly, with the increasing proportion of working wives in many Western nations, husbands participate to an increased extent in grocery shopping activities, and hence influence brand choice. The *Reader's Digest* has, for example, sponsored a number of surveys of husband-wife interaction in making purchase decisions in various European countries, which reveal substantial husband influence and participation in a wide range of products. In Oriental nations, continuance of the extended family relationship implies that several families may continue to live together, and hence, only senior family members are responsible for many purchase decisions.

Similarly, in organizational purchase decisions, in addition to buyers, several other managers may play a key role in purchase decisions, especially where there is a buying committee. Differences in relevant participants in the buying process from one country to another will need to be determined. For example, in Latin American and Oriental countries, there may be a tendency toward centralized decision making. Hence, the buyer merely acts as an agent and may not be the appropriate respondent. Thus, the relevant decision makers will need to be identified. In other countries, there is greater readiness to delegate authority, and hence, the buyer may in fact participate in decision making.

It should, moreover, be noted that in the past an individual has frequently been used as the key respondent, even in situations where multiple participants were involved in the decision-making process. The housewife is, for example, frequently used as the respondent in the study for food and grocery shopping behavior on the assumption that her views will accurately represent those of her family. This has occurred largely because of the high costs of collecting data from multiple respondents, but also because of the limited availability and difficulty of interviewing other respondents such as husbands or children, or senior management within organizations.

It is, however, clear that such strategies may result in data that are not wholly accurate or that are biased, to the extent that they reflect the views of only one participant in the decision-making process. Such problems are particularly likely to be acute in international marketing research in the situations noted previously where participants other than the immediate family or members of the buying organization have an important role in purchase decisions.

Sample Representativity

A second issue to be considered in sampling is the extent to which the sample is representative of the population of interest. This poses questions with regard to the feasibility and cost of obtaining nationally representative samples, as well as the reliability of the procedures used to obtain the samples. In addition, the extent to which findings in one country or target segment can be extrapolated to another needs to be considered.

In most developed countries, information relating to potential target markets and sampling frames, such as telephone listings or electoral lists, is readily available, and quota sampling, and street or mall interviewing are frequently used. The representativity of the sample can then be verified against census or other data. In the developing countries, on the other hand, no sampling frames may exist, and difficulties may arise in reaching the rural or low-income illiterate population. Consequently, different procedures may be needed to obtain representative samples. A procedure such as the following might be used. The major towns or villages are identified. Within each a number of starting points are established, and the interviewer is instructed to visit, for example every nth dwelling, until a specified number of interviews is completed. This is likely to generate a more representative sample than where quota sampling or street interviewing is used. Again, national representativity can be checked against census data, though given the inaccuracy of much census data in developing countries, this may not provide a very accurate indication of sample representativity.

Where the target population is the mass market, some difficulties may be encountered in obtaining a nationally representative sample in countries with low levels of literacy or education. Problems may arise not only in obtaining sampling frames including such people, but also the ability to communicate effectively with them and obtain a relevant response may be limited. Consequently, sampling may focus on urban areas that are likely to constitute the prime targets.

Secondly, the question arises as to whether data from one country or segment within a country, can be extrapolated to other countries or other segments. With increasing communication and travel between countries, particularly on a regional basis in areas such as Europe or Latin America, there is a growing awareness and assimilation of attitudes, behavior, life style, and consumption patterns in other countries. Consequently, the question arises as to whether one country, for example, Belgium, provides an appropriate sampling unit for the rest of Europe. Or, in Latin America, can findings relating to the Brazilian or Argentinian market be extrapolated to other countries? Clearly, sampling a single country is more convenient and cost efficient, but the feasibility will depend on the similarity of behavior among countries relative to this specific product market.

Similarity in response patterns is particularly likely to occur among specific target segments such as senior citizens, businessmen, teenagers, or upscale consumers. To the extent that such groups share similar interests, are faced by similar problems, and have similar responses, so they may tend to have similar purchase and consumption patterns, or to emulate those of their counterparts in other countries. Consequently, it may well be feasible to extrapolate findings related to one such segment in one country, to another country, though extrapolation at the national level entails some dangers.

CULTURAL BIAS IN RESEARCH DESIGN, COMMUNICATION, AND INTERPRETATION

A final issue is that of cross-cultural bias. This occurs because international marketing research typically involves researchers from one cultural environment conducting research in another cultural environment, or communicating with researchers from another cultural environment. These environments may not be understood or correctly interpreted by an outsider, or an individual from another culture (Hall, 1959; Ricks, 1983). Miscommunication can arise due to different styles or modes of communication that are used in different cultures.

In international marketing research, effective communication between researcher and respondents is essential to avoid problems of misinterpretation—either of the research instruments or, alternatively, of response to these. In this regard, there is a certain danger due to the existence of what has been called the cultural self-referent bias (Lee, 1966). In other words, there is always a tendency for a researcher to perceive or interpret phenomena or behavior observed in other countries and cultures in terms of his or her own cultural self-referent. It has, therefore, been argued that all cross-cultural research is inherently ambiguous, and measures or interpretation of these may either be a true reflection of the phenomena observed or, alternatively, of research bias.

Such bias is likely to be particularly acute where a researcher is investigating an unfamiliar sociocultural environment or where he or she lacks experience with sociocultural patterns. As, however, the researcher builds up experience and familiarity with different markets, he or she is likely to develop increased sensitivity to sociocultural specificities. This experience may carry over to other similar markets. Study of the United Kingdom market may, for example, aid in understanding reactions in the Netherlands. Similarly, experience in the French market may prove valuable in investigating the Italian or Spanish markets. Examination of the Far Eastern or African markets would entail, however, mastering totally new and different sociocultural, economic, and political phenomena.

Cross-cultural bias can affect various stages of the research process. It can arise in research design, in communication between researcher and respondent, and in interpretation of the data. Each of these is next discussed in more detail.

Research design: Failure to appreciate adequately the nuances of another culture, and differences in the form in which various attitudes may be expressed or that behavior may be manifested, can constitute a major hindrance in the design of effective international marketing research. In particular, it is important to understand consumption and product usage patterns, as well as the values and cultural behavior patterns underlying these, and their influence on product market structure and market response patterns.

Lack of attention to such factors can lead to designs that do not emphasize adequately the need for identifying and establishing equivalence with regard to relevant constructs to be examined, and appropriate operational definitions or measures of these. The issues of sampling equivalence in terms of relevant respondents or representative samples discussed earlier may be ignored. Similarly, there may be a lack of sensitivity to the importance of adapting research instruments to specific sociocultural environments.

Communication: A second problem is that of communication. This concerns the researcher's ability to communicate instructions about the task to be performed, to the interviewer or the respondent. In other words, it may be difficult for a researcher from one cultural environment to discern whether someone from another environment has effectively understood the task or question. Furthermore, in the interviewer/respondent interaction, it may be difficult to discern whether a response reflects instrument error. This is particularly the case where the response does not fall within the frame of the researcher's experience, or it is not the response expected.

Interpretation: A third problem is that of interpretation. Here, there is the danger that the researcher lacking familiarity with another cultural environment will misinterpret or misunderstand data relating to that culture. Particularly where the attitudes or behavior expressed, or the link between these, differ from that in the researcher's own culture, he or she may experience difficulty in understanding and knowing how to interpret these. Suppose, for example, attitudes toward expression of interest in innovation, or toward sex, are negative. The question then arises as to how this will affect market response. Does this, for example, imply that reaction to a new product or appeals to sex will be negative?

A number of different solutions to deal with the problem of cultural bias have been proposed. A simple procedure entails a four-step approach (see Lee, 1966):

Step 1. Define the business problem or goal in terms of domestic cultural traits, habits, or norms.

Step 2. Define the business problem or goal in terms of the foreign cultural traits, habits, or norms. Make no judgments.

Step 3. Isolate the SRC, that is, self-referent culture, influence in the problem and examine it carefully to see how it complicates the problem.

Step 4. Redefine the problem without the SRC influence and solve it for the foreign market situation.

A major limitation of this approach lies in step 2. This assumes that the researcher *can* define the problem in terms of the foreign environment. This may not always be the case, precisely because the problem may lie in the researcher's lack of sensitivity to such cultural nuances.

Another alternative is to incorporate the perspective of researchers from different cultural backgrounds into research design, data collection, and interpretation, so that cultural bias is minimized as far as possible. In one procedure, the initial plans for research and data collection are developed in a single base country or location. These are then examined and, where necessary, adapted, and additional themes are added by experienced researchers in other countries of interest. Similarly, data interpretation is first undertaken by a researcher familiar with the specific country environment, and then compared across countries. Alternatively, research instruments specific to each country are first developed and then coordinated and harmonized across countries. At this stage, as much commonality as possible is introduced. As in the first case, data are examined both by researchers familiar with a specific cultural or market environment and by those from other countries.

Although this second procedure is preferable, it is likely to be somewhat time-consuming and to pose a number of interaction or organizational problems. Researchers from different cultural environments may often have problems in communicating with each other, and in resolving issues with regard to the need for culture-specific items.

Adoption of the multitrait, multimethod approach (Campbell and Fiske, 1959) may also be desirable. This is based on the principle of multiple operationalism; in other words, that different methods of measuring the same trait should converge toward similar results, and similarly, use of the same method to measure different traits should give divergent results. For example, several different measures of innovativeness, such as self-report, projective, and behavioral, might be developed. Different aspects of innovativeness might also be measured, such as attitudes toward innovation and new products, purchases of new products, or conversations about new products and services. This would help in determining whether specific measures appeared to have any significant type of cultural bias and were, therefore, more appropriate in one country or another. Furthermore, it would indicate whether different traits exhibited any type of cultural bias and were more relevant in a given country or culture.

Problems with regard to communication between researcher and respondent can be diagnosed by the introduction of "comprehension checks." This requires the use of stimuli that evoke no variation in response in different countries or cultures. While these can without too much difficulty be developed for perceptual stimuli, where similarity in structure and processing is widely established, substantially greater difficulties are likely to be encountered in relation to verbal, and especially attitudinal, stimuli. These are inherently more complex and interrelated, and are especially likely to pose problems where they are culturally embedded, as, for example, in relation to food or consumption and purchase behavior.

SUMMARY

In sum, therefore, the need to establish comparability in various aspects of research design and implementation gives rise to a number of issues that center essentially on the question of equivalence in relation to constructs examined, appropriate measures of these, and the samples drawn in each country or culture examined. Various aspects need to be considered in each case. The likelihood of cultural bias stemming from the conduct of research in an environment alien to the researcher should also be evaluated. These aspects are next reviewed.

Construct equivalence has to be assessed first in terms of the *function* performed by the product or activity examined in a particular country or culture. Equivalence in terms of the way in which a *concept* is expressed or perceived by individuals within a culture is also an important consideration. In addition, equivalence in terms of the specific *categories*—for example, product markets or socioeconomic categories—has also to be determined.

In the case of measures and measurement procedures, equivalence has to be determined in terms of the units of measurement used; and in the translation of verbal and nonverbal instruments to ensure comprehension by respondents in different sociocultural environments, and to ensure the equivalence of the response obtained, given a specific response format. Operationally, this is frequently the critical stage in the establishment of measure equivalence, since it requires the development of operational definitions of the constructs to be examined.

Equivalence of the samples drawn in different countries has also to be examined. Here two questions arise. The first concerns whether or not the same respondents—that is, husbands, wives, children, or maids—should be used in different countries and cultures. The second relates to how far a sample is representative of the national market or, alternatively, a regional market such as the EEC or Latin America.

Finally, the potential for cultural bias due to operation in a multicountry environment needs to be assessed. Typically, this will require the development of organizational procedures involving the collaboration of researchers from different national and cultural backgrounds. Comparisons of different perceptions of relevant factors to be examined, appropriate measures of these, and interpretations of data collected can thus prove helpful in identifying possible cultural biases, and "decentering" for the effect of a specific country or culture.

REFERENCES

ANDERSON, R., "On the Comparability of Meaningful Stimuli in Cross-Cultural Research," *Sociometry,* 30 (1967), 124–36.

ANDERSON, RONALD and JACK ENGLEDOW, "A Factor Analytic Comparison of U.S. and German Information Seekers," *Journal of Consumer Research,* 3 (March, 1977), 185–96.

BENNETT, MICK, "Testing Management Theories Cross-Culturally," *Journal of Applied Psychology,* 62 (1977), 578–81.

BERENT, PAUL-HOWARD, "International Research is Different," in Edward M. Mazze, ed., *Marketing in Turbulent Times and Marketing: The Challenges and the Opportunities—Combined Proceedings,* pp. 293–97. Chicago: American Marketing Association, 1975.

BERLIN, B., and P. KAY, *Basic Color Terms: Their Universality and Evolution.* Berkeley, CA: University of California Press, 1969.

BERRIEN, F. KENNETH, "Cross-Cultural Equivalence of Personality Measures," *Journal of Social Psychology,* 75 (1968), 3–9.

BERRY, J. W., "On Cross-Cultural Comparability," *International Journal of Psychology,* 4 (1969), 119–28.

———, "Introduction to Methodology," in Harry C. Triandis and John W. Berry, eds., *Handbook of Cross-Cultural Psychology,* vol. 2, *Methodology,* p. 11. Boston, MA: Allyn and Bacon, Inc., 1980.

BRUNO, ALBERT V. and EDGAR PESSEMIER, "An Empirical Investigation of the Validity of Selected Attitude and Activity Measures," in M. Venkatesen, ed., *Proceedings Third Annual Conference,* pp. 456–74. Chicago: Association for Consumer Research, 1972.

CAMPBELL, DÓNALD T. and DONALD W. FISKE, "Convergent and Discriminant Validation by the Multi-trait Multi-method Matrix," *Psychological Bulletin,* 56 (March 1959), 81–105.

CATTELL, RAYMOND B., "The Dimensions of Culture Patterns by Factorization of National Characters," *Journal of Abnormal and Social Psychology,* 44 (1949), 443–69.

DEREGOWSKI, JAN B., "Perception," in Harry C. Triandis and Walter Lonner (eds.), *A Handbook of Cross-Cultural Psychology,* vol. 3, pp. 21–117. *Basic Processes.* Boston: Allyn and Bacon, Inc., 1980.

DOUGLAS, SUSAN P., "A Cross-National Exploration of Husband Wife Involvement in Selected Household Activities," in William B. Wilkie, ed., *Advances in Consumer Research,* vol. VI, Ann Arbor, MI: Association for Consumer Research, 1979.

——, "Cross-National Comparisons: A Case Study of Working and Non-Working Wives in the U.S. and France," *Journal of Consumer Research,* 3 (June 1976), 12–20.

—— and PATRICK LeMAIRE, "Improving the Quality and Efficiency of Life Style-Research," in *The Challenges Facing Marketing Research: How Do We Meet Them, XXV ESOMAR Congress.* Main Sessions, pp. 555–70. Hamburg, West Germany: Esomar, 1974.

—— and CHRISTINE URBAN, "Life-Style Analysis to Profile Women in International Markets," *Journal of Marketing,* 41 (July 1977), 46–54.

ELDER JOSEPH W., "Comparative Cross-National Methodology," *Annual Review of Sociology,* vol. II. Palo Alto, CA: Annual Reviews, Inc., 1976.

EMBER, CAROL, "Cross-cultural Cognitive Studies," in *Annual Review of Anthropology,* 6 (1977), 33–56.

EYSENCK, S. B. G., O. ADELAJA, and H. J. EYSENCK, "A Comparative Study of Personality in Nigerian and English Subjects," *Journal of Social Psychology,* 102 (1977), 171–78.

FRIJDA, N. and M. JAHODA, "On the Scope and Methods of Cross-cultural Research," *International Journal of Psychology,* 1 (1966), 109–28.

GORDON, L. V., "Comments on Cross-Cultural Equivalence of Personality Measures," *Journal of Social Psychology,* 75 (1968), 11–19.

—— and A. KIKUCKI, "American Personality Test in Cross-cultural Research—a Caution," *Journal of Social Psychology,* 69 (1966), 179–83.

GOUGH, HARRISON G., "A Cross-cultural Study of Achievement Motivation," *Journal of Applied Psychology,* 48 (1964), 191–96.

GREEN, ROBERT and ERIC LANGEARD, "A Cross-National Comparison of Consumer Habits and Innovator Characteristics," *Journal of Marketing,* 49 (July 1975), 34–41.

HALL, EDWARD T., *Beyond Culture.* New York: Anchor Press, 1976.

——, *The Silent Language.* Garden City, NY: Doubleday, 1959.

HEIDER, E. R., "Focal Color Areas and the Development of Color Names," *Developmental Psychology,* 4 (1971), 447–55.

——, "Universals in Naming and Memory," *Journal of Experimental Psychology,* 93 (1972), 10–20.

—— and D. C. OLIVIER, "The Structure of the Color Space in Naming and Memory for Two Languages," *Cognitive Psychology,* 3 (1972), 337–54.

IRVINE, S. H., "Factor Analysis of African Abilities and Attainments: Constructs across Cultures," *Psychological Bulletin,* 71 (1969), 20–23.

KAGITCIBASI, C., "Social Norms, and Authoritarianism: a Turkish-American Comparison," *Journal of Personality and Social Psychology,* 16 (1970), 444–51.

KIKUCHI, AKIO and LEONARD V. GORDON, "Evaluation and Cross-Cultural Application of a Japanese Form of the Survey of Interpersonal Values," *Journal of Social Psychology,* 69 (August 1966), 185–97.

KOHN, PAUL M., "Authoritarianism, Rebellions and their Correlates among British Graduates," *British Journal of Social and Clinical Psychology,* 13, (September 1974), 245–55.

LAPSLEY, DANIEL K. and ROBERT D. ENRIGHT, "The Effects of Social Desirability, Intelligence and Milieu on an American Validation of the Conservation Scale," *Journal of Social Psychology,* 107 (February 1979), 9–15.

LEE, JAMES A., "Cultural Analysis of Overseas Operations," *Harvard Business Review,* 44 (March–April 1966), 106–14.

LEVIN, J. and ELIEZER S. KARNI, "Demonstration of Cross-cultural Invariance of the California Psychological Inventory in America and Israel by the Guttman-Lingoes Smallest Space Analysis," *Journal of Cross-cultural Psychology,* 1 (September 1970), 253–60.

OSGOOD, CHARLES E., WILLIAM E. MAY, and MURRAY S. MIRON, *Cross-cultural Universals of Affective Meaning.* Urbana, IL: University of Illinois Press, 1976.

PESSEMIER, EDGAR A. and ALBERT V. BRUNO, "An Empirical Investigation of the Reliability and Stability of Selected Attitude and Activity Measures," *Proceedings, Second Annual Conference,* pp. 389–403. Chicago: Association for Consumer Research, 1971.

PICK, ANNE D., "Cognition: Psychological Perspectives," in Harry C. Triandis and Walter Lonner, eds., *A Handbook of Cross-cultural Psychology,* vol. 3, *Basic Processes,* pp. 117–54. Boston: Allyn and Bacon, Inc., 1980.

PIKE, KENNETH, *Language in Relation to a Unified Theory of the Structure of Human Behavior.* The Hague: Mouton, 1966.

PRZEWORSKI, A. and H. TEUNE, *The Logic of Comparative Social Inquiry.* New York: Wiley Interscience, 1970.

——, "Establishing Equivalence in Cross-National Research," *Public Opinion Quarterly,* 30 (Winter 1966–67), 105–27.

RICKS, DAVID A., *Big Business Blunders.* Homewood, IL: Dow-Jones-Irwin, 1983.

——, Y. C. FU, and S. ARPAN, *International Business Blunders.* Columbus, OH: Grid, 1974.

ROBERTS, KARLENE H., "On Looking at an Elephant: An Evaluation of Cross-cultural Research," *Psychological Bulletin,* 74, (November 1970), 327–81.

ROSCH, ELEANOR, "Principles of Human Categorization," in *Cognition and Categorization,* E. Rosch and B. Lloyd (eds.). Hillsdale, NJ: Lawrence Earlbaum and Associates, 1978.

SEARS, ROBERT R., "Transcultural Variables and Conceptual Equivalence," in Bert Kaplan, ed., *Studying Personality Cross-culturally,* pp. 445–55. Evanston, IL: Row, Peterson, & Co., 1961.

STRAUS, MURRAY A., "Phenomenal Identity and Conceptual Equivalence of Measurement in Cross-national Comparative Research," *Journal of Marriage and the Family,* 31 (May 1969), 233–39.

TRIANDIS, HARRY,   *The Analysis of Subjective Culture.* New York: John Wiley, 1972.

—— and V. VASSILOU,   "A Comparative Analysis of Subjective Culture," in Harry C. Triandis, *The Analysis of Subjective Culture.* New York: John Wiley, 1972.

URBAN, CHRISTINE,   "Consumer Segmentation for Multi-national Product Planning," in Warren Keegan and Charles S. Mayer, eds., *Multi-national Product Management.* Cambridge, MA: Marketing Science Institute, 1976.

——,   "Life-style Analysis for the Evaluation of Newspaper Audiences," paper presented at the Fourth International Research Seminar in Marketing, Gordes, France, May 31–June 3, 1977.

VILLANI, KATHRYN and DONALD LEHMANN,   "An Examination of the Stability of AIO Measures," in Edward M. Mazze, ed., *Marketing in Turbulent Times* and *Marketing: the Challenges and Opportunities Combined Proceedings Annual Conference,* pp. 484–88. Chicago: American Marketing Association, 1975.

WELLS, WILLIAM D.,   "Psychographics: A Critical Review," *Journal of Marketing Research,* 12 (May 1975), 196–213.

WIND, YORAM and SUSAN P. DOUGLAS,   "Comparative Consumer Research: The Next Frontier," *Management Decision,* 4 (1982), 24–35.

ZALTMAN, GERALD, CHRISTIAN R. A. PINSON, and REINHARD ANGELMAR,   *Metratheory and Consumer Research.* New York: Holt, Rinehart and Winston, 1973.

6

Nonsurvey Data Collection Techniques

The importance of establishing the equivalence and comparability of the concepts, attitudes, and behaviors examined in different countries suggests a need for exploratory research to identify and define relevant phenomena to be examined in subsequent research. This is crucial when the researcher lacks familiarity with a culture or country or with the product market to be investigated. In these instances, qualitative data collection techniques are appropriate as they are unstructured in character. Rather than imposing a specific response format, as in a questionnaire, on the respondent, they focus on probing how people think, feel, and react in response to specific situations or stimuli. In some instances, qualitative research can in some instances be sufficient in and of itself, depending on the nature of the management decision problem.

Thus, qualitative research techniques can be used in two ways in international marketing research. They can be used in exploratory research in order to formulate and define the problem more clearly and to determine relevant questions to be examined in subsequent research. Or, alternatively, they may be used in nonexploratory research where interest is centered on gaining an understanding of a market, rather than quantifying relevant aspects.

Qualitative research techniques are, first of all, useful in the initial stages of cross-national research. In particular, they help the researcher to gain some insight into the problems to be studied and into differences as compared with the domestic market. Often they help in revealing the impact of sociocultural factors on behavior and response patterns in the marketplace. They can therefore be used to pinpoint relevant aspects of the problem to be examined, and to identify and define appropriate concepts and constructs. Operational definitions of these can then be developed and research hypotheses established. These can then be tested in subsequent phases of research using survey techniques.

In some cases, however, qualitative research alone may be adequate, given the problem being investigated. This may be the case where, for example, interest is focused on understanding underlying motivations or attitudes relating to a particular product market or service, or on generating ideas for new products, advertising appeals, or marketing strategies. Here, investigation of relevant issues on a small sample of carefully selected respondents may be sufficient. For example, conducting a number of focus groups might be adequate to generate ideas for new breakfast drink concepts.

In general, four major types of qualitative data collection techniques may be identified: observational data, protocols, projective techniques, and depth interviews. These differ primarily in terms of 1) the degree of structure imposed in data collection, 2) whether data are collected while the respondent is in a real-world shopping or simulated shopping situation, 3) potential reactivity, that is, the extent to which the respondent is aware of being studied, and hence may behave differently, 4) the introspectiveness of data, that is, whether the individual respondents tend to theorize or rationalize their behavior, 5) the subjectivity of the analysis, that is, whether analytic and interpretation procedures and coding schemata are developed prior to data collection, or alternatively, are established *post hoc* by the researcher based on examination of the data, and finally, 6) the sample size, that is, the number of respondents that is generally required, or from which it is feasible to collect data, given typical time and budget constraints. Each of the different data collection techniques is assessed on these criteria, in Table 6.1.

Observational measures typically do not require the respondent to perform a specific task, but rather are based on watching how respondents behave. Generally this is done in a real-world situation, and to the extent that the respondent is not aware of being observed, there is little likelihood of reactivity. Analysis may be prestructured where the movements or signs to be observed are prespecified, or alternatively, these may be subsequently identified by the researcher. Sample sizes vary depending on the specific type of observation. In general, observational procedures tend to be somewhat time-consuming, particularly in the analysis stages.

Protocols or verbalizations of thought processes can either be collected in the field, while the respondent is actually making a purchase decision, or in a simulated shopping environment. In the former case, the respondent is instructed to talk into a microphone while making his or her purchase. In the lat-

TABLE 6.1 Characteristics of selected qualitative methods of data collection

	Structure imposed	Actual shopping environment	Potential reactivity	Introspectiveness	Analysis	Sample size
Observation						
Pure observation	None	Yes	Low	No	Subjective or prestructured	Small
Physical trace measures	None	Yes	None	No	Inferential	Moderate to large
Archival measures	None	N.A.	None	No	Inferential	Moderate to large
Entrapment measures	Moderate	Yes	Some	No	Inferential	Varies
Protocols						
Field	None	Yes	High	Occasional	Subjective	Small
Laboratory	Considerable	No	Moderate	No	Prestructured	Moderate
Projective techniques						
Free response	Varies	No	Low	No	Subjective or prestructured	Small to moderate
Interview						
Depth interview	None	No	Low	Yes	Subjective	Small
Focus group	Moderate	No	Low	Limited	Subjective	Small
EPSY	Considerable	No	Low	Yes	Subjective	Small

Source: Susan P. Douglas, C. Samuel Craig and Jean-Philipe Faivre, "Protocols in Consumer Research: Problems, Methods, and Uses," in Jagdish Sheth (ed.) *Research in Marketing*, Vol. 5, Greenwich, CN: JAI Press, 1981.

ter case, the respondent is given a structured task to perform and asked to talk out loud while making the decision. The technique tends, however, to be highly reactive, and in the case of field protocols, can give rise to introspection on the part of the respondent. Analysis of field protocols is typically subjective, though laboratory protocols can be prestructured. Sample sizes are generally small, especially in the case of field protocols. Like observational data, field protocols are time-consuming and tedious to analyze. In laboratory protocols, on the other hand, the decision task is prestructured and, hence, more easily analyzed.

Projective techniques typically require the respondent to perform a specific task such as word association or sentence completion, or to interpret the actions of others. In the latter case, it is assumed that respondents project their own feelings and reactions in performing this interpretation. There is little potential for reactivity or introspection among respondents. Analysis can either be subjective or prestructured, depending on the extent to which the initial task is structured. Generally, small to moderate sample sizes are used, and the procedure is not overly time-consuming.

Depth interviews and focus groups do not require the respondent to perform any tasks but merely to verbalize opinions. *EPSYs,* on the other hand, require respondents to perform a number of verbal and nonverbal tasks. All three types of interviews are generally conducted in an in-home or laboratory situation and have low potential for reactivity. Depth interviews and EPSYs can tend to become introspective, though this is less likely to occur with focus groups. In all three cases, the analysis is subjective and small sample sizes are used. Depth interviews and focus groups typically last two hours or so, while EPSYs vary from half a day to two days.

The appropriate method to use thus depends to a large extent on the objective of the research and the topic studied. Observational and quasi-observational data are useful where the researcher wishes to gain some idea of purchase behavior and of the impact of the store or retail environment on behavior, and where direct measures cannot be obtained or would lead respondents to change their behavior. Protocols are also designed to capture the impact of the shopping environment on consumer response patterns, but focus on decision processes rather than behavioral acts. Projective techniques are used primarily in the case of sensitive topics, where the respondent would tend to give a biased response if the question were posed directly. Focus and depth interviews can be instrumental in probing underlying motivations and attitudes concerning a particular topic or product market.

The different variants of each of these four types of qualitative data are next examined in more detail. In each case, some specific areas of application are indicated, and the advantages and limitations of different procedures are discussed.

OBSERVATIONAL
AND QUASI-OBSERVATIONAL DATA

Observational and quasi-observational data techniques are commonly used in cross-cultural research in the social sciences. As the name indicates, observational techniques require the researcher to watch or observe behavior of respondents, as, for example, their daily living patterns. This is particularly helpful in cross-cultural research, as it enables the researcher to gain some insights and understanding of a different and unfamiliar culture. Quasi-observational techniques include 1) *physical trace measures,* which are obtained by collecting traces left by different kinds of behavior, such as fingerprints or material wear; 2) *archival records,* which consist of historical or public records of behavioral acts, such as births, deaths, or complaints; and 3) *entrapment* measures, where a respondent is induced to respond to an artificially contrived stimulus, without being aware of its true purpose, for example, confederates playing certain roles. In cross-national research, such techniques are primarily useful in researching sensitive topics, or topics in relation to which the respondent is not able or willing to respond to direct questioning. They also have the advantage, in countries with low levels of literacy, of not requiring any direct response from respondents. Each of these techniques is next discussed in more detail.

Pure Observation

A method of data collection extensively used in cultural anthropology and in investigating cross-cultural phenomena in other social sciences is that of pure observation. Here, the researcher observes behavior patterns in the culture under investigation. In some cases, subjects are not aware of being observed, in which case the technique is totally nonreactive. In other cases, however, the researcher participates in the life of the culture, playing the role of a "participant observer." While initially used to study behavior in specific communities, such as the Hopi Indians or the Italian-Americans in Boston, this technique has more recently been extended to examine behavior in situations such as bars, jewelry stores, clubs, and other interactive situations (Spradley and McCurdy, 1972).

In cross-national research, pure or simple observational techniques can be used in a number of different contexts. First, shopping behavior in open-air markets or in retail stores may be observed. Where purchase behavior is being observed in open markets, the researcher can record the behavior observed, for example, the length of the bargaining or negotiation process, the amount being purchased, the conditions of sale, and so on. Where observation is undertaken in the retail store, the customer's trip through the store can be observed, and counts made of, for example, the number of items examined per product class, their shelf location, and time spent looking at labeling, for each product section. Other factors such as conversations with store personnel, interactions with other shoppers, or, where several family members are present, interaction among them can also be studied. The observation can either be made by individuals posted in the store, or by watching in-store TV monitoring screens, or with hidden cameras in countries where this is legal.

This type of data is particularly useful in providing insights into how people purchase in different shopping environments. It is especially valuable where these differ significantly from one country to another, as for example, between supermarkets in industrialized countries, and bargaining in open-air markets in developing countries, or where the researcher lacks familiarity with the shopping environment.

Where it is feasible to enter individual homes and observe behavior, actual consumption of individual products can be examined. Again, this can either be done by individual researchers or with concealed microphones or TV cameras (Webb, 1978). This latter technique is likely to be more appropriate since this is less likely to be reactive, as respondents are less conscious of being observed. While the consent of respondents has to be obtained to place the equipment in the home, the respondents eventually forget its presence and hence behave naturally.

As in the case of observation in the purchase environment, such data can provide much useful information relating to usage patterns and interaction among family members, which might be difficult to obtain through survey techniques. Furthermore, if the researcher has no prior knowledge about such usage patterns, he or she may not know what questions to ask. For example, in examining attitudes toward coffee, the researcher may not know relevant questions to ask, relating to different techniques of coffee making or taste preferences.

The third type of observation is that of expressive behavior, such as facial expressions, body movements, distances kept between individuals in conversations, and other forms of social interaction (Hall, 1959). These behaviors often differ significantly from one country to another. Use of voice intonation and body movement also vary and have different significance and meaning.

Examination of these factors and their meaning in different countries and cultures is often an important consideration in understanding the interviewer-interviewee interaction and also that between the customer and salesperson. It may thus be desirable to explore these factors prior to designing a survey in unfamiliar cultures, or where the problem relates to the effectiveness of different sales techniques and, particularly, personal selling.

Pure observation thus has several advantages as a methodology in cross-national and cross-cultural research. Where observation is concealed and individuals are not aware of being observed, there are no dangers of reactivity, and individuals behave and respond to different marketing stimuli quite naturally. The researcher can thus gain an understanding of differences in the nature of purchase behavior or social interactions in unfamiliar countries.

On the other hand, pure observation is open to the criticism of subjectivity in interpretation. The onus is placed on the researcher to interpret the meaning of the data collected. Often it is difficult to establish prespecified guidelines with regard to what should be observed and its meaning. The length of time spent examining items on a shelf may, for example, be related to the time available for shopping, or the stock of information and degree of interest in the product category, or it may be purely random. Similarly, the types or classes of behavior that are socially manifested and accepted may vary from one country or culture to another. Hence, observation of actual behavioral patterns may not always provide an appropriate indicator of underlying attitudes and response patterns.

Physical Trace Measures

A second type of observational data is physical trace measures. These differ from pure observation measures insofar as they are traces of behavior rather than actual behavior. They are thus useful in tracking the incidence or frequency of different types of behavior that leave physical traces.

Use of physical trace measures typically requires some ingenuity in devising appropriate measures to track the behavior studied. Examples of physical trace measures include analysis of fingerprints on magazine pages to estimate readership of advertisements and radio dial settings on automobiles brought in for repair to select radio stations to carry the dealer's advertisement (Webb, Campbell, Schwartz, and Sechrest, 1966).

In cross-national research, package shapes and designs common in different countries can be analyzed to assess packaging appeals likely to be the most effective. Similarly, the content of garbage cans can be analyzed to assess the rate of alcohol consumption and use of manufacturer versus private label brands of canned or bottled items. This does, however, require that careful attention be paid to the availability and use of different methods of disposal, such as trash compactors, or cans versus returnable bottles, and the importance of in-home versus on-premise consumption, in order to ensure the comparability of measures. Pantry checks provide another means to check on actual usage of different products or brands where social desirability factors may result in distortion in questionnaire response. Again, however, use of such measures in cross-national research does require careful attention to comparability in storage space availability and habits.

Another type of physical trace measure that focuses on historical artifacts rather than current behavioral traces is the indicators used in the macrosurveys discussed earlier in relation to demand estimation. The presence of physical facilities such as a market square in a developing country might, for example, indicate market potential for piece goods or light agricultural equipment (Carr, 1978). A temple or a fiber mill might suggest potential for mopeds, school supplies, or roofing material. The primary advantage of such measures is that they can easily be obtained at relatively low cost, for example, by aerial photography.

As with pure observational measures, physical trace measures avoid the problems of reactivity associated with the more traditional types of measurement, such as questionnaires. They are also inconspicuous and eliminate difficulties arising from the interaction between an interviewer and respondent. This is particularly advantageous in cross-national research, due to the potential for miscommunication where research is being conducted in a diversity of cultural environments.

On the other hand, physical trace measures suffer from a number of limitations. As with pure observational measures, they are open to criticisms of subjectivity in interpretation, especially in terms of inferences about the link between the indicator or measure used, and the behavior studied. Also, to the extent that the measures used are erosion or accretion measures (that is, of wear or trace), careful attention needs to be paid to the influence of time factors, such as variance in the rapidity with which erosion wears away, or accretion builds up, relative to the period during which measurement takes place.

Archival Measures

A third type of data that resembles the preceding categories is archival records. While not, strictly speaking, observational data, they are nonetheless closely related to these measures and hence are discussed in this context. They differ from other quasi-behavioral measures primarily insofar as they are historical data, including, for example, sources such as official public or government records, mass media, sales records, industrial records, and personal documents. While these can also be classed as secondary data, they differ from the secondary data sources discussed previously insofar as they are used as surrogate indicators of the attitudes and behavior of interest.

A variety of records of different types may be used as surrogate measures of attitudinal and behavioral phenomena. The nuisance created by aircraft noise has, for example, been evaluated based on turnover in real estate transactions, school enrollment records, and complaint records (Webb, Campbell, Schwartz, and Sechrest, 1966). Similarly, anxiety associated with airplane travel has been assessed on the basis of flight insurance sales and consumption of alcoholic drinks in airports.

Content analysis of documents and other types of verbal or visual evidence may also provide appropriate measures of attitudinal and behavioral trends in different countries and cultures. The famous study by McClelland (1961) of achievement motivation in different cultures was, for example, predominantly based on content analysis of different types of data ranging from literature, folk tales, and children's stories, to ceramic designs on urns. To the extent that mass media reflect dominant cultural values and attitudes, these provide a valuable source of information with regard to such factors. Content analysis of the roles in which women are portrayed in advertisements—that is, as wife, mother, sex object, career woman—can be used to assess the role of women in a society. Another measure of the same phenomenon might be provided by comparing the number and circulation figures of women's magazines targeted to housewives (*Family Circle, Good Housekeeping*), the fashion-conscious woman (*Vogue, Glamour*), or working women (*Woman Executive, Self, Savvy*).

Similarly, studies of the diffusion of innovations, and in particular, of drugs among physicians (Coleman, Katz, and Menzel, 1957), have been based on examination of prescription records to determine which doctors prescribed what drugs when. This provides more reliable data than that obtained from the more reactive procedure of interviewing physicians.

Archival records are thus useful sources of information in cross-national research because, like the measures discussed previously, they are unobtrusive. In addition, they enable examination of phenomena over time while other external or environmental conditions vary.

The primary limitation of such measures, as with other observational techniques, is the need to establish the link between the measure or records and the specific behavior or attitude studied. Furthermore, the comparability of this link from one country or culture to another has to be considered. In addition, since archival records are collected for a purpose other than the one studied, it is important to evaluate how and for whom these records are compiled, and what might be potential sources of error or inaccuracy in these records. Factors such as changes in the size of the population for which records are compiled, and also changes in the composition of this group, can, for example, give rise to error in interpretation when cross-national comparisons are to be made.

Entrapment Measures

The fourth type of quasi-observational data is entrapment measures. These differ from the preceding measures insofar as measurement is indirect. Typically, the purpose of the investigation is hidden from the respondent, who is asked to respond to one stimulus when the phenomenon under investigation is in fact different. Often such measures involve the use of experimental techniques in which various stimuli or participants are disguised, or "planted," and respondents' reactions to them assessed.

Simple measures of this type include the use of response rates to mail offers for different series of books to determine which volumes should be published. Similarly, rates of response to coupon advertising of a particular brand or product may be used as an indicator of the effectiveness of advertising copy.

More complex studies, involving role playing, may also be designed. One study, examining the effectiveness of furniture salesmen's performance, entailed the use of actors disguised as pseudoshoppers. The actors were instructed to play different roles such as an indecisive, newly wedded couple, an irascible and difficult-to-please shopper, and a couple with conflicting views and tastes in furniture. Salesmen's performance and ability to motivate sales in relation to each type of shopper were then evaluated.

Insofar as the intent of the research and awareness of being watched is hidden from the respondent, such measures are unobtrusive and nonreactive. They suffer, however, from the danger that the respondent may guess the purpose of the study, or become suspicious that the stimulus or confederate is a plant and may modify behavior accordingly. Furthermore, as in relation to the use of other types of observational and quasi-observational measures in cross-national research, entrapment measures require that specific behavior or acts have the same interpretation and significance in the different countries and cultures studied.

PROTOCOLS

Another qualitative data collection technique that, like observation, is particularly suited to cross-national research, is the protocol. A protocol is a record of a respondent's verbalized thought processes while performing a decision task or while problem solving. This record is obtained by asking the respondent to "think out loud" or talk about anything going through his or her head while making a decision. Protocols can either be collected in a laboratory situation while the respondent is making a simulated purchase decision, or in the field while an actual purchase decision is being made. For further discussion of protocols, see Douglas, Craig, and Faivre (1981).

In contrast to traditional survey techniques, protocol methodologies are specifically designed to avoid the imposition of a prespecified choice model on the respondent, allowing him or her to respond freely in his or her own terms in relation to an actual choice task or decision situation. The researcher does not define or specify the form, or in certain types of protocols, the particular stimuli, to which the subject should respond. Hence, the researcher does not impose his or her own cultural frame of reference on the respondent. Rather, each subject identifies, of his or her own accord, the factors of importance to him or her.

Protocols of organizational decision making can be collected while managers are making actual decisions. Meetings of buying committees have, for example, been recorded (Montgomery, 1975). Alternatively, managers can be asked to recall actual purchase decisions and histories (Wind, 1966; Farley, Hulbert, and Weinstein, 1980), indicating the procedures and decision rules used to arrive at these decisions.

Consumer protocols have also been collected both on actual shopping trips and in simulated shopping environments. When protocols are collected on actual shopping trips, the respondent is typically accompanied by an interviewer, who holds a microphone into which the shopper talks and in some cases helps in pushing the shopping cart. An alternative is to provide the respondent with a tape recorder hung round the neck, or attached to his or her lapel into which the respondent talks while going through the store. This procedure is generally less successful than when an interviewer is used, since the interviewer provides an excuse or target for verbalization and helps to alleviate the embarrassment many shoppers feel in talking alone into a microphone. Field protocols tend, however, to be somewhat unstructured. The data are often partial in character and difficult to analyze. Alternatively, "prompted" or retrospective protocols subsequent to the performance of the decision tasks can be collected, in conjunction with other laboratory tasks such as information display boards or eye fixation tasks (Arch, Bettman, and Kakkar, 1978; Payne, 1976; Russo and Rosen, 1975). The task provides a specific focus for the protocol, giving it a more structured character, and considerably facilitates the analysis.

Uses of Protocols in Cross-National and Cross-Cultural Research

In using protocol methods in cross-national research, a number of potential areas of application may be identified. Among these are projects where attention is centered on examining

1. attributes and cues used in making consumer purchase decisions in different cultural and national environments;
2. product class boundaries and product usage, which may differ in each national and cultural context;
3. the impact of the shopping environment on consumer decisions in different countries.

Cues Used in Selecting Products

The first example shows a protocol collected in a French supermarket (Table 6.2). The rich quality of the data is apparent, as the subject easily ver-

TABLE 6.2   An excerpt from a protocol collected in France

What are we going to look at next—detergents. Well, detergents, that's a difficult item to buy. I must look at the prices and at the special offers (laughter). Ariel 32.50 frs. for 5 kilos. It's always the same weight, it's a good product, is advertised regularly on T.V., but I don't think ever has a promotion on these packages. Skip is also a good product which washes well, and the promotion is either a jam jar or a freezing tray. Well, I think I'll take the freezing tray, because the weight of the gift is included in the weight of the package, and one certainly gets more detergent with a freezing tray than with a jam jar.

Source: A study of consumer information processing at Centre d'Enseignement Superieur des Affaires, Jouy-en-Josas, France. Reprinted from Susan P. Douglas, C. Samuel Craig and Jean-Philippe Faivre, "Protocols in Consumer Research: Problems, Methods, and Uses," in Jagdish Sheth (ed.) *Research in Marketing,* Vol. 5, Greenwich, CN: JAI Press, 1981.

balizes the cues used in brand selection. The weight of the promotion is thought to be included in the weight of the package, and influences the choice of promotion and package. Such a reaction is somewhat unexpected and seems unlikely to be anticipated by a researcher. It is interesting to note that such influences are unlikely to be detected by data-collection techniques such as depth interviews, which do not take place in the store environment.

Product Class Boundaries

Protocol data can also be helpful in providing insights into product categorization and product-related terminology. Often the specific products that are available, and prevailing usage patterns, vary from country to country (Berent, 1975). Consequently, relevant product substitutes and product class definitions tend to differ. These can be investigated by collection of protocol data.

Information from protocols for apparently similar product classes or groups in different countries can be contrasted. In Table 6.3, for example, a

TABLE 6.3   Product-related excerpts from protocols collected in France

---

a)   I need a soft butter for cooking, there, a standard butter, (beurre laitier) and then a butter—wait a minute though—I still have some good quality butter (beurre fin) for the table. I think that will do for the moment.

b)   Ah, fruit, I'll buy some oranges and grapefruit. Since it's hot, we'll make some juice. Lots of juice for the children, and then some for us. When I buy them juice, I generally buy the cheapest, but these, I don't know. These are two kilos for 6.9 frs.; that's certainly less than the others. But those are certainly better for eating. But they've all been treated with something.

Source: A study of consumer information processing at Centre d'Enseignement Superieur des Affaires, Jouy-en-Josas, France. Reprinted from Susan P. Douglas, C. Samuel Craig and Jean-Philippe Faivre, "Protocols in Consumer Research: Problems, Methods, and Uses," in Jagdish Sheth (ed.) *Research in Marketing,* Vol. 5, Greenwich, CN: JAI Press, 1981.

French shopper purchases one product variant, or type of butter, for cooking and another for table use. This implies that in comparing butter purchases in France and other countries, the relevant product class will need to be defined broadly, including both "spread" substitutes, such as margarine, and cooking substitutes, such as oil. Similarly, one type of orange is purchased for making juice and another for eating. Consequently, in examining purchase behavior for fresh oranges, the product class should include not only other fruit and fresh orange substitutes, such as canned or bottled juice, but also other types of juices and fruit drinks, and fresh-orange-juice substitutes, such as frozen, powdered, or dehydrated concentrates, and bottled and carton-packed juices.

Protocols also provide a source of useful information about product usage patterns and attitudes. The shopper in Table 6.4a, for example, in purchasing soap for heavy-duty washing, places emphasis on rubbing to remove dirt and perspiration, rather than on presoaking. Machine washing appears to be regarded as somewhat superficial and as no substitute for a good hand wash. Similarly, in Table 6.4b, the subject has difficulty in comparing cookers and in evaluating the quality of the steel. Comparisons of such statements in protocols collected in different cultures and countries can help in providing insights into differences and similarities of relevant attributes and product cues used in choice behavior.

TABLE 6.4 Extracts from protocols providing product-related information

---

a)   C...I'm going to get some soap (savon de Marseilles) for heavy duty washing.

I...for washing

C...Yes, to rub things. To rub the children's socks when they're really dirty, because the soap powder in the machine doesn't get the underneath dirt out, especially perspiration and for socks. So, I rub them first and then wash, and then put them in the machine. Otherwise, if they come out in the machine....

b)   For the cooker, I need to get some information; I came to look at them but I also need some brochures, any booklets on them, and to look at some articles in periodicals. There are several which have articles about kitchen equipment from time to time because I think there are a number of different qualities at different prices. Ah, look, there are two cookers next door to each other. One costs 1,790 and the other 2,225. I suppose that there's a reason; they look the same—the same brand, and about the same, but the gadgets must be different. I mean whether there's a timing mechanism—that's sometimes useful; it depends on the person. I think there's also a difference in the quality of the steel. One looks more sound than the other. It's the same for refrigerators. That's something I watch out for, because the one I have at home deteriorated very quickly; it was very fragile. For the cooker, what's important is to have a good thermostat for the oven. I'm going to take care with my next purchase; a cooker is very expensive nowadays and I like to keep my equipment a long time.

Source: A study of consumer information processing at Centre d'Enseignement Superieur des Affaires, Jouy-en-Josas, France. Reprinted from Susan P. Douglas, C. Samuel Craig and Jean-Philippe Faivre, "Protocols in Consumer Research: Problems, Methods, and Uses," in Jagdish Sheth (ed.) *Research in Marketing,* Vol. 5, Greenwich, CN: JAI Press, 1981.

Examining the Impact
of Situational Variables

Protocol data can be used to discern the impact of the shopping environment and situational variables on behavior. Their collection in conjunction with a decision task, and hence their *in situ* character, make them particularly appropriate in this regard.

Protocols can be collected to examine the impact of differences in the retail store environment and store layout, such as use of service counters, shelf displays, and gondolas. In many countries, traditional specialized full-service retailers, small self-service stores, and open-air markets account for a higher proportion of retail sales than in the United States. Consequently, factors such as interaction with store personnel or other consumers, crowding, and jostling, often play a major role in consumer decisions. These are often clearly revealed in protocols.

The excerpt in Table 6.5 shows the influence of the saleswomen in the purchase of dye, even to the point of changing previous brand preferences. The excerpts in Table 6.6 reveal negative attitudes toward store layout and display that may tend to affect consumer store loyalty. In many countries, supermarkets compete with specialized retailers for the sale of items such as meat or dairy products, frozen foods, and packaged pastries. Thus, factors such as store layout and display can have significant impact on choice of retail outlet.

Advantages and Limitations
of Protocol Techniques

The absence of a preimposed conceptual framework or verbal stimuli that might generate a culture-specific or pseudo-etic bias make protocols a particularly suitable methodology for use in cross-national research. Protocols can

TABLE 6.5   Store-related excerpt from a protocol collected in France

S:	What sort of dye would you like?
C:	I don't really know, let me ask you. One which lasts well.
S:	I'm not sure what kind you want. I have three brands, Dilon, Idecuir and Ardepo, which is an old brand.
C:	Oh, Idecuir. I know that, it's not bad. I'll take that.
S:	If you know it already.
C:	Yes, I've used it already, unless you can think of another one which is better?
S:	There is another which does for all types of leather, plastic etc.
C:	It also dyes plastic...good, I'll take that one then.

Source: A study of consumer information processing at Centre d'Enseignement Superieur des Affaires, Jouy-en-Josas, France. Reprinted from: Susan P. Douglas, C. Samuel Craig and Jean-Philippe Faivre, "Protocols in Consumer Research: Problems, Methods, and Uses," in Jagdish Sheth (ed.) *Research in Marketing,* Vol. 5, Greenwich, CN: JAI Press, 1981.

TABLE 6.6   Excerpts from protocols providing store-related information

---

a)   This supermarket is so poorly organized. It starts with frozen foods first, and that's not at all what one wants to buy to begin with.

b)   One really does have to hunt for things—all those T.V. stories, you have to get down on all fours to find the cheapest products. Look that must be about the same as Palmolive, and it's cheaper. I'll try it. I must put that straight though.

c)   It's so annoying to have to wait for the bread before it was in front of the cash register, one could just pick it up. This must be easier for them, but not for me. But I prefer this type of bread, because it's fresh I really don't like wrapped bread with preservatives. So let's get in the queue.

Source: A study of consumer information processing at Centre d'Enseignement Superieur des Affaires, Jouy-en-Josas, France. Reprinted from: Susan P. Douglas, C. Samuel Craig and Jean-Philippe Faivre, "Protocols in Consumer Research: Problems, Methods, and Uses," in Jagdish Sheth (ed.) *Research in Marketing,* Vol. 5, Greenwich, CN: JAI Press, 1981.

be especially useful in the initial stages of cross-national research. Here, protocols supplied by respondents from each national context can provide indications as to relevant concepts and how these may most appropriately be defined in each context. Based on this analysis, some initial measures adapted to each context can be developed. For example, protocol data can be used to identify relevant product attributes, attitudinal statements, or life style items to be examined.

Protocol data also enable the researcher to identify the terminology used by consumers when thinking about products, or in relation to purchase situations or the store environment. This can be particularly useful when conducting research in different linguistic environments, where the researcher, although familiar with the formal language, may not be conversant with specific consumer "speech terms," such as "bird," "laid back," and so on.

While protocol methods offer a number of advantages in cross-national research, they also suffer from serious limitations that need to be taken into consideration. These stem primarily from their unstructured character. First, interpretation of cross-national protocol data is highly subjective. Since there is no prespecified conceptual model to provide a framework for analysis, the onus of defining which constructs are relevant, and of determining where there are similarities and differences between countries is placed on the researcher. As in the case of translation, this is best resolved by an iterative, back-checking process and by the use of multiple judges, each with different cultural self-referrents, to analyze the data and develop relevant coding categories.

The validity and ease of collecting protocol data also depend on respondent willingness to cooperate and to talk out loud while making decisions (Wright, 1974). Again, difficulties may be encountered in cross-national research. Cultures differ with regard to their loquaciousness (Mitchell, 1965) and willingness to respond to questions (Brislin, Lonner, and Thorndike, 1973). As a result, this may have an important impact on their capacity to verbalize.

Protocol data are frequently partial in character. They consist predominantly of fragmented pieces of information and phrases. Information stored in memory, relating, for example, to routine purchases and frequently bought brands, may not be verbalized. Consequently, the extent to which it provides a comprehensive picture of all relevant elements of the decision process is not always clear, and certain aspects relevant to cross-national comparisons may be underemphasized. Such limitations can, to some extent, be overcome by use of protocols in conjunction with other methods of data collection, such as behavioral data, supplementary questionnaires, or diary data. For example, protocols can be collected at the same time that husbands and wives select information from display boards in making hypothetical gift, clothing, appliance, or housing decisions, in order to examine cross-national differences in decision-making processes for such items. Videotapes of actual shopping trips or eye-fixation data, can also be collected, as well as in-store protocols, in order to compare the use of visual versus verbal data in cross-cultural and national research.

In essence, therefore, protocols provide a wealth of detail and a breadth of coverage, particularly in relation to the role of situational variables, that is not found in other data collection techniques. Their qualitative character implies, however, that they are best suited for use in exploratory phases of research, to identify relevant concepts to be examined further, rather than to develop precise measures of concepts and behavior.

PROJECTIVE TECHNIQUES

The third type of qualitative data collection procedures entails the use of projective techniques. These may be particularly useful in cross-national research, insofar as they present the respondent with a vague or unstructured stimulus or task and require him or her to respond to it. As in the case of protocol techniques, this does not require the researcher to preimpose a specific response format on the respondent.

A number of different projective techniques may be used in cross-national research. These range from the use of stimuli as unstructured as Rorschach tests, to the use of T.A.T. (Thematic Apperception Test), word association, and sentence completion tasks. These vary primarily in terms of whether the stimuli presented to the respondent are verbal or visual in nature, and in the complexity of the research design.

Rorschach inkblot tests, though extensively used in other social sciences such as cross-cultural psychology, are little used in marketing research and hence are not discussed here. T.A.T.s, on the other hand, have a number of potential applications. Typically, they depict graphically a scenario with two or more persons in a specific consumption purchase or other social interaction situation. Sometimes there is, as in a cartoon, a balloon out of one individual's head, indicating what he or she is thinking or saying, and the respondent is required to fill out the response of the other person in the picture. Otherwise, respondents are asked to indicate what they think the people in the picture are saying or feeling. A picture showing consumers talking to a bank officer might, for example, be used to assess consumer attitudes toward bank officers in different countries.

Design of such tasks in international research poses some difficulties, since it is important to develop stimuli that are equivalent in interpretation and meaning in all countries and cultures. Considerable ingenuity is likely to be required in order to avoid miscomprehension by respondents. Use of line drawings, which are not subject to the problems of interpretation of perceptual cues or culturally determined role models, may be desirable.

Sentence completion and word association tasks entail the use of verbal, as opposed to visual, tasks. In the case of word association tasks, for example, the respondent is given a number of words and asked to indicate others associated with these. Results obtained from use of such techniques in different countries and cultures suggest that these are often highly similar (Berlin and Kay, 1969; Osgood, May, and Miron, 1975). Sentence completion tasks typically pose questions such as: "People who use Tide. . . , People who eat. . ." requiring the individual to project himself or herself into the situation, and indicate his or her perception of the typical Tide user, or the consumer of snacks. If she or he is a Tide user or a consumer of snack products, it is generally assumed that this description also applies to himself or herself.

While projective techniques offer a number of advantages insofar as they do not impose a specific cultural referent on the respondent, they also suffer from a number of important limitations (Lindzey, 1961; Holtzman, 1980). First, interpretation of the data is highly subjective, and the establishment of an appropriate coding and analytic procedure that can be used systematically across different countries poses some problem. Secondly, the comparability of the samples studied in the different countries needs to be assessed to ensure that this does not affect results. Finally, as in relation to other qualitative techniques, establishment of the equivalence of meaning, whether verbal or nonverbal, is likely to pose a major challenge, especially when the linguistic and cultural contexts in which research is being conducted vary markedly.

DEPTH INTERVIEWS

The fourth and final major category of qualitative data collection procedures consists of depth interview techniques, such as individual depth interviews, focus groups, and EPSYs. Depth interviews are essentially unstructured data collection techniques in which an interviewer attempts to elicit discussion and probe in-depth attitudes of an individual or group, with regard to a particular topic. These procedures differ from the preceding techniques insofar as the interviewer plays an active role in eliciting response from subjects, and from survey research, to the extent that there is no prestructured response instrument or questionnaire. Depth interviews can either be individual or, alternatively, group discussions which, in the case of EPSYs, center around game and role playing.

Individual Depth Interviews

Individual interviews are conducted on a one-to-one basis between an interviewer and a respondent. This has the advantage that the interviewer can probe an individual's attitudes and pinpoint responses to specific aspects of a topic. It is particularly useful in the context of industrial marketing research, where it may be desirable to tailor questions to individual company situations or to the respondent's personality or position in the company.

On the other hand, use of individual in-depth interviews does require the availability of highly skilled interviewers. As noted previously, particularly in certain developing countries, it is likely to be difficult to obtain trained interviewers with capabilities in the appropriate language. Furthermore, the conduct of the interview on a one-to-one basis tends to make the procedure relatively expensive and time-consuming. Consequently, there has been a growing tendency in industrialized countries in recent years to move toward the conduct of group interviews.

Focus Groups

Focus groups are group discussions conducted with individuals who are representative of the target market(s) in an informal setting. The discussion is "moderated" by an interviewer who plays a key role in stimulating discussion about feelings, attitudes, and perceptions relating to the topic being studied, and in centering this interchange on relevant issues.

Focus groups are particularly suited to generating and testing ideas for new products, product concepts, and product positioning; studying response to packaging and advertising themes; and diagnosing the possible need for changes in advertising strategy. In particular, they can be used 1) to generate hypotheses to be studied quantitatively in subsequent research; for example, concerning attitudes toward the use of gasoline stations as retail outlets, 2) to elicit information helpful in structuring questionnaires; for example, about the language terms, key phrases, and word terms used by consumers in relation to a specific product category or brand, and 3) to examine the feasibility of transferring a product or advertising theme developed for a market in one country or culture, to other countries or cultures. For a more extensive discussion of focus groups, see Calder (1977).

The primary advantage of group, as opposed to individual, interviews is that the presence of other group members provides a synergy that stimulates discussion. Comments made by one group member may, for example, evoke a response or set off a train of thought or ideas among other group members. Furthermore, the presence and open expression of views by more extrovert group members provides a socially reinforcing situation, which may encourage more timid individuals to verbalize attitudes and views more readily.

On the other hand, the group interview, like the individual interview, suffers from a number of limitations. First, in a focus group, the role of the moderator is crucial to success. In cross-national research, trained moderators, conversant with the appropriate language and also patterns of social interaction in each country or culture, are required. Interpretation and analysis of focus group data is also subjective in character and typically requires considerable skill and experience. In cross-national research, understanding not only of verbal data but also of nonverbal cues such as voice intonation, gestures, and expressions used in other countries and cultures, is often a key ingredient in successful interpretation of findings. Finally, willingness of respondents to talk freely about their attitudes and thoughts on various topics may vary from one country or culture to another. As previously noted, particularly in cultures such as the Middle or Far East, respondents may be extremely reluctant to discuss their feelings. In contrast to the United States, in these countries interaction with acquaintances or neighbors other than in a purely formal context may be uncommon, posing difficulties in the creation of a "natural" focus group situation.

Use of such techniques in multicountry research also poses problems with regard to the comparability of data generated from one country to another. The moderator's role becomes particularly critical; he or she tends to reflect the norms, attitudes, and response patterns typical of a specific cultural context, and these attitudes and responses may be projected into the findings. Similarly, cultural differences in receptivity to the focus group situation may influence results.

EPSYs

In the case of EPSYs (the Etude Projective Synapse), projective techniques are used to stimulate group discussion. As with focus groups, a number of subjects are gathered together to talk about their feelings, attitudes, and thoughts relating to a particular topic. In contrast to the focus group, however, subjects are not only asked to discuss the topic, but also to perform a variety of tasks and to participate in games. The purpose of these is both to provoke discussion and to explore latent feelings and motivations that might not otherwise be revealed. The specific tasks vary, depending on the topic or purpose for which the groups are being conducted. They range from standard projective techniques such as positive and negative associations, word association and sentence completion tasks, thematic apperception tests, and role playing, to more creative tasks such as painting masks and miming.

As with focus groups, EPSYs can be used in a number of different situations. They are, for example, commonly used to examine motivations, attitudes, and feelings with regard to a specific product market as, for example, baby foods or soup. EPSYs, like focus groups, can be used to search for new products and concepts, using brainstorming and word association techniques, and to develop new advertising themes by exploring underlying motivations and attitudes. Differences among different segments can be probed by conducting a focus group for each segment. In addition, EPSYs can be conducted with children, who often express themselves easily and with considerable facility. In general, due to the limited attention span of children, EPSYs conducted with children are somewhat shorter than the normal EPSY, lasting only three to four hours, in contrast to the one to two days that is common for the average EPSY.

EPSYs are also used to predict future attitudinal and consumption trends in a specific product market, or trends in value patterns and attitudes in society. In this case, the typical EPSY in many respects resembles an encounter group. The group remains together for two to three days, discussing various issues raised by the moderator, and engaging in different role-playing situations devised to mirror certain values or attitudinal trends. For a more complete discussion of EPSYs, see Cathelat (1973).

Where the purpose is to diagnose trends related to a specific product market, the tasks center around the invention of an ideal product at some future time. The timespan has to be sufficiently close to be realistic, and sufficiently distant to justify the creation of a new product. Scenarios such as journeys into the future, science fiction, and so on, are often used. If, on the other hand, the purpose is to monitor future trends, the sessions are substantially less structured and are oriented toward the expression of individual desires and motivations, underlying social values and norms, and sociocultural stereotypes. In addition, the imagery associated with products, desired new products, or changes in existing products and communication concepts to meet new value trends and attitudes, are explored.

The primary advantage of the EPSY, as opposed to the focus group, is the combination of projective techniques with group discussion. This helps to focus and to stimulate discussion. Positive and negative associations with the topics are evoked, as well as underlying motivations and feelings related to the topic. The approach is particularly valuable in relation to topics or areas such as future trends, where spontaneous expression of thoughts and reactions may pose some difficulties, and subjects are often not totally conscious of these.

EPSYs suffer from the same limitations noted earlier in relation to focus groups. The analysis poses even greater problems of subjectivity since the difficulties associated with qualitative data interpretation are further compounded by those associated with projective techniques. Consequently, a successful EPSY will depend to a large extent on the skill and experience of the moderator. These factors probably account for their somewhat limited use.

SUMMARY

Nonsurvey data collection techniques play an important role in international marketing research. This role is even more critical than in domestic marketing research, due to the frequent lack of familiarity with cultural mores and behavior in a country. Qualitative data collection procedures can, therefore, be used to identify what aspects should be studied in subsequent phases of research.

Four major types of qualitative data collection procedures may be identified: observational and quasi-observational data, projective techniques, protocols, and depth interviews. These differ primarily in terms of the degree of structure imposed on data collection; whether the respondent is aware of being studied, and hence alters his or her behavior; and whether the focus is on measuring actual behavior, or rather, attitudes and verbal rationalizations about behavior, as well as the typical sample size and scope of the data collected.

The main advantage of qualitative data is that they can be conducted in a relatively short space of time (including both data collection and analysis phases), in contrast to the somewhat more laborious procedures entailed in organizing and administering a survey. This makes them well suited to the exploratory stages of international marketing research in order to provide input into subsequent stages of research and survey design.

On the other hand, analysis and interpretation of qualitative data is frequently open to criticism, due to its subjective nature. Thus, while qualitative data alone are sometimes sufficient to respond to management decision problems, more frequently they provide a source of complementary information to interpret and round out quantitative research.

REFERENCES

ARCH, DAVID C., JAMES R. BETTMAN, and PARDEEP KAKKAR, "Subjects' Information Processing in Information Board Studies," in *Advances in Consumer Research,* vol. 5. Chicago: Association for Consumer Research, 1978.

BERENT, PAUL H., "International Research Is Different," in *Marketing in Turbulent Times* and *Marketing, the Challenges and the Opportunities,"* Combined Proceedings, AMA Conference. Chicago: American Marketing Association, 1975.

BERLIN B. and P. KAY, *Basic Colour Terms: Their Universality and Evolution.* Berkeley, CA: University of California Press, 1969.

BRISLIN, R., W. LONNER, and R. THORNDIKE, *Cross-Cultural Research Methods.* New York: John Wiley, 1973.

CALDER, BOBBY J., "Focus Group and the Nature of Qualitative Research," *Journal of Marketing Research,* 14 (August 1977), 353–64.

CARR, RICHARD P., "Identifying Trade Areas for Consumer Goods in Foreign Markets," *Journal of Marketing,* 42 (October 1978), 76–80.

CATHELAT, B., "Etude Projective Synapse," Centre de Communication Avance, Paris 1973 (unpublished document).

COLEMAN, JAMES S., ELIHU KATZ, and HERBERT MENZEL, "The Diffusion of an Innovation among Physicians," *Sociometry,* 20 (December 1957) 253–70.

DOUGLAS, SUSAN P., C. SAMUEL CRAIG, and JEAN-PHILIPPE FAIVRE, "Protocols in Consumer Research: Problems, Methods and Uses," in Jagdish Sheth (ed.), *Research in Marketing,* vol 5. Greenwich, CN: JAI Press Inc., 1981.

FARLEY, JOHN U., JAMES HULBERT, and DAVID WEINSTEIN, "Price Setting and Volume Planning by Two European Industrial Companies: A Study and Comparison of Decision Processes," *Journal of Marketing,* 44 (Winter 1980), 46–54.

HALL, EDWARD T., *The Silent Language.* Garden City, NY: Doubleday and Co., 1959.

HOLTZMAN, WAYNE H., "Projective Techniques" in *Handbook of Cross-Cultural Psychology,* vol. 2, *Methodology.* Boston, MA: Allyn and Bacon, 1980.

LINDZEY, G., *Projective Techniques and Cross-Cultural Research.* New York: Appleton Century Crofts, 1961.

MCCLELLAND, D.C., *The Achieving Society.* Princeton, NJ: Van Nostrand, 1961.

MITCHELL, ROBERT E., "Survey Materials Collected in the Developing Countries: Sampling, Measurement and Interviewing Obstacles to Intra and International Comparisons," *International Social Science Journal,* 17, (1965), 665–85.

MONTGOMERY, DAVID B., "New Product Decisions: An Analysis of Supermarket Buyer Decisions," *Journal of Marketing Research,* 12 (August 1975), 225–64.

NISBETT, RICHARD and TIMOTHY WILSON, "Telling More Than We Know: Verbal Reports on Mental Processes," *Psychology Review,* 84, (1977), 231–59.

OSGOOD, CHARLES E., WILLIAM H. MAY, and MURRAY S. MIRON, *Cross-Cultural Universals of Affective Meaning.* Urbana, IL: University of Illinois Press, 1975.

PAYNE, JOHN W., "Task Complexity and Contingent Processing in Decision-Making: An Information Search and Protocol Analysis," *Organizational Behavior and Human Performance,* 16, no. 3 (1976) 366–87.

RUSSO, EDWARD J. and LARRY D. ROSEN, "An Eye Fixation Analysis of Multi-Alternative Choice," *Memory and Cognition,* 3 (1975) 267–76.

SPRADLEY, JAMES P. and DAVID W. MCCURDY, *The Cultural Experience.* Chicago: Science Research Associates, 1972.

WEBB, EUGENE J., DONALD T. CAMPBELL, RICHARD D. SCHWARTZ, and LEE SECHREST, *Unobtrusive Measures: Non-Reactive Research in the Social Sciences.* Chicago: Rand McNally, 1966.

WEBB, PETER, "A New Method for Studying Family Decision-Making," *Journal of Marketing,* 42 (January 1978), 12.

WERNER, O. and D. CAMPBELL, "Translating, Working Through Interpreters and the Problems of Decentering," in Raoul Naroll and Ronald Cohen (eds.), *A Handbook of Method in Cultural Anthropology.* New York: Columbia University Press, 1973.

WIND, YORAM, *Industrial Buying Behavior: Source Loyalty in the Purchase of Industrial Components,* unpublished Ph.D. dissertation, Stanford University, 1966.

WRIGHT, PETER L., "On the Direct Monitoring of Cognitive Response to Advertising," in G. David Hughes and Michael L. Ray (eds.), *Buyer/Consumer Information Processing.* Chapel Hill, NC: University of North Carolina, 1974.

7

Survey Research: Instrument Design

While qualitative data collection techniques aid in identifying relevant constructs and concepts to be examined, survey research provides a means of quantifying these concepts and examining relevant relationships in-depth. In this context an important consideration is instrument design. While this also needs to be examined in qualitative data collection, it assumes greater significance in survey research where structured data collection techniques and large sample sizes are typically involved. In particular, it is important to ensure that the research instrument is adapted to the specific national and cultural environment, and is not biased in terms of any one country or culture. Such bias may enter into the design and the development of the instrument, or into its administration, or may result from the scoring procedures used. While the occurence of bias in the design and development of measures is widely recognized, that arising in scoring procedures is less evident.

Since the instrument used in survey research is typically a questionnaire, whether administered by interviewer or self-administered, questionnaire design and question formulation are first discussed. Next, potential sources of bias that may arise as a result of the interviewer-respondent interaction, or of the desires and personal characteristics of the respondent, are reviewed. Procedures for questionnaire translation are then examined, as well as the use of response formats designed to facilitate respondent comprehension and response accuracy.

Throughout, attention is focused on problems specific to the design of questionnaires in international marketing research, such as establishment of equivalence in background or life style variables, and methods of posing questions so as to ensure comprehension by less-educated or illiterate respondents. It is assumed that the reader is already familiar with the basics of questionnaire design, that is, question formulation, sequencing, questionnaire layout, and so on, which are covered in sources such as Oppenheim (1966); Payne (1951); and Sellitz, Wrightsman, and Cook (1976).

QUESTIONNAIRE DESIGN
AND QUESTION FORMULATION

The first step in questionnaire design is to determine what information should be obtained, or what questions asked, and how they should be formulated. Information may be required in relation to three types of variables, namely 1) demographic, background, or respondent identifying characteristics, 2) behavioral or product and brand usage data, and 3) attitudinal, psychographic, and life style variables. It is important to ensure that the questions asked have equivalent meaning and evoke responses that are comparable across different countries and cultural contexts. A decision has to be made about whether open or closed questions are used, and whether direct or indirect questions will provide more accurate response. Furthermore, translation of the questions to ensure comparability in different linguistic and cultural contexts will be required. The response formats should be designed so as to encourage accurate and reliable response and to minimize potential response bias. Each of these issues is next discussed in more detail.

Question Formulation

The issues arising in relation to question formulation differ somewhat, depending on the type of data or content area of the question. As might be anticipated, comparability is much easier to achieve in background and demographic characteristics. It poses certain, though not insurmountable, problems in relation to product- or brand-related data. Most difficulties are, however, likely to be encountered with attitudinal and psychographic measures.

Background and Demographic
Characteristics

As far as background and demographic characteristics are concerned, relatively few problems are likely to be encountered in drawing up questions that generate comparable data from one country to another. Certain categories, such as sex and age, are the same in all countries or cultures, and hence, equivalent questions can be posed. Somewhat greater difficulties may be encountered with regard to other categories such as income, education, and occupation, or the dwelling unit, since these are not always exactly comparable from one culture or country to another.

In addition to the fact that in some countries men may have several wives, marital status can present problems, depending on how the question is put. The growing number of cohabitating couples, especially those who are divorced, creates a particular problem in this regard. Consequently, an ESOMAR (European Society of Opinion and Marketing Research) study group has recommended the use of three major breakdowns to help ensure comparability: 1) married/living together considered as being married; 2) single, and 3) widowed/divorced/separated.

What is included in the category of income may vary from country to country, and incomes vary considerably within countries. The Gallup organization resolves this problem by adopting a method of quartiles within countries, thus giving an indication of relative prosperity, rather than absolute income (Webb, 1982). Similarly, with regard to education, types of schools, colleges, or universities are not always comparable from one country to another. This can be resolved by asking the number of years of schooling, based on the assumption that this provides a more comparable measure than the categories of primary, high school, college, and graduate school, typically used for research in the United States. Alternatively, the age at which full-time education is terminated can be used.

Also certain occupational categories may not be comparable from one country to another. In general, however, the major distinctions or broad categories tend to be the same; that is, farm workers, industrial workers, blue-collar workers, office or white-collar workers, self-employed persons, lower and upper management, and the professions. Alternatively, comparable social hierarchies can be identified.

Another category where differences may occur is in the dwelling unit. In the major Western societies, dwelling units are primarily apartments or multistory houses. In African countries, however, dwelling units may be huts, while in Far Eastern countries many homes are one-story units. Sometimes these have a shop or small business operation in the front room, and one room behind in which the family lives. Often this includes not only the primary family unit—that is, husband and wife and children—but also parents, grandparents, siblings, and their families. Consequently, neither the dwelling unit nor the household unit is comparable.

Behavioral and Product
Market-Related Data

In developing questions related to purchase behavior and consumption or usage behavior, and to specific product markets, two important issues need to be considered. The first concerns the extent to which such behavior is conditioned by a specific sociocultural or economic environment, and hence is likely to vary from one country or cultural context to another. The retail infrastructure is an important moderator of these behavior patterns and can lead to significant differences in shopping patterns. The second issue concerns the extent to which product markets can be defined similarly in all countries and cultural contexts, and hence whether competing and substitute products will be the same.

Since purchase, consumption, and usage behavior form an integral part of day-to-day living and life styles, they may not always be comparable from one sociocultural context to another. Differences may thus occur in terms of the specific processes and behavioral acts that lead up to purchase decisions, as well as in the determinants of these decisions.

Each culture, society, or social group has its own particular conventions, rituals, and practices relating to behavior on social occasions, such as entertaining family or friends on festive occasions—for example, graduation or Christmas. Rules relating to the exchange of gifts, and products, are, for example, governed by local cultural conventions (Levi-Strauss, 1965; Mauss, 1954; Schwartz, 1967). Thus, while in some cultures wine may be an appropriate gift for a dinner host or hostess, in others, flowers are preferred. Similarly, funeral practices differ substantially from one culture to another. The massive use of flowers typical in many Westernized Christian societies is not in keeping with Jewish traditions, and the Jewish culture instead encourages contributions to charity in memory of the deceased (Mitford, 1963). Consequently, questions relating to the gift market, and products positioned as gifts, will need to be tailored to these specific behavior patterns.

Similarly, attitudes with regard to the importance of different types of behavior vary from one culture to another. In the United States, for example, in middle-class society, cleanliness is considered next to godliness. Consequently, considerable importance is attached to activities and product benefits that promote cleanliness, such as household products that keep the house spick-and-span and smelling sweet. In other countries, less importance is attached to cleanliness. In some countries, such as Germany, for example, only products that have an unpleasant smell are considered effective in removing dirt and stains. Consequently, the type of questions, relating to product benefits and attributes, asked in surveys of products such as household cleansing products or personal hygiene, will have to be modified.

The way in which purchases are made may also vary from one country or culture to another. While in the United States, purchasing on credit and the use of credit cards is widely accepted, in other countries, credit may not be available, or attitudes toward credit may be negative. In developing countries, for example, little consumer credit is available. Even in countries where credit is more readily available, as for example the United Kingdom, the tradition of the Protestant Ethic may tend to limit its use. Surveys of financial management practices, and use of credit or debit cards, or of items, such as big ticket items, typically purchased on credit, will therefore need to take such factors into consideration in question formulation.

Significant differences also occur in the retail distribution network. In many developing countries, for example, there are few self-service outlets or supermarkets, except in major cities, and most purchases are made in small Mom-and-Pop-type stores. Even in more developed countries, such as Japan, France, and Italy, importance is attached to freshness in food, and personal service, and consequently, an important proportion of purchases are made through traditional retail outlets. Such shopping patterns affect the formulation of questions relating to the location and timing of purchasing, as well as the importance of investigating salesperson influence on purchase decisions.

In addition to such differences in usage and purchase behavior, relevant product class boundaries or competing and substitute products vary from one country to another. For example, washing machines and other household appliances may be competing with domestic help and professional washerwomen, as well as with other brands of washing machines. Similarly, packaged pasta or macaroni may be competing with pasta made in the home, or alternatively, local specialty stores selling freshly made pasta.

The range and type of items contained in a product class may also vary. For example, the fragrance and perfume markets in Eastern and developing countries are limited to the expensive French perfumes. In Europe, an intermediate level of colognes, fragrances, and perfumes has begun to develop, between the expensive perfumes and the cheap colognes that previously characterized this market. In the United States, on the other hand, a wide range of perfumes and fragrances is available, ranging from the expensive French perfumes to the cheaper local brands. The mass-market colognes obtainable in pint and half-pint sizes in the European market, are, however, typically lacking.

In addition to the lack of comparability with regard to product class boundaries, the competing product set, and the type of products available within a specific product class, differences may be encountered with regard to brand availability and the existence of branding. In some cases, product classes may be dominated by the major international brands, as, for example, cornflakes and other cereal products by Kellogg, tomato juice by Campbell, coffee by Nestlé or Maxwell House, and condensed milk by Nestlé. In other cases, local brands may be much stronger.

Furthermore, in developing countries the markets for consumer packaged goods may not be as well developed. Consequently, products such as canned fruit and vegetables will be competing with fresh fruit and vegetables, while frozen fruit and vegetables are not widely available. Similarly, where there is little fresh cow's milk available, fresh milk is reconstituted from powdered milk or made from soy beans, and is frequently flavored with almond, honey, or chocolate. The major competing products are thus powdered and canned milk.

This implies that in comparing brand preferences and attitudes from one country to another, the use of packaged versus fresh products, and hence the existence of branding, will need to be taken into consideration. In addition, the comparability of brands available in different local markets will need to be studied carefully.

Attitudinal, Psychographic, and Life Style Data

The most significant problems in drawing up questions in multicountry research are likely to occur in relation to attitudinal, psychographic, and life style data. Here, as has already been pointed out, it is not always clear that comparable or equivalent attitudinal or personality constructs—such as aggressiveness, respect for authority, and honor—are relevant in all countries and cultures. Even where similar constructs exist, it is far from clear whether they are most effectively tapped by the same question or attitude statement.

Such considerations underscore the importance of avoiding a pseudo-etic orientation in developing attitudinal and life style measures for cross-national research. Not only should relevant attitudinal and life style constructs and concepts be identified in other countries and cultures, but measures of those specific to an individual country also need to be examined. Similarly, while concepts such as innovativeness, aggressiveness, or sociability may be identified in different countries, different measures may be required.

First, relevant attitudinal or life style constructs need to be identified in each country. These might relate, for example, to specific personality characteristics such as sociability or innovativeness; life style patterns such as leisure behavior, attitudes toward work, or family life; attitudes toward purchasing, use of credit, or patronage of specific types of retail stores; or attitudes toward a specific product market such as detergents, automobiles, or children's clothing. These can be identified by examining qualitative data, through such means as focus groups or protocols.

Previous research examining life style patterns of women in industrialized countries suggests the existence of a common core across different countries (Douglas and Urban, 1977). For women in France, the United States, and the United Kingdom, the basic pattern of life style centers around their acceptance or rejection of the traditional homemaking role. This appears to be closely linked to conservative and traditional moral attitudes. Thus, a common home factor defined in terms of involvement in the homemaking role was identified. Another common element was involvement in social activities outside the home, as well as frustration, lack of optimism, and interest in innovation. Some idiosyncratic constructs were, however, also identified. Interest in intellectual pursuits were only found in the English-speaking countries, while concern with traditional perceptions of male and female roles appeared to be important in France.

Comparisons of the life style profiles of beer drinkers in Canada, the United States, and Mexico also suggested substantial similarities in underlying constructs (Plummer, 1977). In all cases, the heavy beer drinker tended to be self-indulgent, enjoying himself, and liking risk, as well as having a preference for a masculine, male-oriented, and sporting life. Equally, strong similarities were observed in attitudes of subscribers to product testing magazines in the United States and Germany (Anderson and Engledow, 1977). In both cases, similar factors relating to reliability of product testing, degree of rational purchasing, perceived risk, innovation, style-oriented purchasing, the ethics of business, and product satisfaction were identified in factor analyses of sixty variables.

Such similarities, however, do not always emerge. In a comparison of innovators in France and the United States, for example, willingness to try new products and services was found to differ (Green and Langeard, 1977). The United States sample was significantly more willing to try new grocery products and retail services than the French sample. The attitudinal patterns of French women suggested, however, less interest in innovation; hence their response may merely reflect differences in the extent to which innovation is valued in the two countries. Similarly, in a study of ratings of product attributes for soft drinks and toothpaste by student samples in the United States, France, India, and Brazil, significant differences were found in attribute structures for both products (Green, Cunningham, and Cunningham, 1975). In relation to France and India, the United States sample placed greater emphasis on the more subjective and less functional product attributes. The Brazilian sample, however, appeared more concerned with subjective attributes than the United States sample. This, therefore, suggests that in addition to a common core of attributes to provide a basis for comparison, different types of product attributes may need to be emphasized when conducting research in different countries.

The specific items that best tap various attitudinal constructs need to be identified. Yet, even where similar constructs are identified, the specific items making up these constructs may not always be identical. In some cases, the same constructs may be measured by somewhat different items. Thus, for example, sociability may be measured in the United States by a statement such as

"I like to think I'm a bit of a swinger."

While in France this might be measured by

"I do more things socially than most of my friends."

Similarly, in a comparison of the heavy beer drinkers, preference for a male-oriented world and a physical existence was defined in the United States in terms of liking to do better than average in a fist fight, wanting to be a professional football player, thinking that men should not do the dishes, and reading the sports page. In Canada, it was defined in terms of liking to hunt and fish, enjoying war stories and science fiction, and being low in agreement with the women's lib movement. In Mexico, it was related to liking to go to sports events; thinking men were more intelligent than women; liking bull fights, hunting, and fishing; and being a girl watcher (Plummer, 1977). The degree of commonality may also depend on the specific countries or cultures and on the nature of the topic. Relatively similar countries, such as the industrialized Western nations, are likely to have more commonality than Westernized nations have with developing countries. Allowance should, however, always be made for the identification of country- or culture-unique concepts, and also idiosyncratic measures of these, as well as concepts and measures developed in other countries (Wind and Douglas, 1982).

Type of Question

Another issue to be considered is the form in which questions are asked. These may, for example, be closed or open-ended questions. Closed questions require the respondent to reply according to a specific format, and possible responses are prespecified. Open-ended questions, on the other hand, allow the respondent freedom to provide his or her preferred response. Similarly, questions may be posed directly, or alternatively, indirectly so that the purpose of the question is disguised from the respondent.

Open-Ended Versus Closed Questions

An important argument in favor of the use of closed questions is that analysis is considerably facilitated. Responses can be precoded and keypunched directly from questionnaires. On the other hand, they do require that the researcher can specify in advance all relevant response categories. This may not always be the case in cross-national research, if the researcher lacks experience with purchasing behavior or relevant determinants of response in another country or cultural context.

Use of open-ended questions may thus be desirable in a number of situations. Since they do not impose any structure or response categories, open-ended questions avoid the imposition of cultural bias by the researcher. Furthermore, they do not require familiarity with all the respondents' possible responses. On the other hand, they do entail the somewhat tedious process of establishing coding schemes for these responses, and tabulating them once the data have been collected.

In addition, differences in levels of literacy may affect the appropriateness of using open-ended questions as opposed to closed questions. Since open-ended questions require the respondent to respond in his or her own terms, they also require a moderate level of sophistication and comprehension of the topic on the part of the respondent; otherwise responses will not be meaningful. Open-ended questions will, therefore, have to be used with care in cross-cultural and cross-national research in order to ensure that bias does not occur as a result of differences in levels of education.

Open-ended questions are often appropriate in exploratory research, where the primary objective is to identify relevant dimensions, concepts, or terminology associated with the problem studied. They might, for example, be used to elicit content domains relating to products, attitudes toward products, or advertising stimuli, or the associations evoked by such stimuli. In the case of products such as beverages, respondents might be asked to list all the items they perceive as beverages, and the most frequently occurring responses could be examined in each country. Similarly, in eliciting attitudes toward products or advertising stimuli, subjects could be asked to indicate adjectives, words, or phrases that best describe or characterize stimuli such as packages or advertisements. This might also be done using different scenarios, such as for family consumption, when entertaining, and so on.

Direct Versus Indirect Questions

Another consideration is whether direct or indirect questions are utilized. Direct questions avoid any ambiguity concerning question content and meaning. On the other hand, respondents may be reluctant to answer certain types of questions. Similarly, they may tend to provide responses perceived as socially desirable or those that they feel are desired by the interviewer.

Use of indirect questions may aid in bypassing such biases. In this case, rather than being directly stated, the question is posed in an indirect form. Respondents might, for example, be asked to indicate rather than their own preferences, those they would anticipate from the majority of respondents, neighbors, or other relevant reference groups. Alternatively, they might be presented with different examples of purchase decisions, and asked which most closely corresponded to their own. To the extent that respondents may perceive the intent behind such questions, these may not be wholly successful.

Irrespective of the specific way in which questions are formulated, it is important to ensure that they are adequately pretested on an appropriate sample before being administered. While pretesting is important in domestic research, it is crucial in international markets, due to the number of problems that may be encountered in developing questions for international research. Successive iterations are thus likely to be required in order to ensure that sources of response bias are minimized and that respondents fully comprehend questions, so that accurate response and high item-response rates will be obtained.

Use of Nonverbal Stimuli

Another important consideration in instrument design is the extent to which nonverbal, as opposed to verbal, stimuli are utilized in order to facilitate respondent comprehension. Particularly where research is conducted in countries or cultures with high levels of illiteracy, as for example, Africa and the Far

East, it is often desirable to use nonverbal stimuli such as show cards. Questionnaires can be administered orally by an interviewer, but respondent comprehension will be facilitated if pictures of products or concepts, or test packs are provided.

Various types of nonverbal stimuli may be used in conjunction with questionnaires, including show cards, product samples, or pictures. It should be noted that nonverbal stimuli are often used in other data collection techniques, as, for example, EPSYs or projective techniques. The main focus here is, however, on their use in surveys in order to ensure that respondents understand verbal questions, relevant products, and product concepts.

Show cards such as that shown in Figure 7.1 can, for example, be used to assist in answering product usage questions. This particular set was designed to

FIGURE 7.1 Interview show card used in consumer survey in South Africa[a] (assist to answer question "What Is Your Sewing Machine Used For?")

[a] This freehand style of drawing proved to have a good appeal in interviews conducted in the developing countries.

Source: The Singer Company, New York. Reprinted by permission.

aid consumers in understanding the different types of uses that might be made of a sewing machine. Pictures of products, as in the show card in Figure 7.2, can also be used. These ensure that the respondent understands the particular product covered in the survey. These may be particularly useful in rural areas when it is not certain whether the respondent has been exposed to the product and knows what it looks like or what functions it performs. In general, however, these need to be simple, so that respondents can understand them easily. In some countries, as for example, the Far East, difficulties may be encountered in the production of these cards. The quality of the typing, the typeface, and the printing may be poor.

Product samples can also be shown to respondents. A drawback of this approach is that respondents tend to become irritated if the samples are removed for the next interview. Consequently, it is wise to be able to leave a free sample or other reward (Corder, 1978). Alternatively, sketches of the proposed product or service may help the respondent to grasp the concept.

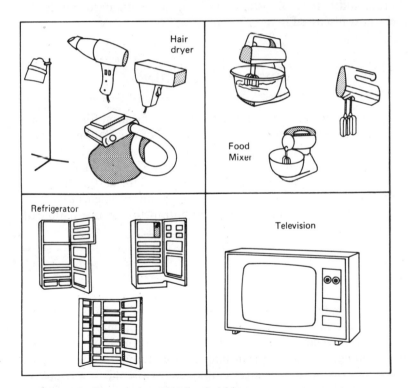

FIGURE 7.2   Show cards used in South Africa

Source: C. K. Corder, ''Problems and Pitfalls in Conducting Marketing Research in Africa,'' in Betsy Gelb (ed.), *Marketing Expansion in a Shrinking World*, Proceedings of American Marketing Association Business Conference. (Chicago: American Marketing Association, 1978), pp. 86–90.

Even where literacy levels are high, it may be desirable to use nonverbal stimuli to complement verbal stimuli, to provide a check on instrument equivalence and potential biases from questionnaire translation and adaptation to different linguistic and cultural contexts. The sample could then be split, and half the respondents asked questions without the nonverbal stimuli, and the other half could be shown the stimuli. The results obtained from the two halves could then be compared to test for potential bias. It should be noted in this context that pictorial stimuli are not culture-free, as perceptual associations and interpretation differ from country to country or culture to culture. However, the types of biases will differ from those occurring in a verbal instrument, and hence comparison of the two procedures will indicate whether there is a need for further testing and instrument development.

Once the basic form of the instruments to be used in the survey has been designed, the next step is to translate these so as to ensure comprehension by respondents, and to avoid errors of miscommunication. The issues involved in translating verbal and nonverbal instruments, and some standard translation procedures, are next discussed in more detail.

INSTRUMENT TRANSLATION

Both verbal and nonverbal instruments require translation for use in different linguistic and cultural contexts. While the need for translation of verbal instruments is widely recognized, and examples of errors arising from mistranslation abound, the need for translation of nonverbal stimuli is less well recognized. It is, nonetheless, important to realize that pictorial stimuli are not pan-cultural and can involve the same miscommunication problems that arise in relation to verbal stimuli. Consequently, attention to the translation of nonverbal as well as verbal instruments will be required.

Verbal Translation

Although little documentation is available (Green and White, 1976), one may suspect that in the case of verbal instruments, the procedure most commonly used in international marketing research is that of direct translation. Following this procedure, a bilingual translator translates the questionnaire directly from a base language into the other languages employed. While this is a relatively rapid and low-cost procedure, it can generate a pseudo-etic bias and result in a number of errors. This is especially likely to occur if the translator is not absolutely fluent in both languages, and familiar with idiomatic expressions and colloquialisms. Among the widely quoted errors of this type are, for example, the translation into French of a "full" airplane as a "pregnant" airplane, and in German, of "Body by Fisher" as "Corpse by Fisher" (Ricks, Fu and Arpan, 1974).

In order to avoid such errors, a procedure widely advocated in the social sciences is that of "back-translation" (Brislin, 1970; Sinaiko, 1963; Werner and Campbell, 1970). A questionnaire is translated from the initial or base language by a bilingual who is a native speaker of the language into which the translation is to be made. This version is then retranslated back into the original language by a bilingual who is a native speaker of the initial language.

Although useful in identifying translation errors and the competency of a translator, back-translation is not always totally effective (Brislin, 1970). Bilinguals often develop a particular language structure and usage. As a result, they do not translate into the idiom commonly used by the mass of the population and tend to use language that is difficult for the population being studied to comprehend.

Bilinguals also tend to have a stock set of rules for translating nonequivalent phrases—for example, "amigo" as "friend"—that may not be caught in the back-translation. Knowing both languages, they may be able to make sense out of poor translation, and carry over language structures and grammar from one language to the other. It has also been found that bilinguals have different personalities in different languages, reflecting the dominant value system or personality traits of the relevant country (Ervin, 1964). This may therefore influence the extent to which their translations are equivalent.

In addition, back-translation starts with the assumption of a base questionnaire or language, and hence a "pseudo-etic" approach. This can be eliminated by a "decentering" process in which successive iterations of translation and retranslation are undertaken (Triandis, 1972; Werner and Campbell, 1970). The original questionnaire is thus modified so that the terminology is equally comprehensive and equivalent in all language contexts, and the dominance of one language structure eliminated. Such a procedure is, however, likely to be somewhat time-consuming and tedious.

Back-translation also assumes the existence of equivalent terms and concepts in all languages, and that a totally loyal translation is required. This may not always be the case. The terms "fair play" and "lonesomeness" are difficult to render in German (Brislin, Lonner, and Thorndike, 1973). Equally, exact equivalents of "husband" and "duty" do not exist in Japanese. Such procedures also imply that a direct and loyal translation may not be possible or appropriate. In some instances, and particularly for the more idiomatic phraseology often used in various types of marketing research such as life style, it may be more desirable to translate into equivalent colloquial phrases. For example, the statement "husbands, more than wives, are deserving of a night out" may best be translated by different phrases in each language.

Such considerations suggest that the use of "parallel" translation may be preferable (Frey, 1970). A committee of translators conversant with at least two of the languages employed, can compare the various translated questionnaires.

The adequacy of alternative versions can then be discussed until agreement is reached on a final version. This technique has been criticized on the grounds that there is no formal control over translations, and personalities may tend to dominate. It appears nonetheless useful in the international marketing research context, especially where a freer and less exact translation is required. Members of local research organizations or marketing subsidiaries can, for example, be used to form the committee. In countries that have multilanguage subgroups, such as Belgium, India, Canada, and South Africa, separate versions of the questionnaire or research instrument will need to be developed. Even if the linguistic subgroup can understand another language, as is, for example, often the case in more developed countries such as Belgium or Canada, translation into the local idiom will enhance willingness to respond and to provide complete and accurate answers.

Irrespective of the specific translation procedure utilized, it is important to verify the quality of the translation and to assess the equivalence of the various versions, prior to use in the field. A difficulty in this regard is that there is no ultimate criterion of translation quality. Four possible means of evaluation have, however, been suggested: 1) evaluation by monolinguals, based on clarity and comprehension, 2) evaluation by bilinguals based on possible meaning errors, 3) testing of subjects' ability to answer questions about the content matter or to perform tasks indicated in the questionnaire, and 4) testing of both original and translated versions on bilingual subjects. The last two procedures are generally considered the most important insofar as a prime objective is that both the original and translated questionnaires elicit the same pattern of response.

Translation of Nonverbal Stimuli

In addition to translating verbal instruments, it is important to recognize that nonverbal instruments and stimuli will require translation, or testing for miscommunication or interpretation in different countries and cultural contexts. This can arise as a result of differences in the interpretation of perceptual cues in different countries and cultural contexts, and the associations evoked by visual phenomena and role models.

African blacks do not always, for example, correctly interpret Western pictorial cues, such as conventions for the representation of three dimensions or use of hatched lines. This may give rise to some difficulties in the use of certain Western conventions in drawing pictures and scenes. The advertisement shown in Figure 7.3 was, for example, incorrectly interpreted as depicting the woman carrying a bottle on her head, rather than a middle-class couple enjoying a drink, with a bottle superimposed on the picture. The use of line drawings such as those shown in Figure 7.1 may thus be desirable, since they do not to the same extent project specific cultural role models.

FIGURE 7.3 Advertisement tested in South Africa

Source: A. P. van der Reis, *Some aspects of the acceptability of particular photographic models to the Bantu.* Peoria: Bureau of Market Research, University of South Africa, 1972.

Once translated, field testing of data collection instruments is necessary in order to identify any final problems. Many examples can be cited where a supposedly good translation of an instrument had to be revised as a result of a field test. This further underlines the desirability of using care in translation, to ensure that errors not found in one stage are ironed out in another. Where both verbal and nonverbal instruments are used, comparison of results obtained with each method can provide a check on overall results.

POTENTIAL SOURCES OF BIAS
IN SURVEY RESEARCH

No matter how carefully the instruments have been designed and how well they have been translated so as to avoid potential problems of miscommunication, some difficulties may arise due to the inherent sources of bias in cross-national surveys. In international, as in the case of domestic, marketing research, major sources of bias arise from the respondent, the nature of the topic, and the interviewer-respondent interaction. More specifically, seven major types of bias of these kinds can be identified, namely those arising from 1) a respondent's desire to be socially acquiescent, 2) the desire to provide the socially acceptable response, 3) the tendency for responses to be influenced by certain underlying cultural traits, 4) specific respondent characteristics, 5) the nature of the topic being studied, 6) extreme response style and yea-saying/nay-saying biases, and 7) tendencies not to respond to specific items in the questionnaire.

Social Acquiescence or Courtesy Bias

The desire to be socially acquiescent, and to provide the response that may be felt to be desired by the interviewer, is particularly prevalent in certain countries and certain cultures. This type of bias appears particularly common in Asia, everywhere from Japan to Turkey (Jones, 1963; Mitchell, 1965), where cultural values imply that it is an obligation for the respondent to see that the interviewer is not distressed, disappointed, or offended in any way. At the extreme, this can lead to a tendency to agree to any assertion, irrespective of the respondent's actual position. In addition, affirmative responses might be given where the respondent does not understand the question but does not want to be impolite or display ignorance by not responding.

Triandis and Triandis (1962) found Greek subjects to show more acquiescence than United States subjects. In Chile acquiescence biases have been found to be more common among less-educated respondents, suggesting that there may also be a relationship between tendencies toward acquiescence and socioeconomic status.

Some of the effects of this bias can be reduced by concealing sponsorship of the study and by more effective training of interviewers. More careful wording of questions in order to disguise the intent and to render them more neutral may also be desirable.

Social Desirability Bias

Another source of bias closely related to the first is the social desirability of items or questions in a given cultural or social context (Gordon, 1968; Berrien, 1968; Frey, 1970; Werner and Campbell, 1970). Replies may be intended not only to please the interviewer, but also to reflect the thing "done" in the respondent's culture. For example, a respondent may say that he votes or purchases a product regularly, whether or not this is the case. This bias is particularly marked among better-educated urban respondents, who will tend to give answers reflecting their greater sophistication and knowledge as to what they *should* answer, rather than their genuine beliefs.

Such biases can be reduced by facilitating the ease of providing a socially nonacceptable response. Questions might be prefaced with phrases such as, "Some people feel this way, some people feel that way. How do you feel?" Questions can also be matched in terms of equally socially desirable responses. Respondents are then requested to respond to items of equal desirability. For example, a number of items to measure social responsibility might be devised, such as

"I always help old ladies across the street."
"I stop to help people if they are stranded."
"I volunteer to collect money for an organization."

Respondents can then be required to choose the item that they think best describes themselves. Improved interviewer training, to eliminate the impression that certain items are perceived as socially desirable, can also aid considerably in this regard.

Topic Bias

Differences also arise with regard to topics that are socially sensitive in different national and cultural contexts. Willingness to respond to questions such as level of income, or topics such as sex or alcoholism, vary from one country or culture to another. In the Scandinavian countries, for example, respondents are considerably more willing to admit to overdrinking than in Latin countries (Lovell, 1973). In India, sex tends to be a taboo topic.

This suggests the need to identify what topics are socially sensitive in each country and cultural context. Measures to reduce bias from this source, such as collecting observational data or using improved interviewer probing techniques, can also be introduced.

Cultural Trait Bias

Yet another source of bias is the tendency for certain dominant cultural traits to affect the nature of response. The Japanese are, for example, more humble, which leads them to undervalue assets or property, while the Middle Eastern respondent is more prone to exaggerate (Mitchell, 1965). Similarly, to the extent that the Irish are more ebullient than the English, one might expect them to tend to give more affirmative responses.

Respondent Characteristics

In general, available evidence suggests that response biases are related to similar respondent characteristics in different countries and cultures. Sex, age, and education all appear to be factors that frequently generate response bias. Yea-saying and nay-saying biases have, for example, been found, as in the United States, to be stronger among women, the less educated, and respondents of lower socioeconomic status, in other countries (Landsberger and Saavedra, 1967). Item nonresponse has been found to be related to similar factors, namely sex, age, and education (Douglas and Shoemaker, 1981).

This suggests that the distribution of different national samples on variables such as sex, income, and education will need to be examined to identify the extent to which such factors are likely to affect the comparability of results. Apparent differences may thus reflect the impact of sample characteristics rather than true national or cultural differences.

Response Style

Differences in response style and tendencies to use extreme points on verbal rating scales, as well as yea-saying and nay-saying biases, have also been found to differ from country to country. This evidence is, however, somewhat sporadic, and, at least to the authors' knowledge, no comprehensive studies of response styles have been undertaken.

Comparison of the use of scale positions among United States and Korean college students (Chun, Campbell, and Hao, 1974) found evidence of extreme response bias among United States respondents. Similar results were found in a study of extreme checking style among Greek and United States subjects (Triandis and Triandis, 1962), and between a Japanese and a United States sample (Zax and Takahashi, 1967). In both cases United States subjects exhibited greater tendencies toward extreme response style than non–United States subjects. German respondents have also been found to exhibit more extreme response style than English respondents.

Another study (Crosby, 1969), however, noting a similar tendency to more affirmative response among French Canadians than English Canadians, examined this by applying other scaling procedures and found it to be in fact a true reflection of attitudes. Ratings by the two groups (a total of 7,000 respondents) of ten desserts were compared on four bipolar and three unipolar scales. Ratings of the French respondents were consistently higher than the English respondents on the unipolar scales, but little difference was observed on the bipolar scales. This suggested either that unipolar scales were biased measures, or alternatively, that bipolar scales were less discriminating. This was tested by using two unipolar and one bipolar measure to evaluate judgments about an abstract, culturally neutral task, that is, the position of a cross-mark relative to a bullseye. Here, no differences were observed between the two groups on any of the scales. It was, therefore, concluded that French attitudes were in fact more positive to desserts, and did not reflect different response biases.

Another form of response bias is the yea-saying, nay-saying bias. This differs from extreme response bias in that yea-saying represents a tendency among some subjects, notably those with enthusiastic, uncritical personalities, to give high ratings to objects that impress them favorably (Wells, 1961). They do not always rate favorably, and will also overreact negatively if they perceive a stimulus as negative. Nay-sayers, on the other hand, are cautious and underexpressive and are more likely to give low ratings.

If tendencies toward yea-saying are stronger in some cultures than in others, this will distort cross-national comparisons. Results in cultures with stronger yea-saying biases will tend to be inflated, (if, as is generally the case, ratings are favorable). The reverse will occur if ratings are negative, though the effect will not be as marked. Chinese in Malaysia, have, for example, been found to exhibit greater response biases than the Indian population (Mitchell, 1965). Evidence of such response bias has also been found among French women (Douglas and LeMaire, 1974). Here, there was a systematic tendency to use more affirmative positions on seven-point Likert scales, and to select more positive statements on forced-choice scales for various life style measures.

Use of correlational techniques to control for extreme response bias has been advocated, by assessing the correlation of responses to similar items (Triandis, 1972). It has, however, been pointed out that correlational techniques are themselves affected by extreme response style. A more detailed statistical analysis, examining response to both positive and negative items, and correcting for the range, thus appears desirable (Chun, Campbell, and Hao, 1974). Alternatively, data can be normalized or ipsatized. These techniques are discussed in relation to data analysis (Chapter 9), and hence are not examined further here.

Use of multiple scaling devices, including unipolar, bipolar, and Likert scales, may be desirable in order to check for the existence of such biases. In addition, where scales equivalent to the Crowne-Marlowe measure (Crowne and Marlowe, 1964)—or other similar scales measuring social desirability, adapted to the specific cultural environment—are available, these should also be included.

Item Nonresponse

Differences in rates of nonresponse to items within the questionnaire are another important source of potential bias in cross-national surveys. Cultures may vary with regard to their loquacity (Brislin, Lonner, and Thorndike, 1973; Mitchell, 1965); their willingness to admit ignorance (Sicinski, 1970); and their interest, involvement, and information relating to a particular topic. All such factors may affect rates of nonresponse to different questionnaire items.

Members of some cultures are willing to be interviewed and to respond to all types of questions. Others may exhibit greater reticence, and hence have higher rates of nonresponse (Brislin, Lonner, and Thorndike, 1973). In Malaysia, the Chinese have been found to be more reticent than Malaysians or Indians in answering questions, giving a higher proportion of "no" or "don't know" answers and fewer responses to open-ended questions (Mitchell, 1965). Similarly, Triandis (1972) found United States subjects more likely than Greek subjects to give "don't know" answers, and to place fewer checkmarks in responding to checklists.

Willingness to respond to different types of questions, such as questions relating to income or age, has also been found to vary from country to country. A recent study of nonresponse to different items in a public opinion survey in eight European countries (Douglas and Shoemaker, 1981) found nonresponse to questions about income to be higher in the United Kingdom and Ireland, than in other EEC countries. Sensitivity, and hence willingness to respond to political questions, appeared to be highest in Germany and Italy. This is consistent with the findings of the classic Almond and Verba (1965) study, which found that 35 percent of the Italian population refused to indicate party allegiance, as compared with 1 percent in the United States.

Willingness to admit ignorance to a number of factual questions relating to international affairs has also been found to differ in three countries (Sicinski, 1970). Norwegians were more inclined than the French or Poles to give wrong answers to questions rather than admit ignorance. Consequently, this resulted in inflated answers for Norwegians, since a certain proportion of answers were correct purely on the basis of chance.

The types of questions in relation to which rates of response are highest tend to be the same from country to country. As might be expected, rates of nonresponse are invariably lowest with regard to background characteristics, such as sex or education; moderate with regard to behavioral variables; and highest in relation to complex attitudinal and opinion questions (Douglas and Shoemaker, 1981; Schreiber, 1975–76).

The impact of item nonresponse in international marketing research depends in large measure on the extent to which different factors underlie nonresponse in different countries or cultures. Differences in rates of nonresponse to different items can be examined by comparing rates for various items across countries. Characteristics of nonrespondents to these items can then be compared with those of the overall sample, to check for any particular characteristics. If, as in the Sicinski study, different factors underlie nonresponse in different countries, and furthermore, respondents and nonrespondents differ with regard to certain characteristics, data will not be comparable, since certain segments or opinion categories will be under-represented or overrepresented in a given country (Sicinski, 1970).

Evidence with regard to this issue is somewhat scanty. The Sicinski study found differences. Another study examining demographic and other characteristics underlying item nonresponse in eight European countries suggests that these are similar to those found in the United States (Douglas and Shoemaker, 1981). In the United States, item nonresponse appears to be related to characteristics such as sex, age, education, and income (Craig and McCann, 1978; Ferber, 1956; Francis and Busch, 1975; Gergen and Back, 1966; Glenn, 1969), as also interest and involvement in a topic (Bogart, 1967; Donald, 1960; Ferber, 1956). In the European study, age and income were less significant than in comparable United States studies, though this may in part be a reflection of the type of data examined, which related predominantly to attitudes to political and economic issues. In general, however, the impact of such factors does not appear to be of major consequence.

A number of strategies may be used to reduce item nonresponse. First, elimination of threatening, monotonous, and ambiguous items will reduce nonresponse. Secondly, response can be increased by improved formulation of items in a manner that engages or involves the respondent (Elder, 1976). On the other hand, care needs to be exercised to ensure, particularly where closed questions are employed, that opinions are not elicited where they do not exist (Mitchell, 1965).

SCALES AND RESPONSE FORMAT

While it is generally recognized that instruments need to be designed to eliminate bias due to the content and mode of presentation to the respondent, there is generally less appreciation or sensitivity to biases that may arise from the specific response format or type of scale used to record response. Low educational or literacy levels in some countries are an important factor to consider in this regard, since they affect the type of scales or response formats that can be used. In designing the way in which responses are recorded, a key issue is whether the same type of response format or scale can be used in all countries and cultures, and whether it is free of cultural bias. Alternatively, some response formats or scales may be subject to bias in certain countries and cultures, and hence, use of different response formats or scales in each context may be more effective.

Pan-Cultural Scales

One type of scale that is said to be pan-cultural is the semantic differential (Osgood, May, and Miron, 1975). This has been extensively tested in a number of countries, where consistently similar results have been obtained in terms of the concepts or dimensions that are used to evaluate stimuli—either objects or subjects—and account for a major proportion of the variation in response.

The semantic differential is a bipolar scale used to rate objects or other items. As shown in Figure 7.4, each end of the scale is designated by adjectives opposite in meaning, such as inexpensive-expensive, reliable-unreliable, or exclusive-common. A five- or seven-point scale is ordinarily used with numbers assigned to each position on the scale. These scales are then submitted to a factor analysis in order to identify common underlying dimensions. This approach has been applied to an extensive range of adjectives, thus permitting the identification of a number of bipolar dimensions that are commonly used to evaluate objects.

This research has also been extended to numerous other countries (Osgood, May, and Miron, 1975), again covering a wide range of different adjectives. In this research, three dominant factors have consistently emerged as common factors in which concepts are evaluated in all cultures and countries. These are an *evaluative* factor, consisting of a good-bad dimension; a *potency* factor, based on a strong-weak dimension; and an *activity* factor, based on a fast-slow dimension. Typically, these three factors account for between 50 and 60 percent of concept meaning, and the evaluative factor is always the most significant.

The semantic differential has thus been argued to be a powerful tool for capturing "affective" meaning and identifying salient dimensions on which items can be evaluated. In addition, the use of several scales to tap a specific dimension is felt to provide evidence that the dimension is in fact widely tapped, and helps to sharpen the meaning of different words and phrases.

Similarly, where research in other disciplines—such as cognitive psychology on concepts such as man, sky, and future—has been conducted, a substantial degree of commonality across cultures has been found. The factors or evaluative dimensions used are, however, somewhat general, and primarily indicate "affect," rather than the cognitive or conative dimensions that are of primary interest in consumer research. In marketing surveys, the concepts examined are more specific and concrete, including, for example, products,

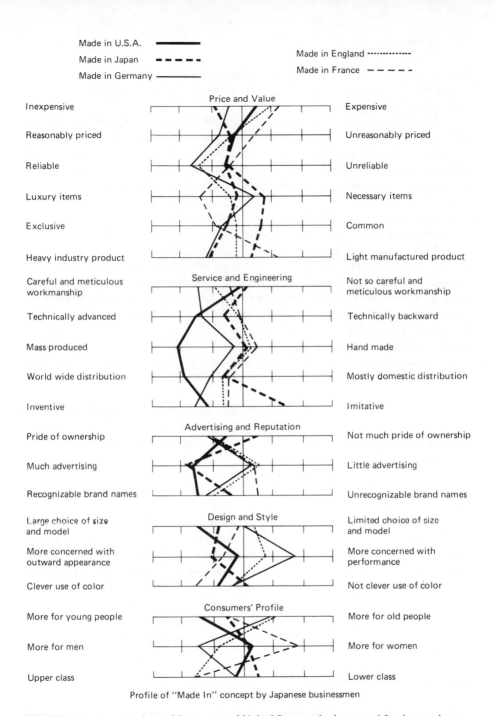

Made in U.S.A. ▬▬▬▬

Made in Japan ▬ ▬ ▬ ▬

Made in Germany ▬▬▬▬▬

Made in England ··············

Made in France ▬ ▬ ▬ ▬ ▬

Price and Value

Inexpensive		Expensive
Reasonably priced		Unreasonably priced
Reliable		Unreliable
Luxury items		Necessary items
Exclusive		Common
Heavy industry product		Light manufactured product

Service and Engineering

Careful and meticulous workmanship		Not so careful and meticulous workmanship
Technically advanced		Technically backward
Mass produced		Hand made
World wide distribution		Mostly domestic distribution
Inventive		Imitative

Advertising and Reputation

Pride of ownership		Not much pride of ownership
Much advertising		Little advertising
Recognizable brand names		Unrecognizable brand names

Design and Style

Large choice of size and model		Limited choice of size and model
More concerned with outward appearance		More concerned with performance
Clever use of color		Not clever use of color

Consumers' Profile

More for young people		More for old people
More for men		More for women
Upper class		Lower class

Profile of "Made In" concept by Japanese businessmen

FIGURE 7.4 A comparison of Japanese and United States attitudes toward foreign products

Source: Akira Nagashima, "A Comparison of Japanese and U.S. Attitudes Toward Foreign Products," *Journal of Marketing,* 34 (January 1970), 68–74. (Published by the American Marketing Association.)

brands, packages, advertising copy, broadcast commercials, or print advertisements. Consequently, there is greater disparity in these stimuli and in their
evaluation from one country to another.

In addition, stimuli are typically evaluated on a variety of different attributes as well as purely on an affective dimension. In a product test, products
might be evaluated, for example, on intentions to purchase; or on salient product features such as distinctiveness, durability, styling or color, functionality,
or ease of use; fit with existing products; or suitability for different occasions,
such as current usage or special occasions; as well as overall preference. Appropriate rating scales that are applicable in all countries or cultures being investigated will thus need to be developed.

This suggests the need for work in developing detailed rating scales for use
in cross-national research. To date, relatively little work, at least in relation to
the types of scales commonly used in the United States, appears to have been
done. One exception is the adaptation of the Myers and Warner Colloquial Instrument and formal rating scale for use in France (Angelmar and Pras, 1978).
The adjectives used in these scales were translated and tested to ensure similar
scaled values and homogeneity in France. Similar adaptations and scale
development, as well as testing of verbal rating scales developed in the United
States, should be undertaken before they are used in other countries or
linguistic contexts.

An alternative approach, rather than attempting to develop scales or
rating devices that are pan-cultural, or as far as possible culture-free, is to apply
techniques that use as a base referent, a self-defined cultural norm. This type
of approach is likely to be particularly useful in evaluating attitudinal positions
where evidence exists to suggest that these are defined relative to the dominant
cultural norm. This has, for example, been found in relation to attitudes to
female and marital roles (Douglas and Urban, 1977; Rodman, 1967).

One such technique is Cantril's self-anchoring scale (Cantril, 1965). This
requires an individual to indicate his or her own anchor point and position
relative to a culture-specific stimulus set. In the research conducted by Cantril,
concerns of different kinds were studied. The same technique could, however,
be adapted to study attitudes toward advertising, toward female roles, social
activities, and so on. While this approach eliminates cultural differences, it has
also been pointed out that it may eliminate differences in adaptation relative to
the cultural norm (Triandis, 1972). It is thus somewhat questionable as to
whether this provides a true (culture-free) instrument.

Response Format

In designing response scales for use in different environmental and cultural
contexts, an important issue is whether response formats, and particularly their
calibration, need to be adapted for specific countries and cultures. It has, for
example, been argued that response procedures and scales will need to be

adapted to specific cultural and educational traditions. Thus, for example, in France a twenty-point scale is commonly used to rate performance in primary and secondary schools. Consequently, it has been suggested that such a scale should be used in marketing research. Such scales are, however, somewhat cumbersome. Furthermore, existing studies suggest that little bias will be introduced by use of five- or seven-point rating scales common in United States research (Douglas and Lemaire, 1974).

In general, verbal rating scales appear to be the most effective, even among less-educated respondents. Even illiterate respondents are accustomed to expressing their feelings in words. Verbal rating scales are familiar and easily grasped by respondents. These scales are quick to administer and require little additional explanation. Some confusion may, however, arise with interpretation of ends of the scale; that is, *1* may be considered as best rather than the lowest point on the scale, regardless of how it is scaled. Also, difficulties can occur in determining equivalents in different languages and, or, countries of verbal descriptors for the scale (Angelmar and Pras, 1978).

Such problems suggest that the use of numerical rating scales (that is, pick x points out of . . .) might be desirable. However, less-educated respondents also appear to have difficulty with such scales. In particular, they have difficulty in identifying the midpoint of the scale as well as the meaning of in-between marks, and again, *1* can be interpreted as being first. In addition, some time is required to explain the concept to less-educated consumers.

This suggests that in countries with low literacy levels, some ingenuity will be required in developing devices to record response. While interviewers can pose questions and record categorical responses concerning behavior and background characteristics, some difficulties can arise in obtaining response to attitudinal questions, where indication of position on a scale by the respondent is required.

Among respondents with low levels of education, however, an appropriate procedure may be to develop pictorial representation stimuli. In the case of life style, pictures of different life style segments or behaviors may be developed (Burke and others, 1976). Respondents are then asked to indicate how similar they perceive such subjects to be to their own life styles. These can be used either to assess the importance of different life style segments in different countries, or alternatively, to develop measures of life style within different behavioral or attitudinal segments or in concept testing.

Another device is the Funny Faces scale. Some research organizations make use of this with less-educated respondents in developing countries. This has been found to be effective among blacks in South Africa (Corder, 1978). The scale is shown in Figure 7.5. It consists of five positions, ranging from very happy to very unhappy. Respondents are shown a concept, or read an attitudinal statement, and asked to indicate their degree of agreement or interest by indicating the corresponding position on this scale. Thus, for example, strong interest would correspond to being very happy.

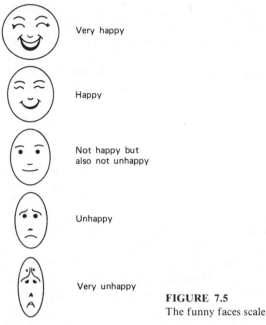

Very happy

Happy

Not happy but
also not unhappy

Unhappy

Very unhappy

FIGURE 7.5
The funny faces scale

Source: C. K. Corder, "Problems and Pitfalls in Conducting Marketing Research in Africa," in Betsy Gelb (ed.),
Marketing Expansion in a Shrinking World, Proceedings
of American Marketing Association Business Conference.
(Chicago: AMA, 1978) pp. 86–90.

Recent research in South Africa (van der Reis, 1981) suggests, however, that some problems may be encountered with the use of such rating scales. In particular, they may be somewhat ineffective in situations where 1) many attributes have to be rated; 2) a scale suitable for a somewhat diverse population, including those with relatively little education, is desired; or 3) a scale that is practical and quick to administer in the field is needed. In some instances, the use of Western pictorial conventions in the Smiling Faces scale appears to be difficult for less-educated respondents to comprehend. The Smiling Faces scale was also found to arouse negative reactions among better-educated respondents, who considered the scale childish and insulting to their intelligence.

Graphic rating scales, that is, continuous line scales, also cause difficulty. Respondents with low levels of education often cannot conceptualize a continuous scale from extreme satisfaction to extreme dissatisfaction, which can be divided into equal intervals. Consequently, the interviewer must spend considerable time explaining the scale. This increases the time required to administer the questionnaire and, hence, may limit its usefulness.

Steps of a ladder can also be used as a scaling device (Cantril, 1965). Respondents are then shown a sketch of a ladder and asked to indicate their position in reponse to a given question, with respect to steps on the ladder. In countries or cultures where ladders are not known, other items can be substituted. For example, for Zulus, a picture of a mountain with successive terraces was substituted, representing the different stages or steps in climbing the mountain. The purpose was, thus, to develop a more familiar set of alternatives for the respondent.

In designing a response format, it is of prime importance to devise a format that the respondent can comprehend and that will enable him or her to respond accurately. As in relation to other aspects of research design, it is important to consider comparability across different national and cultural contexts, but accuracy is of paramount importance.

SUMMARY

In designing instruments for use in survey research, the key issue is often the development of a questionnaire that is clear, easily comprehensible, and easy to administer. Questions need to be formulated so as to obtain the desired information from respondents and to avoid miscommunication between the researcher and the respondent. In multicountry research, the extent to which questions are formulated in precisely the same terms needs to be considered. This is more likely to be feasible in relation to questions relating to demographic and other background characteristics, than for behavioral or product market data. Greatest difficulty is likely to occur in relation to attitudinal and psychographic data. The way in which the question is posed, that is, open-ended versus closed and direct versus indirect formulations, has also to be considered.

Respondent comprehension is likely to be increased considerably by the use of nonverbal stimuli such as show cards, pictures, and photos. These can also be used to provide a check on bias arising from miscomprehension of verbal questions. It is, however, important to note that nonverbal stimuli as well as questionnaires will require translation into the relevant perceptual idiom to avoid misinterpretation.

Instruments need also to be designed to minimize potential sources of bias in international surveys. This can arise first as a result of the questionnaire itself and the topic covered. Secondly, it can arise from the interaction between the interviewer and the interviewee. Thirdly, it can arise from the characteristics of the respondent, such as his or her response style or socioeconomic and demographic origins.

Finally, the format in which the response is obtained needs to be carefully considered. Here, a key issue is whether pan-cultural scales can be used, or whether scales and response formats will need to be adapted to specific countries and cultures. Particularly in developing countries with low levels of literacy, somewhat ingenious devices may need to be used in order to ensure accurate response.

REFERENCES

ALMOND, G. and S. VERBA, *The Civil Culture: Political Attitudes and Democracy in Five Nations.* Princeton, NJ: Princeton University Press, 1965.

ANDERSON, RONALD and JACK ENGLEDOW, "A Factor Analytic Comparison of U.S. and German Information Seekers," *Journal of Consumer Research,* 3 (1977), 185-96.

ANGELMAR, REINHARD and BERNARD PRAS, "Verbal Rating Scales for Multinational Research," *European Research,* 6 (1978), 62-67.

BERENT, PAUL-HOWARD, "International Research Is Different," in Edward M. Mazze, (ed.), *Marketing in Turbulent Times* and *Marketing: The Challenges and the Opportunities—Combined Proceedings.* Chicago: American Marketing Association, 1975.

BERRIEN, F. KENNETH, "Cross-Cultural Equivalence of Personality Measures," *Journal of Social Psychology,* 75 (1968), 3-9.

BOGART, LEO, "No Opinion, Don't Know, and Maybe No Answer," *Public Opinion Quarterly,* 31 (1967), 331-45.

BRISLIN, R., "Back-Translation for Cross-Cultural Research," *Journal of Cross-Cultural Psychology,* 1 (1970), 185-216.

——, WALTER J. LONNER, and ROBERT M. THORNDIKE, *Cross-Cultural Research Methods.* New York: John Wiley, 1973.

BURKE, MIKE, BERNARD CATHELAT, CLAUDE MATRICON, CLAUDE NICOLAY, and FRANCOISE HUGUET, *Rapport Unimedia document roneote non publie,* 1976.

CANTRIL, A., *The Pattern of Human Concerns.* New Brunswick, NJ: Rutgers University Press, 1965.

CHUN, KI TAEK, JOHN B. CAMPBELL, and JONG HAO, "Extreme Response Style in Cross-cultural Research: A Reminder," *Journal of Cross-Cultural Psychology,* 5 (1974) 464-80.

CORDER, C. K., "Problems and Pitfalls in Conducting Marketing Research in Africa," in Betsy Gelb (ed.), *Marketing Expansion in a Shrinking World,* Proceedings of American Marketing Association Business Conference. Chicago: American Marketing Association, 1978.

CRAIG, SAMUEL C. and JOHN M. McCANN, "Item Non-Response in Mail Surveys: Extent and Correlates," *Journal of Marketing Research,* 15 (1978), 285-90.

CROSBY, RICHARD W., "Attitude Measurement in a Bilingual Culture," *Journal of Marketing Research,* 6 (1969), 412-16.

CROWNE, D. P. and D. MARLOWE, *The Approval Motive: Studies in Evaluative Dependence.* New York: John Wiley, 1964.

CUNNINGHAM, WILLIAM H., ISABELLA CUNNINGHAM, and ROBERT T. GREEN,"The Ipsative Process to Reduce Response Set Bias," *Public Opinion Quarterly,* 41 (1977), 379-94.

DONALD, MARJORIE N., "Implications of Non-Response for Interpretation of Mail Questionnaire Data," *Public Opinion Quarterly,* 24 (1960), 99-114.

DOUGLAS, SUSAN and CHRISTINE URBAN, "Using Life-Style Analysis to Profile Women in International Markets," *Journal of Marketing,* 41 (1977), 46-54.

—— and PATRICK LeMAIRE, "Improving the Quality and Efficiency of Life-Style Research," XXV ESOMAR Congress, Budapest, 1974.

—— and ROBERT SHOEMAKER, "Item Non-Response in Cross-National Surveys," *European Research,* 9 (October 1981), 124-32.

ELDER, JOSEPH W., "Comparative Cross-National Methodology," *Annual Review in Sociology,* Palo Alto, CA: Annual Reviews, Inc., 1976.

ERVIN, SUSAN, "Language and TAT Content in French-English Bilinguals," *Journal of Abnormal and Social Psychology,* 68 (1964), 500–7.

FERBER, ROBERT, "The Effect of Respondent Ignorance on Survey Results," *Journal of American Statistical Association,* 51 (1956), 576–86.

——, "Item Non-Response in a Consumer Survey," *Public Opinion Quarterly,* 30 (1966), 399–415.

FRANCIS, JOE D. and LAWRENCE BUSCH, "What We Know About I Don't Knows," *Public Opinion Quarterly,* 39 (1975), 207–18.

FREY, F., "Cross-Cultural Survey Research in Political Science," in Robert W. Holt and John E. Turner (eds.), *The Methodology of Comparative Research.* New York: The Free Press, 1970.

GERGEN, KENNETH J. and KURT W. BACK, "Communication in the Interview and the Disengaged Respondent," *Public Opinion Quarterly,* 30 (1966), 358–98.

GLENN, NORVAL D., "Aging, Disengagement and Opinionation," *Public Opinion Quarterly,* 33 (1969), 17–33.

GORDON, L. V., "Comments on Cross-Cultural Equivalence of Personality Measures," *Journal of Social Psychology,* 75 (1968), 11–19.

GREEN, ROBERT T. and PHILIP WHITE, "Methodological Considerations in Cross-National Consumer Research," *Journal of International Business Studies,* 7 (1976), 81–87.

——, WILLIAM CUNNINGHAM, and ISABELLA CUNNINGHAM, "The Effectiveness of Standardized Global Advertising," *Journal of Advertising,* 41 (1975), 46–54.

—— and ERIC LANGEARD, "A Cross-National Comparison of Consumer Habits and Innovator Characteristics," *Journal of Advertising,* 43 (1977), 25–30.

JONES, EMILY L., "The Courtesy Bias in South East African Survey," *International Social Science Journal,* 15 (1963), 70–76.

KRACMAR, JOHN Z., *Marketing Research in the Developing Countries.* New York: Praeger, 1971.

LANDSBERGER, HENRY A. and ANTONIA SAAVEDRA, "Response Set in Developing Countries," *Public Opinion Quarterly,* 31 (1967), 214–29.

LEVI-STRAUSS, CLAUDE, "The Principles of Reciprocity," in Lewis A. Coser and Bernard Rosenberg (eds.), *Sociological Theory.* New York: Macmillan, 1965.

LOVELL, MARK R., "Examining the Multinational Consumer," *Developments in Consumer Psychology,* pp. 239–62 (ESOMAR Seminar). Maidenhead: ESOMAR, 1973.

MAUSS, MARCEL, *The Gift.* London: Cohen and West, 1954.

MITCHELL, ROBERT E., "Survey Materials Collected in Developing Countries: Sampling Measurement and Interviewing: Obstacles to Intra- and Inter-National Comparisons," *International Social Science Journal,* 17 (1965), 4.

MITFORD, JESSICA, *The American Way of Death.* New York: Simon and Schuster, 1963.

NAGASHIMA, AKIRA, "A Comparison of Japanese and U.S. Attitudes Toward Foreign Products," *Journal of Marketing,* 34 (January 1970), 68–74.

OPPENHEIM, A. N., *Questionnaire Design and Attitude Measurement.* New York: Basic Books, 1966.

OSGOOD, CHARLES E., WILLIAM H. MAY, and MURRAY S. MIRON, *Cross-Cultural Universals of Affective Meaning.* Urbana, IL: University of Illinois Press, 1975.

PAYNE, STANLEY,   *The Art of Asking Questions.* Princeton, NJ: Princeton University Press, 1951.

PLUMMER, JOSEPH,   "Consumer Focus in Cross-National Research," *Journal of Advertising* (1977), pp. 5–15.

RICKS, DAVID, MARILYN Y. C. FU, and JEFFREY S. ARPAN,   *International Business Blunders.* Columbus, OH: Grid, 1974.

RODMAN, HYMAN,   "Marital Power in France, Germany, Yugoslavia, and the U.S.," *Journal of Marriage and the Family,* 29 (May 1967), 320–24.

ROHME, NILS,   "Harmonization of Demographics," *Market Research Society Newsletter,* 118 (November 1981), 12.

SCHREIBER, E. M.,   "Dirty Data in Britain and the U.S.A., the Reliability of 'Invariant' Characteristics Reported in Surveys," *Public Opinion Quarterly,* 39 (1975–76), 493–506.

SCHWARTZ, BARRY,   "The Social Psychology of the Gift," *American Journal of Sociology,* 73 (1967), 1–11.

SECHREST, LEE, TODD FAY, and S. M. ZAIDI,   "Problems of Translations in Cross-Cultural Research," *Journal of Cross-Cultural Psychology,* 3 (1972), 41–56.

SELLITZ, CLAIRE, LAWRENCE S. WRIGHTSMAN, and STUART W. COOK,   *Research Methods in Social Relations,* 3rd ed. New York: Holt, Rinehart and Winston, 1976.

SICINSKI, ANDRZEJ,   "Don't Know Answers in Cross-National Surveys," *Public Opinion Quarterly,* 34 (1970), 126–29.

SINAIKO, H.,   "Teleconferencing: Preliminary Experiments," research paper, p. 108. Arlington, VA: Institute for Defense Analysis, 1963.

TRIANDIS, HARRY C.,   *The Analysis of Subjective Culture.* New York: John Wiley, 1972.

—— and V. VASSILOU,   "A Comparative Analysis of Subjective Culture," in Harry C. Triandis, *The Analysis of Subjective Culture.* New York: John Wiley, 1972.

—— and LEIGH M. TRIANDIS,   *A Cross-Cultural Study of Social Distance.* Washington, DC: American Psychological Association, 1962.

VAN DER REIS, A. P.,   *Some Aspects of the Acceptability of Particular Photographic Models to the Bantu.* Pretoria: University of South Africa, Bureau of Market Research, 1972.

——,   "The Transferability of Rating Scale Techniques to Coloured, Zulu and Northern Sotho Respondents in Attitude Surveys," paper presented at the 3rd SAMRA (South African Market Research Association) Convention. Maseru, Lesotho, 1981.

WEBB, NORMAN,   "International Omnibuses," *Market Research Society Newsletter,* 192 (March 1982), 24.

WELLS, WILLIAM D.,   "The Influence of Yea-saying Response Style," *Journal of Advertising Research,* 1 (1961), 1–12.

WERNER, OSCAR and DONALD T. CAMPBELL,   "Translating, Working Through Interpreters and the Problems of Decentering," in Raoul Naroll and Ronald Cohen (eds.), *A Handbook of Method in Cultural Anthropology.* New York: Columbia University Press, 1970.

WIND, YORAM and SUSAN P. DOUGLAS,   "Comparative Consumer Research: The Next Frontier," *Management Decision,* 20 (September 1982), 24–35.

ZAX, MELVIN and SHIGEO TAKAHASHI,   "Cultural Influences on Response Style: Comparisons of Japanese and American College Students," *Journal of Social Psychology,* 71 (1967), 3–10.

8

Survey Research: Sampling and Data Collection Procedures

Once the types of data to be collected have been identified, and a research instrument designed to collect these data, the next step is to develop appropriate sampling and survey data collection procedures. Although sampling needs to be considered in all types of research, whether survey or nonsurvey, the main focus in this chapter is on sampling in survey research. It is crucial to develop systematic procedures in order to ensure that reliable and comparable data are collected. More specifically, this requires the establishment of a sampling plan based on some target population, the development of a sampling frame or sampling list, and the selection of appropriate survey administration procedures. These relationships are shown in Figure 8.1.

In developing a sampling plan for a particular target population, decisions first have to be made with regard to the appropriate sampling frame; for example, the world, country groupings, countries, or subcountry units. Related to the question of the sampling frame is the choice of sampling procedures. In the case of global and regional samples, the main problem is to select procedures that will ensure representativeness of the target population. The limited availability of comprehensive global or regional sampling frames may suggest that judgment or convenience sampling may be more cost effective than random sampling and may also provide data which are sufficiently reliable and accurate for most purposes. In the case of national sampling units, not only such issues, but also whether the use of equivalent procedures for each sampling unit will yield comparable results, have to be considered. Differences in the

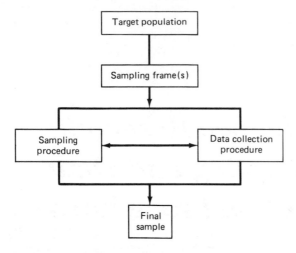

FIGURE 8.1   Elements involved in developing a sampling plan

availability and coverage provided by sampling frames or lists, and in the accessibility of the target population, suggest the use of different procedures for each unit may provide better representation and be more cost effective.

Then, decisions have to be made as to how the survey should be administered. As in domestic research, three major alternatives can be identified—that is, mail, telephone, or personal interview. Again, in the case of multicountry sampling units, the need for comparability from one country or sampling unit to another, and whether equivalent procedures will yield comparable results, has to be assessed.

Survey administration procedures also depend on the availability and adequacy of sampling frames for the target population. Mail surveys require the availability of a mailing list; and telephone surveys, a list of telephone numbers. Personal interviewing provides greater flexibility in that where convenience or quota sampling is applied, a list of the target population is essential. Where national sampling units are concerned, the same issues arise with regard to the use of different administration techniques for different sampling units, as in the case of sampling procedures.

The sample finally obtained, whether a global, regional, national, or subnational sample, should thus be representative of the target population, and in the case of national and subnational sampling units, as comparable as possible across units with regard to representativeness. However, cost considerations and sampling difficulties may, in some cases, limit the feasibility of obtaining totally representative samples.

This chapter examines the various issues involved in sampling, and in the case of multicountry sampling units, ones that are as comparable as possible from one country to another. First, the problem of acquiring sampling frames from which to draw the sample is examined. Second, the implications and advisability of using different sampling techniques are discussed. Third, the suitability and advantages and disadvantages associated with different survey administration methods in international markets are reviewed. Finally, issues associated with field staff selection and training are discussed.

SAMPLING

In designing a sampling plan, the first steps are to determine the level at which sampling is to be conducted (that is, world, country, region, and so on) and to assess whether an appropriate sample frame for the target population exists. Appropriate respondents relative to the unit of analysis have then to be selected. For example, in a consumer survey of grocery products, the wife may be selected as the relevant respondent; or in a survey of office equipment purchasing, the manager of the buying department. The next step is to determine the sampling techniques to be used, the overall size of the sample, and the relevant sample level. Each of these steps is next discussed in more detail.

Selecting the Sampling Frame

Once the target population to be sampled has been determined, the availability of a list of population elements from which the sample may be drawn should be assessed. In an international context, this frequently presents difficulties due to the paucity of information available on industries, businesses, or consumer groups in other countries. Even where sampling frames, such as electoral or municipal lists, directories, telephone books, or mailing lists commonly used in the United States are available, they frequently do not provide adequate coverage, particularly in less-developed countries, and hence, give rise to frame error.

The limited availability of appropriate information or lists from which samples may be drawn often leads to more frequent use of nonprobability sampling in international marketing research. This is particularly true in industrial marketing where interviewing of certain key respondents may be more informative than systematic analysis of representative samples. Where random sampling is desired, as may be the case in consumer research, it can often lead to use of interviewers to develop the sampling frame as well as to administer questionnaires.

In contrast to domestic marketing research, it is important to note that sampling may take place at a number of geographical levels. The most aggregate level at which the sample may be drawn is that of the world. The next level consists of geographic regions such as Europe or Latin America. Following this is the country level, and the geographic units or other subgroups within countries, as, for example, regions, cities, precincts, neighborhoods, or local associations and community groups.

The level at which the sample is drawn will depend to a large extent on the specific product market and research objectives, and on the availability of lists at each level. Some examples of these are shown in Table 8.1. The sequencing of research, and whether, for example, one region or country is investigated first and then another, is also related to the availability of information relative to the specific target segment. The advantages and limitations of sampling at each of these levels are next discussed in more detail.

The World

The first level at which sampling may be conducted is that of the world. This is likely to be appropriate in industrial markets, such as injection molders, surgical equipment, machine tools, and mainframe computers. In industrial markets, worldwide or regional lists of manufacturers can be obtained from sources such as *Bottin International*. This registers names and addresses of more than 300,000 firms in 100 countries, under 1,000 product classifications, by trade and by country. *Kelly's Manufacturers and Merchants Directory* also lists firms in the United States and other major trading countries in the world.

TABLE 8.1   The levels of the sampling frame

Level	Product market examples	Examples of sampling lists
World	Injection molds Machine tools Mainframe computers Hotel services	*Bottin International* *Kelly's Manufacturers and Merchants Directory* *Financial Times, International Business and Company Yearbook*
Regions	Minicomputers Airlines Automobiles Personal computers	*Directory of European Associations* *Europa Yearbook* Regional associations
Countries	Agricultural equipment Construction supplies Most mass-market consumer packaged goods	National associations Banking associations Population lists Telephone listings
Cities	Upscale consumer target segments Communications equipment Advanced surgical equipment	Municipal lists Church organizations Lists of government organizations Public administration

In some cases, trade associations are able to provide such information. These are listed in the *Encyclopedia of Associations,* together with the publications they distribute.

Sampling at the world level is, however, likely to be relatively rare in the case of consumer research. It might occur if the target population is a relatively small transnational market segment. For example, subscribers to the *National Geographic,* or American Express cardholders, might be an appropriate target sample for testing a new foreign travel publication. Similarly, subscribers to *European Research* might be an appropriate sample for testing new marketing research services. The major restriction on sampling at this level is, however, the lack of information relative to the target population.

Country Groupings

The next level at which samples may be drawn is that of a country grouping. This is most likely to be regional. As in the case of global sampling, regional sampling is most likely to be appropriate in industrial markets. Regional listings of manufacturing companies, banks, and other organizations, particularly in the more developed countries, may, for example, be found in publications such as the *Directory of European Associations.*

In some cases regional sampling of consumer markets may also be appropriate. *Paris Match,* for example, has an extensive number of subscribers throughout Europe; and the *Economist,* among English-speaking business people throughout the world. But these will generate a relatively particular sample, and hence, relevance to the desired target population needs to be assessed.

Country

The country is the most commonly used level for drawing a sample in multicountry research. In the domestic market, frames such as electoral lists, population censuses, and telephone books are commonly used for drawing samples at this level. However, such sampling frames are not always available or current in other countries, particularly in developing countries, and coverage will vary. For many years, for example, neither Cairo nor Teheran, with populations of 8 and 5 million respectively, had a telephone book. Some countries, notably in Southeast Asia and Africa, lack any type of population lists. In some cities, even street maps are unavailable, and in extreme cases—for example, Saudi Arabia—streets have no names and houses are not numbered.

Such factors may imply that it is preferable that the researcher construct the sampling list from scratch. In Bangkok, for example, teams have mapped, by hand, individual dwellings in poorer sections of the town so that a random block sample can be developed (Wilson, 1982). In some cases somewhat unorthodox methods may be used. In a northeastern city in Peru, approximately one-third of the population lives on rafts. Fieldworkers chart them and select a sample by picking at random from a set of embarkation points. Typically these methods are associated with the use of interviewers so that the establishment of the sampling list becomes part of the survey administration process.

Different biases may be inherent in the use of these lists. In most countries outside the United States, for example, use of telephone lists (except in the case of industrial research) will provide a relatively skewed sample. Similarly, use of city block data may result in underrepresentation of lower socioeconomic respondents living in caves, hovels, or riverboats.

Subcountry Groupings

The next level at which samples may be drawn is that of subgroups within countries. These might be geographic units such as cities or neighborhoods, or alternatively, ethnic, racial, cultural, age, or demographic subgroupings such as Catholics, Protestants, blacks, Indians, foreigners of different origins, children, cat owners, members of the PTA, or senior citizens. Similarly, in an organizational context, specific industries, or organizations within certain regions, might constitute the relevant population.

The availability of information from which to develop a sample is likely to vary with the specific subgrouping. For geographic units, this is likely to pose the least problem if maps or local electoral lists can be obtained. In some countries, however, even such frames may not be available. Demographic groupings will generally be available from census data, and religious groups from church membership or organizations. Greater difficulties may be encountered with other ethnic groups unless there are local ethnic organizations.

The Choice of Respondent

Once the sampling frame has been determined, the specific respondent to be sampled has to be determined. Here, as in domestic marketing research, an important consideration in studying families and organizations is to determine who is the relevant respondent, that is, the wife or the husband, the production engineer, or the buyer. In addition, a decision has to be made about whether a single respondent is used, or whether multiple respondents will be required, as, for example, husbands, wives, and children in the family; or buyers as well as research and development or production engineers in organizations.

Identification of the relevant respondent(s) in each country is also an important consideration, since these may vary from country to country. In some countries, for example, there may be a tendency among organizations toward highly centralized decision making. Hence, the industrial buyer may be merely an agent. In Anglo-Saxon cultures, on the other hand, there is a greater tendency to delegate authority. Consequently, the buyer may play an important role.

Similarly, where research is being conducted in relation to consumer goods, a decision has to be made as to whether the wife, the husband, or a child is the most appropriate respondent. In relation to frequently purchased consumer goods and groceries, the wife is likely to be selected as being the most readily available respondent. In relation to other products such as automobiles, insurance, or vacations, it may, however, be desirable to consider other respondents. Again, this may vary from one country or cultural context to another. As noted previously, in Latin American countries, upper socio-economic families, and among white non-Afrikans South African families, the maid is frequently responsible for purchasing food and groceries. Therefore, relevant participation in purchase decisions may be difficult to ascertain. Prior examination of such factors is, therefore, necessary to determine the appropriate choice of respondent(s).

The number of respondents to be included from a given household or organization has also to be considered. This is most likely to be relevant in the case of organizations since the cost of collecting data from multiple family members is likely to be prohibitively expensive. The number of respondents depends to a large extent on the degree of involvement of different participants in purchase decisions. In some organizations, for example, buying decisions may also be heavily influenced by the production engineer, research and development engineer, or other users (Wind, 1966), thus suggesting that users as well as buyers should be included in the research.

Sampling Procedures

The next step is to determine appropriate sampling procedures. Here, a first consideration is whether research is to be undertaken in all countries and contexts, or whether alternatively, results and findings are generalizable from one country or context to another.

Ideally research should be conducted in all countries and contexts where marketing operations are planned. There is, however, a trade-off between the number of countries in which research is undertaken and the depth or quality of the research. Given the high costs of multicountry research, management may consider it desirable to use findings in one country as a proxy for another. For example, market response patterns in Scandinavian countries may be sufficiently similar to sample only one of these countries. It is, however, important to realize that such a procedure is fraught with danger. Even though previous experience suggests that response patterns are the same, this may change, or not be relevant in relation to the specific case examined.

In selecting sampling procedures, a key decision is whether random or purposive sampling should be used. This is closely linked to the appropriate survey administration techniques. If sampling lists of the relevant population are not available, probabilistic sampling or random sampling may pose some difficulties, unless field staffs are used to develop an appropriate list. Consequently, in many cases, especially in commercial consumer research, quota sampling is more likely to be used, often with random location starting points or linked to random walk or other systematic procedures (Barnard, 1982). In addition, the sample size has to be determined, as well as procedures for dealing with nonresponse.

Sampling Techniques

Once the number of countries, or other sample units, and the sequence in which they are to be investigated, has been determined, the next step is to select an appropriate sampling technique. A major distinction exists between probabilistic sampling and nonprobabilistic sampling. In probabilistic sampling, each respondent in the target population has an equal chance of being in the sample. In nonprobabilistic sampling, some criteria are established on the basis of which respondents are selected.

In the United States random, or probabilistic, sampling is generally considered to be the most desirable, and comprehensive lists of the target population are frequently available. However, this is not always the case in international marketing research. Lack of published information about the relevant target population, the paucity of sampling lists, and the costs associated with the development of such lists suggest that other methods such as judgment, convenience, or snowball sampling may be more cost effective. This is reinforced in many contexts by the desirability of using personal interviewing procedures rather than mail or telephone surveys. The various types of sampling are next discussed in more detail.

Nonprobabilistic Sampling

Convenience Sampling. A convenience sample may be used. This implies selecting any respondent who is readily available. In developing countries, for example, convenience sampling in the marketplace provides a low-cost procedure for generating a sample (Mayer, 1978). Given the difficulties and costs of sampling frames in such countries and particularly in reaching the rural population, this is often appropriate for developing a sample which, while not strictly representative, may nonetheless be relatively free of any systematic bias.

Judgment Sampling. Another procedure is to select respondents based on judgment. Judgment sampling is based on the assumption that certain persons are better informed than others or may have expert knowledge in a given field. In international marketing research, use of judgment sampling permits the use of area or industry experts for a given country or region, especially in industrial marketing research. It often provides a more efficient method for obtaining information on likelihood of new product acceptance, industry growth, market conditions, and so on, than use of quota or probabilistic sampling.

The sales force is also often a valuable source of information, since they know customer needs and interests. Care should, however, be taken in using them to obtain quantitative estimates of, for example, sales potential. Importers or export agents may also be used as "key informants," though again some bias may be introduced, reflecting their own self-interest.

This procedure may also be used in consumer markets, notably in developing countries. Questioning of village elders, priests, or other local authority figures may provide a reliable method of obtaining information about the number of inhabitants, current purchase behavior, and problems. This may be particularly desirable in countries with high levels of illiteracy, where low-cost procedures are required to provide a general indication of sales potential, rather than a precise estimate of response to alternative marketing strategies.

Quota Sampling.   A procedure used in both industrialized and developing countries is quota sampling. Quotas are established by specifying the number of respondents required within a given category; for example, in consumer research, in different age or income groups, or working versus nonworking wives; or in industrial markets, from a specific industry, or from different firm size groups. Again, this procedure is particularly likely to be appropriate for industrial markets where for many products, customers are likely to be found in specific industries. While this procedure ensures that the sample will be representative of the selected quota characteristics, there is clearly a danger that these characteristics are systematically associated with other factors that will introduce confounding effects (Campbell and Stanley, 1966).

Snowball Sampling.   Snowball sampling is a technique well suited to international marketing research, as it is useful when attempting to estimate characteristics that are relatively rare in the total population. With snowball sampling, initial respondents are selected randomly, and additional respondents are selected from information obtained from the initial respondents. For example, in a three-country study of tourists who had visited the United States during the Bicentennial year, snowball sampling was used. Since the likelihood of finding such respondents was very low, stratified probability methods were used to identify initial respondents. These were then asked to give the names of two other people who would qualify as respondents, thus providing a second sample. Although the initial sample is selected using probability methods, the overall sample is nonprobability, since respondents will tend to give the names of people with similar demographic characteristics to themselves (Green and Tull, 1978).

Probabilistic Sampling

Simple Random Sampling.   Random sampling, although from a statistical standpoint the only valid procedure, poses a number of problems in international marketing research. In the first place, it requires the availability of a frame or list. Respondents are then picked at random from this list, selecting, for example, every *n*th name or person successively until the desired sample size is obtained. These respondents constitute the sample population who are then questioned by personal interview, mail, or telephone. The lack of adequate lists may limit application of this approach, especially in developing countries.

Where a survey is administered by interviewers, an alternative procedure is to use the "random-walk" method. The interviewer then also becomes the sampler. The interviewer is provided with a walk route and instructed to select every *n*th house to interview (Frey, 1970). This actually sounds easier than it is, since the interviewer may have difficulty following the route, or determining exactly what constitutes a "dwelling unit" in urban slums or villages, or where buildings include multiple-dwelling units. Furthermore, as noted previously, if no maps of an area exist, prior mapping of dwellings in an area or villages within a region may be required. The difficulties and costs associated with the application of such procedures suggest why nonprobabilistic sampling tends to be used frequently in international marketing research.

Stratified Sampling.   In some cases it may be considered important to ensure that samples from different countries are representative of certain key characteristics such as income, education, age, proportion of working wives, industrial versus consumer users, purchase frequency of a product, and so on. This is particularly likely to be the case when similar segments are to be targeted in different countries throughout the world. A random sample is then taken from each group or stratum of interest in the population.

In a comparison of consumer innovators in France and the United States, for example, (Green and Langeard, 1975), the French sample was stratified on the variables of age, income, education, and employment status to ensure the same relationship to the national population as the United States sample. This stratification rather than a fundamental difference in innovative behavior, may account for their less frequent communication about grocery products and less frequent TV viewing as compared with the United States sample, since they come from the more sophisticated, better-educated elite of the French population. This procedure also enables investigation of the extent to which differences observed between samples from different countries may reflect such characteristics.

Stratified sampling may either be proportionate or disproportionate. In proportionate stratified sampling, the sample drawn from each stratum is proportionate to the relative size of that stratum in the total population. In disproportionate sampling, other factors—for example, differences in variance in each stratum—may require that the samples taken from each stratum are not proportionate to their relative size.

In estimating market size for small hand-powered tools, for example, two groups or segments may be of interest—"do-it-your-selfers," and an industrial user segment such as craftspersons, repairpersons, and handymen. Greater variation may be expected in the industrial segment in terms of type of usage, frequency of use, type of user, and so on, than in the consumer segment. Consequently, it may be desirable for the sample drawn from the industrial segment to be larger, relative to its size, than that drawn from the consumer segment.

Similarly, in estimating market potential for laundry services, it may be desirable to ensure representativity of homes with young children where both spouses work full time, and homes where one spouse has no paid outside employment. Variance may be expected to be lower among households where both spouses work full time than among households where one spouse does not work outside the home. Hence, it may be desirable for the sample drawn from the latter households to be larger, relative to its proportionate size in the population, than the sample drawn from households with full-time working wives and husbands.

Quota and stratified sampling are frequently confused. While similar to quota samples insofar as representativity on certain key characteristics is desired, stratified samples are drawn probabilistically, while in quota sampling, respondents are selected on a judgmental basis. Thus, a quota sample may contain certain inherent biases that are less likely to occur in a stratified sample.

Cluster Sampling.   A related technique is cluster sampling. While in stratified sampling a random sample is selected from each stratum or subgroup, in cluster sampling a sample of subgroups is selected. It is therefore important that the groups should, as far as possible, be microcosms of the population being investigated.

For example, in assessing appropriate product positioning tactics for toothpaste in Thailand, it may be desirable to select a few key cities such as Bangkok in which to sample, since only the population in urban areas are likely to be of interest and to have running water. This is more cost efficient and avoids the expense and difficulties associated with conducting research in rural areas and, in particular, reduces costs of interviewer travel.

A special case of cluster sampling is area sampling; geographic units, such as cities, or regions, or city areas are the clusters. A sample is drawn from these and is used as the basis for investigation. This is particularly useful where detailed population lists are not available.

Area sampling can be either one stage or multistage. In one-stage area sampling, the geographic units are selected, and all relevant respondents within that unit studied. In multistage area sampling, further sampling within the geographic units takes place. Suppose, for example, a manufacturer of detergents was interested in estimating consumption of powdered detergent in urban households in Taiwan. If one-stage area sampling were adopted, he might select two residential areas in three major urban areas, Taipei, Kaioshung, and Taichung, and estimate consumption per household of detergent in each of these areas. The average of each of the two areas for each city could then be used to estimate consumption of detergent per household in that city.

If, on the other hand, multistage area sampling were adopted, a sample of city blocks within the three major urban areas might first be selected. A sample of households within each of these city blocks might then be selected, and their consumption of detergent determined. The average obtained for the samples for each urban area could then be used to estimate overall consumption of detergent in the area.

Multistage sampling can also be used in conjunction with other sampling approaches. These are next discussed in more detail.

Multistage Sampling.   In addition to deciding whether the sample is drawn probabilistically, another consideration is whether sampling is conducted in a single stage or several stages. Multistage sampling can aid considerably in reducing costs in international marketing research. Efficiency is increased, since the initial stage(s) are used to pinpoint relevant respondents to be sampled in subsequent stages. It is particularly likely to be appropriate for large-scale projects and in developing countries, where sampling frames are not readily available. On the other hand, multistage sampling may be at the expense of some loss in precision, since sampling errors accumulate from one stage to another. In addition, multistage sampling may cause delays, since more time is likely to be required than if sampling is conducted in a single stage. This does, however, depend on the complexity of the sampling procedure. If the initial stage sampling is based on secondary data sources, as, for example, in selecting a sample of regions, states, cities, or industries to investigate, multistage sampling may, on the contrary, increase the efficiency and speed of the research process.

Two principal types of multistage sampling may be identified: double sampling and sequential sampling. These are next discussed in more detail.

Double Sampling.   In double, or two-phase, sampling, samples are drawn twice. In the first sampling phase, data are collected from respondents about certain characteristics—for example, purchasing behavior and frequency, customer demographic variables, company size, and location and availability for future interviewing of respondents themselves, or others within the organization. This information is then used to develop a frame for drawing a second sample, from respondents in the initial sample. Certain respondents are thus interviewed a second time in greater depth.

In evaluating international market potential for microcomputers, for example, it may be desirable to conduct an international telephone survey, to determine which industries and what size companies are the heaviest purchasers of microcomputers in different countries or regions throughout the world. (A preliminary list of companies to phone could be established based on knowledge of heavy-user industries in the domestic market.) Based on data collected from this survey, a list could be drawn up of companies and industries that appear to be heavy users and potentially cooperative respondents. A sample could then be drawn from this list, and these companies investigated in greater depth with regard to purchasing behavior, key characteristics in selecting vendors, who in the firm is responsible for purchasing, who are major users, and so on. Depending on the size of the research budget, users, purchasers, and key participants in the purchasing decision might all be interviewed.

Sequential Sampling. The second type of multistage sampling is sequential sampling. In sequential sampling, the total sample size is not determined in advance. Rather respondents are interviewed one after the other, and the data analyzed simultaneously or at specific points in time, after which a decision is made about whether more respondents should be interviewed. With the increasing use of CRT screens and computerized techniques in telephone and mall intercept interviewing, this procedure is likely to become increasingly popular. Here response data are keyed directly into the computer and analysis of the data updated after each entry.

As discussed subsequently in relation to international telephone interviewing, the decision about whether to interview more respondents can be based on the stability of results from the first 100 respondents in relation to the second 100, and so on. The cost efficiency of research can thus be increased as the minimal feasible sample is interviewed.

In multistage sampling, sample designs may involve a mix of techniques. In the microcomputer example previously described, specific industries may be selected for investigation, based on judgment, and then quota sampled, based on size within each industry. Similarly, in consumer research area sampling may be used to pick certain major cities and villages in developing countries to be investigated and stratified; or block sampling within the cities can then be applied to select households to be interviewed, while in the villages judgment sampling of elders is used.

Sample Size

Another important decision concerns the appropriate sample size. Assuming a fixed budget, there is a trade-off between the number of countries or contexts sampled, the sample size within each country, and the extensiveness of the data collected from each respondent. As in many domestic marketing research projects, a choice has to be made between small samples and high-quality, in-depth research, or larger samples and less extensive data.

Use of statistical procedures to determine appropriate sample size poses some difficulties, since in order to apply these procedures, some estimation of population variance is required (Cochran, 1977). In many cases these may not be available or, where available, may differ from one country to another. Hence, appropriate sample sizes can only be determined on a country-by-country, rather than a transnational, basis. Sample sizes may thus in many cases be determined arbitrarily, on an *ad hoc* basis. Management may, for example, decide that samples of 200 to 300, or ten focus groups in each country, are required. Additionally, if a sequential sampling procedure is used, then the sample size becomes variable, depending on the stability of successive samples. It may also be useful to incorporate Bayesian notions of the cost of collecting additional information, with the value of the information for decision making. In this fashion, sample size becomes a function of the cost of information and its value for management decision making.

Diversity with regard to other factors within country units needs also to be taken into consideration. Differences with regard to the distribution of key determinants and related variables, or sampling characteristics such as income, age, education, and so on, are likely to arise. This suggests that larger-than-normal sample sizes are likely to be required to test for the impact of differences in these variables on cross-national findings. This does, however, entail high sampling costs, and hence may pose budgetary difficulties. Use of large sample sizes, such as those of more than 1,000 respondents in each country, in the *Reader's Digest* European survey or the Leo Burnett/International life style surveys is, therefore, rare (Segnit and Broadbent, 1973).

Small sample sizes may, however, be defensible, particularly in the exploratory stages of research, where there is likely to be less concern with representativity. Use of large samples, while increasing statistical reliability and reducing random error, may increase error from nonsampling sources (Lipstein, 1975; Frey, 1970). Additional interviewers will be required, as well as additional coders, thus increasing the possibility of errors from interviewing and data processing. Consequently, additional quality controls will be required, necessitating expenditures to train competent interviewers and to supervise editing and coding. This is likely to pose problems in international marketing research, particularly in developing countries where the availability of trained interviewers or qualified research staff is limited.

Achieving Comparability in Sampling

Sample Composition.   As noted earlier, a key issue in developing a sampling design is the importance attached to the representativity, as opposed to the comparability, of the samples. If samples that are representative of the target population are drawn, they are unlikely to be comparable with regard to certain key characteristics such as income, age, and education. This can create a problem if, as is frequently the case, such variables affect the behavior or response pattern studied. For example, in comparing interest in tropical fruit in different countries, income or education might be important factors affecting response. Mistaken inferences might be made about national differences or similarities in interest in tropical fruits, when these reflect differences between samples in income distribution, rather than "true" national differences. One might, for example, conclude there was lack of adequate market potential, when in fact a small, high-income segment constituted a potential spearhead for market entry. Equally, a myriad of other factors, such as life style patterns or subcultural influences, may vary across countries. These introduce a confounding effect that may make it extremely difficult to isolate the impact on the behavior studied.

Statistical procedures can be used to evaluate the impact of different sample compositions on results, and to adjust results for these. These are discussed in Chapter 9. Initial applications of such procedures (Douglas, 1980) suggest, however, that substantial differences in composition will be required before there is a significant effect on results.

Selecting a Sampling Procedure.   A further issue is whether the same sampling procedures are used across countries. Sampling procedures vary in reliability from one country to another. Thus, rather than using identical sampling procedures and methods in each country, it may be preferable to use different methods or procedures that have equivalent levels of accuracy or reliability (Webster, 1966). Suppose, for example, in one country, random sampling is of known validity, and in another country, quota sampling is known to be of equivalent validity. The results will be more comparable in terms of response rate and quality of response if two different procedures are used, than if the same sampling procedure were used. Similarly, it is not safe to assume that if the same sampling procedures are used in each country with known biases, the results will automatically be comparable (Holt and Turner, 1970). For example, a sampling procedure that underestimates the number of commercial travelers might have a different effect in various countries, due to a different incidence of commercial travelers.

Similarly, costs of sampling procedures may differ from country to country. Cost savings achieved from using the same method in many countries, and centralizing analysis, coding, and so on, may be outweighed by use of the most efficient sampling method in each country. For example, in one country, random sampling may necessitate the purchase of a special list at a high price, while in another country, quota sampling produces acceptable results at half the cost. Consequently, it may be more appropriate to use the quota method in the latter country while using random sampling in other contexts.

Differences in sampling methods can also be utilized to provide a check on the reliability of results and the potential bias inherent in different methods. In one industrial survey, different sampling procedures with different sources of potential bias were used in five different countries (Webster, 1966). A consistent pattern was found on one of the main variables studied, namely, the percentage of firms in each size category owning the test product. If the same sampling procedure had been utilized in each country, this might not have been detected.

In brief, therefore, use of similar sampling procedures will not necessarily ensure comparability of results, since each procedure is subject to different types of bias, and these vary from country to country. Deliberate variation of procedures, on the other hand, if intelligently used, can provide a means for checking the validity of results, and detecting biases inherent in different types of procedures.

Sampling Error.   In addition to bias that can arise as a result of the interviewer-interviewee interaction, and from the respondent himself or herself, which have been discussed previously, sampling is also a potential source of bias in cross-national surveys. Sampling error can be defined as the error likely to occur because a sample, rather than a census, was employed when gathering data.

Hence, two aspects need to be considered: the first concerns sampling error due to frame error, and the second concerns sampling error due to survey nonresponse. Certain standard techniques are available for increasing response and weighting to account for nonresponse. Where an adequate frame is not available, however, there is little that can be done. This is particularly likely to give rise to problems in international marketing research, due to the unavailability of sampling lists for global or regional target segments, and in developing countries, unless the researcher is willing to develop his or her own list or frame.

Frame Error.   The lack of adequate sampling frames or lists and differences in these from one country to another imply that samples drawn from these may not be strictly comparable from one country to another. Consequently, sampling error may differ from one country or sampling unit to another. In the case of global or regional sampling frames, the *Economist* will, for example, provide better coverage of the business population in English-speaking countries than in French- or Spanish-speaking countries.

If the specific inadequacies of the sampling frame are known, the sample can be weighted to account for these. These will, however, only apply if random sampling procedures are used. If judgment, quota, and convenience sampling methods are used, it may be difficult to evaluate the degree of bias arising from sampling error, and hence the impact on the accuracy of the data collected.

Survey Nonresponse.   Some evidence exists to indicate differences among nations in the rates of nonresponse to surveys. In the classic Almond and Verba (1965) study, the rates of response, or respondents actually interviewed, ranged from 59 percent in the United Kingdom, 60 percent in Mexico, 74 percent in Italy and 74 percent in Germany, to 83 percent in the United States. This, however, is a more significant problem in mail and telephone interviewing, than in personal interviewing, where it can be more effectively controlled. The only exception is in countries where there are high rates of refusal for reasons noted in Chapter 7. The problem is compounded by the inadequacies of many sampling lists discussed earlier.

Available evidence tends to suggest, however, that background characteristics of nonrespondents are likely to be the same. Samples will thus be underrepresented with regard to the same segments, as for example, low-income or less-educated consumers. It is, therefore, important to make adjustments for such factors to ensure comparability of samples, and that national representativeness is not lost. This can be corrected by double sampling on high nonresponse segments. If, however, other factors, such as suspiciousness of interviewers, or hostility in surveys, underlie nonresponse, the relevant determinants and their impact will need to be investigated in each specific case.

Little systematic research appears to have been conducted into ways to increase rates of nonresponse in other countries, or in multicountry surveys. One study of elites found that use of large incentives increased response, and improved the probability of providing complete response (Godwin, 1979).

Another survey in Israel (Jaffe, 1982) suggests that the inclusion of both a monetary incentive and reminder post card can help to increase response rates from 25 percent to 51 percent in a mail survey using a commercial letterhead. Similarly, use of an incentive in a mail survey in Colombia resulted in an increase in returns from 31 percent to 48 percent (Kracmar, 1971).

The efficacy of several return-increasing techniques in various South American and African countries has also been examined (Eisinger, Jahicki, Stevenson, and Thompson, 1974). In Kenya and the Ivory Coast, the effects of registration and personalization in a mail survey were examined. In neither case did personalization significantly increase returns, though registration increased returns by 8 percent in Kenya. Registration was also found to increase returns in Venezuela and Argentina. In all cases, as in the United States, follow-up mailings increased return rates.

In general, existing evidence tends to suggest that techniques that have been found to be effective in the United States are also effective in other countries. The same standard procedures, such as personalization, sponsorship, and follow-ups, are used successfully in other countries, especially by the more sophisticated research organizations. Little has, however, been published with regard to the relative effectiveness of different techniques.

Nonsampling Error.   Surveys have also to be examined for bias arising from nonsampling error. Problems arising from sampling error can generally be readily identified, and hence pose somewhat less of a threat to the quality of data, than the somewhat invidious nature of nonsampling error. Although the impact of such factors has been extensively studied in the United States market, relatively little is known concerning factors that affect the quality of data provided by respondents in other countries. A few studies have been conducted, but these are far from systematic in their coverage, and relate primarily to a single country or area.

Nonsampling error can arise as a result of a number of factors, stemming from the respondent, the interviewer-respondent interaction, recording error, or item nonresponse. In the case of the respondent, factors such as the individual respondent's unwillingness to respond accurately and completely, his or her personality and response set, the purposeful misreporting of data, faulty recall, or respondent fatigue may all generate error. These have largely been discussed in relation to instrument design, and hence will not be further covered here.

Similarly, the interviewer-respondent interaction, if not handled appropriately, can encourage a biased response, as discussed previously. Error from this source can be reduced by improved research design; for example, questionnaires that require less clarification by the interviewer, or, alternatively, by increased interviewer training in, for example, how to administer multidimensional scaling tasks, or how to create a relaxed interviewing environment so as to obtain better respondent cooperation.

Recording error can often be an important source of error. This may arise either due to inaccuracy on the part of the respondent, or lack of care by the interviewer. When survey research is interviewer administered, the latter is likely to be the primary source of error. It is of particular concern in contexts where there is a lack of experienced field staff and interviewer training is required.

Item nonresponse can be another source of error (Craig and McCann, 1978). This arises either because respondents refuse to answer certain questions, or alternatively, state that they have no opinion about certain issues. As indicated in Chapter 7, nonresponse tends typically to be more significant in relation to attitudinal questions than demographic or other characteristics, and gives rise to greater problems in mail than in interviewer-administered surveys. It has also been found, as in the United States, to be higher among women and those with less formal education in a number of European countries (Douglas and Shoemaker, 1981).

Use of some of the more recent technological developments in data collection procedures can help to reduce all three sources of bias. A CRT unit might, for example, be used in a laboratory context or in a mobile unit in the field, parked near a shopping center. The question is flashed on the screen, and the respondent registers his or her response on the screen with an electronically sensitive marker, and this is then directly recorded on disk or tape. This reduces potential bias from the interviewer-interviewee interaction and recording error. Branching techniques can also be programmed into the question sequencing. Thus, if a respondent fails to respond to a question, he or she can be asked an alternate form of the question later on. Latency measures can also be incorporated to provide some indicator of reliability of different respondents, since respondents who are slow in responding tend to give less accurate responses.

DATA COLLECTION PROCEDURES

The next step in the international marketing research process is the selection of appropriate data collection or survey administration procedures. Here, a number of factors need to be considered. In particular, care in the supervision of data collection procedures is needed in order to minimize potential sources of bias and reactivity. It is thus important to identify and use an effective local field research organization. Otherwise, relevant services will have to be developed or organized by in-house staff.

In domestic marketing research, the relative cost, the length of the survey, and time constraints largely determine the choice of questionnaire administration procedures; that is, mail, telephone, or personal interview. In international markets, however, other aspects relating to the development of the marketing research or communications infrastructure also affect the decision, especially in developing countries.

Levels of literacy, as well as the availability of sampling lists, imply that mail surveys, while potentially a low-cost means of reaching the target population, may engender some bias, and hence, personal interviewing may be preferable. Similarly, the quality of the mail service, and in particular, its speed and reliability, will influence the cost effectiveness of mail surveys. Levels of telephone ownership, and in particular, private telephone ownership, affect the feasibility and sampling error associated with telephone surveys. Low levels of literacy, and low wage costs in other countries, may also imply that administration by interviewer is often the most effective procedure. The advantages and disadvantages of each method in international markets are next discussed in more detail.

Mail Surveys

In industrialized countries, the primary advantages of mail surveys are that they typically enable coverage of a wider and more representative sample, and they do not require a field staff. There is no interviewer bias and the costs per questionnaire tend to be relatively low. In addition, respondents may be more willing to provide information about certain issues—for example, sex—and have time to answer questions, such as those relating to life style, at their leisure. On the other hand, nonresponse rates may be high, thus leading to high cost per returned questionnaire, and bias due to nonresponse, especially where response is slow. Control over the questionnaire is lost, and there may be omissions or miscomprehension of questions. Furthermore, certain types of questions, such as probes, cannot be asked.

In international marketing research, such advantages (and limitations) are not always as clear, due to the absence of mailing lists, poor mail services, and high levels of illiteracy. In many markets this does, however, depend on the specific product market being investigated, that is, industrial versus consumer, and also the nature of the survey.

Mail surveys can typically be effectively used in industrial international marketing research. Mailing lists such as Bottin International, or directories for specific industries, are generally available. The key problem is to identify the relevant respondent within a company, and to personalize the address to increase the likelihood of response. Thus, appropriate telephone verification can also aid in increasing response rates.

In consumer research, and particularly in developing countries, use of mail surveys may give rise to some problems. Mailing lists comparable to those in the domestic market may not be available, or not sold, and public sources such as telephone directories may not provide adequate coverage. Lists that are available, that is, magazine subscription lists or membership association lists, may be skewed to better-educated segments of the population. In addition, in some countries, the effectiveness of mail surveys is limited not only by low levels of literacy, but also by reluctance of respondents to respond to mail surveys. As noted previously, levels of literacy are often less than 40 and 50 percent in some Asian and African markets, thus limiting the population that can be reached by mail. Mail surveys are also hazardous in countries such as Brazil, where it has been reckoned that 30 percent of the domestic mail is never delivered, or Nicaragua, where all the mail has to be delivered to the post office. Even in countries where levels of literacy and mail services make the use of mail surveys feasible, a tendency to regard surveys as an invasion of privacy may limit their effectiveness.

Thus, while mail surveys may be effectively used in industrial marketing research, in consumer research, they may be appropriate only in industrialized countries where levels of literacy are high, and mailing lists more available. In other countries they may only be appropriate if it is desired to reach a relatively upscale and well-educated segment of the population. Thus, while costs of administering mail surveys appear low on a per-questionnaire-mailed-out basis, low response rates or poor quality data may limit the desirability of their use, especially in developing countries.

Telephone Interviewing

In the United States the primary advantages of telephone surveys are that they enable coverage of a broadly distributed sample and require no field staff. Costs per respondent are low, due to the availability of WATS lines and special volume rates. Telephone surveys provide a quick way of obtaining information, and nonresponse is generally low. In addition, control over interviewers is facilitated. On the other hand, the interview cannot be too long, and questions have to be short and clear. Furthermore, it is difficult to ask certain types of questions, for example, multidimensional scaling or conjoint analysis questions.

As in the case of mail surveys, in international marketing research these advantages are not always as evident. Low levels of telephone ownership and poor communications in many countries, limit the coverage provided by telephone surveys. In addition, telephone costs are often high, and volume rates may not be available. Again, however, this depends on the specific country and the target population. Consequently, the desirability of conducting a telephone survey will depend to a large extent on the nature of and purpose of the survey.

In industrial international marketing research, use of telephone surveys may be quite effective. The majority of businesses, other than some small or itinerant retailers or craftspersons, are likely to have telephones. It is important, as in the case of mail surveys, to be able to identify the relevant respondent(s). This is, however, facilitated in telephone surveys by the ability to conduct initial probing, or to ask preliminary screening questions. Willingness to respond may, however, depend on relative time pressures at work, and the desired target population. Where the target population is upper management, some resistance is likely to be encountered unless substantial interest in the survey can be aroused. Use of personal contacts, or obtaining sponsorship from some appropriate organization or association, may also be desirable.

In Europe, use of telephone research is becoming widespread and widely accepted due to increasing levels of telephone penetration, and nonresponse rates in personal interviewing. In some cases, this may be "computer-steered" (de Houd, 1982). The interviewer then sits in front of a CRT unit and the questions are presented in logical order on the screen. Replies from each respondent are entered directly into the computer, and hence, many sources of interviewer or key-punching error are eliminated. In addition, results are immediately available on printout.

Another advantage is that for nonspecialized samples, random dialing methods can be controlled by the computer, and each telephone number within a given area given an equal chance of being in the sample. Also, if a respondent is not reached on an initial attempt, he or she can automatically be called back after a number of hours or minutes.

With the decline of international telephone costs, multicountry studies can also be conducted from a single location. This significantly reduces time and costs associated with negotiating and organizing a research project in each country, establishing quality controls, and so on. While additional costs in making international telephone calls are incurred, these may not be highly significant where a centralized location is used (de Houd, 1982).

International calls also obtain a higher response rate. Results obtained by using this technique have been found to be highly stable, the same results emerging from the first 100 interviews as from the next 200 or 500. Interviewer and client control is considerably greater. The questionnaire can be changed and modified in the course of the survey, and interviewing can be extended or stopped to meet the client's requirements. It is necessary to find interviewers fluent in the relevant languages, but in most European countries, this is rarely a problem.

In consumer research, the feasibility of using telephone surveys depends on the level of private telephone ownership in a country, and the specific target population. In countries such as Sri Lanka, only 4 percent of the population have phones, while even in relatively affluent societies such as France and Italy, there are only 29 and 27 public and private telephones, respectively, per 100 inhabitants, and in Portugal only 11.

Telephone linkages vary substantially in quality and are often inadequate for efficient interviewing. As in the case of mail surveys, respondents may be reluctant to respond to strangers or to questions posed by an anonymous interviewer, and be unaccustomed to lengthy telephone conversations. Consequently, telephone surveys may only be appropriate where the research is designed to reach relatively upscale consumer segments who are accustomed to business transactions by telephone, as for example, doctors and lawyers, or those who are able to express themselves easily.

Personal Interviewing

Personal interviewing is the most flexible method of obtaining data. The respondent is clearly identified, and hence the nature and distribution of the sample can be controlled. Also, nonresponse is likely to be low, and all types of questions or data collection techniques can be used. On the other hand, personal interviewing is likely to be the most expensive method of administering a survey. Control of interviewer cheating is, for example, necessary. Furthermore, there is danger of interviewer bias and, in particular, bias from the interviewer-respondent interaction.

As noted previously, personal interviewing tends to be the dominant mode of data collection outside of the United States (Barnard, 1982). There are a number of reasons for this, which includes the difficulty with telephone and mail interviewing indicated earlier. Also, lower wage costs imply that personal interviews may not be as expensive, relative to other methods of administration procedures, as in the United States. On the other hand, use of personal interviewing does require the availability of field staff fluent in the relevant language.

Often, however, given the lack of a pool of trained interviewers in other countries, companies with local research units or international research organizations may train and develop their own field staffs (Barnard, 1982). This provides greater control over the quality of the interviewing conducted in different countries. This is in marked contrast to the practice of "buying field and tab services" from an outside organization that is common in the United States. These interviewers are not necessarily required to work exclusively for a given research supplier, though often they may do so of their own choice.

Personal interviewing is likely to be particularly appropriate in industrial international marketing research. Response to mail surveys may tend to be low and, furthermore, mail surveys do not allow adaptation to specific company situations. In telephone interviews, only a limited amount of information can be obtained from respondents and in relation to specific nonconfidential topics.

Personal interviewing provides a more effective means of adapting questions to a specific company or individual and of probing for answers. Willingness of management to cooperate and provide desired information may depend to a large extent on the competitiveness of the market environment. In certain countries or with certain product markets, such as pharmaceuticals or electronics, management may be considerably more reluctant to provide information than in product markets such as crafts, and so on. In the former case suspicion may be aroused that information may be leaked to competition, or be used to the company's detriment.

Similarly, in consumer research, for the reasons noted previously—that is, lack of sampling lists, inadequate mail services, and high levels of illiteracy—personal interviewing may often be the most appropriate method. The ease with which the cooperation of respondents can be obtained may, however, vary from one country or culture to another. In Latin countries, and particularly in the Middle East, interviewers are regarded with considerable suspicion. In 'Latin countries, where tax evasion is a national pastime, interviewers are often suspected of being tax inspectors. In the Middle East, where interviewers are invariably male, interviews with housewives often have to be conducted in the evenings when husbands are at home.

Thus, while personal interviewing may be the most expensive method of questionnaire administration, in international marketing research it may be the most cost effective. In consumer research in developing countries with high levels of illiteracy, personal interviewing may be mandatory. Yet, even in other situations, low wage rates coupled with higher rates of response, improved quality of the data, and representativeness of the target population may largely offset the higher costs.

RESEARCH STAFF RECRUITMENT AND TRAINING

A key problem in data collection in international markets is the need for reliable and high quality local research staff. This is a particularly important consideration insofar as local field and tab organizations may not be available outside the highly developed Westernized nations. Consequently, it may be necessary for a local research unit or international research supplier to establish their own field organization or import trained foreign staff. Where local interviewers are recruited for field interviewing, training programs may need to be developed to train interviewers.

Research Staff Recruitment

In recruiting research staff, decisions must be made as to what extent and in what positions local personnel should be used and whether trained foreign staff should be imported. Here, distinctions need to be made among research staff concerning individual skills, such as expertise in conducting focus groups, in data analysis, and in field interviewing. In the former case, if local researchers with the requisite skills are not available, one option is to import foreign researchers. In the case of field staff, local recruitment is preferable. Consequently, if an adequate pool is not available, training of local personnel is desirable.

In considering whether to use local researchers or import foreign researchers with specific skills, a number of factors need to be evaluated. As noted previously, this question arises particularly in the context of developing countries where research staff with specific skills, such as the ability to conduct in-depth interviews or focus groups, or skills in research design and analysis, may not be readily available.

The major advantage of using a local researcher for qualitative research or in research design is that he or she will know the local culture and people, as well as the language, and hence, be best able to understand local cultural differences. This may be particularly valuable in conducting qualitative research and lead to greater sensitivity to the specific concerns and interests of the respondent, as well as an ability to create an appropriate climate of confidence during the interview. Familiarity with the local culture is also an important input in adapting research instruments to the specifics of the local market environment. In addition, he or she will be familiar with the local physical, climatic, and research environment. Consequently he or she will be able to operate effectively in this context and cope with any problems arising as a result (Goodyear, 1982).

On the other hand, the local researcher may have more limited research experience than foreign staff and may not have the same specialist skills. In interviewing he or she may have difficulties in adopting a neutral and objective stance relative to respondents, or he or she may lack familiarity with the design of a sophisticated research instrument. In some cases, there may be a scarcity of local researchers with even the minimum required skills, thus necessitating consideration of importing foreign researchers.

An imported foreign researcher may have more experience and more specialized skills than a local researcher. The imported researcher is also likely to maintain a higher level of efficiency and energy, being accustomed to the faster pace of business in more-developed countries (Goodyear, 1982).

However, the imported researcher may experience difficulty in establishing contact with respondents due to language and other barriers. In particular, differences in cultural background may impede the interviewer from establishing the appropriate rapport with a respondent, a key to effective interviewing. Local agents or research organizations may not welcome the intrusion of the imported researcher. Furthermore, he or she may tend to encounter some adjustment problems in operating in a different physical and cultural environment, and hence, lose some degree of momentum (Goodyear, 1982).

The advantages and disadvantages of the different alternatives need to be carefully weighed in selecting research staff. Much depends on the level of skill of researchers in different countries and the extent to which a company or research organization is willing to import foreign researchers or maintain their own research staff in different countries. Whether or not a company or a research organization does maintain its own field staff will, however, depend to a large extent on the volume of business it conducts in each country.

Field Staff Training

A second issue is that of training field interviewers. This is particularly critical in cases where a pool of experienced interviewers is not readily available. In political and social surveys conducted in developing countries, extensive training programs have been developed for interviewing. Upscale individuals in leadership positions, such as village headmen, teachers, and country prefects, have been found to be good interviewers in these situations (Frey, 1970).

Interviewer training should cover basic instruction in the principles of good interviewing. First, it is necessary that interviewers should understand the importance of establishing a good rapport with the respondent and creating a good climate for interviewer-respondent interaction (Morris and van der Reis, 1980). Here, the manner in which the interviewer introduces himself or herself is often a major factor in developing this rapport. In addition, questionnaire administration needs to be clearly understood, with the application of standard procedures and instructions. Introduction of any type of bias, such as generation of any inferences that a certain type of response might be preferred or is right, should be avoided. In essence, the interviewer should be taught to remain as neutral as possible and to avoid interjecting any personal views.

In various instances this has been found to constitute a problem. A study in South Africa (Morris and van der Reis, 1980) found, for example, that local interviewers tended to help and guide respondents rather than allow respondents merely to follow the instructions in the questionnaire. Thus, they tended to influence the respondent and show how a task should be undertaken; for example, they might place the Smiling Faces in order rather than let the respondents do the task alone. Therefore, practice interviews may also be conducted in order to ensure that interviewers have learned the appropriate skills. In this context, use of one-way mirrors to observe the interview may be desirable, in order to avoid disturbing the interviewer or provoking some reaction from the respondent, due to the presence of a third party.

Even in more-developed countries, attention to interviewer training and to briefing and debriefing, is desirable to ensure maximal response rate, and to avoid bias arising from the interviewer-respondent interaction. This is particularly desirable where the interview involves open-ended or complex questions and tasks, such as projective techniques or multidimensional scaling. Such training can also make an important contribution in improving the quality of the data that is collected.

In the United Kingdom, for example, an interviewer card scheme is in operation, in which interviewers from companies belonging to the scheme are provided with an interviewer identity card. This is presented to respondents at the beginning of an interview. The purpose of the scheme is to encourage acceptance of interviewers by the public, and generate increased appreciation for their professionalism (Pottinger, 1982). It also serves to protect the general public from abuse of personal interviews by salespersons. Furthermore, it helps to establish a common standard for field work conducted by member companies.

In order to qualify for this scheme, the work of interviewers from member companies, and also the supervision of their work, is inspected twice annually. This includes levels of training, use of interviewer manuals, the degree of backchecking, and quality control. Certain standards have to be met, and this is reported to have improved the quality of interviewing, especially in the conduct of postal, personal, and phone backchecking.

SUMMARY

In determining appropriate sampling and survey administration procedures, a number of factors have to be taken into consideration. First, the relevant unit or level from which the sample is to be drawn has to be determined. Next is the selection of the technique to be used in drawing the sample. Related to this is the choice of survey administration procedures. In both cases, the impact of such decisions on the comparability and equivalence of the data from one unit to another has to be carefully considered, and weighed against the cost effectiveness of alternative plans and procedures.

In drawing the sample, a number of different levels or units may be considered, including the world, country groupings, countries, or groupings within countries. In making this decision, much depends on the purpose of the survey, the specific product or service concerned, and the target segment, as well as the availability and adequacy of various sampling frames or lists. Surveys concerned with industrial products or with upscale mobile target segments—such as businesspersons or foreign travelers—are, for example, more likely to sample at the world, region or country level than are surveys concerned with consumer packaged goods aimed at a mass market.

The choice of technique to be used in drawing the sample is closely related to the level at which the sample is drawn. In many countries, especially the developing countries, use of systematic random sampling techniques is likely to pose some difficulty. This is due to the lack of sampling lists, street maps, and guides; sprawling urban developments; and scattered rural populations. Consequently, convenience or judgment sampling procedures may have to be used in order to avoid excessive administration costs.

In selecting survey administration procedures, that is, telephone, mail, and personal interview, careful attention has to be paid to the efficacy of each procedure in reaching the sample population, as well as the potential sources of bias associated with each. In many countries, especially the developing countries, telephone surveys will only tap a relatively limited segment, and typically only short questionnaires can be administered by this means. Mail surveys are only effective in countries with high levels of literacy, or in relation to the literate population. Personal interviewing is thus likely to be the most common method of survey administration in cross-national research. This does, however, necessitate the availability or training of competent interviewers in order to minimize bias arising from the interviewer and interviewee interaction.

In brief, differences in market characteristics and the research infrastructure from one country to another, imply that the development of the sampling plan, and survey administration procedures, may entail more creative thought and effort than in the case of domestic marketing research. Means may have to be devised to develop and identify appropriate sampling lists and techniques, and to administer surveys without incurring excessive costs in conditions where the available infrastructure is extremely sparse. In addition, attention has to be paid to the issues of comparability from one sampling unit to another, and to minimizing potential sources of sampling error.

REFERENCES

ALMOND, G. and S. VERBA, *The Civic Culture: Political Attitudes and Democracy in Five Nations.* Princeton: Princeton University Press, 1965.

BARNARD, PHILIP, "Conducting and Co-ordinating Multicountry Quantitative Studies Across Europe," *Journal of the Market Research Society,* 24 (1982), 46–64.

CAMPBELL, D.T. and J.C. STANLEY, *Experimental and Quasi-Experimental Design.* Chicago, IL: Rand McNally, 1966.

COCHRAN, W.G., *Sampling Techniques,* 3rd Ed. New York: John Wiley, 1977.

CRAIG, C. SAMUEL and JOHN MCCANN, "Item Non-Response in Mail Surveys: Extent and Correlates," *Journal of Marketing Research,* 12 (1978), 285–90.

DE HOUD, MAURICE,   "Internationalized Computerized Telephone Research: Is It Fiction? *Marketing Research Society Newsletter,* 190 (January 1982), 14–15.

DOUGLAS, SUSAN P.,   "Examining the Impact of Sampling Characteristics in Multi-Country Survey Research," *Proceedings of 9th Annual Meeting of European Academy for Advanced Research in Marketing,* Edinburgh, 1980.

—— and ROBERT SHOEMAKER,   "Item Non-Response in Cross-National Surveys," *European Research,* 9, (October 1981), 124–32.

EISINGER, RICHARD A., W. PETER JAHICKI, ROBERT L. STEVENSON, and WENDEL L. THOMPSON,   "Increasing Returns in Mail Surveys," *Public Opinion Quarterly,* 38 (Spring 1974), 124–30.

FREY, F.,   "Cross-Cultural Survey Research in Political Science" in Robert E. Holt and John E. Turner, (eds.), *The Methodology of Comparative Research.* New York: The Free Press, 1970.

GODWIN, R. KENNETH,   "The Consequences of Large Monetary Incentives in Mail Surveys of Elites," *Public Opinion Quarterly,* 43 (Fall 1979), 378–87.

GOODYEAR, MARY,   "The Trials, Tribulations and Successes in Doing Qualitative Research in the Developing World," *Marketing Review,* 37 (January/February 1982), 21–26.

GREEN, PAUL E. and DONALD S. TULL,   *Research for Marketing Decisions,* 4th Ed. Englewood Cliffs, NJ: Prentice-Hall, 1978.

GREEN, ROBERT and ERIC LANGEARD,   "A Cross-National Comparison of Consumer Habits and Innovator Characteristics," *Journal of Marketing,* 49 (July 1975), 34–41.

HOLT, ROBERT E. and JOHN E. TURNER, (eds.),   *The Methodology of Comparative Research.* New York: The Free Press, 1970.

JAFFE, EUGENE D.,   "The Efficacy of Mail Surveys in Developing Countries—The Case of Israel," *European Research,* 10 (April 1982), 102–4.

KRACMAR, JOHN Z.,   *Marketing Research in the Developing Countries.* New York: Praeger, 1971.

LIPSTEIN, BENJAMIN,   "In Defense of Small Samples," *Journal of Advertising Research,* 15 (February 1975), 33–42.

MAYER, CHARLES S.,   "Multinational Marketing Research: The Magnifying Glass of Methodological Problems," *European Research,* 6 (March 1978), 77–84.

MORRIS, N. and A.P. VAN DER REIS,   "An Investigation of the Transferability of Rating Scale Techniques to Transport Research in a Developing Country," Pretoria, South Africa. National Institute for Transport and Road Research, Council for Scientific and Industrial Research, 1980.

POTTINGER, JANET,   "The Interviewer Card Scheme," *Marketing Research Society Newsletter,* 191 (February 1982), 10.

SEGNIT, SUSANNA and SIMON BROADBENT,   "Life-style Research," *European Research,* 1, no. 1 (January 1973), 6–19; 1, no. 2 (March 1973).

WEBSTER, LUCY,   "Comparability in Multi-Country Surveys," *Journal of Advertising Research,* 6 (December 1966), 14–18.

WILSON, WILLIAM J.,   "Pitfalls in International Research," *Marketing Review,* 37 (December/January 1982), 17–20.

WIND, YORAM,   *Industrial Buying Behavior: Source Loyalty in the Purchase of Industrial Components,* unpublished Ph.D. dissertation, Stanford University, 1966.

9

Multicountry Data Analysis

Once procedures for collecting data have been determined using either survey or nonsurvey methods, the next step is the choice of appropriate methods and procedures for data analysis. These two phases are interrelated as certain types of analysis; for example, multidimensional scaling requires specific types of data. There are a number of issues to be considered in relation to how data analysis is conducted and organized. Where research is conducted in a single country, these are the same as in domestic research. In multicountry research, the issues become more complex due to the existence of multiple units of analysis (that is, countries). First, the data need to be coded and edited, and the quality and reliability of the data must be examined. Once this has been accomplished, and the comparability of the data from one country to another determined, the next step is to conduct within-country and across-country analysis. In the case of nonsurvey research, this may merely be qualitative analysis. In the case of survey research, however, some type of quantitative analysis is likely to be conducted. Here, as in domestic marketing research, either univariate or bivariate methods of analysis, or alternatively, multivariate techniques, may be used.

Multicountry data analysis is more complicated than single-country analysis due to the hierarchical or multitier character of the research design, entailing analysis not only at the country level, but also across regions and eventually at a global level. In domestic marketing research, decision problems, and hence analysis, typically relate to a single national sample or unit of analysis. In multicountry research, however, management is concerned not only with developing marketing strategy or tactics relative to a single national market, but also with assessing the extent to which such strategies or tactics can be standardized across different national markets or geographic areas. Consequently, analysis needs to be conducted not only within countries, but also across countries. This poses a number of issues with regard to how and where the different phases of analysis are conducted.

The importance of this preliminary phase of coding and data checking suggests that it is likely to be desirable to decentralize this phase of analysis. Researchers from the country concerned are likely to be best qualified to check and code open-ended or other data. Issues of data reliability between different national samples can then be assessed, prior to statistical analysis and comparison of findings from different national samples.

In the second phase of the analysis, where results are examined both within countries and between countries, and particularly where sophisticated multivariate procedures are used, it is generally preferable to centralize the data. This ensures that comparable procedures, techniques, and computer programs are applied. Furthermore, if data are to be analyzed cross-nationally, the operation must be centralized.

In this chapter the problems associated with both phases of data analysis are examined, as well as procedures for minimizing difficulties. The discussion focuses primarily on the analysis of quantitative data. It is assumed that the reader is already familiar with standard marketing research texts (Green and Tull, 1978; Lehmann, 1979; and Churchill, 1983), and with the procedures commonly used to edit, code, and analyze data. First, issues arising in relation to the quality and reliability of the data are examined, and procedures for testing and comparing the reliability of quantitative data from different countries or units of analysis are discussed. Again, attention is focused on issues arising in relation to multicountry data, and familiarity with standard reliability measurement procedures is assumed. Next, methods of analyzing cross-national data are examined, including use of both univariate and multivariate techniques. Here, knowledge of statistical methods commonly applied to analyze domestic marketing data is assumed, and emphasis is placed on how analytical procedures and methods are used to test for similarities and differences between data from different countries or units of analysis.

QUALITY AND RELIABILITY OF DATA

An important consideration in collecting data in multicountry research is the quality of the data obtained. A sampling plan can be set up to ensure comparability of the samples from country to country, and the instrument may be well designed to minimize cultural bias. Cost-efficient survey administration procedures may be established. Yet, there may still be a number of underlying problems that might affect the quality and comparability of the data obtained from different countries or units of analysis that need to be carefully evaluated.

In the first stage of the analysis, an important consideration is the editing and coding of the data, and the examination of the data from different units for potential sources of bias that might imply that they are not comparable. Here, the key issue is to identify sources of cultural bias, and where comparable data are collected, to ensure that the same codes are used for all countries or units of analysis. Reliability has then to be examined, and in some cases appropriate adjustments may have to be made to ensure that the data are as equivalent as possible from one country to another.

Editing and Coding

An important aspect of the preliminary analysis is the editing and coding of the data. In editing, the same checks need to be applied as in domestic research, namely, for omission, interviewer error, ambiguity, inconsistency, lack of cooperation, and ineligible respondents. This may require that some or all of the responses from a respondent are thrown away, or that recontacting the respondent is required. A byproduct of this is that experience is gained in the effectiveness of instrument and survey administration procedures, as well as of different interviewers and other administration procedures.

In order to ensure consistency across different national samples, it is desirable that guidelines for editing and follow-up procedures are established centrally. For example, a rule that 25 percent of respondents should be contacted to ensure that they have in fact been interviewed, might be established. In general, the actual editing will be carried out by the local field organization, although some cross-checks may be centrally made.

An important problem in this regard concerns laws of data privacy with regard to individuals (Cole, 1981). In Germany, for example, either the names and addresses of respondents and questionnaires must be sent into the office separately, and no identifying system for matching them up is permitted; or an employee has to separate the names and addresses from the questionnaires as soon as they are received. This seriously affects backchecking. In fact, the only backchecking that can lawfully be done is to check from a name and address list that an interview has actually been carried out. No information on the questionnaire can be checked. Theoretically, recall interviews become impossible. In practice, however, marketing research organizations have usually managed to negotiate some arrangement that permits them to retain names and addresses for recall purposes, if they have agreement—usually in writing—from respondents.

In the case of coding, a key issue is to ensure the data are as comparable as possible across different samples in order to facilitate cross-national analysis. For close-ended questions this poses relatively few problems since different responses can be precoded, indicating how they should be entered in machine-readable form. In a few cases, some difficulties may, however, be encountered in ensuring comparable codes, as for example, for local brands, education, and so on. In the case of coding open-ended questions, substantially greater difficulties are likely to be encountered. It is desirable that coding categories be established by analysts familiar with the local market environment. Lists of items that might fall into each of these categories can then be generated, and as far as possible, categories harmonized or coordinated across countries.

In general, therefore, it is desirable to establish a central coding book, prior to key-punching, in order to ensure that, where questions are comparable, the codes used are the same for all countries, and that, for example, non-responses are coded in the same way (Barnard, 1982). Some flexibility will, however, be needed to code responses to questions that will vary from country to country, as, for example, brands, specific product attributes, product variants, or media that are not comparable from one country to another.

Once coded, questionnaires or other recording sheets can be key-punched onto cards, or keyed directly into the system. Where data analysis is centralized and time delays are crucial, country data files may be directly transmitted to the central location. Where facilities for interviewing by CRTs (cathode ray tubes) are available, data can be even more rapidly transmitted, and feedback obtained in the field, concerning results.

Data Reliability

Once the quality of the data has been considered, coding procedures have been developed, and the data edited, the next step is to examine the reliability of data. This is particularly important in countries or contexts where little research has been conducted, or with which the researcher has little prior experience. In these cases, the reliability of different types of data or measures may not be well documented, and particularly in the case of attitudinal data, will need to be verified and established.

When examining reliability—in contrast to considering whether a measure measures what it purports to measure, as in the case of validity or equivalence—attention is centered on whether the same result is obtained when a measure is repeated, in a different context, fashion, or time. Despite all efforts to design an instrument that is adapted to all countries and cultures, it may not be equally reliable in all these contexts. Different forms of attitudinal, life style, and other measures, may, in particular, vary in their level of reliability. The stability of data over time may also vary. It is thus important to compare the reliability of data obtained in different countries or contexts, since this may attenuate the precision of estimation, and reduce the power of statistical tests.

In cross-national research, reliability can be examined, based on external criteria, such as repeated measures, that is, test-retest reliability, or consistency of results reported by different judges, that is, interjudge reliability. Alternatively, internal consistency can be assessed using split-half reliability measures, or measures such as Cronbach's Alpha or Kuder-Richardson 20 can be applied (Nunnally, 1978). In both cases, levels of reliability are then compared across countries. In general, examination of reliability based on external criteria is preferable in cross-national research, since internal consistency measures may reflect sampling difficulties, as well as those arising from the instrument. This does, however, substantially increase costs, as well as increasing the burden of data collection and incurring delays in data processing.

Despite its significance, reliability of data in cross-national research has received relatively little attention (Davis, Douglas, and Silk, 1981; Schreiber, 1975–76). Available evidence suggests, however, that the reliability of data varies from country to country, and can give rise to problems, especially with regard to attitudinal and life style data.

A study of public opinion data, applying measures of test-retest reliability has, for example, investigated the reliability of information provided on age and education in the United Kingdom and the United States over time (Schreiber, 1975–76). For age, 91 percent of the United States sample, and 98 percent of the British sample, gave consistent reports in both waves of measurement. However, for education, the figure was only 74 percent in the United States sample, compared with 66 percent in Britain. This suggests that even for "objective" characteristics, such as age or education, reliability may not be as high as might be expected.

Another study based on questionnaires administered to couples in five countries applied interjudge measures of reliability to demographic, behavioral, and life style variables (Davis, Douglas, and Silk, 1981). The study was based on data from husbands and wives in countries from two linguistic groupings,—that is, two English-speaking countries, the United States and the United Kingdom, and three French-speaking countries, France, Belgium, and French Canada.

Here, somewhat higher levels of reliability were found for "hard" variables—for example, demographics—than for "soft" variables—for example, life style/attitudinal variables. In all, three types of measures were examined: 1) demographic and background characteristics, 2) self-reports of behavior in the form of ratings of involvement in household tasks and decisions, and 3) life style or psychographic variables. These thus spanned the diversity of constructs and types of measures commonly employed in consumer surveys.

In the case of the background characteristics and the measures of involvement in household tasks and decisions, husbands' and wives' responses to the same items were cross-tabulated, and a measure of agreement between them computed based on Cohen's k coefficient (Cohen, 1960). This measure, k, reflects the excess of observed over chance agreement, given the particular marginal distributions observed for the two sets of husbands' and wives' responses. In contrast to measures of association or correlation, the measure focuses on agreement based on the frequency of response in the main diagonal, rather than the overall contingency table.

For the background characteristics, the k values were generally quite high, indicating strong and consistent reliability across variables and samples. This suggests that the reliability of measures such as income or age is not, in general, likely to pose a major problem in cross-national surveys. In examining agreement for involvement in household tasks and decisions, the k coefficient showed less agreement than for background characteristics. It was therefore concluded that although husband and wife agreement in involvement in tasks and decisions exceeded that which might be expected by chance, the degree of agreement was generally moderate. Furthermore, there was some between-sample variation. In the case of the life style variables, an internal consistency measure was used to assess reliability applying the Kuder-Richardson (Formula 20) coefficient. This varied for different variables as well as for the samples, but the measures did appear to possess good discriminant ability, although this varied by country.

In situations where longitudinal data are routinely available, test-retest measures of reliability can be made. This is, however, likely to be relatively rare except in the case of panel data or advertising ratings. Data suitable for calculating measures of interjudge reliability are likely to be even rarer, due to the high costs of collecting data from two or more household members. Consequently, reliance is most likely to be placed on internal consistency measures of reliability. These might include statistics on internal consistency of multiple-item measures, as well as split-half reliability measures.

Linguistic and conceptual nonequivalence in questionnaire instruments used in cross-national surveys can thus produce differences in the reliability of measurements. This can, therefore, pose a threat to the validity of conclusions about similarities and differences in markets based on measures commonly used in cross-national surveys. Examination of reliability, while costly and time-consuming, is nonetheless critical, and more attention should be paid to include checks of this type as standard procedures in multicountry research.

This is particularly important in the early stages of research in foreign markets and in countries where only limited research experience has been accumulated. Understanding of the limitations and possible errors associated with different types of measures needs to be acquired. Progress can thus be made toward the development of improved techniques of data collection and measurement, and also of data analysis, and thus, toward greater confidence in the reliability of results.

METHODS OF ANALYSIS

Once data have been coded and edited, the quality and the reliability of the data examined, and various sources of bias identified, the next step is to conduct the desired type of analysis. Here, it is important that, wherever feasible, adjustments are made to ensure that the units of measurement are as comparable as possible across national samples. These may include, for example, procedures for the establishment of currency equivalents or metric equivalents and, in the case of attitudinal data, scale adjustment to ensure some degree of numerical equivalence. Various procedures may be utilized to adjust scales. They may, for example, be standardized or normalized. If scales are standardized, the mean for each subject is made equal to zero, and deviation is expressed in terms of standard deviation around that point. In normalization, the individual differences are expressed in terms of deviation from a group (that is, country) mean. Another alternative procedure is ipsatization (Straus, 1969; Cunningham, Cunningham, and Green, 1977). This is similar to normalization in that an individual's score is adjusted for the group, or country, mean. Once all such tests and adjustments have been made, the data are then ready for cross-national analysis.

In analyzing cross-national data, as noted previously, the existence of multicountry or other data units implies the desirability of adopting a two-stage or sequential approach to analysis. In the first stage, data are analyzed *within* countries or other relevant organizational units. In the second stage, the comparability of findings *across* different countries or organizational units is investigated, and the significance of observed differences and similarities examined.

In the first *within* country phase of analysis, the relationships among the independent variables—for example, among different attitudinal or socioeconomic variables; or among various dependent variables, such as purchases of different brands, or preferences for different product benefits—are examined. This enables identification or verification of relevant constructs to be examined in subsequent stages of analysis. For example, in the case of life style variables, it may be desirable to reduce the number of variables examined; or in the case of preference or purchase data, to identify relevant bundles of benefits or purchases. Then the association between the dependent and the independent variables can be studied. Here, techniques similar to those used in domestic marketing research are applicable and hence are not discussed further.

In the second, cross-national, phase of the analysis, the comparability of findings from one country to another is investigated. Here, an important consideration is whether the comparison is made on an implicit judgmental basis, or whether differences and similarities are explicitly analyzed. In the first case, the interpretation of the significance of observed variation across countries is based on subjective judgment incorporating previous management or researcher experience. In the second case, analytic techniques are applied to test the magnitude of differences and similarities between different countries or units of analysis. Various different procedures may be used, applying various univariate and multivariate methods. Subsequent discussion focuses on the advantages and limitations of these techniques in multicountry analysis.

This discussion assumes that the reader is already familiar with the underlying statistical formulas and computational procedures, and merely illustrates use of these formulas and procedures in international marketing research, based on examples drawn from available published sources. Readers not familiar with these techniques are referred to standard sources, such as Snedecor and Cochran (1967), Hays (1973), Winer (1971), and Siegel (1956).

Univariate and Bivariate Analysis

Univariate and bivariate analysis can be used to test the significance of differences, relative to one or two variables, between two samples. Such analysis tends in general to be descriptive rather than inferential, and thus is typically most appropriate in the initial phases of research, to identify areas where similarities and differences may exist.

Cross-Tabulation

Where cross-tabulations have been performed, chi-square tests can be conducted. This is a technique for determining the probability that differences between the expected and observed number of cases in each cell are significant. Where results are cross-tabulated by national sample data or by different subgroups within a country, chi-square can be used to test for independence between national samples or subgroups.

Chi-square analysis has been used to test for differences in levels of perceived risk for three products—bath soap, toothpaste, and instant coffee —between United States and Mexican consumers (Hoover, Green, and Saegert, 1978). Consumers were asked to respond, on a four-point Likert scale, to two questions relating to perceived risk for each product, namely, the degree of danger they felt in trying a brand they had not used before, and how certain they were that an untried brand would work as well as their present brand. The scores on both scales were summated to provide an overall measure of perceived risk, and chi-square analysis used to test for the significance of differences between countries for each product. This is shown in Figure 9.1. In all cases the computed chi-square was significant, indicating significant differences in risk perception between national samples.

An example of the second use is provided in a study by Hempel (1974) which examined the significance of differences between husbands and wives in the United States and the United Kingdom in their perceptions of role involvement in five house-buying decisions relating to the neighborhood in which the house was purchased, the style of house, when to purchase, an acceptable price, and where to apply for a mortgage. This analysis is shown in Table 9.1. In eight out of ten cases, significant differences were observed between husbands and their wives; but only in three cases, were there significant differences between

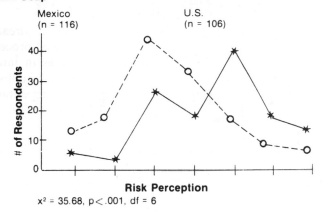

Bath Soap

x² = 35.68, p<.001, df = 6

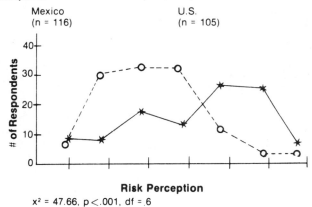

Toothpaste

x² = 47.66, p<.001, df = 6

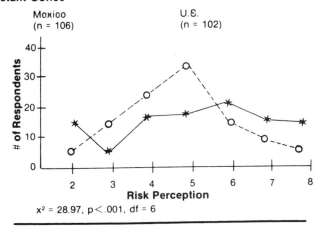

Instant Coffee

x² = 28.97, p<.001, df = 6

Nationality: Mexico O----O   U.S.A. *——*

FIGURE 9.1 Frequency of responses in the seven risk perception categories for the two nationalities for three products

Source: Robert J. Hoover, Robert T. Green, and Joel Saegert, "A Cross-National Study of Perceived Risk," *Journal of Marketing,* 42 (July 1978), 105.

TABLE 9.1 Cross-cultural comparisons of role differentiation perceived by husbands and wives in house-buying decisions

Buying decision		PERCENT DISTRIBUTION OF ROLES PERCEIVED BY HUSBAND & WIFE								CHI-SQUARE AND LEVEL OF SIGNIFICANCE	
		Connecticut (N = 145)				N.W. England (N = 183)				Husband vs. Wife	Connecticut vs. England
		WW	WJ	WH		WW	WJ	WH			
Neighborhood	HW	4	11	1	(16)	7	7	1	(15)	C: 6.66	H: 3.56
	HJ	6	66	6	(78)	7	65	2	(74)	E: 42.20[a]	W: 1.19
	HH	1	4	1	(6)	2	7	2	(11)		
		(11)	(81)	(8)		(16)	(79)	(5)			
Style of house	HW	7	16	1	(24)	3	14	0	(17)	C: 18.81[a]	H: 5.11
	HJ	7	60	2	(69)	7	64	3	(74)	E: 12.24[c]	W: 2.16
	HH	1	4	2	(7)	2	6	1	(9)		
		(15)	(80)	(5)		(12)	(84)	(4)			
When to purchase	HW	4	3	1	(8)	1	5	1	(7)	C: 38.15[a]	H: 2.41
	HJ	6	45	10	(61)	1	57	10	(68)	E: 10.11[c]	W: 21.80[a]
	HH	2	13	16	(31)	2	17	6	(25)		
		(12)	(61)	(27)		(4)	(79)	(17)			
Acceptable price	HW	0	1	1	(2)	2	2	1	(5)	C: 7.65	H: 1.59
	HJ	4	36	17	(57)	2	51	8	(61)	E: 40.31[a]	W: 10.70[b]
	HH	1	20	20	(41)	2	18	14	(34)		
		(5)	(57)	(38)		(6)	(71)	(23)			
Where to apply for mortgage	HW	1	1	0	(2)	1	6	0	(7)	C: 42.94[a]	H: 4.89
	HJ	4	24	6	(34)	1	35	8	(44)	E: 38.16[a]	W: 7.16[c]
	HH	1	21	42	(64)	1	17	31	(49)		
		(6)	(46)	(48)		(3)	(58)	(39)			

a = The frequency differences in the contingency tables on which these decision matrices are based were statistically significant the .001 level; b = .01 level; c = .05 level.

HW = husband perceived wife as dominant; HJ = husband perceived joint decision; HH = husband perceived self as dominant; WW = wife perceived self as dominant; WJ = wife perceived joint decision; WH = wife perceived husband as dominant.

Source: Donald J. Hempel, "Family Buying Decisions: A Cross-Cultural Perspective," *Journal of Marketing Research* 11 (August 1974), 295–302.

the American couples and the British couples; there were always differences for wives. Chi-square analysis is, however, a test of independence and as such provides no indication of the degree of association between two variables. Additional statistics, such as the contingency coefficient, phi, tau, or gamma, can be computed to provide an indication of the association between variables. For example, one might like to have some indication of the degree of husband-wife agreement between countries. This can be done by using the data in Table 9.1 and computing a contingency coefficient (see Siegel, 1956, for computational procedures and limitations).

The examples given so far have illustrated two-way cross-tabulations. In analyzing cross-national data, the researcher may want to use three-way or n-way cross-tabulations. For example, sex, purchase rate of a particular product, and country can be cross-tabulated. The computed chi-square statistic provides an indication of the overall degree of independence. Partial gammas can then be computed to provide a measure of the relationship between two variables, controlling for the third (or more) variable. In a cross-national context, this would allow determination of whether the relationship between sex and consumption of a particular product is affected by the country. (See Nie and others, 1975, pp. 228–229, for a discussion of the procedure.)

T-Tests

T-tests provide a relatively simple way of testing for differences in data obtained from national samples. A T-test is a statistic that provides a measure of the significance of differences between means drawn from two sample populations. It thus indicates whether there is a statistically significant difference between values on a given variable for two samples.

In international marketing research, T-tests can be used to test whether mean scores on a given variable are significantly different between countries. Alternatively, they can be used to test whether different subgroups or segments within countries exhibit significant differences in behavior, attitudes, and so on; and the level of significance in each country can then be compared.

T-tests have, for example, been used to test whether the perception of American and French directors of purchasing, toward five "made in" concepts, differed significantly (Cattin and Jolibert, 1979). The concept of "made in" five different countries—the United States, France, Germany, Japan, and England—were rated on twenty bipolar scales, such as expensive, mass produced, much advertising, clever use of color, and upper scale. Mean-scaled values for each scale were obtained for each of the two national samples, and T-tests performed to assess the significance of differences between the two samples. (See Table 9.2.)

T-tests have, also, been used to test whether differences in social class characteristics within the United States and France, namely between full-time

TABLE 9.2 American (A) and French (F) mean perceptions of the "made in" concepts

BIPOLAR DIMENSIONS[a]	MADE IN USA A[b] F[b]	MADE IN FRANCE A F	MADE IN GERMANY A F	MADE IN JAPAN A F	MADE IN ENGLAND A F	
			Price and value dimensions			
Inexpensive (1)	5.11 5.04 (−.39)[c]	5.02 4.52 (−3.49)	5.43 5.38 (−.31)	3.34 2.12 (−7.04)*	4.84 3.82 (−6.28)*	Expensive (7)
Reasonably Priced (1)	4.09 4.30 (1.14)	5.01 4.28 (−4.89)*	4.60 4.45 (−.85)	2.71 2.17 (−3.15)*	4.67 3.57 (−7.23)*	Unreasonably Priced (7)
Reliable (1)	2.87 3.11 (1.34)	4.22 3.22 (−6.21)*	1.93 2.53 (3.01)*	2.78 4.06 (7.03)*	4.01 4.14 (.73)	Unreliable (7)
Luxury Items (1)	2.68 4.78 (10.41)	3.25 3.00 (−1.40)	3.84 4.87 (5.64)*	3.65 4.87 (6.18)*	3.97 4.00 (.14)	Necessary Items (7)
Exclusive (1)	3.96 3.09 (−4.95)*	3.40 3.82 (2.59)*	3.13 3.23 (.57)	4.58 4.19 (−2.02)*	3.64 3.69 (.31)	Common (7)
Heavy Industry Products (1)	2.26 2.86 (3.58)	4.55 4.41 (−.84)	2.25 2.17 (−.51)	3.49 4.28 (3.33)*	3.88 3.88 (−.03)	Light Manufacture Products (7)

[a]Each extreme of the bipolar dimensions was assigned a 1 or 7 as shown.

[b]A stands for the mean perception of the American respondents and F for the mean perception of the French respondents.

[c]The t-value corresponding to the significance of the differences between American and French perceptions are shown below each pair of mean values. A positive t-value indicates that the American respondents perceive the corresponding concept as possessing more of the extreme that has a 1.
*means that the corresponding t-value is significant at the 5% level.

Source: Philippe Cattin and Alain Jolibert, "An American vs. French Cross-Cultural Study of Five 'Made In' Concepts," *American Marketing Association Proceedings*. Chicago: American Marketing Association, 1979. Reprinted with permission.

working women versus homemakers, would affect media exposure variables (Urban, 1977). Here, the analysis was conducted separately for each national sample; that is, T-tests were performed to examine differences in media exposure variables between working women and homemakers in each country, and the results were compared across countries (see Tables 9.3a and 9.3b). This showed that while there were significant differences in media usage between full-time working women and homemakers in the United States, relative to TV and radio, in France, there were differences only with regard to TV.

One-Way and Two-Way Analysis of Variance

Analysis of variance can be used to test for the significance of differences within a national sample or between different national samples. One-way analysis of variance tests whether the means of several samples are significantly different for a single variable. Two-way analysis of variance extends this logic to the situation where there are two influencing variables. Two-way analysis of variance thus tests for the effect of two variables, as well as interactions between these two variables. (See Winer, 1971, for detailed discussion of procedures and limitations.)

In international marketing research, one application of one-way analysis of variance would be to test whether a number of means differ. For example, if in the "made in" example discussed earlier (see Table 9.2) there was interest in knowing whether there were differences in perceived value across "made in" concepts, analysis of variance could be applied to the five mean responses for the United States sample. The same analysis could then be applied to the French sample. This use of analysis of variance is not appreciably different from the way in which it would be used in domestic marketing research. An extension of its use would be to test for the significance of differences on a variable between two countries. For example, analysis of variance has been used to test the significance of differences between Venezuelan and United States subjects in their preferences for three suits in two conditions (Green, Saegert, and Hoover, 1979). In one condition the subjects rated the suits independently in terms of the quality; and in the other, group pressure was exerted. Analysis of variance was used to test for the significance of differences in the mean quality ratings in the two situations, and the results obtained for the United States sample compared with those obtained for the Venezuelan sample. This showed that the Venezuelan sample appeared to be more susceptible to conformity pressure than the United States sample.

Analysis of variance has been used to test for national differences in brand loyalty and perceived risk for three products—bath soap, toothpaste, and coffee (Hoover, Green, and Saegert, 1978). Brand loyalty scores were compared within perceived risk scores and nationality, using a two-way analysis of

TABLE 9.3a Summary means on media usage by major demographic groups

UNITED STATES WOMEN

	Total sample $\bar{x}$	Employment status			Education			Income		
		Full-time $\bar{x}$	Home-maker $\bar{x}$	t	College $\bar{x}$	Grammar $\bar{x}$	t	High $\bar{x}$	Low $\bar{x}$	t
Television	2.37	2.15	2.53	7.60**	2.23	2.41	2.00*	2.25	2.43	2.57**
Radio	2.18	2.26	2.13	1.97*	2.23	2.02	1.91	2.28	2.07	2.38*
Newspapers	4.01	4.08	3.91	1.66	4.23	3.60	3.50**	4.45	3.66	5.64**
Magazines	1.84	1.85	1.82	.54	1.95	1.72	2.09*	1.96	1.78	2.02*
n	(2819)	(783)	(1012)		(811)	(226)		(520)	(931)	

**p < .01
*p < .05

246

TABLE 9.3b Summary means on media usage by major demographic groups

FRENCH WOMEN

	Total sample $\bar{x}$	Employment status			Education			Income		
		Full-time $\bar{x}$	Home-maker $\bar{x}$	t	College $\bar{x}$	Grammar $\bar{x}$	t	High $\bar{x}$	Low $\bar{x}$	t
Television	2.64	2.44	2.86	3.93**	1.83	2.85	14.11**	2.38	2.86	3.02**
Radio	1.32	1.33	1.37	.44	1.01	1.38	2.96**	1.11	1.36	1.97*
Newspapers	4.67	4.66	4.73	1.08	4.61	4.72	16.03**	4.60	4.67	.88
Magazines	4.33	4.28	4.36	1.02	4.25	4.56	2.67**	4.18	4.39	1.88
n	(1048)	(390)	(413)		(129)	(431)		(142)	(325)	

In the French data, media usage scales for newspapers and magazines range from 1 (regular use) to 5 (never use). For television and radio use, the scales are 1 (1 hour a day or less) to 9 (9 hours a day or more). In the U.S. data, 1 represents "never use" for all four media categories, and the maximum scale values are 5 (for television), 6 (for magazines and radio) and 7 (for newspapers).

**p < .01
*p < .05

Source: Christine D. Urban, "A Cross-National Comparison of Consumer Media Use Patterns," *Columbia Journal of World Business* (Winter 1977), pp. 62–63.

TABLE 9.4 Analysis of variance summary table for instant coffee in United States and Mexico, with brand loyalty as criterion variable (N = 204)[a]

Source of variation	Sum of squares	Degrees of freedom	F Ratio	Probability
A (Perceived risk)	.1965	6	10.92	< .01
B (Nationality)	.1125	1	37.51	< .001
A × B (Interaction)	.0594	6	3.30	< .01
Error	.5700	190	—	—

[a]N differs from 222 due to 18 respondents who indicated that they did not use instant coffee.

Source: Robert J. Hoover, Robert T. Green, and Joel Saegert, "A Cross-National Study of Perceived Risk," *Journal of Marketing* 42 (July 1978), 107.

variance. An example of one of these analyses, for instant coffee, is shown in Table 9.4. The two-way analysis of variance shows that there are differences in brand loyalty due to perceived risk and nationality, and also a significant interaction between the two. Analysis of variance can easily be extended to three-way or n-way analysis. The major limitation in the extension becomes the difficulty in interpreting the higher-order interactions.

Univariate and bivariate analyses perform a useful function in cross-national research. They enable presentation of results in a simple form that is clearly understood by management. However, they do not always facilitate an understanding of why differences occur between countries. They are not appropriate where many variables are to be studied, since examination of numerous cross-tabulations is tedious and cumbersome. While this can to some extent be alleviated by n-way cross-tabs (discussed earlier), this requires large sample sizes in order to ensure adequate cell size. Consequently, where several variables are to be examined, it is generally desirable to use multivariate analysis.

Multivariate Analysis

In many situations, the researcher is interested in the effect of more than one variable on a particular dependent variable. In this instance, multivariate statistical techniques, such as analysis of covariance, multiple regression, discriminant analysis, and conjoint analysis, can be used. In other situations, the relationship between a number of variables may be of interest to the researcher. Here suitable techniques include factor analysis, three-mode factor analysis, cluster analysis, and multidimensional scaling.

While in many instances multivariate techniques are used in international research in the same way as in domestic research, of particular interest is their application in cross-country analysis. Here, a key problem is to test for the significance of differences between countries in the dependent variables, or the relationship between dependent and independent variables, while checking that these are not due to any spurious factors related to research design or sampling procedures. A number of techniques, such as analysis of covariance (Winer, 1971) and three-mode factor analysis, (Tucker, 1964, 1966) offer the researcher powerful tools in this regard.

In the subsequent discussion of multivariate techniques, it is assumed, as in the case of univariate and bivariate techniques, that the reader is already familiar with these. Attention is therefore focused on applications in multi-country research. Readers not familiar with the basic principles underlying these techniques are referred to standard sources such as Cooley and Lohnes (1971), Johnston (1972), Green (1978), and Morrison (1976).

Analysis of Covariance

Analysis of covariance is an extension of analysis of variance. It can incorporate the effect of other variables, used as covariates, on the dependent variable(s). In cross-national research, it is particularly useful insofar as it enables the researcher to take into consideration the impact of sampling characteristics, such as income and age, on survey results. This is of particular interest when nationally representative samples are used. Especially if a diverse group of countries is examined, these are unlikely to be comparable in composition with regard to key variables, such as income, occupation, education, or age. This can create a major problem, particularly if such variables are related to the dependent variable, that is, the behavior studied. For example, in comparing interest in exotic tropical fruit in different countries, income or education might be an important factor affecting response. Mistaken inferences about national differences or similarities in interest in tropical fruits might therefore be made, when these actually reflect differences between samples in income distribution, rather than "true" national differences. One might, for example, conclude there was lack of adequate market potential, when in fact, a small high-income segment constituted a potential spearhead for market entry.

In applying covariance analysis, each national sample is treated as an experimental group. Although this implies nonrandom assignment to treatment groups, this has been found not to generate biased estimates (Overall and Woodward, 1977). The relevant socioeconomic and demographic or other sample characteristics likely to affect treatment response (that is, the dependent variable) are then used as covariates.

Next, the group response means and associated F statistics from the analysis of variance are compared with the corresponding means and F statistics in the covariance analysis (that is, after adjustment for the background characteristics). This indicates the extent to which the results are affected by sampling characteristics.

National or group response means can be adjusted for variance in the covariates, so that the impact of such variables is removed from the analysis. The magnitude of this adjustment can also be examined. Here, caution has to be exercised in the interpretation of results where there is the possibility of an association or common factor underlying the treatment means and the covariates.

The significance of the F statistics associated with each of the covariates can also be examined, to identify which specific sampling characteristics, such as age or income, are most strongly related to the dependent variable. Here, again, caution in interpretation needs to be exercised, due to the likelihood of multicollinearity among sampling characteristics such as age and income. Also, these are often variables of a discrete nature, thus violating the linearity assumptions of the underlying model. Some preliminary analysis and data reduction procedures—for example, factor analysis or a step down MANOVA procedure—may therefore be desirable (Homans and Messner, 1976).

Univariate analysis of covariance has been applied to examine the impact of sampling characteristics on the allocation of responsibility among husbands and wives for seventeen household tasks and decisions in five countries (Douglas, 1980). Previous research findings (Davis, 1976) provided substantial evidence that sampling characteristics such as age, income, and so on, are likely to affect response measures. Consequently, it was considered important to examine their effect when comparing differences between countries. Two-way analyses of variance by sex (husband and wife) and country, followed by analyses of covariance, were therefore conducted for seventeen measures of involvement in different household activities, using eleven socioeconomic and demographic characteristics as covariates. This is shown in Table 9.5.

Inspection of Table 9.5 clearly shows that some of the differences observed between the groups disappear once the impact of sample background characteristics is taken into consideration. For example, eleven out of the seventeen scores showed significant differences in the analysis of variance, compared with only seven in the analysis of covariance. Adjustments in the scores were relatively small (that is, less than .20). The significance of the relationship between the background characteristics and the dependent variables was not examined, due to the problems of multicollinearity among the sampling characteristics.

Multivariate Analysis
of Covariance

Multivariate analysis of covariance is a generalization of the analysis of the covariance model to the case involving more than one dependent variable (see, for example, Winer, 1971). It explicitly takes into account intercorrelation

TABLE 9.5 Summary table for the analyses of variance and covariance of involvement scores by sex and country

F STATISTICS FOR SHARED DIMENSION

Activity	Analysis of variance			Analysis of covariance			
	Country	Sex	Interaction	Country	Sex	Interaction	11 Covariates
Savings	9.94**	1.06	0.46	6.33*	1.57	0.7	5.85*
Bills	3.53	1.18	0.07	2.64	2.37	0.22	2.18
Checkbook	7.31**	0.19	0.31	3.44	0.69	0.30	2.52
Garbage	9.99**	3.07	0.48	7.18*	3.77	0.33	3.83
Vacuum cleaning	4.71*	0.01	0.35	3.30	0.02	0.38	10.12**
Repairman	8.41**	8.28**	0.72	5.60*	8.40**	1.01	5.07*
Garage	8.78**	7.79	0.97	3.14	4.16	0.63	3.36
Travel	5.34*	0.10	0.09	2.36	0.00	1.15	3.81
Furniture	3.72	0.15	0.22	2.50	0.13	0.16	1.82
Evening	0.28	0.20	1.51	0.76	0.00	1.18	1.71
Suit	62.10**	3.25	0.33	24.42**	3.40	0.20	2.05
Record	1.93	7.62**	0.12	1.68	5.74*	0.19	3.04
Car	2.36	1.33	0.60	0.97	0.78	0.51	2.63
Clothes	17.25**	2.76	0.37	5.33*	1.73	0.23	0.94
Supermarket	19.92**	0.63	0.47	11.25**	0.00	0.85	5.22
Garden	10.23**	0.37	0.31	6.74*	0.09	0.41	3.31
Bath	5.83*	0.47	0.61	3.46	1.35	0.75	1.15

*Significant at the .05 level
**Significant at the .01 level

Source: Susan P. Douglas, "Examining the Impact of Sampling Characteristics in Multi-Country Survey," Proceedings, European Academy for Advanced Research in Marketing, Edinburgh, March, 1980.

among dependent variables. Thus, differences significant in a univariate analysis may disappear in an overall multivariate analysis, and conversely, differences that do not appear in a univariate analysis may emerge in a multivariate analysis.

In cross-national research, multivariate analysis of covariance can be used when analyzing within country data to control the effect of sampling characteristics on the interaction between other variables; for example, different measures of response to advertising commercials for brand users and nonbrand users. Results for different countries can then be compared. As in univariate analysis of variance, multivariate analysis of covariance can also be applied to data pooled across countries, to take out the effects of sampling characteristics, or other variables such as attitudinal characteristics, when making comparisons between countries.

In a study comparing purchase behavior of working and nonworking wives in France and the United States, multivariate analysis of covariance was used to assess whether differences between these two groups within each country were greater or less than between the two countries (Douglas, 1976). While the samples were initially matched with regard to age, working, and educational status, it was considered important to examine the effect of other background characteristics such as income, number of children, and type of dwelling, on differences and similarities between the two country groups as also between the working and nonworking groups.

A two-by-two factorial design, by working and nonworking wives, and by France and the United States, was used. Multivariate analysis of covariance was conducted relative to five sets of variables: eight grocery shopping variables; frequency of purchasing ten convenience products and services; nine clothing shopping characteristics; seven fashion attribute ratings; and ten attitudinal measures (Table 9.6). This enabled examination of differences between the five sets and provided useful summary measures. This was particularly advantageous since there were likely to be interrelationships within each set of variables.

This showed that in a number of cases, variables such as the number of children and income, affected response means, and hence, their impact needed to be examined more closely. There was, however, little evidence of any systematic relationship between such variables across all purchase and attitudinal variables, which might suggest that these reflected a common factor underlying the various treatment groups and these covariates.

Attitudinal factors were also expected to play some role in the differences observed between the samples in purchase behavior. A second covariance analysis was undertaken, in which the ten attitudinal measures (female role perception, pride in home, opinion leadership, fashion interest, optimism, and so on) were used as covariates. This indicated that attitudes had little effect on

TABLE 9.6 Summary table of the multivariate analyses of covariance for the purchasing and attitudinal variables (with 10 socioeconomic and demographic covariates) (Approximate F statistics)

Source of variance	PURCHASING VARIABLES			ATTITUDINAL	
	8 grocery shopping characteristics	10 convenience product services	9 clothing shopping characteristics	rating of 7 fashion info sources	ratings on 10 attitudinal scales
United States versus France	18.94*	11.52*	5.36*	6.51*	3.38*
Working versus nonworking wives	2.20*	1.35	1.57	1.19	2.06*
Interaction	2.87*	1.36	1.28	0.53	0.92
Covariates					
Number of children	4.61*	0.66	3.28*	2.25*	0.94
Wife's age	0.83	1.88	2.57*	1.43	1.22
Daily help	1.01	0.68	0.52	1.78	2.66*
Wife's education	1.44	2.65*	0.63	0.78	4.25*
Number of cars	1.63	0.95	1.41	0.96	1.23
Husband's occupation	1.07	2.47*	0.68	1.90	0.99
Husband's education	0.23	0.65	0.50	2.03	2.63*
Income	1.23	2.27*	2.68*	2.17	2.18*
Number of rooms in home	1.86	1.20	1.79	0.44	1.20
Live in apartment	1.13	0.95	1.12	0.18	1.01

* Significant at the .05 level.

Source: Reprinted with permission from: Susan P. Douglas, "Cross-National Comparisons and Consumer Stereotypes: A Case Study of Working and Non-Working Wives in the U.S. and France," *Journal of Consumer Research,* 3 (June 1976), 16.

purchase behavior but did have some influence on sources of fashion information used.

Multiple Regression

Regression analysis is a robust statistical technique. In simple regression, the dependent variable is assumed to depend on a single independent variable. In multiple regression, a number of variables are assumed to underlie variance in the dependent variable. For further discussion of regression techniques, see Cohen and Cohen (1975) and Johnston (1972). In cross-national research, multiple regression can be used to examine the extent to which certain variables account for variation in one variable within countries, and the results compared from one country to another, either qualitatively, or by explicit statistical testing. Data from different countries can also be pooled, and countries entered as dummy variables in the regression.

In a study of the relationship between performance and various marketing variables, in three geographic areas—the United States, Europe, and other foreign markets—multiple regression analysis was applied (Douglas and Craig, 1981). Two measures of performance, market share and ROI, were identified, and two sets of multiple regressions were run; one with market share as the dependent variable, and one with ROI as the dependent variable. In both cases, the independent variables were the seven marketing mix variables and firm type (consumer versus industrial). These two regressions were run separately for each of the three market areas. The regressions with market share as the dependent variable are shown in Table 9.7. This showed a high degree of similarity between the United States and other foreign markets. As has been found in other studies, the key factors associated with high market share were high-quality, premium-priced products, and expenditure on research and development, while sales force expenditure and the percent of new products were negatively associated with high market share. This did not, however, appear to carry over into European markets, where other factors appeared to be operating. Where an explicit test of differences in the beta coefficients from one sample to another is required, the Chow-test can be applied (Fisher, 1970).

TABLE 9.7 R^2 and beta coefficients for the regressions with market share as dependent variable

	U.S. markets (n = 678)	European markets (n = 38)	Other foreign markets (n = 35)
Sales force expenditure	−.18[b]	.06	−.40[b]
Media and promotion expenditure	−.01	−.33	−.66[b]
Other marketing expenditure	.03	.31[a]	−.18
Relative price	.17[b]	−.19	.44[a]
Product quality	.31[b]	.37[b]	.11
New products	−.14[b]	−.11	−.34[b]
Product research and development	.27[b]	.01	.46[b]
Firm type	−.07[a]	.85[b]	.26[a]
Unadjusted R^2	.23[b]	.60[b]	.57[b]

[a] Significant at .05 level.
[b] Significant at .01 level.

Source: Susan P. Douglas and C. Samuel Craig, "Some Decision Variables Related to Performance in International Operations," Annual Meeting of Academy of International Business, Montreal, 1981.

Multiple regression can also be conducted on data pooled across countries. Each country is then entered as a dummy variable (0,1). If, for example, the effect of income, age, and household size on purchases of automobiles were to be compared across four countries, a single multiple regression could be run, with the automobile purchase data in the first four countries as the dependent variable; the data on the income, age, and household size in each country as independent variables; and the four countries represented by three dummy variables. This would only enable examination of whether there were differences between countries, that is, whether the dummy variables were significant. However, differences with regard to the effect of the independent variables in the different countries could not be determined from this type of analysis.

Multiple Discriminant Analysis

Discriminant analysis is similar in principle to regression except that the dependent variable is categorical rather than continuous. Discriminant analysis attempts to predict group membership based on a number of independent variables. It also indicates which variables are significant in discriminating between groups. It might, for example, be used to predict the purchase of private versus manufacturer brands, based on variables such as income, price sensitivity, or quantity of butter purchased per month. The reader is referred to Tatsuoka (1970) for more detailed discussion of the underlying assumptions and statistical formulation.

In international marketing research, discriminant analysis can be used to identify which variables are significantly different between two or more national samples or units of analysis. Each national sample or unit is thus treated as a categorical variable or group, and differences in relevant independent variables examined. Similarly, it can be applied to test for differences beween subgroups or segments within a country, and the results compared across countries.

Multiple discriminant analysis has, for example, been used by the Singer Company in a study of the factors underlying profitability in its North and South American and European Markets (Ferber and DeSa, 1977). Initial examination of the factors affecting profitability suggested the existence of two major groups of countries, based on per capita income, that is, highly developed countries and less-developed countries. In highly developed countries, profitability was thought to be a function of accounting and environmental variables, while in less-developed countries, profitability was thought to be related to the product mix. Multiple discriminant analysis was applied to a number of profit-and-loss statement and product mix variables, selected by means of regression analyses, to test for differences between the two groups.

The results of this analysis are shown in Table 9.8. These suggest that, in fact, variables such as market share, fixed costs, and sales ratios are related to profitability in the developed countries, while in the developing countries, product mix variables were more critical.

Discriminant analysis has also been used to examine differences in magazine readership between working and nonworking wives in the United States and France (Douglas, 1977). The results of this analysis are shown in Table 9.9. Here, since the magazines typically read in the two countries were different, two separate discriminant analyses were conducted, one for each country. This showed that in the United States, homemaker magazines were more frequently read by nonworking wives, though shelter magazines were read more frequently by working wives; but few differences with regard to other types of magazines were observed. Similarly, in France, overall differences in readership patterns between working and nonworking wives were slight.

Conjoint Analysis

Conjoint analysis assumes that an individual's overall evaluation or judgment of an object or product can be broken down into part worth judgments

TABLE 9.8   Discriminant analysis[a]

MODEL I DATA

Variable means by group and difference in means

Variable	Mean 1	Mean 2	Difference
X– 1	294.46	201.57	92.89
X– 2	307.38	494.50	–187.12
X– 3	394.54	471.43	–76.89
X– 4	399.23	210.71	188.52
X– 5	212.08	144.07	68.01
X– 6	433.08	445.00	–11.92
X– 7	540.00	136.43	403.57

Discriminant function coefficients

A_1	A_2	A_3	A_4	A_5	A_6	A_7
0.00032	–0.00016	–0.00040	0.00032	0.00091	–0.00043	0.00024

Mahalanobis	D-Square -	7.83138
	$F_{(7, 19)}$	5.73141

Pop. no.	Sample size	Mean z[b]	Variance z	Std. dev. z
1	13	0.15386	0.01777	0.13330
2	14	–0.15940	0.00770	0.08772

TABLE 9.8 (*cont.*)

		MODEL I DATA		
Rank	First group values of z	Second group values of z	First group item no.	Second group item no.
1	0.48384		13	
2	0.28002		6	
3	0.26975		7	
4	0.18782		5	
5	0.17128		11	
6	0.15855		8	
7	0.13518		10	
8	0.13498		1	
9	0.08397		12	
10	0.03067		2	
11	0.02589		9	
12	0.02335		4	
13	0.01484		3	
14		-0.00082		1
15		-0.01098		10
16		-0.10342		3
17		-0.10563		2
18		-0.10973		11
19		-0.12829		12
20		-0.17706		8
21		-0.18657		14
22		-0.18717		6
23		-0.20833		4
24		-0.21847		9
25		-0.23087		7
26		-0.26665		13
27		-0.29756		5

[a]These are not separate tables but represent the essentials of one computer printout.
[b]z is the "linear discriminant function" defined by $z = A_1X_1 + A_2X_2 + \ldots + A_nX_n$.

Source: Robert C. Ferber and Edward D. DeSa, "Modelling One Company's International Marketing Locations," *Columbia Journal of World Business,* 12 (Winter 1977), 44–52.

about different product or object attributes. This is discussed in detail in Green and Wind (1973). In conjoint analysis, a number of overall evaluations of different combinations of levels on these attributes are obtained. These are then decomposed to assess the utilities assigned to different levels of attributes.

In multicountry research, conjoint analysis can be used to examine buyers' preferences for, and evaluations of, products with regard to different product attributes in different countries. These preferences can then be compared across countries to assess differences and similarities.

Conjoint analysis has, for example, been used to assess buyers' perceived needs and preferences for car models in Britain, France, Germany, and Sweden

TABLE 9.9   Results of the discriminant analysis of the factor scores for U.S. magazine readership

	Mean factor scores		Univariate F ratios
	Working wives (n = 57)	Nonworking wives (n = 49)	
Homemaker magazines	−0.14	0.17	3.8*
Shelter magazines	0.08	−0.09	1.6*
News magazines: 2 (New Yorker)	0.08	−0.09	1.3
News magazines: 1 (Time)	0.04	−0.05	0.1
Service magazines	0.01	−0.02	0.1
Family magazines	−0.03	0.03	0.0

*Significant at the .05 level

Results of discriminant analysis of factor scores for French magazine readership

	Mean factor scores		Univariate F ratios
	Working wives (n = 54)	Nonworking wives (n = 48)	
General interest magazines	−0.37	0.39	21.2*
Women's fashion magazines	−0.21	0.27	7.9*
Shelter magazines	−0.17	0.16	3.4*
TV magazine 1	−0.10	0.08	1.4
TV magazine 2	0.03	−0.01	1.0
Catholic magazines	0.05	−0.04	0.6
Romantic story magazines	−0.06	0.09	0.5
Business magazines	−0.04	0.04	0.2
Women's magazines	−0.02	0.04	0.0

*Significant at the .05 level

Source: Susan P. Douglas, "Do Working Wives Read Different Magazines from Non-Working Wives," *Journal of Advertising*, 6 (Winter 1977), 42.

(Colvin, Heeler, and Thorpe, 1980). A sample of consumers in each country was required first to evaluate a set of twenty-seven product attributes, pairwise. This enabled identification of a reduced set of alternatives. Respondents were then required to rate a new car model on these attributes at two levels: a "low" awareness level where respondents were only shown photographs of the exterior of the car, and a "high" awareness level where respondents were given a

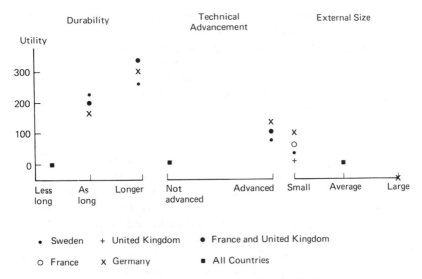

FIGURE 9.2 Utility values for four countries for three attributes

Source: Michael Colvin, Roger Heeler, and Jim Thorpe, "Developing International Advertising Strategy," *Journal of Marketing,* 44 (1980), 73-79.

full photographic and verbal briefing on exterior and interior appearance, features and performance, and so on. Both current and new models were evaluated in this way. From this, utility values for the various attributes in each country were obtained. These showed significant differences between countries in technical advancement and external size, as indicated in Figure 9.2. The utilities obtained for each individual in the conjoint analysis were then used to predict purchase intentions for different model types.

Cluster Analysis

The purpose of cluster analysis, as the name indicates, is to group variables, objects, or individuals into clusters that are more similar to each other than to variables, objects, or individuals in another cluster. For a more complete discussion, see Green, (1978); Sneath and Sokal, (1973). Two major types of cluster analysis can be identified. Hierarchical clustering starts by linking together the two most similar objects or variables, based on a measure of distance or similarity, the next two most similar, and so on, until all variables or objects are in a single cluster. See, for example, Johnson, (1967). In centroid clustering, objects or variables are divided first into two groups or clusters, such that, overall, a member of a cluster is more similar to a typical group member than to members of another group. See, for example, Howard and Harris, (1966). Objects and variables are then divided into three, four, or as many groupings as are desired, based on the same principle. Cluster analysis can thus be used in multicountry research to identify different subgroupings within countries, and to assess whether these are similar across countries. It can also be, and is commonly, used to identify groups of countries that appear to be similar in terms of some relevant factors.

A simple type of hierarchical cluster analysis is the McQuitty procedure. This has been used to examine similarity in involvement in different household tasks and decisions in five countries—that is, the United States, the United Kingdom, France, Belgium, and French Canada—from two linguistic groups (Douglas, 1979). The purpose of the analysis was to assess whether similarities would be greater within the linguistic groupings, that is, the United Kingdom and the United States as opposed to France, Belgium, and French Canada; or between North America as opposed to European countries.

A sample of couples from each of the five countries was asked to indicate the degree of involvement of the husband, as opposed to the wife, in seventeen household activities. Two separate dimensions of husband-wife involvement were distinguished: the relative involvement of the husband as opposed to the wife, and the proportion of couples who shared responsibility for an activity. Spearman correlations of rank order on seventeen activities were calculated between all possible pairs of the five groups (ten in all) for each of the two dimensions of husband-wife involvement. McQuitty hierarchical clusterings for these two sets of correlations were then performed (McQuitty, 1960). These are shown in Figure 9.3. These showed, in both cases, greater similarities within the two linguistic groupings than between North American and European continents.

Cluster analysis has also been used to group countries into clusters that are similar in terms of certain relevant characteristics. Typically, these clusters have been developed based on macroeconomic data such as GNP per capita, degree of urbanization, population, imports and exports, percentage of the population in agriculture, and level of literacy. This assumes that these factors imply similar marketing environments, and hence, lead to meaningful groupings for planning international marketing strategies.

One of the most detailed analyses of this type applied the BC Try system to fifty-six variables for ninety-three countries (Sethi and Curry, 1973). The variables were first factored to identify clusters of variables and to reduce problems of intercorrelation. This yielded six clusters: aggregate production and transportation, affluence and life styles, purchasing power of money, international trade, economic advancement, and health and entertainment. The countries were then clustered in two, three, four, five, and six dimensions. The span diagram for the six-dimension solution is shown in Figure 9.4. The two-dimension solution essentially resulted in a division between the highly in-

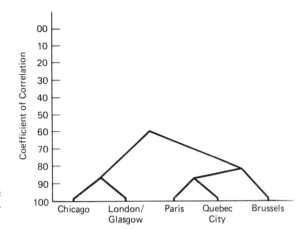

FIGURE 9.3a
McQuitty clustering of the five groups based on shared involvement measures[a]

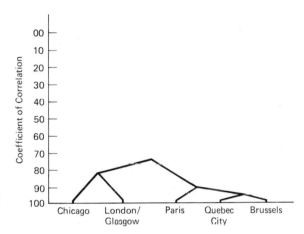

FIGURE 9.3b
McQuitty clustering of the five groups based on the degree of husband involvement measure[b]

[a] The shared involvement measured was calculated on the basis of the proportion of "sometimes husband, sometimes wife" and "both" responses relative to the total response for the activity.

[b] The degree of husband involvement measure was calculated on the basis of the proportion of "mainly husband" responses relative to the total of both "mainly husband," and "mainly wife" responses.

Source: Susan P. Douglas, "A Cross-National Exploration of Husband-Wife Involvement in Selected Household Activities," *Advances in Consumer Research,* vol. 5, Ann Arbor: Association for Consumer Research, 1979.

dustrialized nations and the developing countries. Further splitting resulted in a breaking down of the first group into two groups of developed countries, and a splintering of the second group into one main group of developing countries, and three small groups of six or less countries.

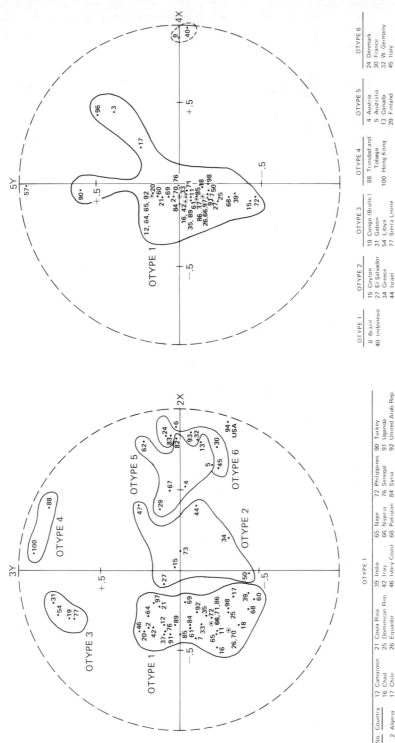

FIGURE 9.4 Span diagram of country types (6 dimensions)

Source: S. Prakash Sethi and David Curry, "Variable and Object Clustering of Cross-Cultural Data: Some Implications for Comparative Research and Policy Formulation" in S. Prakash Sethi and Jagdish Sheth, *Multinational Business Operations Marketing Management.* Pacific Palisades, CA: Goodyear Publishing Co., 1973.

Factor Analysis

Like cluster analysis, factor analysis is concerned with examining inter-relationships among a set of variables. Essentially, factor analysis groups together variables into factors consisting of intercorrelated variables. In contrast to cluster analysis, factor analysis uses the intercorrelation among variables to develop the factor structure while cluster analysis relies on a measure of distance between objects. Factor analysis can be used for two basic purposes. It can be used to reduce the number of variables to be analyzed and to ensure that there is no multicollinearity between variables. Alternatively, it can be used to identify underlying relationships or structure within the data. (See Harman, 1967, for a complete reference on factor analysis.)

Various types of factor analysis can be identified. Principal components analysis is probably the most commonly used. This identifies factors based on the correlation matrix of variables, and forms a number of "factors" that effectively summarize the interrelationships among the variables. A number of reduced variables are thus obtained that can be used in subsequent stages of the analysis. In Q-type factor analysis, on the other hand, rather than grouping variables, objects are grouped based on variables, thus transposing the original data matrix.

Factor analysis has been used in international marketing research to reduce the number of variables to be analyzed, and to identify comparable constructs to be compared in subsequent phases of the analysis. In comparing magazine readership, for example, in the United States and France, the frequency of reading different magazines in each country was first factor analyzed to reduce the number of variables to be handled (Douglas, 1977). This also eliminated any potential problems of multicollinearity in the subsequent phases of the analysis. The results of this analysis are shown in Table 9.10. The groupings that emerged were somewhat different in the two countries. In the United States the three most frequently read groups of magazines were family magazines, news magazines, and homemaker magazines. In France, on the other hand, readership was more disparate, the most frequently read magazines being a group of women's magazines, fashion magazines, business magazines, and two TV magazines.

Factor analysis has also been used to examine interrelationships among variables based on national data. These relationships can then be compared across countries. In one study of women's life style patterns in three countries, the United States, the United Kingdom, and France, for example, factor analysis was performed on a battery of life style statements collected independently in each country (Douglas and Urban, 1977). In each case, five factors were extracted: the first four were highly similar in all three cases, and consisted of a home factor, a social factor, a frustration factor, and an innovation factor. The specific variables defining these factors did, however, vary from country to country. Table 9.11 shows the variables defining the home factor in the three countries.

TABLE 9.10   Results of factor analysis of U.S. magazine readership[a]

(percent of variance explained and factor loadings)

Family magazines	*(40.3%)*	News magazines: 1	*(25.1%)*
Family Circle	.83	*Time*	.54
Woman's Day	.77	*MS*	.48
Homemaker magazines	*(13.9%)*	News magazines: 2	*(8.7%)*
McCalls	.77	*New Yorker*	.65
Ladies' Home Journal	.63	*Holiday*	.52
American Home	.48		
Shelter magazines	*(6.7%)*	Service magazines	*(5.3%)*
House & Garden	.80	*T.V. Guide*	.54
Better Homes & Gardens	.49	*Reader's Digest*	.46

Results of the factor analysis of French magazine readership[a]

(percent of variance explained and factor loadings)

Women's magazines	*(25.7%)*	Women's fashions magazines	*(20.8%)*
Marie-Claire	.81	*L'Echo de la Mode*	.80
Elle	.71	*Femme d'Aujourd'hui*	.53
La Maison de Marie-Claire	.64		
Business magazines	*(10.6%)*	TV magazine	*(9.6%)*
L'Express	.87	*Tele-Poche*	.70
General interest magazines	*(8.3%)*	TV magazine 1	*(9.6%)*
Jours de France	.80	*Tele 7 Jours*	.62
Paris Match	.70		
Romantic magazines	*(6.7%)*	Catholic magazines	*(6.0%)*
Bonnes Soirées	.90	*La Vie Catholique*	.72
		L'Echo de Notre Temps.	.58
Shelter magazines	*(4.8%)*		
Maison et Jardin	.56		

[a] Columns show percent variance explained in parentheses and factor loadings.

Source: Susan P. Douglas, "Do Working Wives Read Different Magazines from Non-Working Wives," *Journal of Advertising,* 6 (Winter 1977), 43.

Other studies have not only examined factor patterns of data from country samples, but also have applied procedures to test explicitly for the similarity of the factor patterns between countries. One study of attitudes toward advertising among young and old subscribers to product test magazines in the United States and Germany applied a complex technique suggested by Meredith

TABLE 9.11 Key statements from the home factor

United States	Factor loading	United Kingdom	Factor loading	France	Factor loading
I am a homebody	.67	I am a homely kind of person	.62	In the evening I would rather stay at home than go out	.54
A woman's place is in the home	.70	A house should be dusted and polished at least three times a week	.44	A woman's place is in the home	.59
I love to work on improving our home	.65	The kind of dirt you can't see is worse than the dirt you can see	.44	I enjoy most household tasks	.61
I am a very neat person	.59				
All men should be clean-shaven every day	.66	All men should shave every day	.54	Obedience and respect for authority are the most important things to teach a child	.55
On a job, security is more important than money	.65	On a job, security is more important than money	.49	It is the duty of every Frenchman to defend his country no matter what the circumstances	.53
Today, most people don't have enough discipline	.66	Today, most people don't have enough self-discipline	.46		
I have somewhat old-fashioned tastes and habits	.59	There is too much emphasis on sex today	.53		

Note of explanation: Factor loadings measure the degree to which each variable is associated with the factor in question; the higher the loading figure, the stronger the association. For instance, on the statement "I am a homebody" above, 67% of the variance of this variable is explained by the home factor. This variable, taken together with other variables having a high loading on same factor, helps in determining the meaning of the factor.

Source: Susan P. Douglas and Christine D. Urban, "Life-style Analysis to Profile Women in International Markets," *Journal of Marketing*, 41 (July 1977), 48.

(Anderson, Engledow, and Becker, 1980). This entails rescaling the original factor matrix for each country sample to ensure comparable variance and forming a correlation matrix from these rescaled factor patterns. This is then used to form an average factor matrix. Differences in factor patterns between countries were then examined by developing indexes of deviation between the patterns in the average factor matrix and the rescaled factor matrix for each country. Differences in the overall pattern of the factor matrixes were examined by computing coefficients of congruence (Harman, 1967). These are shown in Table 9.12.

Higher-order factor analysis provides another means for comparing factor structures across countries. In a study comparing attitudes and behavior of subscribers to product testing magazines in the United States and Germany, first and second order factor analyses were conducted on data for each country (Anderson and Engledow, 1977). Path diagrams were then utilized to trace the relationships between variables in the first- and second-order factors. These are illustrated in Figure 9.5 for the German sample.

First-order and second-order factors were compared visually, and factors

TABLE 9.12 Pattern target and indices of similarity

Advertising variables	Pattern target		INDICES OF DEVIATION			
			1970		1976	
	Economic	Social	U.S.	W.G.	U.S.	W.G.
Advertising						
1. is essential	.708	− .032	.03	.09	.01	.09
2. does not insult intelligence	.279	.795	.04	.12	.02	.02
3. results in lower prices	.749	.215	.02	.03	.03	.03
4. does not persuade people to buy things they do not want	− .129	.876	.01	.01	.01	.01
5. presents a true product picture	.618	.451	.01	.01	.01	.04
6. helps raise the standard of living	.876	− .035	.01	.03	.00	.02
7. results in better products	.852	.140	.01	.06	.01	.02
Overall Index of Deviation			.13	.35	.09	.23
Coefficients of Congruence						
1970: U.S.	.998	.975				
W.G.	.996	.904				
1976: U.S.	.997	.988				
W.G.	.997	.946				

Source: Ronald D. Anderson, Jack L. Engledow, and Helmut Becker, ''Advertising Attitudes in West Germany and the U.S.: An Analysis over Age and Time,'' *Journal of International Business Studies* (1980), p. 35.

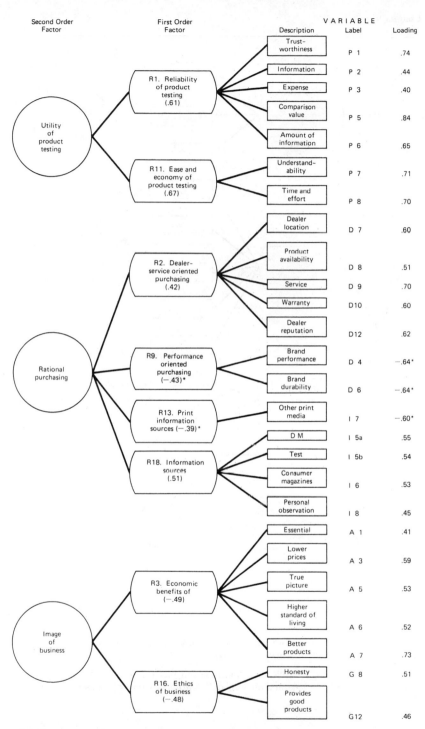

FIGURE 9.5 Relationships among variables, first order factors, and second order factors; German study

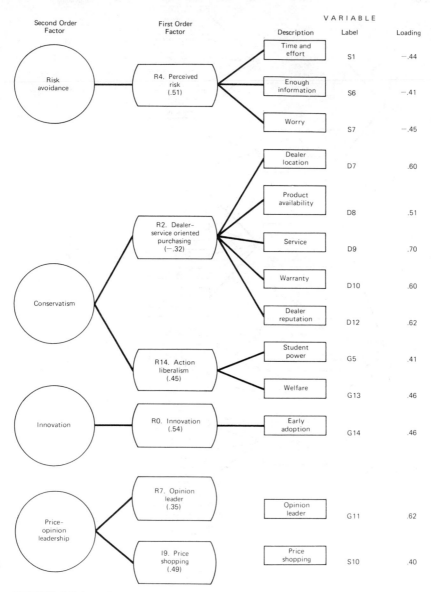

FIGURE 9.5 (*cont.*)

*Examination of correlation matrices or variables or first order factors shows that a bipolar interpretation is not appropriate, despite negative loadings.

Source: Adapted with permission from: Ronald Anderson and Jack Engledow, "A Factor Analytic Comparison of U.S. and German Information Seekers," *Journal of Consumer Research,* 3 (March 1977), 185–96.

that were considered similar enough (five of the seven) in composition in each country, matched. In the case of the first-order analysis, this resulted in the identification of fourteen pairs of factors, and in the second order analysis, five pairs of factors. These pairs were then compared by rotating the United States factors to the German space, and calculating coefficients of congruence for each of the factors, to provide measurable comparisons of the factor patterns. For the five common factors, the coefficients of congruence ranged from .60 to .88.

Another type of factor analysis that appears particularly appropriate for multicountry research is three-mode factor analysis (Tucker, 1964, 1966). Three-mode factor analysis enables the identification of three sets of factors, one for the stimulus pattern, one for behavior of subjects, and one for the points of view among subjects. In addition, a core matrix shows the interrelation among the sets of factors. Although this has been used in cross-cultural psychology, it has not, at least to the authors' knowledge, yet been used in international marketing research.

Multidimensional Scaling

Multidimensional scaling is a technique that allows the researcher to develop a mapping of individuals' perceptions of objects. It assumes that individuals evaluate objects, such as product concepts or other stimuli, relative to each other, rather than independently. A measure of similarity between each pair of objects examined is developed, based on perceptual or preference data. This is then used to generate a mapping, indicating the relative proximity of the various objects or stimuli to each other. The mapping may be two-, three-, or *n*-dimensional in character, depending on the number of dimensions that appear to underlie similarity judgments. This is evaluated, based on a measure of closeness of fit to the original data, each time an additional dimension is added (see Green and Carmone, 1970, for a more complete discussion).

When perceptual data are used, respondents are asked to make similarity judgments about objects or other stimuli. Preference data, on the other hand, consist of ratings or rankings of objects or stimuli on different attributes, such as price or taste. Judgments can also be made under different scenarios, as for example, suitable for the family, or when entertaining guests.

Preference data can then be combined with perceptual data to develop joint-space maps. The perceptual data determine the initial configuration of objects, and the preference data are superimposed on the mapping. If, for example, PREFMAP is used, the data are shown as vectors from the origin, each representing a specific attribute or scenario. The proximity of an object to a vector (as measured by a line drawn horizontally to the vector) thus indicates its rating on that attribute or scenario. The ideal points of subjects and of groups can also be projected on the mapping, indicating where the subject's or group's ideal object would be positioned.

In international marketing research, multidimensional scaling can be used in a variety of ways. As in the case of other multivariate techniques, it can be used to analyze national data as well as similarities and differences across countries. For example, product positioning or concept evaluation studies can be conducted in a number of countries. Consumers in different countries, might, for example, be asked to indicate the similarity of different vegetable- or fruit-flavored crisps relative to other snack products such as regular potato chips, fruit, dried fruit mixes, cookies, or salty crackers. They might also be asked to rate these on the basis of different attributes such as fattening, nutritious, expensive, or liked by all the family. Joint-space maps of both perception and preference can then be generated for each national sample. Similarities of mappings can be compared across countries using the Cliff Match program.

Alternatively, the analysis can be conducted across countries. The initial perceptual configuration of stimuli is thus developed, based on data pooled across national samples. This indicates the overall positioning of the products or other stimuli. Preference data are then grouped by country and may either be shown as ideal points for each national sample or vector ratings on attributes for each national sample. In the preceding example, a single overall perceptual configuration of snack products could be developed. Preference ratings for attributes could also be collected for each sample and projected on this mapping. For example, there would be a vector for fattening for French consumers, another for fattening for German consumers, and so on.

Another way in which multidimensional scaling has been applied to international data, is to develop mappings of countries based on perceived similarities in characteristics such as political or economic profiles, or sociocultural factors (Wish, Deutsch, and Biener, 1972). In this case, subjects were asked to rate twenty-one countries in terms of perceived similarity on a number of characteristics including political alignment, perceived friendship among nations, and a number of other characteristics. These data were then analyzed by means of the INDSCAL scaling procedure (for further details see Green and Carmone, 1970). Two-dimensional mappings for all subjects for the first two dimensions, and for the third and fourth dimensions, are shown in Figure 9.6. This shows that the most important dimension in determining perceived similarities among countries was political alignment. The second most important factor was the level of economic development; the third, geographic location; and the fourth, sociocultural and racial characteristics. The correlation of each of these dimensions with ratings of the countries on eighteen bipolar scales, shown in Table 9.13, indicates more clearly how these dimensions may be defined.

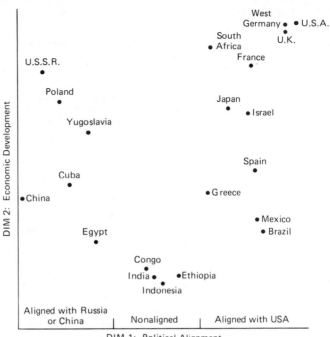

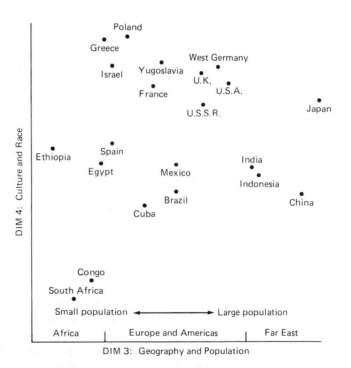

FIGURE 9.6
A four-dimensional
mapping of countries

Source: Myron Wish, Morton Deutsch, and Lois Biener, "Differences in Perceived Similarities of Nations" in A. Kimball Romney, Roger Shepard, and Sarah Nerlove, *Multi-Dimensional Scaling: Theory and Applications in the Behavioral Sciences.* New York. Seminar Press, 1972.

TABLE 9.13 Correlations of INDSCAL dimensions with mean ratings of nations on eighteen bipolar scales

	Dim. 1: Political alignment	Dim. 2: Economic development	Dim. 3: Geography and population	Dim. 4: Culture and race	Multiple correlation
1 Aligned with U.S.A.	.965	.379	.012	.299	.974
2 Individualistic	.818	.103	−.124	−.159	.876
3 Peaceful	.500	−.043	−.065	.201	.596
4 Many rights	.740	.535	.273	.499	.874
5 I like	.606	.301	.246	.700	.890
6 Good	.556	.482	.395	.660	.861
7 Similarity to ideal	.498	.735	.390	.736	.940
8 Can change status	.548	.676	.384	.631	.885
9 Stable	.233	.755	.318	.641	.846
10 Population satisfied	.350	.703	.241	.708	.842
11 Internally united	.022	.423	.116	.672	.698
12 Cultural influence	.321	.546	.415	.560	.738
13 Educated population	.336	.890	.268	.741	.973
14 Rich	.461	.906	.255	.405	.936
15 Industrialized	.316	.924	.407	.537	.975
16 Powerful	.142	.748	.556	.356	.885
17 Progressing	−.000	.461	.544	.434	.715
18 Large	−.099	.056	.522	−.203	.614

Source: Myron Wish, Morton Deutsch, and Lois Biener, "Differences in Perceived Similarities of Nations" in A. Kimball Romney, Roger Shepard, and Sarah Nerlove, *Multi-Dimensional Scaling: Theory and Applications in the Behavioral Sciences.* New York: Seminar Press, 1972.

SUMMARY

In multicountry research as in domestic marketing research, data analysis needs to be carefully planned in advance. Not only do the specific types of analyses and data collection procedures need to be specified, but in addition, the location *where* different phases of the analysis are to be carried out, needs to be determined. These issues are particularly important if timing is a major factor and tight deadlines have to be met.

Although time-consuming and tedious, it is important to check the quality and validity of the data collected, prior to conducting any type of quantitative or qualitative analysis. Data need to be examined for possible sources of bias, and differences between countries that might lead to, or account for, differences in research findings investigated. In this context, checks and procedures to minimize coding errors, as well as sampling and nonsampling errors, need to be established. This phase of analysis is generally best conducted locally.

The reliability of data from different countries should also be examined and tested, and compared from one country to another. Differences in reliability from one country to another will attenuate the precision of estimates, and hence, their effect needs to be diagnosed and taken into consideration when interpreting results.

Once data have been edited and carefully checked, they are then ready for analysis. Here, two types of analysis need to be conducted. First, data need to be analyzed at the country level, that is, for the country unit; and then, differences across countries compared. This latter phase can either be based on qualitative judgment or, alternatively, on explicit quantitative procedures.

As in domestic marketing research, a wide variety of quantitative techniques can be applied to analyze multicountry data. These range from univariate and bivariate techniques such as chi-square and T-test, to multivariate techniques such as regression and discriminant analysis, analysis of variance and covariance, clustering, factor analysis, and multidimensional scaling.

Univariate and bivariate techniques can be used both in the within- and between-country phases of analysis. In the former case, they are mostly used to test for independence or association of cross-tabulated data. In the latter case, they can be applied to test for the significance of differences between samples from different countries. In general, however, the complexity of most marketing problems suggests that it may be more desirable to make use of the rich potential of multivariate techniques.

Multivariate techniques can also be used both in the within- and between-country phases of analysis. In the within-country phase, applications are the same as in domestic marketing research. In the between-country phase, techniques such as analysis of variance, regression and discriminant analysis, conjoint analysis, factor and cluster analysis, and multidimensional scaling can all be applied to examine differences between countries. Analysis of covariance and three-mode factor analysis are particularly advantageous in this regard, since they allow for simultaneous examination of within- and between-country variation. With these exceptions, most existing statistical techniques are not adapted to examining hierarchical structures, and hence, need to be applied and interpreted with caution.

REFERENCES

ALMOND, G. and S. VERBA, *The Civic Culture: Political Attitudes and Democracy in Five Nations.* Princeton, NJ: Princeton University Press, 1965.

ANDERSON, RONALD D. and JACK ENGLEDOW, "A Factor Analytic Comparison of U.S. and German Information Seekers," *Journal of Consumer Research,* 3 (March 1977), 185–96.

———, JACK L. ENGLEDOW, and HELMUT BECKER, "Advertising Attitudes in West Germany and the U.S.: An Analysis over Age and Time," *Journal of International Business Studies* (1980), p. 35.

BARNARD, PHILIP, "Conducting and Coordinating Multicountry Studies Across Europe," *Journal of the Marketing Research Society,* 24 (1982), 46–64.

CATTIN, PHILIPPE and ALAIN JOLIBERT, "An American vs. French Cross-Cultural Study of Five 'Made In' Concepts," *American Marketing Association Proceedings.* Chicago: American Marketing Association, 1979.

CHURCHILL, GILBERT A., *Marketing Research,* 3rd ed. Hinsdale, IL: Dryden Press, 1983.

COHEN, JACOB and PATRICIA COHEN, *Applied Multiple Regression/Correlation Analysis for the Behavioral Sciences.* New York: John Wiley, 1975.

———, "A Coefficient of Agreement for Nominal Scales," *Educational and Psychological Measurement,* 20 (Spring 1960), 37–46.

COLE, EILEEN, "The Data Privacy Dilemma," *The Market Research Society Newsletter,* 186 (September 1981), 24–28.

COLVIN, MICHAEL, ROGER HEELER, and JIM THORPE, "Developing International Advertising Strategy," *Journal of Marketing,* 44 (Fall 1980), 73–79.

COOLEY, WILLIAM W. and PAUL R. LOHNES, *Multivariate Data Analysis.* London: John Wiley, 1971.

CRAIG, C. SAMUEL and JOHN McCANN, "Item Non-Response in Mail Surveys: Extent and Correlates," *Journal of Marketing Research,* 12 (1978), 285–90.

CUNNINGHAM, WILLIAM H., ISABELLA CUNNINGHAM, and ROBERT T. GREEN, "The Ipsative Process to Reduce Response Set Bias," *Public Opinion Quarterly,* 41 (Fall 1977), 379–94.

DAVIS, HARRY L., "Decision Making within the Household," *Journal of Consumer Research,* 2 (March 1976), 241–60.

———, SUSAN P. DOUGLAS, and ALVIN J. SILK, "Measure Unreliability: A Hidden Threat to Cross-National Marketing Research," *Journal of Marketing,* 45 (Spring 1981), 98–109.

DOUGLAS, SUSAN P. and C. SAMUEL CRAIG, "Some Decision Variables Related to Performance in International Operations," paper presented at A.I.B. meetings, Montreal, Canada, October 15–17, 1981.

——— and ROBERT SHOEMAKER, "Item Non-Response in Cross-National Surveys," *European Research,* 9 (July 1981), 124–32.

———, "Examining the Impact of Sampling Characteristics in Multi-Country Survey Research," *Proceedings of 9th Annual Meeting of European Academy for Advanced Research in Marketing,* Edinburgh, 1980.

———, "A Cross-National Exploration of Husband-Wife Involvement in Selected Household Activities," in William Wilkie (ed.), *Advances in Consumer Research,* vol. 5. Ann Arbor, MI: Association for Consumer Research, 1979.

——— and CHRISTINE URBAN, "Using Life-Style Analysis to Profile Women in International Markets," *Journal of Marketing,* 41 (July 1977), 46.

———, "Do Working Wives Read Different Magazines from Non-Working Wives," *Journal of Advertising,* 6 (Winter 1977), 40–43.

———, "Cross-National Comparisons and Consumer Stereotypes: A Case Study of Working and Non-Working Wives," *Journal of Consumer Research,* 3 (June 1976), 12–20.

EISINGER, RICHARD A., W. PETER JAHICKI, ROBERT L. STEVENSON, and WENDEL L. THOMPSON, "Increasing Returns in Mail Surveys," *Public Opinion Quarterly,* 38 (Spring 1974), 124–30.

FERBER, ROBERT, "Item Non-Response in a Consumer Survey," *Public Opinion Quarterly,* 30 (1966), 207–218.

—— and EDWARD D. DESA, "Modelling One Company's International Marketing Locations," *Columbia Journal of World Business,* 12 (Winter 1977), 44–52.

FISHER, F. M., "Tests of Equality Between Sets of Coefficients in Two Linear Regressions: An Expository Note," *Econometrica,* 38 (1970), 361–66.

GODWIN, R. KENNETH, "The Consequences of Large Monetary Incentives in Mail Surveys of Elites," *Public Opinion Quarterly,* 43 (Fall 1979), 378–87.

GREEN, PAUL E., *Analyzing Multivariate Data.* Hinsdale, IL: Dryden Press, 1978.

—— and DONALD S. TULL, *Research for Marketing Decisions,* 4th ed., Englewood Cliffs, NJ: Prentice-Hall, 1978.

—— and YORAM WIND, *Multiattribute Decisions in Marketing: A Measurement Approach.* Hinsdale, IL: Dryden Press, 1973.

—— and F. J. CARMONE, *Multidimensional Scaling and Related Techniques in Marketing Analysis.* Boston: Allyn and Bacon, 1970.

GREEN, ROBERT, JOEL SAEGERT, and ROBERT J. HOOVER, "Conformity in Consumer Behavior," *Proceedings of American Marketing Association Educators Conference.* Chicago: American Marketing Association, 1979.

HARMAN, HARRY H., *Modern Factor Analysis,* 2nd ed., Chicago: University of Chicago Press, 1967.

HAYS, WILLIAM L., *Statistics for the Social Sciences,* 2nd ed., New York: Holt, Rinehart and Winston, 1973.

HEMPEL, DONALD J., "Family Decisions: A Cross-Cultural Perspective," *Journal of Marketing Research,* 11 (August 1974), 295–302.

HOMANS, RICHARD E. and DONALD J. MESSNER, "On the Use of Multi-Variate Analysis of Variance and Covariance in the Analysis of Marketing Experiments," *Proceedings, American Marketing Association.* Chicago: American Marketing Association, 1976.

HOOVER, ROBERT J., ROBERT T. GREEN, and JOEL SAEGERT, "A Cross-National Study of Perceived Risk," *Journal of Marketing,* 42 (July 1978), 102–8.

HOWARD, N. and B. HARRIS, "A Hierarchical Grouping Routine IBM 360/65 Fortran IV Program," University of Pennsylvania Computer Center, October, 1966.

JOHNSON, S. C., "Hierarchical Clustering Schemes," *Psychometrika,* 32 (September 1967), 241–54.

JOHNSTON, J., *Econometric Methods.* New York: McGraw-Hill, 1972.

LEHMANN, DONALD, *Market Research and Analysis.* Homewood, IL: Irwin, 1979.

MCQUITTY, LOUIS L., "Hierarchical Syndrome Analysis," *Educational and Psychological Measurement,* 20 (Summer 1960), 293–304.

MORRISON, DONALD F., *Multivariate Statistical Methods,* 2nd edition. New York: McGraw-Hill, 1976.

MYERS, JOHN, *Marketing Research.* Englewood Cliffs, NJ: Prentice-Hall (forthcoming).

NIE, NORMAN H. and others, *Statistical Package for the Social Sciences,* 2nd edition. New York: McGraw-Hill, 1975.

NUNNALLY, J. C., *Psychometric Theory,* 2nd ed. New York: McGraw-Hill Book Company, 1978.

OVERALL, JOHN E. and J. ARTHUR WOODWARD, "Common Misconceptions Concerning the Analysis of Covariance," *Multi-Variate Behavior Research,* 12 (April 1977), 171–85.

SCHREIBER, E. M., "Dirty Data in Britain and the U.S.A.: The Reliability of 'Invariant' Characteristics Reported in Surveys," *Public Opinion Quarterly,* 39 (Winter 1975–76), 493–506.

SETHI, S. PRAKASH and DAVID CURRY, "Variable and Object Clustering of Cross-Cultural Data: Some Implications for Comparative Research and Policy Formulation," in S. Prakash Sethi and Jagdish Sheth, *Multinational Business Operations Marketing Management.* Pacific Palisades, CA: Goodyear Publishing Co., 1973.

SIEGEL, SIDNEY, *Nonparametric Statistics for the Behavioral Sciences.* New York: McGraw-Hill, 1956.

SNEATH, H. A. and R. R. SOKAL, *Numerical Taxonomy.* San Francisco: Freeman, 1973.

SNEDECOR, GEORGE W. and WILLIAM G. COCHRAN, *Statistical Methods,* 6th ed. Ames, IA: The Iowa University Press, 1967.

STRAUS, MURRAY A., "Phenomenal Identity and Conceptual Equivalence of Measurement in Cross-National Comparative Research," *Journal of Marriage and the Family,* 31 (May 1969), 233–39.

TATSUOKA, MAURICE M., *Discriminant Analysis: The Study of Group Differences.* Champaign, IL: Institute for Personality and Ability Testing, 1970.

TUCKER, L. R., "The Extension of Factor Analysis to Three-Dimensional Matrices" in N. Frederik (ed.), *Contributions to Mathematical Psychology.* New York: Holt, Rinehart, and Winston, 1964.

———, "Some Mathematical Notes on Three-Mode Factor Analysis," *Psychometrika,* 31 (1966), 279–311.

URBAN, CHRISTINE D., "A Cross-National Comparison of Consumer Media Use Patterns," *Columbia Journal of World Business* (Winter 1977), pp. 62–63.

WINER, B. J., *Statistical Principles in Experimental Design,* 2nd edition. New York: McGraw-Hill, 1971.

WISH, MYRON, MORTON DEUTSCH, and LOIS BIENER, "Differences in Perceived Similarities of Nations" in A. Kimball Romney, Roger Shepard, Sarah Nerlove (eds.), *Multi-dimensional Scaling: Theory and Applications in the Behavioral Sciences.* New York: Seminar Press, 1972.

10

The International
Marketing Information
System

Once research has been conducted, and the data collected and analyzed, the next step is to incorporate this information into management decision making. This is in many respects one of the most crucial aspects of the research process. All too frequently, research may be conducted and a number of conclusions or implications for marketing strategy and tactics drawn, and yet these are not acted upon. While there are any number of reasons that management may not take action, ranging from internal political considerations to external competitive factors, a key reason is that the information may not reach the relevant decision makers or be available in a form that is readily accessible or easily understood.

Construction of the international marketing information system involves integration of three types of data: 1) secondary data, 2) company data, and 3) primary data. Information based on secondary data sources relating to different country markets, as well as from specific research projects needs to be integrated or coordinated with data from internal company sources relating to performance in specific countries and product markets. Measures such as ROI, advertising/sales ratios, sales/expense ratios, and promotion effectiveness provide historical information on past performance and effectiveness, while secondary and primary data provide indications as to which future strategies are likely to work.

Secondary data collection often provides an important input for strategic decisions relating to initial market entry, expansion plans, estimates of market size and potential, and changes in market environmental conditions. Primary data are typically collected prior to making tactical marketing decisions, relating, for example, to product extension and positioning, standardization of advertising campaigns, transferability of other promotional ideas, and other aspects of the marketing mix. Company sales and performance data, on the other hand, provide information on how effective different strategic or marketing decisions have been, and how well they have been implemented.

The wide variety of different types of data to be absorbed by management, as well as the sheer volume and scope of information available from different countries, product markets, and organizational units throughout the world, suggests the need for systematic procedures to collect, organize, and integrate this information into a form that can be used by management. This can be accomplished by the establishment of an international marketing information system. This should be designed so as to ensure, first, that the information that is collected, is relevant to management decisions, and also, that it is available in an easily accessible and usable form. Secondary data need to be updated and continually monitored to pinpoint and evaluate future market opportunities. Experience developed with product introduction and positioning, and with testing advertising campaigns or promotional tactics in different countries and market environments, and in relation to different market segments, needs to be assimilated to assess the most effective approach in tapping these opportunities. Sales and performance data complement this information and provide specific measures of the effectiveness of different marketing strategies and tactics. These three sources of information can thus be integrated into a computerized international marketing information system, providing ready access and regular updating of this information for different countries, product markets, and organizational units.

The data bank should, therefore, contain information relating to relevant macroeconomic, social, political, and technological indicators for the product markets in which a company is involved in different countries throughout the world. For countries where the company already has operations, it should contain data relating to market size and structure, for example, sales and market share for major competitors. In addition, internal information relating to company sales and performance data should be included. A key role of this information system is, thus, to facilitate assessment of the link between each of these types of information, and more specifically, between the macromarket indicators, market structure, and company performance and marketing strategy.

The international marketing information system can thus be used

1. to aid in decisions relating to international market expansion, as, for example, whether new countries are potential candidates for market entry, or existing products might be carried into new markets;
2. to monitor performance in different countries and product markets based on criteria such as ROI and market share, so as to diagnose where existing or potential

future problems appear to be emerging, and hence where there is a need to adapt current marketing tactics or strategies.

3. to scan the international environment, in order to assess future world and country scenarios, and to monitor emerging and changing environmental trends.

4. to assess strategies with regard to the allocation of corporate resources and effort across different countries, product markets, target segments, and modes of entry, to determine whether changes in this allocation would maximize long-run profitability.

The development of an international marketing information system requires, first, consideration of management information requirements for strategic planning and decision making, to determine the relevant components of the system. Next, it requires organization of data collection and the development of procedures to process and analyze these data as well as to update the system. In addition, routines to access information and to present it in a form easily comprehensible to management, will be required. Finally, the specific applications and way in which this information can be utilized in management decision making needs to be considered in order to ensure its integration into the planning and decision making process. Each of these issues is next examined in more detail.

INFORMATION COMPONENTS OF THE INTERNATIONAL MARKETING INFORMATION SYSTEM

In constructing an international marketing information system, information required in making the two key types of decisions discussed earlier—that is, strategic and tactical decisions—needs to be determined. In general, an international marketing information system is likely to be useful primarily in relation to strategic decision making—in coordinating information relating to different countries, for making decisions with regard to market entry and expansion and resource allocation. Furthermore, it can be helpful in controlling and evaluating performance in different countries and product markets. Yet, it is also important to integrate experience gained from primary research since this can aid not only in short-term tactical decisions, but may also provide a valuable input into strategic decision making.

The need for both long- and short-term perspectives suggests that three types of information will be required. The first consists of data relating to the macroeconomic environment of the country, as for example, GNP and population size. The second concerns data relating to specific product and supply markets, their size and competitive structure, and the third relates to company sales and performance in specific product markets.

Macroeconomic Data

The types of macroeconomic data that are of potential use in international marketing decisions have already been discussed in Chapter 3 and hence do not require further elaboration here. It should, however, be noted that the specific variables to be considered will depend to a large extent on company objectives and individual product markets. Company international information banks should thus be tailored to meet specific corporate needs. This provides greater relevance for management purposes than general information banks focusing predominantly on the general business climate.

Company international information banks should, however, not be too heavily skewed toward specific product market data. General indicators of long-run global and national economic, financial, and social trends are also needed in order to monitor such developments. Such indicators might, for example, include labor unrest, number of strikes, and number of building starts. A balance should thus be struck between general and environmental indicators, and indicators more directly related to specific corporate and marketing objectives. Integration of a general information bank with specific company indicators may thus provide a desirable strategy.

Market Size and Structure

The next level of the information bank consists of data relating to specific product businesses and sources of supply. In the case of product markets, data relating to production, sales, or consumption of specific products and product types within the market, will be needed. Where feasible, this might be obtained in units and dollar sales volume. Sales data broken down by specific product lines is also desirable. For example, personal toiletries might be broken down by shampoos, antiperspirants, soaps, and so on; and then within the shampoo market, by hair type, fragrance, and so on. Furthermore, where obtainable, breakdowns by major geographic regions, by cities as opposed to rural areas, by different types of distribution outlets, and also by customer types are useful. For industrial products, breakdowns by user industry and industry size might be included; and for consumer products, by sex, age, and income, or other relevant customer groupings.

In the case of consumer durables, information about product ownership, or the stock of existing products, as well as the secondhand market for products such as cars and various types of industrial machinery, is also desirable. Information about sales of complementary or substitute products, such as margarine, butter, and oil, might also be included. These may aid in understanding current sales patterns and fluctuations in them, as well as signaling likely future trends.

Data with regard to the competitive market structure is also an important consideration in developing long-run marketing strategy. Information about the number of competitors, market share by company, product line, and brand provide baseline statistics in this regard. Again, where feasible, breakdowns by region and type of distributive outlets might be obtained. Other information relating to competitive strategies and current trends in the relevant industry or product market can also be helpful as a benchmark for company strategy, such as typical advertising or promotional expenditure ratios used in the industry, trade margins, trends in investment in new product and plant facilities, hiring and dismissal of employees, and so on. However, such information is likely to be available only for industrialized nations and well-established product markets.

In the case of sources of supply, data of primary concern include availability of various raw materials and labor, as well as their prices and price fluctuations. In the case, for example, of the labor market, the availability of workers in different trades and skills, unemployment rates by type of trade, and average hourly or weekly rates by industry, might be helpful. Similarly for materials such as steel or industrial components, monthly unit production figures, and also price ranges for different grades of steel or types of components from different suppliers, might provide valuable information.

Company Sales and Product Market Performance

Internal company data are also an important component of the information system. The same types of information as those necessary in domestic marketing decisions are likely to be required, but in this case, relating to each country or organizational unit. The exact form that this information will take is, however, likely to vary from company to company, depending on the nature and organization of existing operations. Important differences in this regard are likely to arise between industrial and consumer goods companies, due to differences in marketing strategy and organization.

Regardless of interfirm variation, certain data will be common to all companies. These include, for example, ROI, market share as a percentage of total industry sales, market share relative to the top or leading three competitors, trends in market share, marketing expenditure relative to sales ratios, and growth in sales by product line.

Parallel to the product market data, and depending also on the size of the market and the degree of product line diversity, these data may be broken down to reflect territorial or regional measures of performance. For example, market share estimates and trends may be available by specific geographic regions, sales and sales trends by region, expenditure relative to sales ratios by region, and so on. Again, sales and marketing expenses might be broken down by type of distribution channel—for example, direct or indirect—or different types of outlets. In industrial markets, sales and performance measures might also be evaluated relative to specific end-user markets, and for consumer goods relative to different consumer segments.

In addition to such general performance measures, more specific measures relating to individual marketing tools, such as sales force, advertising, sales promotions, distribution efficiency, and sales turnover, might be included. These will, however, vary depending on the type of company. Industrial companies may, for example, collect more detailed information relating to performance by different types of sales persons, distribution costs, and so on. Consumer companies, on the other hand, may be more concerned with media and sales promotion expenditures and retail store volume.

In contrast to other types of data, these data, will only be available in relation to the specific national or product markets in which the company is already involved. Under certain circumstances it may be feasible to extrapolate from one country to another, based on similarity in market conditions. Different performance standards, such as profitability, from a specific type of region or territory might be extrapolated from one country to another. For example, performance ratios for major metropolitan areas, as opposed to smaller cities, might be hypothesized to be comparable from one country to another.

Other Sources of Information

In addition to information from documentary sources, which can be directly compiled and fed into the system, two other sources of information are also important in making international marketing decisions. These are human sources of information, and observation of physical stimuli. These sources are particularly useful insofar as they aid in interpreting and understanding documentary information.

Human sources of information include all forms of intrapersonal and nonwritten communications, such as conversations, meetings, telephone conversations, or sales representatives' reports. These contacts may either be *internal,* that is, between managers or employees within a company, or alternatively, *external,* for example, with government or trade officials, advertising agencies, or distributors. The Japanese make extensive use of human sources of information. This is systematically collected and disseminated by the Japanese Ministry of International Trade and Industry (*Business Week,* December 14, 1981).

Internal intrapersonal communications are integral to the successful functioning of any organization. In international marketing, the establishment of an effective system of intrapersonal communications is particularly crucial due to the far-flung character of operations. As has frequently been observed, many of the key problems in multinational operations revolve around the relations between the corporate headquarters and local management (Weichman and Pringle, 1979; Hulbert, Brandt, and Richers, 1980).

Consequently, mechanisms for facilitating communication between corporate headquarters and local management are needed to coordinate and control operations in different parts of the globe. Typically, these consist of regular visits by corporate headquarters staff to regional or national operations (Brandt and Hulbert, 1976). The reverse movement may also be desirable to alleviate feelings among local management, of excessive control and supervision by corporate headquarters. Local management can also provide input into global planning. In a recent survey of eight multinationals operating in Brazil (Hulbert, Brandt, and Richers, 1980), local management provided information used in marketing planning in more than half of the cases.

The same study also found the salesforce was used as a source of information in marketing planning in 75 percent of the firms studied. In particular, the salesforce was useful in providing estimates for sales forecasting. It should, however, be noted that these may contain some downward bias if they are perceived as being used to set salesforce goals.

Use of *external* sources of information is also an important consideration, and can provide a highly valuable input into management decision making. Government and trade officials can, for example, provide much information concerning government economic and social policy and regulation, and their impact on various product markets; possible support and assistance in marketing products such as nutritional supplements, contraceptives, and farming or medical equipment; or current trends in different industries. This is often helpful, not only in determining whether to enter a particular country, but also in determining the mode of operation and appropriate marketing strategy in that country.

Similarly, conversations with or information collected from advertising agency personnel, or distributors, can frequently be helpful in developing marketing mix tactics. Opinions with regard to the value of different measures of advertising copy effectiveness, or the advisability of a given media plan may, for example, be solicited. Distributors might, for example, provide information relating to in-store promotions, and problems likely to be encountered in physical distribution and flow of merchandise, as well as at point of sale.

The importance of intrapersonal communication may be attributed in part to the confidentiality of certain types of critical information; for example, information of a political nature or relating to the evaluative character of this information. The dynamics of personal interaction may also provide certain types of information that cannot be communicated in writing, as well as influencing the perceived value of such information. Face-to-face communication often has a greater impact than documentary sources, and in many respects, it provides a more efficient method of communication since it focuses on salient points of interest.

Observation of physical stimuli also constitutes an important input into international marketing decisions. Management may, for example, only become directly aware of the distance between two countries through actually traveling between them. Similarly, observation of different conditions in another country—for example, consumer shopping practices, climatic conditions, the nature of the distribution network, how products are displayed in-store, or the type of advertising and other promotional stimuli—may be the best way to appreciate their significance. The latter type of information may be particularly crucial in relation to international, as opposed to domestic, marketing decisions, due to the differences in environmental conditions from one market or country to another.

Information from personal sources and direct observation can thus play an important role in interpreting and selecting relevant data provided by documentary sources. The dominant role attached to documentary sources in the design of global information systems may be misplaced. Lack of familiarity with overseas conditions and the absence of an intuitive basis on which to select and interpret relevant information, results in a need for and reliance on more selective sources of information. Explicit integration and allowance for information from personal and physical sources in the system takes into consideration the active role of the decision maker in the collection and interpretation of data, and provides for more efficient information utilization.

Once the specific types of data to be contained in the information system have been determined, the next step is to establish procedures for the collection and processing of these data, in order to provide an appropriate and comprehensive basis for management decision making.

DATA COLLECTION AND PROCESSING
FOR THE INTERNATIONAL MARKETING
INFORMATION SYSTEM

In developing an international marketing information system, a number of issues are likely to arise with regard to data collection and processing. First, problems can arise with regard to the comparability of data collected in different countries, due to differences in relevant definitions, data collection procedures, as well as accounting practices, from one country to another. Secondly, procedures for filing and coordinating such data are required. This is often a source of potential conflict or disharmony among different organizational units. Thirdly, routines for processing, updating, and maintaining the information are required.

Data Comparability

The issues with regard to the comparability of macroeconomic and product market data have already been discussed elsewhere and hence are not repeated here. Some more specific considerations arise, however, in relation to internal company data. Incorporation of data from foreign operations into an international data bank system initially appears relatively straightforward. Data comparability from one country to another presents, however, a major obstacle. It is important to realize that the value of a number supplied by a subsidiary in one country is not necessarily identical to the supposedly comparable figure supplied by a subsidiary in another country. Consequently, values or figures need to be adjusted into equivalent units so they can serve as a meaningful input for marketing decisions.

Sales volume measures, for example, may be expressed in real or monetary units. Real units, while accurately reflecting the number sold, may be misleading, as noted in Chapter 5, in that the nature of the product can vary from country to country, corresponding to different market requirements. Automobiles and pharmaceutical products, for example, frequently require modification to conform to specific national product regulations, thus entailing different costs.

Monetary units may thus be doubly misleading. The price of the product may reflect not only design differences, but in addition, differences in pricing policy, transfer pricing practices, and local taxation rules, as for example, VAT. In addition, monetary units require conversion by an appropriate exchange rate. This gives rise to further difficulties in that exchange rates are floating and may sometimes artificially reflect shifts in capital funds or temporary balance of payments. Procedures or mechanisms that adjust for such factors are thus required.

These difficulties are further compounded by variations in accounting procedures and standards in different countries (Choi and Mueller, 1978). While some movement is being made toward the standardization of accounting procedures across countries, and the issue has been raised as to whether separate standards should be set for MNCs, as yet, little resolution on this appears to have been reached (Gray, Shaw, and McSweeney, 1981). Costs may not be estimated in the same way or may include different expense items. Rules for depreciation, or how the book value of assets is estimated, may vary from one country to another. In addition, as noted previously, methods of compensation tend to vary from country to country. Companies in countries with high rates of taxation, for example, often provide substantial fringe benefits, rather than salary increases, to compensate management. Countries have different rates of social security payments, and methods for allocating and billing them. Some adjustment has, therefore, to be made in order to make calculations of salesforce costs as a percentage of total sales, comparable.

Companies with intrafirm transactions between subsidiaries in different countries may price so as to maximize profits in countries with low rates of taxation (Burns, 1980). Thus, for example, subsidiaries in high-tax countries will bill subsidiaries in low-tax countries at cost, to maximize profits in low-tax countries. Conversely, subsidiaries in low-tax countries may include a profit margin in prices charged to subsidiaries in high-tax countries. This will, therefore, generate some bias in comparisons of performance in high- versus low-tax countries.

Even seemingly unambiguous measures of performance, such as market share, may be misleading. The definition of the relevant product market may vary from country to country as, for example, in the case of soft drinks or pharmaceuticals, thus, understating or overstating a firm's share of the market. In examining sales response to various marketing mix elements, differences in distribution channels and their efficiency, in media availability and effectiveness, or in market structure and pricing may have to be taken into consideration. Distribution channels such as supermarkets, used in one country, may not exist in another, and hence, margins and distribution costs may be higher. Advertising sales ratios may be affected by the availability of various media and their reach. In some countries, TV advertising may not be available. Consequently, print or radio media may be more widely used. Media mixes thus vary considerably, rendering strict comparison of advertising and sales ratios of limited value.

Data Collection

The lack of comparability in data from different national contexts suggest that a number of difficulties are likely to be experienced in developing efficient procedures for data collection for an international information system. Rules for transforming data so that they are comparable from one context to another have to be devised, and methods for implementing these translation rules need to be established. This can be a major source of conflict between local subsidiaries and headquarters management.

In the absence of uniform and widely accepted international standards, one solution to alleviate such problems is for a company to establish its own rules. Central headquarters thus establishes guidelines for translation rules and a reporting format. To do so, information is obtained from local operating subsidiaries, concerning measurement standards, local accounting procedures, and taxation laws and other fiscal requirements. A standardized system is then established for cost accounting and reporting results. Local subsidiaries will thus initially compile and process data according to standard company accounting procedures. Reports are then submitted to central headquarters, based on these standards. In some cases, this may entail keeping a double set of books—one based on local accounting procedures, and the other on international reporting standards.

Another alternative is to standardize information centrally. Local subsidiaries thus compile data and other required information in local units and according to the local standards. Details of the procedures used locally, and local accounting standards, are then submitted to central headquarters. Central headquarters management is then responsible for converting the data to a uniform base and for its integration into the international information bank.

The development by central headquarters of guidelines for reporting procedures has the advantage that greater allowance is made for input from local subsidiaries. Local subsidiaries not only provide information about local accounting procedures, but also transform data according to the translation rules. This allows for greater sensitivity to differences in local operating conditions and reporting standards. On the other hand, it increases the burden placed on local subsidiaries, and can result in complaints with regard to the time required to fill out such reports. This is likely to be particularly marked in situations where little or minimal feedback is obtained from central headquarters, or alternatively, where this information is perceived as being used for the purposes of control or the development of plans subsequently imposed by corporate headquarters.

Centralization of data standardization, on the other hand, offers the advantage of avoiding such potential conflicts with regard to data collection and reporting by local subsidiaries. However, sensitivity to local environmental differences is likely to be lost. Furthermore, difficulties may be encountered in reconciling information, and ensuring that these are comparable from one country to another.

A compromise solution can be achieved by establishing coordinating procedures based on input from local subsidiary and central headquarters management. To the extent that staff from local subsidiaries in different countries participate in setting up coordinating procedures, conflicts or inconsistencies in accounting standards and rules can be discussed and ironed out. Valuable input can thus be obtained from local subsidiaries with regard to the relevance of different reporting practices, and the problems associated with the use of different types of measures or standards, such as ROI or market share as a basis for evaluating performance in a specific local or national context.

On the other hand, significant problems may be encountered in applying this procedure. Local subsidiaries are likely to be less concerned with developing an efficient and consistent reporting system worldwide, than with the selection of procedures and standards that facilitate their own task and put their own operations in a favorable light. Furthermore, use of a coordinating committee approach is likely to be time-consuming and tedious, since it entails extensive discussion and the need for collaboration.

Data Processing, Analysis, and Maintenance

Closely related to the question of the format in which information is reported, is that of the way in which data are processed and integrated into the information system. Here, as might be expected, greater difficulties are likely to be encountered in relation to product market data, or data from internal company sources collected from local subsidiaries, than with regard to macroeconomic data.

Data with regard to macroeconomic indicators are, as noted previously, readily available from various sources, and currently existing data banks. Some, such as Business International, are already computerized, and hence, merely require linking up with the company's information system. Others, particularly those publicly available, are not computerized and may require computerization. This investment allows for greater customization to specific company requirements than is possible in the case of standard information banks. However, these data need to be updated regularly, typically on an annual or biannual basis, or whenever relevant data become available. Procedures for updating on a more frequent basis, based on estimated or projected future trends, can also be developed if greater precision is required.

Product market data are likely to pose somewhat greater problems insofar as such data are not always readily available on an ongoing basis. If Nielsen or other comparable commercial audit services are available, these may provide an appropriate basis. Otherwise, reports or studies conducted by sources such as the U.S. Department of Commerce or the Economist Intelligence Unit, may be used. Typically, however, this requires integrating or patching together data from different sources and diverse origins, and can pose significant problems in establishing their comparability. In cases where published sources are not available, it may be desirable to obtain cooperation of local subsidiaries in making relevant estimates.

In the case of internal company data, somewhat greater problems may be encountered. Here, the key issue is to ensure not only that requisite information is collected in an appropriate form, but also that procedures are established for obtaining this on a systematic basis without incurring significant time delays. This problem is likely to be particularly acute if subsidiaries are required to engage in intensive recording for central headquarters, for purposes, such as global planning, not perceived as directly related to their own preoccupations.

Such difficulties may to some extent be alleviated by the use of telex or the development of a computerized global information system. Information could thus be transmitted to corporate headquarters via telex, or entered directly into the data base on a computer terminal. In the latter case, the information is also accessible to local subsidiary management and may be used in guiding tactical decisions related to specific country markets. Some problems may, however, be encountered in the establishment of such systems, due to government regulation of the transmission of such information across international boundaries.

Once procedures have been developed for collecting and updating information on a systematic basis, procedures for analyzing these data need to be implemented. Here, a key issue is the uses to be made of the international information bank, and in particular, how this is integrated into management decisions.

Programs for retrieving data have thus to be adapted to these specific needs. These needs are next discussed in more detail.

APPLYING THE INFORMATION SYSTEM

The international marketing information system can provide a useful input in relation to four major types of decision situations; first, in monitoring international market expansion opportunities, that is, entry into other countries; secondly, in monitoring performance in different countries and product markets throughout the world; third, in scanning the world environment and anticipating change; and finally, in integrating strategies across countries and product markets worldwide, to assess whether reallocation of company resources and effort might be desirable.

Monitoring Market Expansion Opportunities

The international information system can provide a valuable input in international expansion decisions, and in particular, in assessing whether a country is ripe for in-depth investigation and evaluation. The types of data that can be used for these decisions, and also, the various procedures for assessing countries based on macroeconomic data, have already been discussed in Chapter 3 and hence will not be further examined. Typically, the information system provides an initial input and is used in conjunction with informed opinion to arrive at a final decision.

One major United States industrial company that maintains a computerized information system for monitoring expansion opportunities in international markets is American Can. The primary equity exposure of the company in a foreign market consists of the establishment of a manufacturing plant. Sales of the output from that plant are typically negotiated in advance, either with a domestic customer with potential market sales in the foreign market or alternatively, with a potential foreign customer. Consequently, the primary focus is on assessing the favorability of the investment climate and the risks associated with investment in that country. As a result, the data base consists primarily of macroeconomic variables that are used to develop composite indexes of factors such as the political or economic situation, the availability of labor and the quality of the infrastructure, and various operational factors. These are then summarized in terms of two major dimensions, the economic desirability of a country and the risk or potential payback from operations in that country.

This information provides an important input into decisions with regard to which countries appear to provide attractive opportunities for market entry and is particularly useful in signaling those that merit further investigation. It may also be helpful in assessing whether additional investment in a given country is warranted.

Prism

The information that is collected consists primarily of macroindicators relating to the investment climate of a given country, and to factors that may influence the costs or difficulties of operating in a given environment. In addition to standard indicators of the investment climate, such as per capita income, market size, and inflation, a number of variables relating to the quality of the infrastructure, the availability of capital, and bureaucratic delays are also considered to be important factors in country assessment, since production is the keystone of overseas operations.

In total, information is collected, from a variety of external sources, on over thirty variables that are considered critical in assessing relevant political, economic, and operational dimensions. Four subindexes are developed that assess the political climate, the economic climate, the management of operations, and the labor and infrastructure situation.

In constructing these indexes, the variables are weighted based on their importance to United States management, with special emphasis placed on elements that are likely to lead to short-term changes in the investment climate. Thus, for example, in assessing the political climate, political stability is considered to be three times more important than the next most important variable, political freedom. In assessing the economic climate, four variables—per capita income, market size, market growth, and inflation—are considered almost equally important. Information on these variables is collected from a variety of external sources, including Business International, B.E.R.I., Freedom House, and the Overseas Development Council.

To make overall country assessments, two composite indexes of economic desirability and risk (payback) have been developed, composed of the same factors as the four subindexes. The weights attached to the different factors vary (see Table 10.1), and a number of factors appear in both indexes. In the economic desirability index, for example, the quality of the infrastructure, followed by the availability of financing, are considered the most crucial factors. In the payback index, political stability is the most important, and corporate tax level least important. While quality of the infrastructure is the most important factor in assessing economic desirability, it is fourth in importance in evaluating payback.

In screening countries to assess the attractiveness of their investment climate, a number of different procedures are used. Since the industrialized Western nations invariably score highest in absolute terms on the indexes, both the economic desirability and the risk indexes are related to consumer buying

TABLE 10.1 Foreign investment screen relative factor weights for indexes

MAJOR INDEXES

. A. Payback index		B. Desirability index	
	%		%
Political stability	26.0	Quality of infrastructure	13.6
Political freedom	7.0	Availability of financing	10.1
Civil liberties	7.0	Labor situation	9.1
Quality of infrastructure	6.7	Market growth	8.6
Nationalization probability	6.3	Currency convertibility	6.6
Desire for foreign investment	5.6	Per capita income	7.1
Bureaucratic delays	5.4	Market size	7.1
Market size and growth	4.4	Inflation	6.8
Inflation	3.6	Physical quality of life	6.0
Labor situation	3.5	Bureaucratic delays—red tape	5.1
Currency stability	3.3	Enforceability of contracts	4.4
Balance of payments	3.3	Balance of payments	3.4
Likelihood of internal disorder	3.2	Currency history	3.2
Availability of financing	2.4	Corporate tax level	2.2
Restrictions on capital movements	2.3	Local management	2.0
Enforceability of contracts	1.8	Cultural interaction	1.7
Government intervention	1.5	Reserves/imports ratio	1.3
Limits on foreign ownership	1.4	Government intervention	0.8
Cultural interaction	1.4		
Limits on expansion	1.1		
Local management and partners	1.0		
Physical quality of life	1.0		
Corporate tax level	0.8		

Source: Business Research, American Can Company, 1981.

power. Country ratings on these indexes are then plotted against per capita income. The attractiveness of a country's investment climate can then be assessed relative to its stage of economic development. Figure 10.1 shows the economic desirability index plotted against per capita consumer spending. Countries that rate substantially above those at an equivalent level of development, are considered particularly bright prospects. This assessment thus provides a means of gauging the likelihood of exceeding or falling short of return on investment goals normally obtained in countries at a given level of development.

In making the assessment, certain cutoff values may be established, above which risk is too high, or potential income too low, to warrant further investigation. If, for example, risk minimization is desired, all countries below a certain level might be eliminated. Countries to be further examined could then be selected on the basis of high purchasing power relative to their economic level, or simply high ranking. Similarly, if the product to be marketed requires a high level of personal income, a minimum cutoff for income can be established.

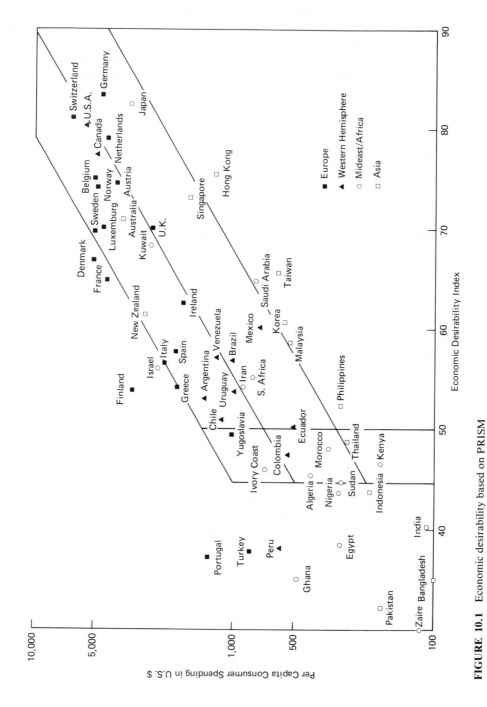

FIGURE 10.1 Economic desirability based on PRISM
Business Research, American Can Company, 1981.

Further selection can then be based on absolute position on either or both indexes; or position relative to the norm for a given level of development. On the other hand, if a mass-market product is to be introduced into the country, both upper and lower limits on income can be established, as well as a minimum level of risk. Further selection can then, as in the preceding cases, focus on identifying countries rating above average on one or both indexes.

An analogous procedure can be used to pinpoint geographic regions or multicountry areas that offer good prospects for development. As index values are recalculated and updated, the position of countries can be tracked over time. This provides an ongoing evaluation of areas of particular interest, as well as pinpointing or monitoring areas of rapid change.

The evaluation provided by this appraisal provides an important input in the preliminary stages of management assessment of investment opportunities in foreign markets. In particular, it is helpful in revealing which countries merit further analysis. Furthermore, the specific factors included in the appraisal, as well as the criteria used, can be varied and adapted to the specific project envisaged or business group concerned.

This evaluation is then used in conjunction with other sources of information in making actual investment or market entry decisions. Secondary studies on the outlook for the industry in a particular region or country are also examined. For certain areas, an advisory council of outside regional experts, including members from industry and academic circles, meets twice yearly to advise on investment projects in the area.

The information system provides a systematic analytical approach to evaluating countries, and as such, constitutes a valuable input into management decision making. It is particularly useful in the initial stages of the decision-making process, complemented by other documentary sources and expert opinion, and can be tailored to specific projects and decisions. Its integration into actual decisions is, however, largely contingent on management judgment and experience, and qualitative interpretation of the various indexes.

Monitoring Company Performance

Another use of the international data bank is to monitor company performance in different product markets and countries throughout the world. The international data bank can be helpful in controlling company activities in different countries and subsidiaries throughout the world, and in providing a benchmark for the comparison of performance under different environmental and market conditions.

In evaluating performance in domestic markets, a number of standard measures are typically used, such as, for example, market share and ROI. This is based on the assumption, which has consistently been supported by various studies in the United States, that high market share is related to high levels of profitability (Gale 1975; Buzzell, Gale, and Sultan, 1975). Furthermore, emphasis on product related variables such as product quality has been consistently found to lead to high market share (Craig and Douglas, 1982).

Use of such criteria for evaluating performance and emphasis on similar marketing mix variables in an international context assumes that similar relationships will hold in foreign markets. A number of factors suggests, however, that this may not necessarily be the case. Differences in demand factors, as, for example, the degree of concern for product quality or new product development, as well as more fragmented markets, and differences in competition and the character of the marketing and media infrastructure, suggest that the same marketing and competitive strategies may not necessarily be equally effective. In addition, some evidence exists indicating that different market mix strategies appear to be successful in markets outside the United States and that strategies associated with high market share and ROI in those countries also differ (Douglas and Craig, 1983).

This raises some issues concerning appropriate measures of performance in international markets. Where operations are decentralized, and each national subsidiary operates autonomously, the types of measures used by central headquarters to evaluate performance are likely to be predominantly financial, as for example, ROI.

Focus on the use of financial criteria, however, does not take into consideration market potential and the extent to which this is currently exploited. Certain countries may, for example, be experiencing rapid rates of economic growth, and consequently, have greater potential for market development and expansion than countries with relatively stagnant or low rates of market growth. This needs to be considered not only in the perspective of existing products and product lines, but also in that of the addition of new lines and product market expansion. Thus, markets that are growing are likely to be better candidates for expanding or upgrading existing product lines and for adding new items. Certain economies may thus be achieved in relation to the sales and marketing organization within a country, either because overhead expenses are extended over a broader range of products, or as a result of scale economies.

Furthermore, in some cases, low levels of ROI may predominantly reflect poorer product performance or inappropriate or ill-adapted market strategies. Changes in marketing tactics may improve performance and thus result in changes in ROI. Situational factors such as political instability or economic fluctuations may affect rates of return in the short run. This is particularly likely to occur in relation to products with a substantial proportion of imported components that are subject to short-run trends or currency fluctuations. Such factors may have an artificial impact on rates of return. Manipulation of transfer pricing may also imply that financial measures are biased and do not accurately reflect actual performance.

In addition to the likelihood of bias, emphasis on financial criteria implies a focus on short-run profitability. This may not always be appropriate, particularly in international markets, where company goals may center on market expansion and growth, in order to build world market share and remain competitive in world markets, rather than on short-run profitability. Such considerations suggest that factors other than purely financial criteria should be taken into account in evaluating performance in international markets. Criteria such as market growth and productivity levels should also be examined. Measures such as sales per salesperson, advertising-to-sales ratios, promotional-expenditure-to-sales ratios, and employee turnover rates, might for example, be evaluated, providing both a more detailed evaluation and a broader horizon for evaluating performance.

In using these criteria to evaluate and compare performance in different countries, differences in operating conditions and the market environment need to be taken into consideration. These might be evaluated based on aggregate measures at the country or industry level, as for example, rate of growth of GNP or rate of market growth. These can be used as benchmarks in evaluating and comparing performance from one country to another. The evaluation is thus made relative to differences in environmental factors, as well as in absolute terms.

Scanning the International Environment

A third use of the international marketing information system is to scan the environment in order to monitor changes and emerging trends in different countries throughout the world. It is particularly crucial to keep abreast of such developments, especially in view of the rapid rates of change in many international markets. Furthermore, these can have a profound impact on the company's ability to compete effectively in world markets, and maintain desired levels of profitability.

In scanning the environment, a number of elements need to be taken into consideration, including social, political, ecological, economic, and technological trends. A key problem, here, given the morass of possible trends and information sources that could be examined, is to select trends and indicators that are pertinent to the specific company and the product markets in which it is involved.

Trend monitoring should be tailored to factors believed to have the most significant impact on investment patterns and strategic decisions. This is a function not only of a company's priorities in terms of resource allocation across different markets, but also of the different constraints under which a company operates in different environments.

A recent survey of the opinions of United States and European executives about the aspects of the external environment that had the most significant impact on strategic decisions (O'Connell and Zimmerman, 1979) showed that both United States and European executives consistently considered economic and technological domains most important in terms of both present and future impact. However, differences occurred in perceptions of the importance of the social environment. Europeans ranked the social domain fourth in actual impact, and third in potential impact. United States executives, on the other hand, ranked the social domain fifth in both cases, though its potential impact was perceived as increasing substantially. This would appear to reflect the greater significance of social constraints, such as labor unions and employment policies, on business operations in Europe.

The same survey also revealed that the major problems in environmental scanning were how best to organize for environmental scanning and the difficulty of applying a systematic approach. Furthermore, doubts were frequently voiced about how to interpret trends in the social, political, and ecological domains, particularly in terms of the timing of the impact of these trends on strategic decision making. These are domains that pose threats, rather than opportunities as in the case of economic and technological trends. Hence, while they cannot be ignored, there is some inherent bias to "screen out" such factors.

Large multinational corporations with experience in scanning systems often have a full-time staff devoted exclusively to environmental scanning (Thomas, 1980). I.B.M. and G.E. have, for example, had specialized scanning units for about a decade. In the case of I.B.M., the staff group consists of a domestic staff of twenty-five and an overseas staff of thirty-five, while G.E. has had an environmental studies group at headquarters for many years. C.P.C. International and Ciba-Geigy have all conducted environmental analysis for more than ten years, while Royal Dutch Shell and General Mills have operated scanning systems for about five years.

The specific information that is monitored, and the type of techniques used to process this information, do, however, vary considerably from company to company. I.B.M., for example, looks mainly at economic conditions, but also considers consumerism, privacy, and data security, and makes use of econometric modeling. G.E. monitors a wide range of factors including international defense, social, political, legal, economic, technological, manpower, and financial environments, making use of cross-impact matrices and scenario analysis. Shell applies scenario analysis, but, as noted previously, for a narrow range of alternatives. C.P.C. International also monitors a wide range of factors at the national and regional market level. At the national market level, C.P.C. monitors law, consumer behavior, market structure, labor organization, and attitude of the government to MNCs. At the regional level, politics, social and economic trends, technology, psychology, and education are monitored. At General Mills, public policy is monitored worldwide by headquarters staff, while at the national level overall movements in consumer attitudes are monitored using information from outside consultants.

The scope and content of scanning thus varies considerably from one company to another (see Table 10.2). The scope varies, from a primary concern

TABLE 10.2 Scanning in three multinationals

	SCOPE	RANGE	FUTURITY	ORGANIZATIONAL LEVEL	SPECIAL FEATURES
IBM	Mainly economic conditions. Also other environmental factors, e.g., consumerism, privacy and data security, international political and economic relationships.	Nationwide and global	Not discussed	IBM scans the environment through two organizational mechanisms—one being the operating units affected and the second the corporate staff.	Macro forecasts circulated to senior management four times a year, 25 professionals in Corporate Economic Department in U.S. plus 35 with units abroad
General Electric	Tunnel visions of international, defense, social, political, legal, economic, technological, manpower, and financial environments.	Nationwide plus some global	10 years historical plus alternative scenarios 10 years into the future	Environmental studies group at headquarters plus divisional management	Has had an environmental analysis group for over a decade. Uses cross impact matrices to arrive at sets of alternative futures, is experimenting with computer models of the external environment
CPC International	Law, consumer behavior, market structure, labor organization, attitude of government to MNCs.	National market	10–20 years for strategic plan	Global headquarters, regional headquarters, field units	Planning system gives equal voice in planning to the divisions and to headquarters, although final decisions are made at headquarters. Maximum opportunity provided for these voices to be heard.
	Politics, social and economic trends, technology, psychology, education, etc.	Regional			

Source: Philip S. Thomas, "Environmental Scanning—The State of the Art," *Long-Range Planning*, 13 (February 1980), 21-28.

with economic conditions as at I.B.M., to the projections of a wide range of different aspects of the environment as at G.E. In general, the orientation is global and is combined with a country-level analysis, though C.P.C. International also has a regional perspective. The horizon also varies, ranging from the medium term (five years) to the long term (twenty years).

The experience of these corporate giants suggests the importance of environmental scanning in order to anticipate future social, political, economic, and technological conditions. A major problem is, however, how to integrate this information with that used in assessing the investment climate in different countries, and with various measures of company performance in different markets, in developing a global marketing plan. Appropriate frameworks and procedures for systematic global planning are discussed in the next section.

Integrating Market Entry, Performance, and Change

For companies that are already involved in international markets, the key issue is not so much one of selecting countries that offer the best prospects for international market expansion, but rather of determining how to allocate resources across different countries, product markets, target segments, and modes of operation. Decisions thus concern not only investment in different countries and product markets, but also *divestment* from unprofitable or less profitable operations, and a shift from these into operations with higher expected rates of return.

In order to make these decisions, information will be required relating to the investment climate and product or target market potential in all the countries and regions to be considered for possible entry, and also on performance in markets where the company already has existing operations. An information system designed to aid in making such decisions should include data at all three levels discussed earlier, that is, macroeconomic data, such as GNP per capita; product market data, such as sales or production; and internal company data, relating to ROI, sales, and other indicators of performance, in different countries and product markets. An important consideration in designing this information system is how to integrate the macroeconomic and product market data with company performance data when making investment and divestment decisions. The macroeconomic and product market data provide an input with regard to factors that are likely to impinge on future profitability, while the internal sales and performance data provide an historic record of past performance.

The product portfolio approach, which has attained considerable popularity in recent years in planning domestic marketing strategy, provides an appropriate conceptual framework for analyzing international market expansion strategies. The same basic principles can be applied, while extending the scope of the analysis to include the country, mode of operation, and target segments as additional dimensions to be considered in portfolio design.

The product portfolio approach to planning market strategy is based on the assumption that maximum long-run return will be attained by achieving a balanced mix of products, at different stages of maturity, with different cash flow positions and capital requirements (Day, 1977). The optimal portfolio of products will thus contain a mix of products, including mature products that produce large cash flows and require little financing, "stars" that are also market leaders but are growing fast and hence require cash to finance the rate of growth, and new products in rapidly growing markets that require heavy investment in order to acquire a solid position in these markets. The cash flow generated by the mature products can thus be used to finance the new, rapidly growing products.

The combination of products to be included in the firm's portfolio is assessed primarily on the basis of two principal dimensions—rate of market growth, and market share. The market growth dimension synthesizes the expected risk-return trade-off at the product market level, while the market share dimension indicates the firm's success in capturing this market.

Extending this approach to international marketing strategy requires the inclusion of several additional dimensions to the analysis (Wind and Douglas, 1981). Not only does the appropriate combination of products to be included in the firm's portfolio have to be considered, but also the appropriate combination of countries, modes of operation within these countries, target segments, and marketing strategies to achieve maximum long-run profitability on a worldwide basis. The extent to which economies can be achieved through the use of standardized products, advertising, or other strategies across different countries, or through the sharing of a common salesforce, or of conducting joint promotional activities, or of marketing complementary products has also to be considered.

A comprehensive international portfolio model would thus include the following dimensions:

    countries
    modes of operation
    product markets
    target segments
    marketing strategies

and evaluate the optimal combination of these to achieve long-run profitability. This approach does, however, need to be customized for the individual company, depending on its organizational structure and objectives with regard to international market expansion. The specific dimensions to be included will, thus, depend on the company and the degree of product or business diversification, as well as the nature of the product market.

In examining the appropriate combination of countries to be considered in the firm's international portfolio, stable, mature, low-growth markets such as the Western European nations can be counterbalanced with high-growth, high-risk countries such as the Middle and Far Eastern markets or certain Latin American countries. The level of risk associated with a given country, can, however, be attenuated by the mode of operation in that country. Thus, for example, licensing, contract manufacturing, or joint venture may provide a means of reducing equity involvement or exposure in a high-risk market.

In determining the optimal combination of products and product lines to be marketed worldwide, consideration has to be given, not only to the optimal product mix in each country based on the cash flow generated by each product, but also to the trade-off between new product development and the transfer of products and brands from one country to another. Thus, for example, the issue arises as to whether a successful or standard product, such as cornflakes or popcorn, should be marketed in countries where it is not currently available, or whether more varieties, for example, health cereals, should be developed, and marketed in existing country markets in order to obtain greater penetration of these markets. Alternatively, new products and brands should be developed for these markets.

In this context, economies that may be achieved by more efficient use of the salesforce or distribution facilities in a given country need to be weighed against the savings in product research and development costs associated with transferring products from one country to another. The costs of product modification and adaptation to other market environments have, however, also to be considered.

A fourth component of the multinational portfolio consists of the combination of market segments targeted worldwide. A company may decide to target a specific market segment worldwide, as, for example, to market cosmetics to young working women worldwide. Typically, this has the advantage that the same or similar marketing tactics can be used. Substantial economies can, for example, be achieved through the use of standardized advertising campaigns in international markets. Alternatively, a company might decide to target the mass market in different countries, or a variety of market segments. Furthermore, the segments targeted might differ from country to country. For example, all segments might be targeted in one country, and only upscale women in another country. Again, these decisions are likely to hinge on the degree of adaptation in tactics required in a given sociocultural environment, the economies obtained through joint use of distribution facilities and the salesforce marketing to different segments, and the degree of competition encountered in relation to these different segments.

The primary advantage of the portfolio approach is that it provides a global perspective for developing marketing strategy rather than a country-by-country perspective. Guidelines for allocation of resources, whether in terms of financial or management time and effort, can thus be established on a regional or global basis rather than for each country separately. This can aid not only in decisions with regard to which countries and product markets to invest in, but also from which countries and product markets to divest, and how far strategies should be integrated across different countries, segments, and product markets. Furthermore, the analysis can be conducted in relation to different units and combinations of units, depending on the specific objectives and organizational structure of the company. For example, a company with a single product line and mode of operation, such as exporting, might only be concerned with a portfolio composed of countries as indicated in Figure 10.2. On the other hand, a more diversified company might wish to consider portfolios consisting of different combinations of countries, modes of operation, products, market segments, and marketing strategies, also shown in Figure 10.2.

Management would thus be asked to provide information with regard to their objectives in international markets, as for example, the desired level of profit, the level of risk, and sales growth. The relative importance or weight attached to each of these under different future scenarios, for example, optimistic versus pessimistic, would also be evaluated, both in the long and the short term. Sales growth might, for example, assume greater importance under a pessimistic scenario than an optimistic one. Similarly, profitability might be less important under a pessimistic scenario, and less important in the short run, than under an optimistic scenario, or in the long run. Such objectives and their importance under different assumed conditions would thus provide the basis for evaluating alternative portfolio combinations.

Following financial portfolio analysis, assessment of alternative portfolios will require data on measures of risk and return, for each of the units to be considered in the portfolio. Thus, for example, if the country is the only level to be considered, only measures at this level will be needed. As noted previously, various indicators of risk might be considered, depending on the specific type of risk to be considered. As indicated in Chapter 3, political risk might be assessed based on the number of previous expropriations, the degree of political stability, expert rating, or a composite index. Similarly, financial risk might be assessed in terms of foreign exchange risk, or the rate of inflation, or based on a composite index. The specific indicators to be used will, however, depend to a large extent on management objectives and the specific product market concerned.

In markets where a company already has operations, return can be evaluated based on standard measures of performance, such as ROI, market share, or sales-to-expense ratios; or at a more detailed level, advertising-to-sales ratios, salesforce effectiveness, or other criteria that are deemed by management to be appropriate measures of performance. The specific measure to be used, and its operational definition will depend to a large extent on the nature of the market, and the accounting system of the company. Thus, for example, market share might be defined in terms of overall market share, served market share, or relative market share to the top or top three competitors.

A Country Portfolio

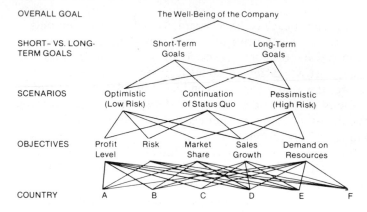

A Portfolio of Countries by Mode of Entry,
Market Segment, Product, and Market Strategy

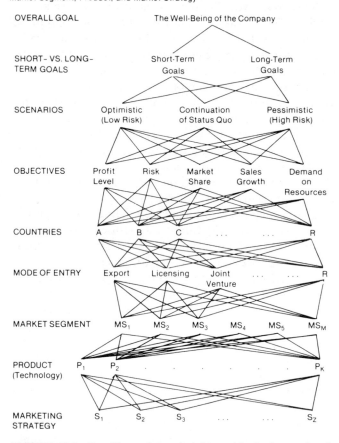

FIGURE 10.2   Two illustrative analytic hierarchies for international portfolios

Source:Yoram Wind and Susan P. Douglas, ''International Portfolio Analysis and Strategy: The Challenge of the Eighties,'' *Journal of International Business Studies,* 12 (Fall 1981), 76.

If countries, as well as different products and modes of operation and marketing strategies, are to be included in the analysis, measures of risk and return will need to be developed for each unit in the analysis. For example, risk and return will need to be assessed for each product included in the analysis, as well as for alternative modes of operation and marketing strategies.

In countries and product markets where the company is not currently involved, surrogate indicators of risk and expected return or market potential will need to be developed. Alternatively, barometric analysis can be conducted. The procedures for demand estimation discussed in Chapter 4 can effectively be applied in this context. Again, these should be tailored to the specific industry or product market concerned. Similarly, if alternative modes of operation are to be considered, estimates of risk and return for these will need to be developed, based on the anticipated degree of competitive activity, the desired level of equity involvement and marketing expenditure, expected market share, and ROI.

SUMMARY

Information is a key element in developing and implementing effective international business strategies. Maintenance of an international marketing information system is an important priority for companies committed to international markets and to global market expansion. This can provide an important input, enabling management to keep up to date on developments worldwide, and can also play a major role in integrating worldwide operations.

The three major components of the international marketing information system are macroeconomic data, data relating to specific product markets, and internal company sales and performance data. In each case, the specific information that is collected should be tailored to individual company requirements and objectives, and will also vary depending on the product or services concerned.

A number of issues arise with regard to the comparability of information obtained in different countries, due to differences in reporting systems and procedures in different countries. Generally, it is desirable to develop a standardized recording format for use worldwide. This can then be used by local management in transmitting reports. Computerization of the reporting system also facilitates and speeds up transmission of information, and broadens the horizon of potential uses of the global information system.

The information system can thus be helpful in a variety of decision areas. In particular, the information system can provide an important input in decisions relating to initial market entry and expansion into new countries and product markets. It can be an invaluable aid in evaluating performance in different countries and product markets. It can also be used to scan the global environment and to monitor emerging trends and changes in existing patterns. Finally, a global information system is essential in developing strategies that are integrated worldwide and that provide for the optimal combination of countries, product markets, modes of operation, and marketing strategies to maximize long-run profitability. Current developments in telecommunications and in computer and communications technology also offer promise for expanding the scope of global information systems, as well as facilitating their use and integration into management decision making.

REFERENCES

BRANDT, WILLIAM K. and JAMES M. HULBERT, "Patterns of Communications in the Multinational Corporation: An Empirical Study," *Journal of International Business Studies,* 7 (Spring 1976), 57–64.

BURNS, JANE O., "Transfer Pricing Decisions in U.S. Multinational Corporations," *Journal of International Business Studies,* 11 (Fall 1980), 23–39.

BUZZELL, ROBERT D., BRADLEY T. GALE, and RALPH G.M. SULTAN, "Market Share— A Key to Profitability," *Harvard Business Review,* 53 (January-February 1975), 96–106.

CHOI, FREDERICK D.S. and GERHARD G. MUELLER, *An Introduction to Multinational Accounting.* Englewood Cliffs, NJ: Prentice-Hall, 1978.

CRAIG, C. SAMUEL and SUSAN P. DOUGLAS, "Strategic Factors Associated with Market and Financial Performance," *Quarterly Review of Economics and Business,* 22 (Summer 1982), 101–12.

DAY, GEORGE S., "Diagnosing the Product Portfolio," *Journal of Marketing,* 41 (April 1977), 8–19.

DOUGLAS, SUSAN P. and C. SAMUEL CRAIG, "Examining Performance of United States Multinationals in Foreign Markets," *Journal of International Business Studies* (forthcoming).

GALE, BRADLEY T., "Selected Findings from the PIMS Project: Market Strategy Impact on Profitability" in Ronald C. Curhan (ed.), *Combined Proceedings.* Chicago: American Marketing Association, 1975.

GRAY, SIDNEY J., JACK C. SHAW, and BRENDAN McSWEENEY, "Accounting Standards and Multinational Corporations," *Journal of International Business Studies,* 12 (Spring/Summer 1981), 121–36.

HULBERT, JAMES, WILLIAM K. BRANDT, and RAIMAR RICHERS, "Marketing Planning in the Multinational Subsidiary: Practices and Problems," *Journal of Marketing,* 44 (Summer 1980), 7–15.

"Japan's Strategy for the '80s," *Business Week,* December 14, 1981, p. 39.

O'CONNELL, JEREMIAH and JOHN W. ZIMMERMAN, "Scanning the International Environment," *California Management Review,* 22 (Winter 1979), 16–23.

SCHOEFFLER, SIDNEY, ROBERT D. BUZZELL, and DONALD F. HEANY, "Impact of Strategic Planning on Profit Performance," *Harvard Business Review,* 57 (March-April 1979), 137–45.

THOMAS, PHILIP S., "Environmental Scanning—The State of the Art," *Long Range Planning,* 13 (February 1980), 20–28.

WEICHMAN, ULRICH and LEWIS PRINGLE, "Problems that Plague Multinational Marketers," *Harvard Business Review,* (July-August 1979), pp. 118–24.

WIND, YORAM and SUSAN P. DOUGLAS, "International Portfolio Analysis and Strategy: The Challenge of the 80s," *Journal of International Business Studies,* 12 (Fall 1981), 69–82.

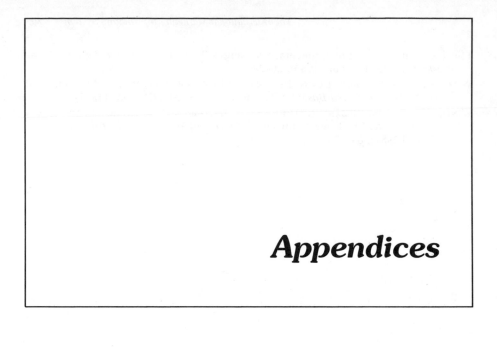

Appendices

APPENDIX I
SELECTED SECONDARY DATA SOURCES

International Organizations

1. United Nations Room A-3317,
New York, N.Y. 10017

The United Nations is a prolific publisher of useful statistics and economic surveys covering United Nations member countries. For a periodic list of United Nations publications see the monthly listings.

Among the more useful sources for international marketing research are

The Statistical Yearbooks
The Demographic Yearbook
The Yearbook of Industrial Statistics
The Yearbook of Labor Statistics
The Yearbook of National Accounts Statistics
Statistical Yearbook for Asia and the Pacific
Statistical Yearbook for Latin America
World Trade Annual

2. The World Bank
1818 H Street, NW,
Washington, D.C. 20433

The World Bank also publishes a number of reports and statistics, including

The World Development Report
The World Bank Tables

3. OECD
1750 Pennsylvania Avenue, NW,
Washington, D.C. 20433

OECD publishes a number of statistics, as well as economic surveys of its twenty-four member countries, and key industries in Europe. Key publications include

Main Economic Indicators
Labor Force Statistics
Country Economic Surveys

U.S. Goverment Publications

1. U.S. Department of Commerce,
Washington, D.C. 20230

The U.S. Department of Commerce publishes a variety of information of interest to the international marketer. These include

Global Market Surveys
Country Market Sectorial Surveys
Overseas Business Reports
Foreign Economic Trend Reports
Index to Foreign Market Reports
Market Share Reports

2. U.S. Department of Labor,
Washington, D.C. 20402

Monthly Labor Review

3. U.S. Department of Agriculture,
Washington, D.C. 20250

Agricultural Economy and Trade
The World Economic Situation

Commercial Organizations

1. Business International Corporation,
Dag Hammarskjold Plaza,
New York, N.Y. 10017

Business International has an extensive publishing program. It maintains a computerized data base containing economic, demographic, trade, and other statistics on 131 countries. A copy of the printout is published annually. Other useful publications include

Investment, Licensing and Trading Conditions Abroad for 56 countries
International Business
Business Asia, Business Europe, Business Latin America,
Business Eastern Europe
Doing Business in . . . series

2. The Economist Intelligence Unit,
75 Rockefeller Plaza,
New York, N.Y. 10019

The Economist Intelligence Unit also publishes a number of studies of interest to international marketers. Among these are

Marketing in Europe
Retail Business
Quarterly Economic Review
Special Industry Reports
Multinational Business

3. Predicasts
200 University Circle Research Center,
11001 Cedar Avenue,
Cleveland, Ohio 44106

Predicasts has the companion service to U.S. Predicasts in the form of *Worldcasts*. These are short- and long-term forecasts for economic indicators in selected countries and certain industries. They are published by geographic region and by product.

Predibriefs—industry news reports for twenty-nine industries are also published.

4. Euromonitor, 18 Doughty Street, London WC 1N2 PN

Euromonitor has a number of publications of interest to the international marketer. These include

International Marketing Data and Statistics
European Marketing Data and Statistics
Consumer Europe (market data for 280 products in thirteen European countries)
Retail Trade International (for thirty-six countries)
Consumer Markets in Latin America

Other Sources

1. Tax and Trade Guides

Several U.S. based accounting firms publish guides on doing business in country. . . . These typically cover investment, trading and business practices, employment, and accounting and taxation. Among these are

Arthur Andersen, *Tax and Trade Guide* series
Cooper & Lybrand, *International Reference Manual*
Ernst & Whinney, *International Series*
Price Waterhouse, *Information Guide* series
Touche Ross International, *Tax and Trade Profiles*
Haskin and Sells, *International Tax and Business Services*

2. Directories and Miscellaneous

Bottin International. Los Angeles, CA: Bottin International.
Business Guide to Privacy and Data Collection Legislation. New York: ICC Publishing, 1981.
Directory of European Business Information. Irene Kingston and William A. Benjamin, eds. New York: Find/SVP.
Encyclopedia of Associations. Detroit, MI: Gale Research Co.
Encyclopedia of Geographic Information Sources, 3d ed. Detroit, MI: Gale Research Co., 1978.
Europe's 5000 Largest Companies. New York: Dun and Bradstreet.
Exporters Encyclopedia. New York: Dun and Bradstreet, annual edition.

Foreign Commerce Handbooks.

Kelly's Manufacturers and Merchant's Directory. New York: Kelly's Directories Ltd.

Principal International Businesses. New York: Dun and Bradstreet.

Sources of Aid and Information for U.S. Exporters. Donna M. Jablonski, ed. Washington, DC: Washington Researchers, 1979.

World Almanac. New York: Newspaper Enterprise Association, Inc.

World Directory of Chambers of Commerce. New York: ICC Publishing, 1981.

World Directory of Industry and Trade GATT Associations.

World Sources of Market Information. E. Blauvelt and J. Durlacher, eds. Cambridge, MA: Ballinger, 1982.

APPENDIX II
PRINCIPAL MARKET
RESEARCH/MARKETING ASSOCIATIONS

(Address and telephone number)
SYMBOLS: * Membership basis individuals
          + Membership basis organizations

International

Association

*	ECMRA	European Chemical Marketing Research Association Room 14, 5th Floor, Morley House, Regent Street, London W1R 5AB (United Kingdom) (01-637-1221)
*	ESOMAR	European Society for Opinion and Marketing Research Wamberg 37, 1083 CW Amsterdam, (Netherlands) (020/44.49.45)
*	EVAF	European Association for Industrial Marketing Research Room 14, 5th Floor, Morley House, Regent Street, London W1R 5AB (United Kingdom) (01-637-1221)
*	WAPOR	World Association for Public Opinion Research 1500 Stanley, Suite 520, Montreal, Quebec H3A 1R3, (Canada) (514/849.8086)

Argentina

	AAM	Asociacion Argentina de Marketing Alsina 1609, 50 piso, Of.12 Buenos Aires 1088 (46/7172)
+	CEIM	Camara de Empresas de Investigacion de Mercado Quito 3850 1212 Buenos Aires (812-3588)

Australia

+	AMRO	Association of Market Research Organisations POB 109, Gordon, New South Wales 2072 (02/43-2566)
*	MRSA	Market Research Society of Australia POB 109, Gordon, New South Wales 2072 (02/43-2566)

Austria

*	VMO	Verband der Marktforscher Osterreichs c/o INFO, Institut fur Markt-und Meinungsforschung GmbH Mariahilferstrasse 99, A-1060 Vienna (56.95.95)

Belgium

	BMMA	Belgian Management and Marketing Association 1 Chemin des Moines, 1640 Rhode St. Genese (02/358.01.16)
+	FEBELMAR	Federation of Belgian Market Research Institutes Rue Paul Lauters, 1, 1050 Brussels, (02/649.00.55)

Brazil

*	SBPM	Sociedade Brasileira de Pesquisa de Mercado Rua Afonso de Freitas 695 04006 Sao Paulo, (011/549.2824)
+	ABIPEME	Associacao Brasileira dos Institutos de Pesquisa de Mercado Av. Paulista 2367 - 19th Floor, 01311 Sao Paulo SP (011/287.6511)

Canada

+	CAMRO	Canadian Association of Marketing Research Organisations 15 Toronto Street, Suite 702, Toronto, Ontario, M5C 2E3 (416/364.1233)
*	IMRAC	Industrial Market Research Association of Canada 2 Bloor Street West, Box 100–375, Toronto, Ontario, M4W 3E2 (416/671.7200)
*	PMRS	Professional Marketing Research Society POB 5155, Terminus A, Toronto, Ontario, M5W 1N5 (416/487.4893)

Denmark

*	DMF	Dansk Markedsanalyse Forening Gallup Markedsanalyse A/S, Gammel Vartovvej 6, DK 2900 Hellerup (01/29.88.00)
+	FMD	Foreningen af Markedsanalyseinstutter Danmark Flintholm Alle 2413 2000 Copenhagen F (01/10.66.44)

Finland

+	FAMRA	Finnish Association of Marketing Research Agencies c/o Finnpanel Oy, Lauttasaarentie 28–30 00200 Helsinki 20, (90/6923.073)

| * | SM | Suomen Markkinointitutkimusseura RY
Suomen Gallop Oy,
Lauttasaarentie 28–30,
00200 Helsinki 20
(90/6923.125) |

France

| * | ADETEM | Association Nationale pour le Developpement des Techniques de Marketing
30 Rue d'Astorg,
75008 Paris,
(266.51.13) |
| + | SYNTEC | Chambre Syndicale des Societes d'Etudes et de Conseils
3 Rue Leon Bonnat,
75016 Paris,
(524.43.53) |

Germany (Fed. Rep.)

| + | ADM | Arbeitskreis Deutscher Marktforschungsinstitute EV
Burgschmietstrasse 2,
8500 Nurnberg
(09911/395.231) |
| * | BDM | Berufsverband Deutscher Markt und Sozialforscher EV
Marktplatz 9,
6050 Offenbach,
(06611/8059.266) |

Greece

| | GIM | Greek Institute of Marketing of the Greek Management Association
40 Zan Moreas - 67 Sygrou,
Athens - 404,
(01/922.51.98) |

India

| | IMM | Institute of Marketing and Management
62-F Sujan Singh Park,
New Delhi 10003,
(69/9224) |

Ireland

| | MSI | The Marketing Society of Ireland
c/o Radio Telefis Eireann,
Donnybrook,
Dublin 4
(01/693111) |

Italy

| *+ | AISM | Associazione Italiana per gli Studi di Marketing
Via Olmetto 3, 20123 Milan
(02/863.293) |

Israel

IMA   Israel Marketing Association
                  4 Henrietta Szold Street,
                  Tel Aviv

Japan

+   JMRA   Japan Marketing Research Association
                  No. 20 Sankyo Building, + + 506,
                  11-5 Iidabashi 3-chrome,
                  Tokyo 102
                  (09–81/03.265.3677)
    JMA   The Japan Marketing Association
                  Daisan Dentsu Kosan Building
                  No. 16-7, 2-chrome, Ginza,
                  Chuo-ku,
                  Tokyo.

Kenya

MSK   Marketing Society of Kenya
                  P O Box 69826,
                  Nairobi
                  (23086)

Mexico

ANEC   Asociacion Nacional de Economistas Consultores A.C.
                  Antonio Caso 86, Mexico 4,D.F.

Netherlands

*   NVM   Nederlandse Vereniging van Marktonderzoekers
                  Koningslaan 34, Amsterdam
                  (020/73.95.51)
    NIMA   Nederlands Instituut voor Marketing
                  Van Alkemadelaan 700
                  2597 AW The Hague
                  (070/26.43.41)

New Zealand

*   MRSNZ   Market Research Society of New Zealand
                  c/o Massey University,
                  Palmerston North
                  (69.099)

Nigeria

NIM   Nigerian Institute of Management
                  7 Alhaji Murtala Animashaun Close
                  P O Box 2557, Surulere,
                  Lagos
                  (01-830565)

Norway

*	NMF	Norsk Markedsforsknings Forening c/o Siemens A/S Postboks 10, Veitvedt, Oslo 5 (02/15.30.90)

Pakistan

	MAP	Marketing Association of Pakistan 403 Burhani Chambers, Abdullah Haroon Road, Karachi (78741)

Philippines

+	MORES	Marketing and Opinion Research Society c/o Unisearch POB 1176, Manila 2800 (504011)
	PMA	Philippine Marketing Association 3rd Floor, J & M Building, 7848 Makati Avenue Makati, Metro Manila (86.17.71)

Portugal

	SPC	Sociedade Portuguesa de Commercializacao (Marketing) Av. Elias Garcia 172 - 2 - Esq Lisbon (77.44.57)

South Africa

*	SAMRA	South African Market Research Association P O Box 781454, Sandton 2146
+	AMRO	Association of Marketing Research Organisations P O Box 56213, Pinegowrie 2123

Spain

*	AEDEMO	Asociacion Española de Estudios de Mercado, Marketing y Opinion Urgel, 152, Atico 2a, Barcelona 36, Apartado 5027, Barcelona 7 (3/253.85.09)

Sweden

+	FSM	Foreningen Svenska Marknadsundersokningsinstitut Upplandsgatan 7, 111 23 Stockholm (08/11.33.97)

| * | M-GRUPPEN | Foreningen for Marknadsforskning och Marknadsanalys
Box 19006,
104 32 Stockholm
(08/10.36.60) |

Switzerland

*	VSMF/ASSEM	Verband Schweizerischer Marktforscher / Association Suisse des Specialistes en Etude du Marche c/o IHA Institut für Marktanalysen AG, Obermattweg 9, CH-6052 Hergiswil /NW (041/95.22.22)
+	SILK	Schweizerische Institutsleiter - Konferenz c/o Isopublic AG Witokonerstrasse 297, 8053 Zurich (01/53.72.72)
	GFM	Schweizerische Gesellschaft für Marketing Bleicherweg 21, 8022 Zurich / Postfach 1057 (01/202.34.25)
	GREM	Groupement Romand du Marketing 2 Av. Agassiz, 1001 Lausanne (021/202811)

Thailand

| | TMA | Thailand Management Association
308 Silom Road,
Bangkok 5
(233.0233) |

United Kingdom

+	ABMRC	Association of British Market Research Companies c/o Gerry Levens and Company 195 Lavender Hill SW11 5TB (01-228-6654)
*	AQRP	Association of Qualitative Research Practitioners 29 Burchington Road London N8 HHP (01-340-6679)
+	AMSO	Association of Market Survey Organisations c/o BJM Research Partners Limited 67 Clerkenwell Road, London EC1R 4BH (01-404-5577)
+	BAMRA	British Agricultural Marketing Research Association Cedar Flat, Upper Bolney, Nr. Henley-on-Thames, Oxon, (04912-39221)

*	IMRA	Industrial Marketing Research Association 11 Bird Street, Lichfield, Staffs, WS13 6PW (05432–23448)
*	MRS	The Market Research Society 15 Belgrave Square, London SW1X 8PF (01–235–4709)

United States

*	ACR	Association for Consumer Research 250 South Wacker Drive, Chicago, Ill. 60606 (312/648–0536)
*	AMA	American Marketing Association 250 South Wacker Drive, Chicago, Ill. 60606 (312/648–0536)
*	ARF	Advertising Research Foundation 3 East 54th Street, New York, N.Y. 10022–3180 (212/751–5656)
+	CASRO	Council of American Survey Research Organizations POB 182, Port Jefferson, New York, N.Y. 11777 (516/928–6954)

Yugoslavia

YUMA	Jugoslavensko Udruzenje za Marketing Makanceva 16, 41000 Zagreb (041/447.240)

Source: *The International Research Directory of Market Research Organizations.* 6th Ed. London: The International Research Directory, 1982. Reprinted by permission.

Countries covered in the International Marketing Research Survey

Argentina	Luxembourg
Australia	Malaysia
Austria	Mexico
Belgium	Netherlands
Brazil	New Zealand
Canada	Nigeria
Chile	Norway
Colombia	Pakistan
Cyprus	Philippines
Denmark	Poland
Ecuador	Portugal
Egypt	Puerto Rico
Finland	Singapore
France	South Africa
Germany (Federal Republic)	Spain
Greece	Sweden
Guatemala	Switzerland
Hong Kong	Syria
Hungary	Taiwan
India	Thailand
Indonesia	Trinidad
Ireland	Tunisia
Israel	Turkey
Italy	United Kingdom
Ivory Coast	United States (New York State)
Japan	United States (Rest)
Jordan	U.S.S.R.
Kenya	Venezuela
Korea	Yugoslavia
Lebanon	

A more complete listing of market research organizations in fifty-nine countries can be found in the *International Research Directory of Market Research Organizations*. A sample page indicating the information available on each company is shown on the next page. Questionnaires to complete these entries were mailed to a total of 1819 names and addresses compiled from a variety of sources. A total of 1100 responses were obtained for an overall response rate of 60.4 percent.

COUNTRY **Australia**

COMPANY NAME

CONTACT   FOUNDED

ADDRESS
                                         TELEX

TELEPHONE   CABLE

PARENT COMPANY   SUBSIDIARY COMPANIES

MEMBER INTERNATIONAL RESEARCH CHAIN

MEMBER PROFESSIONAL RESEARCH/MARKETING ORGANIZATIONS

SERVICES PROVIDED BY COMPANY

COMPREHENSIVE ☐
                ☐ EXECUTIVE   ☐ FIELDWORK   ☐ DATA
AVAILABLE   ☐ CONSULTANCY   ☐   PROCESSING
SEPARATELY ☐

RESEARCH TECHNIQUES/AREAS   S = SPECIALISE   X = OFFER

AD HOC CONSUMER ☐	CONTINUOUS CONSUMER ☐	INTERNATIONAL RESEARCH ☐	CANNIBUS RESEARCH ☐	RETAIL AUDITS ☐
ADVERTISING RESEARCH ☐	DESK RESEARCH ☐	QUALITATIVE RESEARCH ☐	PACKAGING RESEARCH ☐	SOCIAL RESEARCH ☐
ATTITUDE RESEARCH ☐	INDUSTRIAL RESEARCH ☐	MEDIA RESEARCH ☐	PRODUCT TESTING ☐	TELEPHONE SURVEYS ☐

PRODUCT GROUP EXPERTISE

COUNTRIES RESEARCHED LAST TWO YEARS

STAFF   FIELDFORCE

EXECUTIVE ☐   ALL OTHERS ☐   SUPERVISORS ☐   INTERVIEWERS ☐
              (FULL TIME)

TURNOVER US $

UNDER 99,000: ☐   250,000 TO 499,000: ☐   1,000,000 TO 1,999,000: ☐   NOT AVAILABLE: ☐

100,000 TO 249,000: ☐   500,000 TO 999,000: ☐   2,000,000 AND OVER ☐

APPENDIX III
LISTING OF MARKETING RESEARCH
ORGANIZATIONS IN 48 COUNTRIES

Argentina

A & C-Analistas de Empresas y Consultores de
Direccion
    Buenos Aires 824-3086/7
                           84-5055/0442
Audits & Surveys, Inc.
    Buenos Aires 30-4309
                           33-2324
                           33-2337
Investigadores & Analistas de Mercado, SA
    Buenos Aires ....
IPSA S.A. Audits & Surveys Latinamerica
    Buenos Aires 33-2324/2337
A.C. Nielsen Argentina, S.A.
    Buenos Aires 46-2332

Australia

Australian Sales Research Bureau Pty. Ltd.
    Melbourne .... (03) 623121
    North Sydney .... (02) 927755
Beacon-Research International
    North Sydney .... (09) 922 5622
Burke Marketing Research-Australia
    Sydney ....
The Roy Morgan Research Centre Pty. Ltd.
    Melbourne .... (03) 625871
    North Sydney .... (02) 927755
A.C. Nielsen Pty. Ltd.
    North Sydney 92 5881
Reark Research Pty. Ltd.
    South Yarra .... (03) 240-8733
Frank Small & Associates
    Darlinghurst 334101
SRG Australia Pty. Ltd.
    Sydney 29-4406

Austria

INFO-Research International
    Vienna .... (0222) 565695-9
A.C. Nielsen Company, Ges.m.b.H.
    Vienna 63 6797

Bahrain

Pan Arab Research Center
    Bahrain 233372

Belgium

Cegos Benelux
    Brussels 241-6586
The Economist Intelligence Unit (Europe) S.A.
    Brussels 538-29-30
Kline SA
    Brussels .... (02) 230.54.90
A.C. Nielsen Company (Belgium) S.A.
    Brussels 11 2296
SUMA-Research International
    Brussels .... (02) 537 2008

Brazil

Audi Market Ltda.
    Rio de Janeiro .... (021) 226-5393
                           286-2596
                           246-6950
    Sao Paulo .... (011) 71-7729
                           71-8828
                         549-2771
Audits & Surveys, Inc.
    Rio de Janeiro 224-9398
                         224-3505
    Sao Paulo 285-5238
                        285-2179
Cegmark International Inc.
    Sao Paulo 285.00.70
IPSA Do Brasil Ltda. Audits & Surveys Latin-
america
    Sao Paulo 285-2179
                        285-5238
                        284-1727
LPM-Burke Levantamentos e Pesquisas de
Marketing Ltda.
    Sao Paulo ....
Marplan Research International
    Sao Paulo 230-1422
MAVIBEL-Research International
    Sao Paulo .... (011) 212 6522

A.C. Nielsen Lda.
    Sao Paulo.............................287-3811
Store Audits/Q.E.D. Do Brasil Propaganda e
Pesquisa Ltd.
    Sao Paulo......................(011) 62 8938

Canada

Audits & Surveys, Inc.
    Toronto .... (416) 486-8486
Burke International Research Corporation
    Agincourt ....
Canada Market Research Ltd.
    Toronto .... (416) 964-9222
Canadian Facts
    Montreal .... (514) 353-0210
    Ottawa...
    Toronto ....(416) 924 5751
    Vancouver .... (604) 669-3344
The Creative Research Group Ltd.
    Montreal .... (514) 288-3500
    Toronto .... (416) 484-9500
Decima Research Ltd.
    Toronto .... (416) 928-0900
Groupe Innova Inc.
    Montreal .... (514) 288-3500
Market Aides Ltd.
    Toronto .... (416) 663-5695
Market Facts of Canada Ltd.
    Toronto .... (416) 964-6262
Market Opinion Research
    Toronto .... (416) 868-0135
Marplan Research International
    Toronto ....(416) 925-3231
Moran, Inc.
    Montreal .... (514) 735-2541
A.C. Nielsen Company of Canada Ltd.
    Toronto .... (416) 441-2222
Opinion Place/Marketing Insights Ltd.
    Winnipeg...................... (204) 774-1879
R.I.S.-Christie Ltd.
    Toronto .... (416) 868-1020
Starch INRA Hooper Inc.
    Toronto .... (416) 425-1824
Telmar Communications of Canada Ltd.
    Toronto .... (416) 961-3915

Chile

IPSA S.A. Audits & Surveys Latinamerica
    Santiago 60-872
Marplan Research International
    Santiago 743056

Colombia

Interamerican Research
    Bogota .... (127) 243-5311
                                       242-1391
Robinsons Inc.
    Bogota ....

Cyprus

Africa Market Research Company
    Nicosia.................................... 45413
Middle East Marketing Research Bureau
    Nicosia............................(021) 45413

Denmark

IFH-Research International
    Copenhagen ....(01) 866677

Egypt

Egyptian Marketing Services Bureau
    Cairo 822826

England

Burke Marketing Research
    London ....
Business Decisions Ltd.
    London ....(01) 580-9636
CSS International
    London 01-834-2223
    Manchester 061-831-7511
Denjon International Ltd.
    London ....(01) 240-1666
The Economist Intelligence Unit Ltd.
    London 01-493 6711
European Market Research Bureau Ltd.
    London .... (01) 567 3060
Eyescan
    London .... (01) 727 1563/4
Frost & Sullivan, Ltd.
    London 01-486-8377/9
Gordon Simmons Research Ltd.
    Claygate ....(44) 372 67311
    London ....(44) 1 240 0256
Louis Harris International
    Richmond........................ 01-948-5011
Haug International
    Windsor ....(07535) 51018

IAL-Industrial Aids Ltd.
  London .... (01) 828 5036
IFT Marketing Research Ltd.
  Claygate ....(44) 372 67311
  London ....(44) 1 240 0256
JRH Marketing Services, Inc.
  London ....(01) 741-1121
Makrotest Ltd.
  London 998.77.33
Management Horizons (U.K.) Ltd.
  Richmond..................... (441) 940-4866
Market & Opinion Research International
  London 01-222 0232
Market Behavior Ltd.
  London .... (01) 723 4257
Marplan Research International
  London 7237376
McCollum/Spielman/& Company, Inc.
  London .... (44) (1) 379-6464
MIL Research Group Ltd.
  London 01-637-1444
MPI Marketing Research, Inc.
  London..
MRB International Ltd.
  London ....(01) 567-3060
A.C. Nielsen Company Ltd.
  Oxford.................... (STD 0865) 64851
Public Attitude Surveys Ltd.
  High Wycombe................. (0494) 32771
Quantime, Ltd.
  London ....(01) 637-7061
RBL-Research International
  London .... (01) 488 1366
                                (01) 353 3494-5
Robinsons International Ltd.
  London 01-235-9502/3
Russell International Marketing Services
  London 01-373-4947
Survey Research Group Ltd.
  London 388-5021
Telmar Communications, Ltd.
  London 011/44/1/9300/4117
Welling, Minton & Vanderslice (UK) Ltd.
  Alton............................. (0420) 88809
Roger Williams Technical & Economic Services
(UK), Inc.
  London ....(01) 405-0327

Finland

IFH-Research International
  Helsinki .... (00) 694 3762

France

Burke International Research S.A.R.L.
  Paris...
Cegos-Idet
  Boulogne 620.60.00
Express Europe
  Clichy 011-33-1-737-5555
Frost & Sullivan, Inc.
  Paris................................. 079-10-10
Louis Harris France
  Paris............................. 01-260-9654
IRM Europe, S.A.
  Paris............................. 562-92-35
MIL France SARL
  Paris................................. 742 97 13
MPI Marketing Research, Inc.
  Paris...
National CSS, Inc.
  Paris................................. 261 56 35
A.C. Nielsen Company
  Paris................................578-6120
SECED-Research International
  Paris............................ (01) 584 1525

Germany

Burke International Marktforschung GmbH.
  Frankfurt/Main ....
Eyescan
  Wuppertal 49 202 476 597
Frost & Sullivan, Inc.
  Frankfurt am Main..................59 01 36
  Munich 19 41 80
Haug Associates, Inc.
  Hamburg.....................(040) 8 99 22 04
IVE-Research International
  Hamburg........................ (040) 441190
Laves Chemie
  Frankfurt ....(0611) 774026/7
Makrotest G.m.b.H.
  Dusseldorf 66.21.97
Marplan Research International
  Offenbach am Main..................80 59-1
MIL Research KOLN
  Koln...........................(0221) 13 50 11
A.C. Nielsen Company G.m.b.H.
  Frankfurt 0611/74 08 21

Greece

KEME-Marketing Research Centre Hellas Ltd.
  Athens 7018082

LHR-Research International
   Athens .... (01) 779 5749
A.C. Nielsen Hellas Ltd.
   Athens 923-1454

Guatemala

Marplan Research International
   Guatemala City......................... 65335

Hong Kong

ASI Market Research, Inc.
   Hong Kong ....(5) 438-662
                                      436-053
                                      431-404
Frank Small & Associates
   Hong Kong 5-6911175
Survey Research Hongkong Ltd.
   Wachai 5-732296

Indonesia

PT In-Search Data
   Jakarta 591729
Frank Small and Associates
   Jakarta 796057

Ireland

A.C. Nielsen of Ireland Ltd.
   Dublin 765112

Italy

Burke Research S.r.l.
   Milan...
Cegos Italia Spa
   Milan....................................86.43.41
CER-Research International
   Milan...................(02) 653663/659 5838
Marplan Research International
   Milan................................... 865-619
MPi Marketing Research, Inc.
   Rome...
A.C. Nielsen Company
   Milan....................................809311

Japan

ASI Market Research, Inc.
   Tokyo..................................432-1701
Burke/Institute of Social Behavior
   Tokyo...
The Central Research Services Inc. (Chuo
   Chosa-Sha)
   Tokyo........................(03) 591-7201-5
Frost & Sullivan, Inc.
   Tokyo................................. 5831161
IRM Inc.
   Tokyo...........................(03) 583-1161
Japan Market Research Bureau
   Tokyo...........................(03) 449-2511
Marplan Research International
   Tokyo..................................265/5411
McCollum/Spielman/& Company, Inc.
   Tokyo........................... 03-461-7938
A.C. Nielsen Company
   Tokyo................................710-6551

Jordan

Jordan Centre for Marketing Research &
Surveys
   Amman.................................... 43351

Kenya

RBEAL-Research International
   Nairobi 558825/559429

Kuwait

M.E.M.R.B. (Kuwait) WLL
   Kuwait 421843
Pan Arab Research Center
   Kuwait .... (965) 442 100

Lebanon

Cegmark International, Inc.
   Beirut 23.19.31
Pan Arab Research Center
   Beirut...........................802972/802977

Malaysia

Frank Small & Associates
　　Kuala Lumpur 921166
Survey Research Malaysia Sdn. Bhd.
　　Kuala Lumpur 486122

Mexico

Burke Investigaciones de Mercadotecnia Inter-
　　nacionales S.A.
　　Mexico 5 ....
Datos, de Mexico, S.A.
　　Mexico 5 5-11-35-80
　　　　　　　　　　　　　　5-11-38-94
Gaither Internacional, S.A. de C.V.
　　Mexico 5 .... (905) 520-6097
A.C. Nielsen Company
　　Mexico City 531-3080
Robinsons Inc.
　　Mexico 6 ....

Morocco

Societe D'Etudes Marketing Marocaine
　　Casablanca 259461

Netherlands

A.C. Nielsen (Nederland) B.V.
　　Amsterdam 020-44 49 72
SOCMAR-Research International
　　Rotterdam .... (010) 13 21 89

New Zealand

A.C. Nielsen Pty. Ltd.
　　Wellington 735-736

Nigeria

RBNL-Research International
　　Lagos 661123
　　　　　　　　　　　　　　661126
　　　　　　　　　　　　　　661128

Peru

IPSA S.A. Audits & Surveys Latinamerica
　　Lima 22-0197

Philippines

Consumer Pulse, Inc.
　　Manila 693-8705
Frank Small and Associates
　　Manila 988702

Portugal

Cegoc
　　Lisbon 65.45.44
IEM-Research International
　　Lisbon .... (019) 684106
A.C. Nielsen Company
　　Lisbon 554412

Saudi Arabia

Pan Arab Research Center
　　Jeddah 6531214
　　Riyadh 4038949
Saudi Marketing & Research Consultants
　　Jeddah 6438626

Singapore

Frank Small and Associates
　　Singapore 2965064
Survey Research Singapore (Pte) Ltd.
　　Singapore 2528595

South Africa

A.C. Nielsen Company
　　Johannesburg 836-7891
Research International
　　Durban .... (031) 326171

Spain

Haug Associates, Inc.
    Madrid.............................. 455 80 42
INDECSA-Research International
    Madrid............. (01) 261 3971/262 3614
A.C. Nielsen Company
    Madrid............................ 448–81–00
T.E.A.-Cegos
    Madrid............................ 458.83.11

Sweden

Burke Marketing Research AB
    Gothenburg......................................
IFH-Research International
    Stockholm ....(08) 231595
A.C. Nielsen Company
    Stockholm 08/740 5060
Squires, Schalin & Co. AB
    Stockholm ....(08) 14 28 40
Testologen AB
    Sollentuna ....(08) 35 94 60

Switzerland

EIM S.A.
    Geneva...........................(22) 47.86.87
The Marketing Group International SA
    Geneva......................... (022) 42 79 30
A.C. Nielsen S.A.
    Lucerne......................... (041) 303333
Stratmar/TMG
    Geneva...

Taiwan

Frank Small and Associates
    (Hong Kong) 8911175–9

Thailand

Deemar Company Ltd.
    Bangkok............................... 2344520
Frank Small and Associates
    (Hong Kong) ....(5) 8911175–9

Tunisia

Cegmark International, Inc.
    Tunis 892–322

Turkey

BRU-Research International
    Istanbul.......................... (011) 486065

United Arab Emirates

M.E.M.R.B. (Gulf) Company
    Sharjah 358484
Pan Arab Research Center
    Abu Dhabi...............................334350
    Dubai 470070

Venezuela

Jesus Aponte y Asociados, S.A.
    Caracas ....(02) 32–11–23
                             32–86–38
Datos, C.A.
    Caracas 979–5611

Source: *International Directory of Marketing Research Houses and Services,* Green Book, 20th Ed., Pat Ryan (ed.), New York: American Marketing Association, 1982. Reprinted by permission.

Author Index

Subject Index

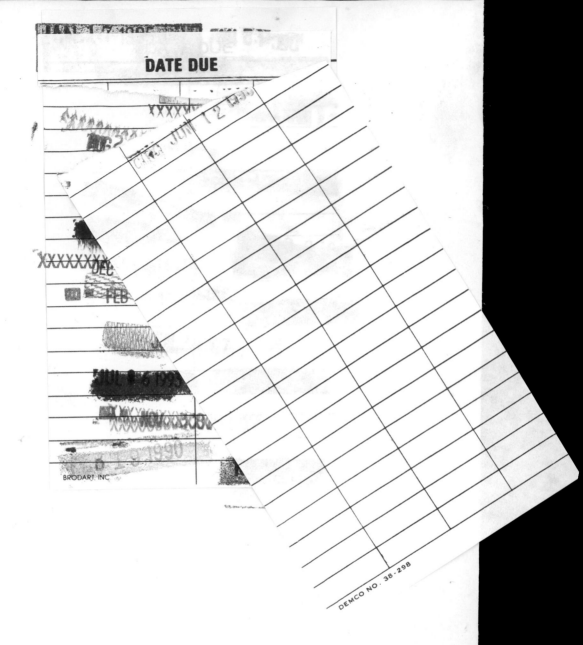